The POLITICS
of JUSTICE

AMERICAN POLITICAL INSTITUTIONS AND PUBLIC POLICY

Stephen J. Wayne
Series Editor

VICTORY
How a Progressive Democratic Party Can Win and Govern
Arthur Sanders

THE POLITICS OF JUSTICE
The Attorney General and the Making of Legal Policy
Cornell W. Clayton

AMERICAN POLITICAL INSTITUTIONS AND PUBLIC POLICY

The POLITICS of JUSTICE
The Attorney General and the Making of Legal Policy

CORNELL W. CLAYTON

M.E.Sharpe Inc.
Armonk, New York • London, England

Copyright © 1992 by M. E. Sharpe, Inc.

All rights reserved. No part of this book may be reproduced in any
form without written permission from the publisher, M. E. Sharpe, Inc.,
80 Business Park Drive, Armonk, New York 10504.

Available in the United Kingdom and Europe from M. E. Sharpe,
Publishers, 3 Henrietta Street, London WC2E 8LU.

Library of Congress Cataloging-in-Publication Data

Clayton, Cornell W., 1960–
The politics of justice: the attorney general and the
making of legal policy / Cornell W. Clayton.
p.   cm. —
(American political institutions and public policy)
Includes bibliographical references and index.
ISBN 1-56324-018-1 (cloth)
ISBN 1-56324-019-X (pbk)
1. United States. Dept. of Justice.
2. United States. Dept. of Justice. Office of the Attorney General.
3. Attorneys-general—United States.
4. Justice, Administration of—Political aspects—United States.
5. Political questions and judicial power—United States.
6. Law and politics.
I. Title.
II. Series.
KF5107.C5   1992
353.5008′8—dc20
92-30711
CIP

Printed in the United States of America

The paper used in this publication meets the minimum requirements of
American National Standard for Information Sciences—
Permanence of Paper for Printed Library Materials,
ANSI Z39.48–1984.

MV   10   9   8   7   6   5   4   3   2   1

To Wendy for years of patience

Contents

List of Figures

Foreword

The M.E. Sharpe series on American Political Institutions and Public Policy intends to examine contemporary U.S. political developments and to discern their impact on issues of public policy. Cornell W. Clayton's *The Politics of Justice: The Attorney General and the Making of Legal Policy* is the second publication in the series. It is a fascinating study of politics and governance: how one government affects the other and how both affect public policy.

Surveying the historical evolution of the office of the Attorney General, Clayton sees significant recent changes in the role, position, and influence of the person who holds that office. He attributes many of these changes not only to the increased demands placed on government and the increased complexity of public policy issues but also to the decreased capacity of the governmental system to meet those demands and attend to those issues. Disproportionately, the burden of overcoming the American political system's constitutional and institutional constraints, and the political divisions that currently exacerbate these constraints, has fallen on the President. The President, in turn, has regularly turned to his Attorney General for help, sometimes to achieve through the judiciary what he could not obtain from the legislature.

The President's increasing reliance on the Attorney General as political ally, policy adviser, and administration coordinator for a range of domestic social issues (the Attorney General has chaired the Cabinet Council on Domestic Affairs in the last two administrations) has helped transform the Justice Department from a judicial to an executive branch agency and the Attorney General from the nation's top legal official to its top legal policymaker. This reliance has also thrust the Justice Department and the people who have been chosen to head it into the public controversies that typically accompany political issues, which contrast sharply with the more narrowly defined questions of law that primarily concern the legal community. Professor Clayton contends that constitutional conflicts have become more regularized, and in the process, the judicial system has been politicized. Policy issues have also become more judicialized.

All these important and far-reaching systematic changes, captured in this rich, institutional portrait, have generated considerable tension within and among the branches of government. By illustrating these tensions and indicating their political sources and institutional consequences, *The Politics of Justice* raises an important issue for contemporary students of government: How should the achievement of short-term policy benefits be weighed against longer-term institutional costs? Specifically, is the politicization of the Justice Department by recent Presidents to implement their policy agenda a good idea? Clayton does not shy away from answering this question. His prescription, together with his description and analysis, should give readers concerned with effective government within the framework of the U.S. constitutional system pause for thought.

Stephen J. Wayne
Georgetown University

Acknowledgments

The idea for this book began in a book shop in Georgetown in 1982 when I stumbled upon Victor Navasky's fascinating account of Robert Kennedy's tenure as Attorney General. The questions raised by Navasky about the mixture of law and politics in the Justice Department have agitated me ever since. I could not have known in 1982 that controversy would engulf the Reagan Justice Department during the next six years. It proved to be an exciting, and at times frustrating, period to study this complex and important institution.

Although many people have offered helpful insights as this project developed, I am most indebted to Gillian Peele, who provided patient guidance and rigorous criticisms during the past five years. I am also indebted to Louis Fisher of the Library of Congress, who made valuable suggestions for improving this book and has done so much through his own work to reinvigorate the public law tradition and the study of normative institutional theory. Many others have also provided help or encouragement during the writing of this manuscript. Thanks are due Deborah Owen, Gary Malecha, Susan Olson, Howard Ball, Jennifer Brice, and Terrence Cole: their advice and efforts were all to the good and do not account for whatever weaknesses remain.

Cornell W. Clayton

Attorneys General
of the United States

Name	Term	President
Edmund Randolph	1789–1794	Washington
William Bradford	1794–1795	Washington
Charles Lee	1795–1801	Washington and Adams
Levi Lincoln	1801–1805	Jefferson
John Breckenridge	1805–1806	Jefferson
Caesar A. Rodney	1807–1811	Jefferson and Madison
William Pinkney	1811–1814	Madison
Richard Rush	1814–1817	Madison
William Wirt	1817–1829	Monroe and Adams
John M. Berrien	1829–1831	Jackson
Roger B. Taney	1831–1833	Jackson
Benjamin F. Butler	1833–1838	Jackson and Van Buren
Felix Grundy	1838–1839	Van Buren
Henry D. Gilpin	1840–1841	Van Buren
John J. Crittenden	1841–1841	Harrison and Tyler
Hugh S. Legare	1841–1843	Tyler
John Nelson	1843–1845	Tyler
John Y. Mason	1845–1846	Polk
Nathan Clifford	1846–1848	Polk
Issac Toucey	1848–1849	Polk
Reverdy Johnson	1849–1850	Taylor
John J. Crittenden	1850–1853	Fillmore
Caleb Cushing	1853–1857	Pierce
Jeremiah S. Black	1857–1860	Buchanan
Edwin M. Stanton	1860–1861	Buchanan
Edward Bates	1861–1864	Lincoln
James Speed	1864–1866	Lincoln and Johnson
Henry Stanbery	1866–1868	Johnson

William M. Evarts	1868–1869	Johnson
Ebenezer R. Hoar	1869–1870	Grant
Amos T. Akerman	1870–1872	Grant
George H. Williams	1871–1875	Grant
Edwards Pierrepont	1875–1876	Grant
Alphonso Taft	1876–1877	Grant
Charles Devens	1877–1881	Hayes
Wayne MacVeagh	1881–1881	Garfield
Benjamin H. Brewster	1881–1885	Arthur
Agustus H. Garland	1885–1889	Cleveland
William H. Miller	1889–1893	Harrison
Richard Olney	1893–1895	Cleveland
Judson Harmon	1895–1897	Cleveland
Joseph McKenna	1897–1898	McKinley
John W. Griggs	1898–1901	McKinley
Philander C. Knox	1901–1904	McKinley
William H. Moody	1904–1906	Roosevelt
Charles J. Bonaparte	1906–1909	Roosevelt
George W. Wickersham	1909–1913	Taft
James C. McReynolds	1913–1914	Wilson
Thomas Watt Gregory	1914–1919	Wilson
A. Mitchell Palmer	1919–1921	Wilson
Harry M. Daughtery	1921–1924	Harding
Harlan Fiske Stone	1924–1925	Coolidge
John T. Sargent	1925–1929	Coolidge
William D. Mitchell	1929–1933	Hoover
Homer S. Cummings	1933–1939	Roosevelt
Frank Murphy	1939–1940	Roosevelt
Robert H. Jackson	1940–1941	Roosevelt
Francis Biddle	1941–1945	Roosevelt
Tom C. Clark	1945–1949	Truman
J. Howard McGrath	1949–1952	Truman
James P. McGranery	1952–1953	Truman
Herbert Brownell, Jr.	1953–1957	Eisenhower
William P. Rogers	1957–1961	Eisenhower
Robert F. Kennedy	1961–1964	Kennedy
Nicholas deB. Katzenbach	1965–1966	Johnson
Ramsey Clark	1967–1969	Johnson
John N. Mitchell	1969–1972	Nixon
Richard G. Kleindienst	1972–1973	Nixon
Elliot L. Richardson	1973–1973	Nixon
William B. Saxbe	1974–1975	Nixon
Edward H. Levi	1975–1977	Ford

Griffin B. Bell	1977–1979	Carter
Benjamin R. Civiletti	1979–1981	Carter
William French Smith	1981–1985	Reagan
Edwin Meese III	1985–1988	Reagan
Richard Thornburgh	1988–1991	Reagan and Bush
William P. Barr	1991–	Bush

The POLITICS
of JUSTICE

1

Introduction

On March 4, 1789, the first Congress of the United States convened in New York City. The meeting can aptly be described as an extension of the Constitutional Convention itself; many of the same participants were present, and the task they confronted was to complete the construction of the government initiated under the document recently ratified by the several states. During the course of the summer, Congress fashioned the contours and character of the executive and judicial branches of the new federal government. Among the measures enacted at the end of its first session was a bill providing for a "meet person, learned in the law, to act as Attorney General for the United States."

For more than sixty years, the U.S. Attorney General's position was only part time. Incumbents maintained private law practices in addition to their official duties. It was not until 1870 that Congress created a law department to assist the Attorney General, and not until the 1920s that the Justice Department began to take on its modern bureaucratic structure. The Department of Justice—the institutionalized Attorney General—has since grown enormously. Today its budget is nearly $7 billion, it employs more than 80,000 persons, and it has law enforcement responsibility in virtually every area of American public life.

Despite the size and power of the department he or she administers, the Attorney General would not capture the public's imagination if not for the fact that the government's legal policy in recent decades has become the subject of intense partisan debate. Attorneys General have increasingly found themselves the target of scrutiny in the popular press and congressional investigation, as well as the subject of campaign rhetoric. For better or worse, the names of many recent Attorneys General—Edwin Meese, Griffin Bell, John Mitchell, Ramsey Clark, Robert Kennedy—have become widely recognized by the general public.

The controversies that have surrounded recent Attorneys General present a marked contrast to the relative obscurity in which the office operated throughout most of its existence. Prior to the 1930s, government legal policymaking was generally viewed as a "legal" rather than "political" enterprise. Attorneys General were known to a relatively small number of academic lawyers and law enforcement professionals. Perhaps nothing illustrates the changing nature of the

3

office as much as the confirmation process. Before the 1950s, public hearings were not even held. When President John F. Kennedy appointed his brother Robert Attorney General in 1961, the first special-interest group appeared at a confirmation hearing. By the time Congress confirmed Griffin Bell in 1977, some thirty-three separate interest groups appeared; when Edwin Meese was confirmed in 1986, more than fifty interest groups testified at the hearings.

The transformation in the conventions and perceptions that define the Attorney General's role as the government's chief legal policymaker, however, are symptomatic of more fundamental changes in the American political system. The twentieth-century metamorphosis of the federal government from a limited to a positive state greatly magnified the tensions inherent in our system of separated powers. This development, coupled with the erosion of American political parties and the regularization of split-ticket voting in the post–1968 period, has altered fundamentally the style of American politics. While the operations of nearly all major political institutions changed, the central role that "the law" plays in the constitutional system put particular stress on the legal policy establishment.

The impact of these developments on the Attorney General's office became apparent as Presidents increasingly began to view the Department of Justice as a partisan instrument for effecting their policy agenda. President Franklin D. Roosevelt used the Justice Department to carry out an attack on the Hughes Court to keep it from interfering with his New Deal policies. In the wake of the court-packing plan in 1937, President Roosevelt and his successor, Harry S. Truman, appointed the next thirteen Supreme Court justices. The new members of the Court embraced a New Deal jurisprudence which, following the lead of the executive, permitted government regulation in the economic sphere, but placed greater restrictions on government intervention in the cultural or noneconomic one.

The shift in the Court's jurisprudence that took place during the 1940s set the stage for an alliance between the executive and judicial branches that during the next two decades liberalized American public policy. While conservative, southern Democrats dominated Congress, Presidents began turning to the courts as an alternative forum to achieve policy goals, especially in areas such as civil rights and criminal justice reform. In sharp contrast to the 1930s, the Justice Department during this period actively encouraged courts to resolve political disputes and supported expansion of judicial reliefs. The Justice Department's briefs in cases such as *Henderson v. United States* (1950), *Brown v. Board of Education* (1954), or *Baker v. Carr* (1962), urged a jurisprudence diametrically opposed to the one it supported in cases twenty years earlier. The department also supported the Court's policy innovations through rhetoric and legislative proposals.

By 1968, the Justice Department's activist alliance with the judiciary had become so controversial that Republican candidate Richard M. Nixon made an explicit campaign promise to appoint a new Attorney General if elected. The promise was noteworthy, not because Nixon would carry it through—any incoming administration would be expected to appoint a new Attorney General—but because it reflected how politicized and partisan the office had become. American voters elected Nixon, and he appointed his campaign manager, John Mitchell, to head the Department of Justice. Mitchell immediately set out to reverse departmental policies. He attacked judicial activism in a series of speeches, and in cases such as *Swann v. Charlotte–Mecklenburg Board of Education* (1971) he had the department file briefs urging the Court to restrict its scope of constitutional authority and limit its remedial power. The Justice Department's policy positions in a variety of controversial areas such as school busing and Fourth Amendment search-and-seizure were reversed. And the department played a large role in the Nixon administration's efforts to centralize control over the administrative bureaucracy, helping to screen agency access to the courts.

The ignominious end to the Nixon administration, brought on by Watergate, forced a public reappraisal of presidential power, especially the desirability of White House domination of the administrative state. The Nixon administration's use of impoundment power, budget centralization techniques, personnel screening practices, and selective enforcement strategies in order to bypass Congress's policymaking authority, led historian Arthur Schlesinger, Jr., to write in 1973, that "the pivotal institution of American government, the Presidency, has got out of control and badly needs new definition and restraint."[1]

Arguments for "depoliticizing" the administrative bureaucracy appealed particularly to those who wanted to reform the Department of Justice, which had been severely damaged by revelations of its involvement in the Watergate cover-up. Upon taking office, Presidents Gerald R. Ford and Jimmy Carter promised to restore political neutrality and professional integrity at the Justice Department. Both appointed Attorneys General (Edward Levi and Griffin Bell respectively) who eschewed partisan politics and instituted administrative reforms aimed at buffering the department from direct White House interference. Congress also intensified its oversight of the department and even considered severing Justice from presidential control by limiting presidential removal authority over the Attorney General. Lawmakers rejected this plan for radical surgery, though they enacted a less ambitious reform in 1978 by creating the independent prosecutor's office.

By the late 1970s, however, the zeal for grand institutional reforms was on the wane. The dismal performance of the Carter administration forced a new assessment of the presidency. By the 1980 election, fears of an "imperial presidency" had dissipated, and President Ford's warning that the presidency had become seriously "imperiled" had emerged in its place. In this environment of executive resurgence, Ronald Reagan moved to reassert political control over the administrative bureaucracy. The Reagan administration's conservative social policy agenda and its deregulatory economic philosophy made the Justice Department a key element in its strategy of governance. The boast by Terry Eastland, Assistant Attorney General for Public Affairs during the Reagan years, that "no administration has thought longer and more deeply about law since that of FDR, and we have thought more deeply than that administration," was no overstatement.[2]

Edwin Meese's unabashed partisanship while serving as Attorney General provoked unparalleled controversy. During the President's first term, Meese had served as the ideological alter-ego of the Reagan White House. From his position as White House Counselor, he engineered many of the controversial changes in government policy associated with the "Reagan Revolution," and it came as no surprise that his nomination in 1984 to be Attorney General drew sharp reaction. Meese's confirmation came only after a year-long debate in the Senate Judiciary Committee and a separate investigation by the independent counsel's office.

Under Meese's direction, the Justice Department intensified its selective enforcement strategies, refusing to prosecute under statutes which it opposed. In litigation, it abruptly abandoned legal positions the federal government had advocated for more than two decades and asked the Court to overturn precedents in wholesale fashion. In his speeches, Meese lashed out at the Court's jurisprudence, arguing it should use a standard of "original intent" and challenged the Court's authority as final arbiter of the Constitution. So sharp was his rhetorical assault, that several members of the Court took the unprecedented step of responding publicly to his criticisms.

The controversy surrounding the Reagan Justice Department came to a climax in 1987, when the administration's nomination of Robert Bork to the Supreme Court was defeated in a dramatic Senate showdown.[3] The following year, embattled in the press, the subject of a second investigation by the independent counsel's office, and faced with evaporating support within the administration, Edwin Meese resigned. The appointment of Richard Thornburgh, a moderate Republican and former Governor of Pennsylvania, at least temporarily reduced the level of controversy engulfing the Justice Department. Nevertheless, the reverberations of the Reagan administration's politicization of the department are still being felt.[4] The Attorney General became an issue during the 1988 presidential campaign when Democratic candidate Michael Dukakis pledged to "appoint an Attorney General who knows what justice is."[5] Congress's heightened scrutiny led to the rejection of two Bush administration nominees to fill high-level posts in the department.[6] And fearing another Bork-style confirmation battle, in 1990 the administration nominated to the Supreme Court a virtually unknown jurist, David Souter, who had little federal experience and no political background.[7] All of this is symptomatic of how politicized the process of making legal policy has become in the United States.

This book sets out to explain the nature and causes of this development, the controversy it has created, and its impact on the institution at the head of the legal policy bureaucracy. Three factors are critical to that explanation. First, the institutional evolution of the Attorney General's office from an elite barrister, perceived as a judicial institution, into an administrator of a massive executive branch bureaucracy has left fundamental tensions in the office's role. Second, the acceptance of more integrative modes of political jurisprudence and the growth of interest group litigation have led to the judicialization of larger and larger areas of public policy. This in turn has created a more politically autonomous judiciary and increased the importance of litigation and judicial selection as instruments of presidential policymaking.

Third, because Democrats have tended to control Congress and Republicans the White House, since 1968 there has been a tendency for policy disputes to be transformed into institutional conflicts over constitutional powers. The conflict has been further exacerbated by reforms inside Congress, which have led to a more liberal brand of Democratic leadership and by reforms in the presidential nominating process, which increased the influence of the conservative wing of the Republican party. This polarization of ideology, both within and between the two elected branches, has had dire consequences for democratic control of public policy. Presidents have increasingly relied on administrative strategies of policymaking, while Congress has increasingly sought to "micro-manage" administration. The result is a new style of administrative law: one in which the judiciary is more intricately involved in the administrative process, and where control over agency litigation becomes an important lever for bureaucratic management.

Apart from understanding the recent controversy, there is another reason why a study of the Attorney General and the Department of Justice is valuable at this juncture. Scholars of American government have long recognized the importance of the separation of powers. Yet, in an era of electoral dealignment and party weakness, the institutional friction inherent in the separation of powers is greatly magnified. The result is a political system less democratic and more prone to legal and administrative conflicts.[8] The expanding role that the courts and the legal bureaucracy play in making public policy illustrates the degree to which a new set of institutional relations has emerged in the United States. Although this book is not intended primarily as an analysis of the peculiar strengths and weaknesses of the American system of government, focusing on the changing role of the Attorney General may yield insight into general developments and problems in constitutional government in the United States.

Because the study of federal legal policy straddles the disciplines of law, politics, and public administration, few scholarly studies of the subject exist. A smattering of general histories of the Justice Department and a handful of biographical sketches provide a rich source of detailed information on the activities of particular Attorneys General.[9] These accounts, however, offer little in the way of systematic treatment of the subject. Only three studies of a systematic variety exist: a short monograph entitled *Role of the Attorney General*, published in 1968 by the American Enterprise Institute;[10] *The Jurocracy*, a 1976 study by Donald Horowitz examining Justice Department litigating relations with other federal agencies;[11] and "The President, the Attorney General and the Department of Justice," a short monograph written by Professor Daniel Meador in 1980. A recent study of the Solicitor General's office, *The Tenth Justice: The Solicitor*

General and the Rule of Law, by Lincoln Caplan, was published in 1987.[12]

Rather than recognizing the full impact of trends in divided government and other broad institutional developments on the politics of legal policymaking, these studies have treated such relationships only in passing. This book attempts to explain those relationships. Chapter 2 traces the evolution of the Attorney General's office from a small part-time position into the head of a powerful bureaucracy. This development mirrors the growth of the federal government generally, where periods of crisis and ideological realignment have acted as ratchets to increase the government's size and power. Chapter 3 examines the origin and nature of the Attorney General's office as a political actor. Particular attention is paid to its roles in judicial selection, government litigation, and its ability to shape the legal-political environment through speeches and rhetoric. The book then turns to examine the constitutional setting of the Attorney General's office and the political conflict over Justice Department policy. Chapter 4 analyzes disputes over appointment and removal authority. The picture that emerges is marked by periods of intense interbranch conflict brought on by constitutional crisis such as the Civil War, the New Deal, and Watergate. Chapters 5 and 6 focus on the changed nature of American politics since the 1930s. Chapter 5 examines the growing role of courts in the political process and the changing relationship between the executive and judicial branches. Chapter 6 centers on administrative law and the Justice Department's role in conflicts between the executive and Congress. These chapters emphasize how constitutional conflict has become more regularized and the role of government legal institutions more politicized in recent years.

A variety of sources contributed to this study. In addition to historical documents and secondary sources, interviews with former Attorneys General and other Justice Department and White House officials helped steer my research. Obtaining information from the Justice Department, like most Washington, D.C., bureaucracies, can be challenging even at the best of times. During a period when it was the subject of congressional investigations and intense press coverage, department personnel were especially sensitive to outside requests for information. Here I owe a considerable debt to friends who set up interviews, obtained statistical information, and secured access to the department's library and archives.

I should emphasize at the outset that a study of this length cannot presume to present a comprehensive picture of government legal policy or all of the institutions involved in its making. Neither is this intended to be a comprehensive history of the Attorney General or the Department of Justice. More than twenty years ago, the noted legal scholar Arthur Miller wrote:

> The office of Attorney General is one of great complexity, when it is seen in its entirety. What gets public attention is usually only the tip of the iceberg, underneath which may be discerned a vast number of ways in which the chief law officer of the government functions within the governmental framework.[13]

His statement is even more true today. This study is an attempt to chart only a small portion of the underside of the iceberg.

Notes

1. Arthur M. Schlesinger, Jr., *The Imperial Presidency* (Boston: Houghton Mifflin, 1973), x.

2. Quoted in David O'Brien, "The Reagan Judges: His Most Enduring Legacy," in Charles O. Jones (ed.), *The Reagan Legacy: Promise and Performance* (Chatham, N.J.: Chatham House, 1988), 63.

3. The 58–42 Senate vote against confirmation was the largest margin in the history of rejected Supreme Court nominations.

4. For a discussion of controversies involving the Justice Department under Richard Thornburgh see Joan Biskupic, "Thornburgh's Bumpy Start Surprises Some on Hill," *Congressional Quarterly*. August 26, 1989, 2215.

5. See comments by Michael Dukakis, delivered before the Democratic National Convention, Atlanta Georgia, July 18–21, 1988.

6. The administration's nomination of William Lucas to become Assistant Attorney General for the Civil Rights Division was rejected by the Senate Judiciary Committee. The administration was also forced to back away from its choice to be Deputy Attorney General, Robert Fiske, Jr., because of opposition on the Judiciary Committee. See Joan Biskupic, "Lucas Comes Under Sharp Fire at Confirmation Hearings," *Congressional Quarterly*, July 22, 1989, 1871, and Ann Devroy, "Dispute on Justice Nominee Persists," *Washington Post*, June 22, 1989.

7. See Terry Eastland, "Anonymity: A Feather in Souter's Cap?" *Los Angeles Times*, July 28, 1990.

8. The literature on the "new politics" is voluminous and is discussed in detail in chapter 5. An especially good recent discussion is Benjamin Ginsberg and Martin Shefter, *Politics by Other Means* (New York: Basic, 1990).

9. The best general history of the Attorney General's office and the Department of Justice is Homer Cummings and Carl McFarland, *Federal Justice* (New York: Macmillan, 1937). The most recent history of the department is Luther Huston's *The Department of Justice* (New York: Praeger, 1967). See also Albert Langeluttig, *The Department of Justice of the United States* (Baltimore: John Hopkins Press, 1927); James Easby-Smith, *The Department of Justice: Its History and Functions* (Washington, D.C.: Lowdermilk & Co., 1904); R.L. Malone, "The Department of Justice: The World's Largest Law Office," *ABA Journal* 39 (1953), 381; Sewall Key, "The Legal Work of the Federal Government," *Virginia Law Review* 25 (1938), 165; Frank Buckley, "The Department of Justice—Its Origin, Development and Present Day Organization," *Boston University Law Review* 5 (1925), 177; and John A. Farlie, "The United States Department of Justice," *Michigan Law Review* 3 (1905), 352. Biographical and autobiographical works include: James Easby-Smith, "Edmund Randolph—Trail Blazer," *Journal of the Bar Association of the District of Columbia* 12 (1945), 419; Francis Biddle, *In Brief Authority* (Garden City: Doubleday, 1962); Richard Harris, *Justice* (London: Bodley Head, 1970); Elliot Richardson, *The Creative Balance* (London: Hamish Hamilton, 1976); Victor Navasky, *Kennedy Justice* (New York: Atheneum, 1977); Griffin Bell and Ronald Ostrow, *Taking Care of the Law* (New York: Morrow, 1982); and Richard Kleindienst, *Justice* (New York: Praeger, 1985).

10. Luther Huston, Arthur Miller, Samuel Krislov, Robert Dixon, *Roles of the Attorney General of the United States* (Washington, D.C.: AEI, 1968).

11. Horowitz, *The Jurocracy* (Lexington, Mass.: D.C. Heath, 1977).

12. Caplan, *The Tenth Justice* (New York: Vintage, 1988). There are also two major studies done on the United States Attorneys offices, Witney Seymour North, Jr., *United States Attorney* (New York: Morrow, 1975) and James Eisenstein, *Counsel for the United States* (Baltimore: John Hopkins Press, 1978).

13. Miller, "The Attorney General as President's Lawyer," in Huston et al., *Roles of the Attorney General*, 41.

2

History of the
Attorney General and the
Department of Justice

The United States inherited its Attorney General's office from England. The office was embedded in colonial government and later grafted into the institutions of the new republic. Despite their common heritage, the English and U.S. offices have evolved in different directions. Whereas the British office has maintained a relatively apolitical nature as an elite legal counsel and barrister for the government, the U.S. office has become highly politicized and has developed a major administrative role. The modern-day character of the U.S. Attorney General's office is largely the result of its constitutional environment and historical development. Today it sits at the top of the Department of Justice, a large bureaucracy with massive authority. However, the U.S. Attorney General's office has not always been so large or complex. This chapter briefly traces the development and evolution of the U.S. Attorney General and contrasts it with the office in Britain.

The British Attorney General

The title of Attorney General can be traced back to 1398, when the Duke of Norfolk first employed *attornies generalx* as witnesses to his banishment.[1] During the medieval period, the king and noblemen customarily employed attorneys to appear in court on their behalf. These representatives held various titles, but commonly were referred to as *attornatus regis*. Unlike today's government legal officers, these early attorneys for the Crown were appointed on a temporary basis to handle individual cases or to practice in certain courts only.[2]

As the legal profession in England expanded and became more complex, the Crown's legal business was consolidated. In 1472, William Hussee was appointed as the Crown's chief legal representative and given the title "Attorney General." Since that time, only one person at a time has served as England's

Attorney General. Although Hussee was the Crown's chief legal counsel, he was not the only one. An order of barristers called the King's "serjeants" continued to share legal authority with the Attorney General. By 1604, however, the Attorney General had asserted control over the serjeants and become the Crown's sole representative in English courts.[3]

The English office had no statutory origin, relying instead on common law and custom for definition of its authority and function. Nearly from the beginning it had a quasi-political role in addition to its legal functions. In 1673, Attorney General Francis North was seated in the House of Commons and began advising members on the legal aspects of prospective legislation. Later, as the concept of cabinet government developed, the office naturally became a member of the ministry.[4]

Today the Attorney General is an integral player in British government. Typically a member of the House of Commons, the Attorney General is usually active in the majority political party and appointed by the Prime Minister. The Solicitor General serves under the Attorney General and acts as the latter's chief deputy. These two officers are known collectively as the "Law Officers of the Crown."[5] In addition, the Attorney General has supervisory authority over the Director of Public Prosecutions (DPP). This official, however, serves at the pleasure of the Home Secretary and is customarily independent of routine direction by the Attorney General.[6]

Although the Attorney General administers no government department, he nevertheless has special obligations to the political executive in Britain. Edwards has classified the functions of the Attorney General into three categories: providing legal advice to the Cabinet, supervising important public prosecutions, and representing the Crown in legal affairs.[7] Not surprisingly, the union of political and legal roles on occasion has left the office vulnerable to criticism that its legal judgments are clouded by political considerations. Recent controversies over the prosecution of Clive Ponting and Peter Wright under the Official Secrets Act underscore this vulnerability.[8]

However, the British Attorney General's office remains far less controversial than its counterpart in the United States. Despite their shared history, the American and British offices operate in quite different constitutional environments. In Britain, well-defined conventions isolate the office's legal and political roles. The Attorney General, though legally a member of the ministry and exercising prerogative powers, is by political and constitutional tradition independent when carrying out law enforcement functions. It "is not in the power of government," said Prime Minister Balfour in 1903, "to direct the Attorney General to direct a prosecution."[9] While the Attorney General may seek advice from Cabinet colleagues on important cases, their opinions may not overrule his judgment, according to convention. Thus, while the Attorney General may seek out Cabinet members, contact regarding prosecutions should not be initiated in the opposite direction.

As mentioned, the powers and function of the British Attorney General's office have no origin in statute but are instead rooted in custom and tradition. Undergirding its independence is a 1924 episode that occurred while Ramsay MacDonald was Prime Minister and Sir Patrick Hastings was Attorney General. Hastings allegedly dropped a sensitive prosecution as a result of political pressure from the Prime Minister. The truth of the accusation remains a matter of debate; Hastings vowed throughout that he made the decision without interference. In any event, the episode precipitated the downfall of the MacDonald government and appears to have established as a constitutional rule the office's independent status.[10] In explaining the office's political independence, leading constitutional scholar, Geoffrey Marshall, writes:

> Since the prerogative of the Crown is exercised by convention on the advice of Ministers, there seems nothing inherently improper in the Ministry's formulating a collective view about the use of the prerogative in a particular case and directing the Attorney-General to comply with it. There is no doubt that they could enforce their view by the sanction of dismissal. . . . Nevertheless it cannot be doubted that since 1924 the holders of the Attorney General's office in both the major political parties have asserted that by convention in matters related to the institution and withdrawal of prosecutions the Attorney-General exercises his function independently of the Cabinet and could properly refuse to be instructed by them.[11]

The fact that the Attorney General may properly refuse direction from the Cabinet does not mean that under ordinary circumstances he should. All recent Attorneys General have argued the propriety and prudence of consulting political colleagues when a case raises important policy questions.[12] Nevertheless, the office's freedom from political accountability is well established. As Marshall notes: "In Britain the independence of the Attorney General, the principle public prosecutor, is legally insecure but conventionally safe."[13]

The conventions that surround the office in Britain are possible as a result of its constitutional setting. Unlike Americans, the British have no constitutional qualms about vesting executive functions in officers independent of the political executive. Underlying Britain's political institutions is the theory of "mixed government," not separation of powers.[14] There, the division or balance is not between specialized functions or departments of government, but between total constitutional principles (monarchical, oligarchical, and democratic) for dividing sovereign authority. These constitutional principles are intended to be represented respectively in the institutions of the King, the House of Lords, and the House of Commons. Consequently, there is no requirement that institutions control distinct and separate governmental functions. Because functions can be mixed in constitutional theory, officers performing executive functions may be partly or wholly independent of the political executive, the Cabinet.[15]

Above all, the political independence of the Attorney General in Britain is possible because the law is not as highly politicized as in the United States. The active policymaking role that the federal judiciary plays in the American system stands in marked contrast to the relatively apolitical function of judges in the British system. This difference is due not, as is commonly believed, to the existence of a written constitution. There is no reason why British courts could not actively create policy based on the principles of natural justice the way judges in the United States cite the Constitution. Instead, the role the courts play in political policymaking is a function of fragmentation in political authority. Divisions in sovereign authority permit essentially political disputes to be transformed into constitutional quarrels, carried out in the legal arena. As the British legal scholar Patrick Atiyah notes, "it is the constitutional-political role of the legislature and the executive that determines the (political) role of judges and the courts."[16]

The fusion of executive and legislative authority in Britain shields the administrative bureaucracy from the types of interbranch conflicts that routinely occur in the American system. The fact that policy disputes between the executive and Parliament cannot arise on a regular basis limits the policymaking opportunities for British courts, thus curtailing the political value of the legal policy bureaucracy.

The Colonial American Attorney General

From the outset, legal administration in America differed significantly from that in England. During the colonial period, each colony had a local Attorney General or equivalent official who acted as the delegate of the English Attorney General. These officers were vested with the same common-law powers as their English prototypes. The first colonial Attorney General, Richard Lee of Virginia, was appointed in 1643. The appointment of other colonial legal officers soon followed.[17]

Like the English Attorney General, these local officers had minor political duties in addition to litigating and prosecutorial responsibilities. Generally they were appointed by the colonial governor to serve as legal advisors to both the governor and legislature. Some even held elected seats in the legislature.[18] As the size and population of the colonies grew, so did the government's legal work. Expanded work loads usually prompted the appointment of subordinate officers to assist the colonial Attorney General. These officers were usually called solicitor general or deputy attorney general.[19]

Despite their integration into local government, colonial Attorneys General were supervised from afar and were responsible for representing the British government in colonial courts.[20] In practice, however, several factors gave these officers independence. Geography and slow communication in the seventeenth and eighteenth centuries made day-to-day supervision impossible. Moreover,

vesting the power of appointment in colonial political leaders perpetuated parochial loyalties, especially during periods of tension between central and colonial
governments. Thus, central control was more symbolic than real; in fact, colonial
legal administration was highly decentralized.[21]

The decentralized nature of government legal administration in the United
States changed little in the immediate aftermath of the American Revolution.
The Continental Congress was too preoccupied with the exigencies of war and
the maintenance of national unity to focus on establishing a coherent legal system. No national court system or system for legal administration was erected
under the Articles of Confederation.

This began to change, however, when claims against the new national government started making their way into state courts—some form of representation
became necessary. Congress's solution was to appoint an attorney, or "procurator," in each state to represent the national government in local courts.[22] No
central oversight existed for these federal procurators—each autonomously interpreted and pursued the government's legal interests within his respective jurisdiction. The chaos and disorder in legal policy that developed soon led to calls
for the creation of a national legal office. Only a month after the first procurator
was appointed, a special congressional committee proposed creating the position
of a federal Attorney General.[23] Lingering fears of centralized authority, however, as well as the press of wartime business, stymied such proposals for the
remainder of the Continental Congress.

Only after the Constitution of 1787 was ratified did Americans finally gain a
national legal office. When the first Congress met in 1789, its initial order of
business was to flesh out the details of the new federal executive branch. In
August and early September, Congress adopted and President Washington
signed a number of measures creating new departments. The War, Treasury, and
State departments were born, each to be headed by a secretary with broad discretionary powers.[24]

It is significant that the Attorney General's office was not established until
nearly a month later, when Congress turned its attention to the judicial
branch. On September 24, 1789, President George Washington signed "An
Act to Establish the Judicial Courts of the United States."[25] The Judiciary Act
provided for a Supreme Court, lower federal courts, district attorneys, and the
appointment of

> . . . a meet person, learned in the law, to act as attorney-general for the United
> States, who shall be sworn or affirmed to a faithful execution of his office;
> whose duty it shall be to prosecute and conduct all suits in the Supreme Court
> in which the United States shall be concerned, and to give his advice and
> opinion upon questions of law when required by the President of the United
> States, or when requested by the heads of any of the departments, touching any
> matters that may concern their departments, and shall receive such compensa-
> tion for his services as shall by law be provided.[26]

By using the title "Attorney General," Congress no doubt had in mind the British office with which it was familiar. Although the office itself might not be new, uprooting it from its English history and grafting it into the constitutional structure of the new government presented formidable problems. A new legal order had been established; the office could no longer rely entirely on English common law for definition. Moreover, the provisions of the Judiciary Act that outlined the Attorney General's functions and authority were vague. Consequently, the role the office plays in American government emerges largely out of custom and practice in the early years of the new republic.

The U.S. Attorney General

The office confronting the first U.S. Attorney General, Edmund Randolph of Virginia, appointed by George Washington in 1789, was nothing like the powerful post that exists today. It was not seen as a policymaking position; Randolph's $1,500 per annum salary was less than half the $3,500 received by heads of the executive departments.[27] The position was so unattractive that President Washington had to lure Randolph with the promise of increased remuneration in his private law practice. The salary, Washington said, "appears to have been fixed at what it is from a belief that the station would confer pre-eminence on its possessor, and procure for him a decided preference of professional employment."[28] The first Attorney General had no extended office or establishment to assist in performing his functions. Although the Judiciary Act established federal district attorneys in each of the U.S. judicial districts, these officers were presidential appointees and not responsible to the Attorney General.[29]

Despite the office's meager rewards, Randolph, a former governor of Virginia and close personal friend of Washington, felt obliged to accept. On February 2, 1790, he arrived in New York, presented himself to the Supreme Court, and took the oath of office. The United States had its first Attorney General.[30]

Unlike other cabinet offices, the Attorney General's post was conceived as a part-time position. The low pay was interpreted as authorization for the occupant to maintain private practice. Early Attorneys General resided in the capital city only when the Supreme Court was in session.[31] Randolph expressed frustration with the arrangement when he wrote to Washington: "I am a sort of mongrel between the State and the U.S.; called an officer of some rank under the latter, and yet thrust out to get a livelihood in the former—perhaps in a petty mayor's or county court."[32]

Nevertheless, Randolph's personal relationship with the President made him a powerful figure in Washington's administration. Washington sought Randolph's counsel on more than just legal matters.[33] Indeed, Washington came to rely so heavily on Randolph's political advice that Thomas Jefferson complained to a friend in 1790: "the government is directed solely by Randolph."[34] In 1792, Washington invited Randolph to attend cabinet meetings even though he headed no department.[35] The close relationship between Randolph and Washington set an important precedent that continues to define the character of the office to this day. Presidents have always sought to appoint a close personal friend or confidant as Attorney General and the office's conventional inclusion in the cabinet institutionalized its role as a political advisor.

After Randolph came a succession of Attorneys General who, though individually distinguished, had little impact on the office or its functions: William Bradford (1794–1795), Charles Lee (1795–1801), Levi Lincoln (1801–1805), John Breckenridge (1805–1806), Caesar Rodney (1807–1811), and William Pinkney (1811–1814). Both Bradford and Breckenridge died in office, but the others went on to serve distinguished political careers. Lincoln served as Governor of Massachusetts and was appointed (he died before serving) Associate Justice of the Supreme Court. Rodney and Pinkney each served in both the House of Representatives and the U.S. Senate. The Attorney General's position, however, retained its rather peculiar part-time character. In his pioneering study of early administrative history, historian Leonard White summed up the unique situation: "he [the Attorney General] had no establishment . . . [and] was assigned to duties only in connection with the operation of the courts. He received no reports and was in a curious way disconnected from the actual conduct of the government's everyday business."[36]

The work load of the early office was meager. Its statutory duties were to represent the federal government in the Supreme Court and to render legal opinions to the executive.[37] The newness of national judicial-administrative institutions and the reluctance to view the law as a policy instrument meant few cases reached the Supreme Court docket in early years. District attorneys usually disposed of cases involving the federal government in state or federal district courts.[38] As the volume of government business gradually increased the office's work became more demanding. In 1814, Congress, which was relying on the Attorney General as its general legal counsel, considered legislation requiring him to reside year-round in Washington, D.C. William Pinkney, who did not want to forsake a lucrative practice in Baltimore, opposed the measure and immediately resigned. In any event, the bill did not pass. In appointing Richard Rush to succeed Pinkney, however, President James Madison obtained an informal promise from Rush that he would live in the capital, at least while Congress was in session.[39]

Rush's successor, William Wirt, became the first Attorney General to establish an official residence in Washington.[40] His continual presence led to further growth in the office's duties as President James Monroe noted in 1817: "being at the seat of government throughout the year, [Wirt's] labors have increased by giving opinions to the different departments and public offices. . . . The removal of the office to Washington has more than doubled the entire business under this head."[41] In a 1927 study of the Justice Department, political historian Albert Langeluttig called Wirt "the first great American Attorney General."[42] Wirt served in the office twelve years, longer than any incumbent before or after. His tenure completely redefined the office, expanding its duties and formalizing procedures.[43] On the flyleaf of the earliest Justice Department record book appears Wirt's own handwriting:

> Finding on my appointment, this day, no books, documents, or papers of any kind to inform me of what has been done by any one of my predecessors, since the establishment of the Federal Government, and feeling very strongly the inconvenience, both to the nation and myself, from this omission, I have determined to remedy it, so far as depends on myself, and to keep a regular record of every official opinion which I shall give while I hold office, for the use of my successors.[44]

This note is the beginning of the compiled opinions of the Attorney General, which Congress ordered collected and printed starting in 1841.[45] Wirt's own opinions as Attorney General filled over 500 pages of the first volume. Recognizing the office's increased work load, in 1818 Congress increased Wirt's salary to $3,500 and provided him with a clerk and office expenses. The expense funds, however, were only a one-time appropriation. Not until 1831 did Congress begin making regular appropriations for office expenses and book purchases.[46]

Wirt's most important contribution as Attorney General took the form of an opinion to President Monroe regarding the nature of the office itself. In his opinion, Wirt said "republican orthodoxy" required that "the influence of every office should be confined within the strict limits prescribed for it by law." In particular, he said, the Attorney General should no longer act as legal counsel for Congress. Because the Judiciary Act made him an advisor to the executive only, Wirt decided to cease providing Congress with routine opinions regarding the constitutionality of legislation. The practice, he said, had evolved from a sense of "courtesy," not statutory duty, and had become too burdensome.[47]

Wirt's successor, John Berrien, was the first Attorney General asked to resign as a result of a disagreement with the President on an issue of law. Berrien refused to acquiesce in President Andrew Jackson's strategy to disestablish the National Bank. When asked by Jackson to provide a legal opinion allowing him to unilaterally withdraw funds from the bank, Berrien refused. Reportedly, Jackson then told his Attorney General "you must find a law authorizing the act or I will appoint an Attorney General who will."[48] When Berrien still resisted, Jackson carried through on his threat and the Attorney General became a casualty of Jackson's 1831 cabinet purge.

After obtaining Berrien's resignation, Jackson appointed Roger Taney Attorney General. Taney promptly wrote an opinion authorizing divestiture of the bank. One hurdle remained; despite Taney's opinion, Treasury Secretary William Duane refused to act on Jackson's plan. Jackson fired him and moved the ever-compliant Taney into the Treasury post.[49] Eventually the funds were removed and the bank closed. Congress sent a resolution to Jackson that reauthorized the bank and censored Jackson's actions in removing his cabinet officers.

The President responded with his famed letter of protest. Actually authored by Taney, the letter shaped an argument destined to be repeated by future Presidents. Under the Constitution, the letter said, "the entire executive power is vested in the President." It follows that he alone has power to remove "those officers who are to aid him in the execution of the laws."[50]

Although Jackson's authority to remove Berrien and Duane was never challenged in court, an important precedent was established at a time when conventions surrounding the Attorney General's office were still malleable. Cabinet officers, even the Attorney General, apparently served at the pleasure of the President.[51] Congress in 1835 punished Taney for his earlier "political opinion" by rejecting his nomination to the Supreme Court. Following the 1836 Senate elections, however, he was renominated and confirmed as Chief Justice.[52]

Following the National Bank controversy, the Attorney General's office returned to obscurity. Between 1833 and 1853, the United States had ten Attorneys General: Benjamin Butler (1833–1838), Felix Grundy (1838–1839), Henry Dilworth Gilpin (1840–1841), Hugh Legare (1841–1843), John Nelson (1843–1845), John Mason (1845–1846), Nathan Clifford (1846–1848), Issac Toucey (1848–1849), Reverdy Johnson (1849–1850), and John Crittenden (1841 and 1850–1853). Crittenden is of singular interest because he became the only individual appointed to the office twice: by President William Henry Harrison in 1841 and by Millard Fillmore in 1850.[53]

Crittenden's successor, Caleb Cushing, served as Attorney General from 1853 to 1857. Highly talented and energetic, Cushing was the most outstanding member of President Franklin Pierce's cabinet.[54] He transformed the Attorney General's office into a full-time position, and he condemned any admixture of public office and private practice. The duties of the office, he said, are "quite sufficient to test to the utmost all the faculties of one man . . . [and] the government has the same precise claim on his services, in time and degree, as on those of the Secretary of State or the Secretary of the Treasury."[55]

As Attorney General, Cushing tackled new duties and responsibilities that increased the office's political power and linked it more firmly to the President's administration. Responsibility for advising the President on pardons and judicial nominations was transferred from the State Department. The Interior Department surrendered the duty of handling accounts for the federal courts. Routine legal correspondence, formerly handled by lawyers scattered throughout the executive departments, became centralized in the Attorney General's office.[56] Congress also added to the office's statutory duties during this period, giving it the job of advising treaty commissioners, examining government land titles, adjudicating claims under Indian treaties, representing the government in the newly created Court of Claims, administering government patents, advising the Sinking Fund Commission, and compiling and publishing federal laws.[57] To complete all these new duties, Congress authorized the appointment of an Assistant Attorney General in 1859 and raised the Attorney General's salary to $6,000, finally placing it on the same level as heads of the executive departments.[58]

Like William Wirt, Cushing left his mark as Attorney General by authoring an opinion regarding the office itself. In a letter to President Pierce, he outlined two developments that had come to define the office.[59] First, Cushing pointed out that the office had undergone an institutional transformation from a judicial to an executive branch post. Originally a "quasi-judicial" office, through custom and convention it had became "subordinated" to the President, he said.[60] Second, Cushing argued that to effectively dispatch the legal business of the government, especially litigation in the Supreme Court, the office needed greater authority to control district attorneys and other government law officers. Fragmentation in the government's legal authority had impeded the development of coherent legal policy. He recommended that Congress pass legislation to create a department of law and bring the district attorneys under the Attorney General's supervision.[61]

Before there was time to implement Cushing's recommendations, the nation was plunged into Civil War. Not surprisingly, the Attorney General was inundated during this period by legal work resulting from war and Reconstruction.[62] Between 1857 and 1870, nine Attorneys General served: following Cushing came Jeremiah Black (1857–1860), Edwin Stanton (1860–1861), Edward Bates (1861–1864), James Speed (1864–1866), Henry Stanbery (1866–1868), William Evarts (1868–1869), and Ebenezer Hoar (1869–1870). The legal exigencies of the war and President Lincoln's use of emergency powers affirmed still further the view that the Attorney General's office had become a subordinate of and advocate for the President. Three months after taking office, Edward Bates was asked to find legal justifications for Lincoln's wartime policies. In their book *Federal Justice*, Homer Cummings and Carl McFarland portray how Lincoln's suspension of the writ of habeas corpus brought the administration into direct conflict with Taney's Supreme Court. The writ, of course, is the traditional means of preventing imprisonment without trial. The Constitution allows the writ to be suspended, but not without congressional authorization, which Lincoln did not obtain. When Taney issued a writ on behalf of an active secessionist in *Ex parte Merryman* (1861), Lincoln refused to comply with the order.[63] To justify the President's action, Bates drafted a curious opinion—although the President could not unilaterally suspend the writ, Bates argued, he could suspend the privilege of the writ by refusing to release those held for rebellious acts. In other words, the courts could not be stopped from ordering, but the executive could lawfully refuse to obey.[64]

In the *Prize Cases* (1863), Bates confronted another wartime legal dilemma, this time regarding presidential authority to order a naval blockade of Southern seaports.[65] From the outset of hostilities, the government had maintained that the conflict was a domestic insurrection, not a war. The terminology was important; if it were an insurrection, foreign governments would be discouraged from recognizing the Confederacy. Therefore the government could prosecute secessionists for high treason rather than treat them as prisoners of war. In arguing the *Prize Cases*, however, Bates was forced to rely on the laws of war to justify the

North's naval blockade of the South and its capture of neutral ships. Critics attacked the government's legal duplicity—either the conflict was not a war, in which case the capture of prizes was illegal, or it was a war, in which case the government was forced to admit the existence of opponents in arms. Fortunately for Bates, the Supreme Court extricated the government from its dilemma by concluding that the legal conditions of war did not require both parties be recognized as sovereign states. "It is not the less a civil war, with belligerent parties in hostile array, because it may be called an insurrection by one side, and the insurgents be considered as rebels or traitors," the Court noted, thereby upholding the blockade and leaving undisturbed the government's contention that the conflict was an insurrection.[66]

Bates later found himself authoring opinions supporting the Emancipation Proclamation and demands for redress of wartime crimes committed by the Confederacy.[67] He was, however, aware that the executive was capable of committing excesses, even in times of war. Cummings and McFarland point out that his sense of duty to the law led him into conflict with military leaders and Republican radicals often impatient with the civil legal process. In particular, he and Secretary of War Edwin Stanton often battled over government legal policy. Stanton, who had himself served as Attorney General under President James Buchanan, thought Bates too hesitant to take the war into the legal arena. Frustrated by the slow process of confiscating Confederate property in civilian courts under the Confiscation Acts, Stanton established provost courts to facilitate direct military appropriations of enemy property.[68] Furious with this intrusion into civil administration, Bates appealed to Lincoln, who issued an order requiring the Attorney General's approval for all proceedings under the Confiscation Acts.[69] Bates later wrote, "there seems to be a general and growing disposition of the military, wherever stationed, to engross all power, and to treat the Civil Government with contumely, as if the object were to bring it into contempt."[70]

The most serious confrontation between Bates and Stanton occurred over efforts to extend the jurisdiction of military courts over the civilian population. Bates objected to this practice and refused to authorize or defend it while he was Attorney General. When Bates resigned in 1864, Stanton prevailed on Bates's successor, James Speed, to write two opinions authorizing the extension of jurisdiction.[71] From his home in Missouri, Bates railed against "the corruption and degradation of the Law Department" and against his "imbecile successor" for caving in to Stanton.[72] A year later, in *Ex parte Milligan* (1866), the Supreme Court vindicated Bates.[73] The laws and usage of war, the Court said, "can never be applied to citizens in states which have upheld the authority of the government, and where the courts are open and their process unobstructed."[74] The Court's decision in *Milligan* discredited Speed, who later resigned, and dealt a severe blow to the legal policies of the military administration.

Speed's successor, Henry Stanbery, was destined to become a casualty of the conflict that brewed after the war between President Andrew Johnson and radical

Republicans in Congress. In 1868, Stanbery resigned to act as Johnson's personal attorney during his impeachment trial. At the trial's conclusion, Johnson renominated Stanbery as Attorney General; however, the Senate refused to reconfirm him.[75]

Two years later the Attorney General was again embroiled in Reconstruction politics. With legislation to create a law department being debated in Congress, President Ulysses S. Grant asked his Attorney General, Ebenezer Hoar, to step down. Hoar apparently had made himself unpopular in Congress by failing to consult lawmakers on judicial nominations. Grant, wanting to bolster Southern support, saw the advantage of removing Hoar and appointing a Southerner in his place. Consequently, on June 23, 1870, Amos Akerman, a Georgian, was appointed Attorney General and eventually became the first head of the U.S. Department of Justice.[76]

The Drive to Centralize Government Legal Work

Creation of the Justice Department in 1870 was the culmination of efforts since Randolph's day to centralize the government's legal work. In addition to the district attorneys, Congress also created legal officers in several of the executive branch departments. Many of these officers were titled "solicitors" for their respective department, e.g., the Solicitor of the Treasury. Solicitors had authority to represent their departments in legal affairs independent of the Attorney General.[77] Without the ability to control government litigation in the lower courts and the legal activities of other executive branch officers, the Attorney General was unable to coordinate government legal policy. In a sense, the early Attorney General was no better off than William Hussee had been in 1472. He was the government's chief legal representative, but he was only one among many.

Historians have debated whether Congress intended a fragmented and decentralized system of legal administration, or whether the system's odd structure was merely an oversight during the hectic development of the new nation.[78] Whether Congress intended such a system or not, the problems presented by decentralized administration became apparent immediately. Edmund Randolph found himself unable to control even routine matters pertaining to the federal government's legal business. In December 1791, he wrote President Washington:

> Many instances have occurred in which the heads of the Departments have requested that suits should be prosecuted in different States under my direction. It has been always my inclination to conform to their wishes; but the want of a fixed relation between the attorneys of the districts and the Attorney General, has rendered it impossible for me to take charge of matters on which I was not authorized to give instructions. . . . [Moreover] from the same source it may frequently arise that the United States may be deeply effected by various proceedings in the inferior courts, which no appeal can rectify.[79]

Washington transmitted the letter to Congress and asked for legislation to rectify the situation, however his proposal, the first of several attempts by Presidents to centralize the government's legal authority, failed in Congress.[80] President Madison made another request in 1814, asking Congress to expand the Attorney General's authority to bring suits in lower courts as well as to incorporate district attorneys under his supervision. Once again, however, the request was denied.[81]

Congress's failure to enact legislation, however, did not assuage the need for reform. The problems of coordination and control only worsened as the government's business expanded. In 1829, President Jackson recommended the creation of a full-scale department of law.[82] His proposal grew out of concern about debts owed the government following the War of 1812. Congress assigned an officer in the Treasury Department to collect the debts, but because that officer was an accountant, not an attorney, he was unable to bring suit to recover the money. Jackson wanted the Attorney General to take over debt collections and proposed that Congress create a department to assist him.

Legislation to establish Jackson's law department was drafted and introduced in Congress. The bill, however, became a pawn in the political struggle between Jackson, John Calhoun, and Senator Daniel Webster.[83] Congress, still feuding with Jackson over the National Bank, was not anxious to create another department or further centralize executive power. Playing on old fears of central authority, Webster used his formidable parliamentary skills to stop the Jackson plan and introduced a countermeasure. Webster's bill, which passed Congress in 1830, created a Solicitor of the Treasury and gave the office independent litigating authority to collect debts in federal and state courts. In addition, the bill gave the office power to supervise district attorneys and U.S. marshals "in all matters and proceedings, appertaining to suits in which the United States is a party."[84] The provision granted the Solicitor of the Treasury controls not even the Attorney General possessed. After 1830, then, federal legal administration was distinctly two-headed.[85] The Attorney General acted as an elite legal barrister, representing the federal government only when an issue made it all the way to the Supreme Court. The Solicitor of the Treasury, on the other hand, became the government's chief law enforcement official in the lower courts.

Once the precedent was established, Congress went on to create solicitor positions in other executive departments: General Land Office in 1836,[86] Court of Claims in 1855,[87] War Department in 1863,[88] Navy Department in 1865,[89] and in the Internal Revenue Service and Department of State both in 1866.[90] Although the relationship between these new officers and the Attorney General was usually amicable, lack of coordination continued to hinder the development of coherent legal policy at the federal level. President Jackson again called on Congress to create a law department in 1832. Once more Congress rejected the idea.[91] President James Polk unsuccessfully called for creation of a law department in 1845.[92] President Millard Fillmore's Secretary of the Interior, Alexander Stuart, was the first to propose that a law department be called the "Department of Justice." Stuart predicted that a central legal department would save money through administrative efficiency; but Congress, still leery of central legal authority, once again declined to act.[93]

Not until 1854 did Congress itself propose consolidating the government's legal work. In an effort to reduce government cost, the Senate Committee on Retrenchment and Reform asked Attorney General Caleb Cushing and other executive department heads for recommendations on streamlining administration. Rather than reply directly to the committee, Cushing sent his aforementioned letter to President Pierce on the nature and operation of the Attorney General's office.[94] Cushing recommended that Congress centralize all government legal work into a single department. Pierce transmitted the letter to Congress, which promptly asked Cushing to reduce his suggestions to bill form. Cushing's proposal met the same fate as previous centralization attempts. The Senate Judiciary Committee, labeling the plan as too costly, refused to let the bill out of committee.[95]

It took a crisis to force Congress to act. At the outbreak of the Civil War in 1861, the Attorney General's office was overworked, understaffed, and lacked authority to coordinate government litigation. An avalanche of legal claims brought about by the war quickly demonstrated the inefficiency of the existing legal-administrative system. Lacking assistance from a central office, district attorneys resorted to hiring outside counsels to help meet the surge in litigation. Because the Attorney General was already overloaded, additional appropriations were needed to augment legal services in the various executive departments which began contracting out routine legal business. The cost of outside services soon began draining the treasury. Between 1864 and 1867 alone, the federal government spent over half a million dollars on private legal services.[96] Congress's urgent desire to economize now became the impetus behind—rather than a hindrance to—creation of a law department.

By 1867, three congressional committees were considering legislation aimed at improving legal administration. Attorney General Henry Stanbery recommended that, at the very least, Congress create an office of "Solicitor General" to assist in carrying out government litigation. Stanbery also wanted all other executive branch legal officers transferred to a single department.[97] Before Congress could act on Stanbery's recommendation, however, the impeachment trial of Andrew Johnson intervened. The unpopularity of Johnson and Stanbery temporarily dampened congressional enthusiasm for the new law department.

Finally, in 1870, with Ulysses S. Grant in the White House and the Reconstruction controversy beginning to fade, Congress created the long-awaited law department. On February 25, Representative Jenckes of Rhode Island reported from the Committee on Retrenchment an act establishing a Department of Justice. In explaining the act to the Senate, Jenckes spelled out existing problems:

> We have found that there has been a most unfortunate result from this separation of law powers. We find one interpretation of the laws of the United States in one Department and another interpretation in another Department. . . . It is for the purpose of having a unity of decision, a unity of jurisprudence, if I may use that expression, in the executive law of the United States, that this bill proposes that all the law officers therein provided for shall be subordinated to one head.[98]

After only perfunctory opposition, the bill was enacted and signed by the President on June 22, 1870. The Department of Justice came into formal existence on July 1, 1870.[99]

The Attorney General and the Department of Justice

The creation of the Justice Department in 1870 permanently altered government legal administration in the United States. In particular, it transformed the nature of the Attorney General's office itself, changing it from an elite one-man barrister in the Supreme Court into a major administrative position. The 1870 act clearly intended to make the Attorney General the titular head of government legal administration.[100] Section 3 placed all executive branch solicitors and attorneys under the direct control of the Attorney General. Section 16 extended the office's control over the district attorneys. Section 5 secured control over government litigation generally, providing that "the Attorney General may, whenever he deems it in the interest of the United States, conduct and argue any case in which the government is interested, in any court of the United States, or may require the solicitor general or any officer of his department to do so."[101] The act also established three new officers: the Solicitor General, who became the second-ranking officer in the Justice Department, and two Assistant Attorneys General. Commenting on Congress's intent behind the 1870 act, the Supreme Court noted in *Perry v. United States* (1893) that the language of the act is "too comprehensive and too specific to leave any doubt that Congress intended to gather into the Department of Justice, under the supervision and control of the Attorney-General, all the litigation and all the law business in which the United States are interested."[102]

The Justice Department Act, however, merely incorporated the Attorney General's office as it existed and made it head of the new department. The act thus codified the office's old roles along with its new. Since 1870, the Attorney General has worn several hats: Supreme Court barrister, cabinet-level political advisor, department administrator, and chief law enforcement officer. Because Congress placed the authority of the Justice Department entirely under the discretionary control of the Attorney General, the Justice Department can literally be said to have but one function—assisting the Attorney General. The Supreme Court declared in 1927: "the Attorney General is the head of the Department and its functions are all to be exercised under his supervision and direction."[103]

Although the size, powers, and functions of the Justice Department have since been augmented by statute and executive orders, the 1870 act still provides the statutory foundation for the Attorney General's office and its functions. These functions are summarized in the 1986 Attorney General's Report to Congress:

> The Attorney General is responsible for supervising and directing the administration and operation of the offices, boards, divisions, and bureaus which comprise the Department. He also furnishes advice on legal matters to the President, the Cabinet, and the heads of the executive Departments and agencies of the government. In addition, the Attorney General represents the United States in legal matters generally, and makes recommendations to the President concerning appointments to federal judicial positions and to positions within the Department, including U.S. Attorneys and Marshals.[104]

If the Attorney General's institutional nature has remained fundamentally unaltered since 1870, the political significance of its functions has not. There are two reasons for this change: First, the legal-political environment in which it operates changed radically during the twentieth century. Second, the Justice Department has grown in both size and authority. Shifts in the legal-political environment will be discussed in later chapters, but one must first understand something of the alterations in government legal administration brought about by the sheer size of the modern-day Department of Justice.

The growth of the Justice Department into a powerful bureaucracy mirrors the transformation of the federal government from one of limited means and ends into a positive, social-regulatory state.[105] The nationalization of America's political power since the last quarter of the nineteenth century was accomplished primarily through the enactment of congressional statutes that vested massive amounts of new regulatory and law enforcement power in executive branch agencies such as the Department of Justice. While changes in the size or budget of the Justice Department can be measured quantitatively, such analyses provide little insight into the reasons for such growth. Knowing the number of employees in a government bureaucracy or the size of its budget tells us little about its actual power. For instance, the Bureau of the Census is extremely large, but it exercises little control over public policy. Likewise, relatively small agencies, such as the Federal Reserve Board, possess extraordinary power. An examination of quantitative factors is only valuable as a starting point. Other factors, such as the creation of divisions and management structures within the department, or changes in statutory authority, must also be examined. All these elements must be integrated into any account of bureaucratic growth of the Justice Department since 1870.

Budgetary Growth

The first regularly appropriated budget for the Department of Justice was for fiscal year 1872. At a meager $209,500, the budget was less than half the appro-

Figure 2.1. **Justice Department Budget 1920–1990 in Appropriated Dollars**

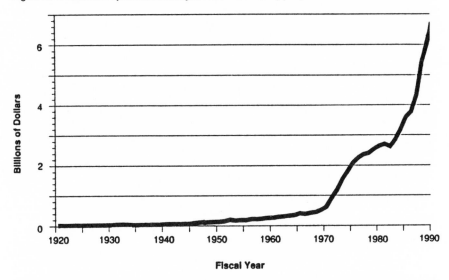

Fiscal Year

Source: Budget figures taken from *United States Statistical Abstracts* (1920–1990)

priation for the Post Office Department that same year.[106] During its first one hundred years the Justice Department's budget grew at a steady rate, reaching an appropriation of $17 million by 1920 and $641 million by 1970. After 1970 its budget grew at a much faster rate. Between 1970 and 1980 it nearly quadrupled to $2.641 billion. Then, between 1980 and 1990 the budget tripled itself again to $6.755 billion.[107] Figure 2.1 depicts the expansion of the department's budget.

Inflation accounts for some of the department's budgetary growth. Even after adjusting for inflation, however, one can see that the budget has increased dramatically. Figure 2.2 traces the Justice Department's budget since 1920 using constant dollars. Using adjusted figures, we can see that the department's budget underwent three periods of real growth: from 1920 to 1932, from 1970 to 1977, and from 1983 to 1990.

Following each of the first two periods of real growth, the department's budget went through a period of retrenchment. After increasing by nearly 400 percent between 1920 and 1932, the budget contracted slightly during the next six years. Beginning in 1940, it resumed a steady, slower rate of growth. In 1970, a second spurt of real growth occurred as the budget increased by 300 percent in just seven years. Immediately after this period came five years of budgetary retrenchment. Finally, a third growth spurt began in 1983 and continues today.

If the growth in the Justice Department's budget cannot be explained by inflation alone, neither can it be explained entirely by overall growth of the federal government. Although the federal budget as a percentage of gross national product (GNP) has increased sharply since the turn of the century, the

Figure 2.2. **Justice Department Budget 1920–1990 in Constant 1990 Dollars**

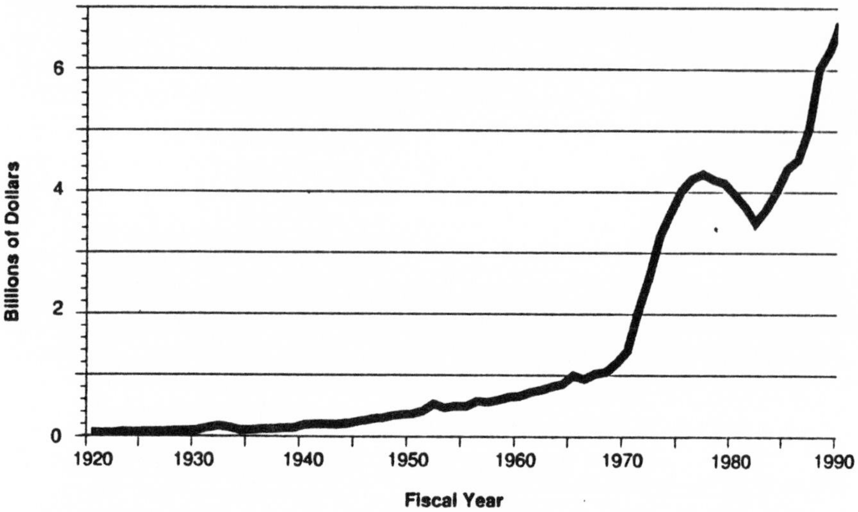

Fiscal Year

Source: United States Statistical Abstract (1920–1988); and Budget of the United States Government for Fiscal 1990 with implicit price index calculations made by author.

Justice Department's budget has increased relative to that of the government as a whole. Its share of the federal budget increased from 2 percent in 1920 to 4 percent in 1960 and 7 percent in 1974. In the mid-1970s, it dropped back to roughly 5 percent of the GNP and has remained constant since.[108]

What caused the growth spurts? Some resulted merely from the transfer to Justice of functions previously performed by other departments or agencies. For example, the Immigration and Naturalization Service, which currently consumes 16 percent of the department's budget, was reassigned from the Treasury Department in 1940. Longer-term patterns of growth, however, cannot be explained by such isolated transfers. Instead, one must view them in the context of the evolution of the federal government's power and responsibilities.

The expansion of the federal government during the twentieth century has not occurred evenly or systematically. Studies of increases in the federal bureaucracy have identified "ratchets"—periods of crisis or ideological realignment—when the government assumed new authority. Once authority was established by law, bureaucracy expanded in its wake. In his study of the federal bureaucracy, political scientist Robert Higgs identifies several "critical episodes" since the turn of the century—the Progressive Era, the New Deal, World War II, and the Great Society—during which federal authority was ratcheted upwards and expansion of the federal bureaucracy followed.[109]

Higgs's description of the way government grows fits the picture that emerges when we examine changes in the Justice Department's budget. Growth has been neither steady nor evenly distributed within the department. Rather, as the federal government assumed new regulatory and law enforcement roles, bureaucratic divisions were erected or expanded. For instance, revenue and antitrust statutes passed during the Progressive and New Deal periods eventually led to the creation of the antitrust and tax divisions. Criminal justice, environmental protection, and civil rights statutes associated with the Great Society era led to the creation of several more divisions and offices charged with enforcing those statutes during the 1960s and 1970s. The Office of Justice Programs, established in 1968, for example, now consumes 6 percent of the Department's budget. Finally, the extraordinary growth experienced during the 1980s can largely be attributed to expanded federal efforts aimed at immigration control and drug enforcement. The Drug Enforcement Administration, for example, created in 1973, today consumes nearly 8 percent of the department's budget and is likely to continue to grow during the 1990s. Thus, by examining changes in management structure and bureaucratic development, one gains a better appreciation of the nature, not just the amount, of growth in the Justice Department.

Bureaucratic Development

In 1870, the Justice Department consisted of only four general officers (the Attorney General, the Solicitor General, and two Assistant Attorneys General), sixteen clerks, and three messengers.[110] As long as the department remained small, there was little need for management subdivisions or area specialization. Of the few attorneys, some worked only on a part-time or contract basis, and their assignments remained flexible.[111] In the Attorney General's reports to Congress, the department's activities were described without identifying which functions were performed by which officers. The solicitors in the departments of Treasury, Labor, and Commerce, though formally members of the Justice Department, continued to operate semi-autonomously. They remained in offices attached to their former departments and issued reports to Congress included as appendices to the Attorney General's.[112]

Congress responded to increases in the government's legal work by creating temporary positions rather than increasing the Justice Department's full-time staff. Special Assistant Attorneys General were appointed to handle such matters as litigation involving polygamy and the Mormon Church, Indian deprivation suits, and government land-patent disputes in the western territories. Reports from these officials also appeared as appendices to the Attorney General's annual report.[113]

As the Justice Department began to grow, the need for specialization and hierarchical management structures increased. By 1900, Congress had established nine Assistant and Special Assistant Attorneys General. There was one Assistant Attorney General each for the Court of Claims, Post Office, and Interior Department, and three more performed general duties.[114] There were also three Special Assistant Attorneys General: one for Indian depredations suits, one for litigation before the Spanish Treaty Claims Commission, and one for pardons.[115]

In 1903, Congress created two new posts, an appointment clerk and the office of Assistant to the Attorney General (not to be confused with Assistant Attorney General).[116] The former assisted in screening presidential nominees for federal judgeships or for district attorney and federal marshal offices. The latter became an administrative deputy to the Attorney General and was the department's third-ranking officer just below the Solicitor General. At that time, 260 non-supervisory employees worked in the main Justice Department and nearly 1,300 in field offices throughout the United States.[117]

Attorney General Charles Bonaparte reported to Congress in 1907 that the duties of the Solicitor General, the Assistant to the Attorney General and of the several Assistant Attorneys General within the department "have now grown so responsible and onerous that they are shut out from private practice and compelled to devote their entire time to the service of the Government."[118] Bonaparte suggested that Congress increase the salaries of these officials and create an "Assistant Secretary of Justice" to relieve them of their administrative tasks and allow them to focus more fully on their "legal duties."[119]

Bonaparte also recommended that the government would save money by establishing its own detective force. Prior to this time, the department employed private investigators on a contract-only basis. Although Congress refused to establish the Assistant Secretary of Justice position, two years later it did appropriate money for a permanent staff of investigators which later became the nucleus for the Federal Bureau of Investigation (FBI).[120]

Bonaparte's successor, George Wickersham, took the first real steps toward erecting a permanent management structure in the Justice Department. In 1909, Wickersham organized the department's personnel into four function-based divisions: the Bureau of Investigation; Bureau of Public Lands; Customs Division; and Bureau of Pardons. He also instituted a merit recruitment and promotion program for career employees, and clarified the supervisory authority of the Assistant to the Attorney General.[121]

Wickersham's modest effort prefigured more comprehensive restructuring by Attorney General A. Mitchell Palmer in 1919, at which time two developments led to a massive increase in the federal government's legal work. First, Progressive Era statutes expanding federal regulatory authority gave the department new responsibilities and involved it in burdensome new litigation involving other agencies. Second, American involvement in the First World War led to a surge of new civil claims against the government.[122]

To cope with the increased workload, Palmer reorganized the Justice Department. The Solicitor General and Assistant to the Attorney General remained the department's second- and third-ranking officers. Under them, however, were created eight functionally based divisions, each headed by an Assistant Attorney General: Antitrust; Criminal Prosecutions; Defence of Claims (later renamed the Civil Division); Tax and Internal Revenue; Public Lands; Customs; Admiralty and Insular Affairs; and the Division for Miscellaneous Matters, which included subdivisions for Investigation and for Field Services.[123]

Palmer's reorganization of the Justice Department established the foundation for its subsequent development. Although it has continued to grow in size, the functional mode of division and the major subdivisions erected in 1919 still lie at the heart of the department. The Antitrust, Civil, Tax, Criminal, and Lands divisions, as well as the Bureau of Investigation and field service offices all form part of the present-day organization.

The Antitrust Division carries out the Attorney General's responsibilities under the nation's antitrust laws, such as the Sherman Antitrust Act of 1890 and Clayton Antitrust and Federal Trade Acts of 1914.[124] The objective of these and other antitrust laws enforced by the department is to "promote competition in open markets."[125] Both the language and goals of these statutes, however, are vague. What they mean in terms of enforcement action against particular corporations is left to the discretion of the Attorney General. Thus, the Antitrust Division is capable of playing an important role in shaping the nation's business and economic climate. The division is divided into nine sections: Economic Litigation, Economic Regulation, Communications and Finance, Transportation Energy and Agriculture, Litigation, Appeals, Foreign Commerce, Professional and Intellectual Property, and Legal Policy.[126]

The Civil Division represents the federal government in civil litigation. Its functions can be broken into four separate areas: defending executive branch policies in court; bringing suit to collect money owed the government; defending the United States or its officers against tortuous claims; and enforcing federal consumer-protection laws, immigration laws, and other program initiatives. It has branches and offices for Commercial Litigation, Torts, Federal Programs, Consumer Litigation, Immigration, Policy and Legislation regarding civil matters, and Appellate Litigation.[127]

The Tax Division represents the government in civil and criminal litigation arising from Internal Revenue statutes. It assists the Internal Revenue Service (IRS) in collecting revenue, and helps to establish legal guidelines for the IRS and taxpayers. The division is divided into four Civil Trial Sections (one each for the north, south, west, and central regions), a Criminal Section, an Appellate Section, and an Office of Review.[128]

The Division for Criminal Prosecutions, renamed the Criminal Division in 1928, carries out the Attorney General's plenary responsibility to enforce federal criminal statutes. In addition to setting prosecutorial guidelines, it coordinates the activities of the U.S. attorneys, who are the government's front-line prosecutors. The division encompasses the following sections and offices: Organized Crime and Racketeering, Public Integrity, Fraud, General Litigation and Legal Advice, Appeals, Internal Security, Narcotics and Drugs, Policy and Management, International Affairs, Special Investigations, Legislation, Administration, Enforcement Operations, and Asset Forfeitures.[129]

The Division of Public Lands was retitled the Land and Natural Resources Division in 1965. The name change reflects the evolution of federal land policy from land dispossession to land retention and management. The division's original responsibility to represent the government in title disputes under homesteading, railroad, and other statutes aimed at transfer of title to federal property, has gradually shifted to representing federal land management agencies such as the Forest Service, National Park Service, and Bureau of Land Management. Environmental statutes added during the 1970s, especially the Clean Air Act of 1970, Water Pollution Control Act of 1972, Resource Conservation and Recovery Act of 1976, and Comprehensive Environmental Response, Compensation and Liability (Superfund) Act of 1980 have also given the division a major environmental regulatory role. The division is currently divided into eight sections: Environmental Enforcement; Wildlife and Marine Resources; Land Acquisitions; Appeals; Environmental Defense, Policy Legislation and Special Litigation; Indian Resources; and General Litigation.[130]

Attorney General Palmer's report to Congress for 1920 was the first to include a separate report by the Solicitor General on government appellate litigation. Early Solicitors General had operated as administrative deputies with wide-ranging responsibilities.[131] The 1870 act, however, specifically said the Solicitor General could be required "to conduct and argue any case in which the government has an interest . . . in the Supreme Court . . . or any court of the United States."[132] This provision was not included in the statutory descriptions of other department officers. Thus, as specialization began to emerge in the Justice Department, the Solicitor General naturally became the department's chief litigator.

In 1895, Attorney General Judson Harmon issued an order requiring the Solicitor General's authorization before any government appeal could be taken to the Supreme Court. In 1919, Palmer extended the order to cover appeals to circuit courts as well.[133] The specialized litigating role of the Solicitor General became further entrenched when the position of Assistant to the Attorney General was created in 1903 and that of Deputy Attorney General in 1953. These new officers relieved the Solicitor General of administrative responsibilities and freed him to concentrate on litigation. Today, the office's only function is the control of government appellate litigation. In addition to authorizing appeals, the office conducts most cases involving the government as a party before the Supreme Court, and usually decides when the government will intervene as *amicus curiae* in the Supreme Court.[134]

Palmer's reorganization also created a division for central support of field services. Today there are three major offices in the Justice Department to support its field services: the Executive Office for United States Attorneys, the United States Marshal's Service, and the Executive Office for United States Trustees.

The Investigative Division was the final one set in place by Palmer's reorganization. During the early 1920s, it attracted controversy over its involvement in the infamous "Palmer Raids," investigations into the lives of alleged communists and anarchists. The controversy led Palmer's successor Attorney General Harlan Stone to reorganized the division's twenty-four investigators and place them under stricter supervision and control. In 1924, the new investigative unit was titled the Bureau of Investigation and a young investigator named J. Edgar Hoover was named its first head.[135]

Hoover headed the FBI for nearly fifty years, building it into a national investigative force of legendary repute. His conviction that federal investigations should be shielded from political control, combined with his formidable bureaucratic skills and institutionalized influence on Capitol Hill, molded the FBI into a fiefdom within the Justice Department. In clashes with his superior, the Attorney General, over the bureau's budget and mode of operation, Hoover often prevailed.[136] Indeed, when asked to pinpoint the greatest single challenge confronting the Attorney General, James Bennett, a former Assistant Attorney General, remarked "they all have the same problem—the control and management of J. Edgar Hoover."[137]

Although Hoover's directorship ended two decades ago, the FBI remains an oddity in the Justice Department. It is the department behemoth, employing more than 23,000 people and operating on a budget of more than $1.7 billion.[138] Attorneys General have made several attempts to reel back the independence the FBI gained under Hoover, but it still enjoys greater autonomy than any other division in the department. Although the director is under the Attorney General's supervision, he is the only major bureau chief or division head appointed to a fixed term. Moreover, the FBI carries on a unique relationship with Congress. As recently as 1989, Attorney General Thornburgh ordered FBI Director William Sessions to halt the "informational meetings" that directors have held routinely with congressional leaders since Hoover's reign. The meetings obviously were meant to maintain the FBI's independent ties to Congress.[139]

The FBI's primary responsibility is to gather evidence in criminal and civil cases to which the government is party, and to carry out foreign counterintelligence investigations. The bureau currently has eleven divisions: Legal Counsel, Inspection, Identification, Training, Laboratory, Administrative Services, Records Management, Technical Services, Intelligence, Criminal Investigation, and an Office for Congressional and Public Affairs.[140]

The Bureau of Prisons joined the Justice Department in 1930. Although the federal prisons system had been managed by Attorneys General since 1891, it was not until 1930 that Attorney General William Mitchell created a bureau for its administration. The bureau currently operates more than forty-seven federal institutions housing over 42,000 individuals.[141] After the FBI, the Prisons Bureau is the second largest component of the department, employing more than 15,000 on a budget of $1.7 billion.[142]

The Justice Department underwent a minor reorganization under Attorney General Homer Cummings in 1933. Cummings abolished the division of Admiralty, merging its functions into the Civil Division, and established the Office of Legal Counsel (OLC).[143] OLC provides institutional support to the Attorney General in his role as legal advisor to the President. Responsibility for drafting the formal opinions of the Attorney General, rendering legal advice to executive department officials, and reviewing executive orders was transferred to the OLC from the Solicitor General.[144] Because this office routinely is asked to develop legal positions to support the administration's policy initiatives, it often is viewed as one of the most politicized units in the department.

In 1940, the Immigration and Naturalization Service (INS) was transferred to Justice from the department of the Treasury. Originally established in 1891, INS enforces all federal immigration and nationality laws. The service operates field offices throughout the United States and in several foreign countries.[145] Today, the INS is the third largest subdivision in the Justice Department, employing more than 18,000 individuals on a budget of over $1 billion.[146]

In 1945, Attorney General Francis Biddle elevated the office of Chief Clerk to an Assistant Attorney General level, and established the Administrative Division. Renamed the Justice Management Division (JMD) in 1985, it controls and oversees departmental resources, and provides administrative support and services to the operational subdivisions and offices. JMD also works with other federal management agencies such as the Office of Management and Budget, General Services Administration, and Office of Personnel Management.[147]

The department underwent yet another major restructuring in 1953, during Attorney General Herbert Brownell's tenure. The Assistant to the Attorney General was elevated to second in command of the Justice Department and the title was changed to Deputy Attorney General. The Solicitor General thereafter became the third-ranking officer and was relieved of his remaining administrative duties, freeing him to carry out the government's appellate litigation.[148] Brownell also eliminated the Customs Division, merging its functions into the Civil Division.

The Civil Rights Act of 1957 spawned the Civil Rights Division. It enforces federal civil rights laws, including provisions of the 1957, 1960, and 1964 Civil Rights Acts, as well as the 1965 Voting Rights Act, 1968 Fair Housing Act, 1974 Equal Opportunity Act, 1973 Rehabilitation Act, and affirmative action guidelines of Executive Order 12250. The division currently is divided into nine sections: Educational Opportunities, Housing and Civil Enforcement, Special Litigation, Appeals, Coordination and Review, Criminal Prosecution, Employment Litigation, Voting, and Administrative Management.[149]

Under the 1964 Civil Rights Act, Congress also created the Community Relations Service. The service helps communities cope with problems that arise from the implementation and enforcement of civil rights laws, especially the social fallout from racial integration of southern schools under the Supreme Court decision in *Brown v. Board of Education* (1954). The Community Relations Service reaches out with conciliation and mediation services for troubled communities to resolve racial-ethnic conflict. It also cares for Cuban and Haitian entrants into the United States as authorized by Title V of the Refugee Education Assistance Act of 1980 and Executive Order 12341.[150]

Since 1970, the Justice Department has undergone several more reorganizations. It established new agencies to administer federal programs and policy initiatives emerging during the 1960s and 1970s, and then Watergate led to a series of reforms aimed at "depoliticizing" the Justice Department. Many of these reforms were short-lived, however, as the Reagan administration's commitment to restoring strong central control of the administrative bureaucracy led to counterreform during the 1980s.[151]

During the Nixon administration, several offices and agencies came into being. Under the Omnibus Crime Control Act of 1968, Congress established the Law Enforcement Assistance Administration (LEAA). Renamed the Office of Justice Programs (OJP) in 1984, the office administers federal law enforcement assistance programs and research agencies: the National Institute of Justice, Bureau of Justice Statistics, Office of Juvenile Justice and Delinquency Prevention, and Bureau of Justice Assistance.[152] The OJP budget exceeded $400 million in fiscal 1990.[153]

In 1973, Attorney General Mitchell established the Office of Legislative Affairs (OLA). In addition to responding to congressional requests for information, OLA routinely monitors committee hearings and provides legal advice in the form of testimony to Congress. It also formulates and coordinates the legislative initiatives of other divisions and offices of the department.[154] By screening other divisions' contacts with congressional oversight and appropriating committees, OLA gives the Attorney General a convenient mechanism for controlling the department's legislative initiatives.

The Drug Enforcement Administration (DEA) also was created in 1973. DEA enforces federal narcotics and controlled substance laws. Along with its investigation and enforcement roles, the DEA administers a variety of educational and preventive programs aimed at reducing the availability and attractiveness of illicit drugs. The agency currently is divided into five major divisions and offices: Office of Chief Counsel, Office of Congressional and Public Affairs, Planning and Inspection Division, Operations Division, and the Operational Support Division.[155]

Following the Watergate scandal, Attorneys General Edward Levi and Griffin Bell sought to restore public confidence in the department. Their reforms sought to decentralize decision making inside the department and to buffer personnel from direct political influence. In 1975, Levi established the Office of Professional Responsibility (OPR), which investigates complaints of criminal and ethical misconduct against Justice Department officials or other high-ranking executive branch officials. On completing an investigation, the office usually prepares a recommendation for further action. Under the 1978 Ethics in Government Act, it specifically is charged with assisting the Attorney General in carrying out preliminary investigations prior to the appointment of special counsels.[156]

Bell sought further to separate the department's prosecutorial functions from its political functions by creating the Office of Associate Attorney General in 1977. Both the Associate and the Deputy Attorney General reported directly to the Attorney General. The Solicitor General's position was further removed from the policymaking hierarchy, as it became the fourth-ranking post in the department. Under the new management structure, the Deputy supervised law enforcement divisions and the Associate was directly responsible for civil litigating and nonlitigating divisions.[157]

Griffin Bell also established the Office for Improvements in the Administration of Justice (OIAJ) in 1977. OIAJ was charged with finding ways to improve the operation of the federal court system and federal legal administration and was intended to move the Justice Department into a role similar to the one played by a European-style ministry of justice.[158] During its existence, OIAJ sponsored several conference and legislative proposals to improve judicial management and buffer Justice Department personnel from overt political pressures.[159]

The redeployment of an "administrative presidency strategy" by the Reagan administration led to the reversal of many reforms implemented in the late 1970s. In 1981, Attorney General William French Smith recentralized the leadership structure of the department. The Deputy Attorney General was again made second-ranking officer of the Justice Department with the Associate Attorney General placed under his supervision.[160] Smith also replaced OIAJ with the Office of Legal Policy (OLP). During the Reagan administration, OLP functioned to further centralize Justice Department decision making and to coordinate activities of its various divisions on matters relevant to the administration's political objectives. In addition to publishing academic reports on controversial legal issues, OLP also carried out the primary screening role in the administration's judicial selection process.[161] Because OLP's mission was to translate the administration's political agenda into legal policy, its efforts often created friction with other divisions in the department.[162]

The Institutionalized Attorney General Today

Today the Attorney General is an institutionalized office. The title signifies both the individual who holds the office and the vast bureaucracy under his control.[163] Few substantive changes to the department's management structure have been made since the mid-1980s. Under Richard Thornburgh OLP's name was changed to the Office of Policy Development (OPD) and the role of the office became less overtly partisan. It continues to act as a center for policy development, but the ideological nature of the office has been de-emphasized.[164]

Attorney General William Barr has also followed Thornburgh's decision to leave the Associate Attorney General's position vacant, in effect returning the department's top management to the pre-1977 structure, with all division, bureau, and office heads reporting through the Deputy Attorney General's office.[165] Figure 2.3 reflects the department's current management structure.

The Justice Department is divided into more than thirty major divisions, bureaus, agencies, and offices. The size and diversity of these subagencies gives an idea of the nature and breadth of the department's responsibilities. For fiscal year 1990, the department's budget exceeded $6.7 billion, and it employed more than 80,000 persons.[166] Figure 2.4 provides a breakdown of its personnel and budget by major function and division.

Organizational charts, however, can mislead with regard to the actual control that the Attorney General exerts over subordinates. Like other large bureaucracies, the Justice Department is not a monolith. Rather, it is a collection of diverse drives and interests that does not respond immediately to commands from the top.[167] Although the Attorney General is the head of the department, he cannot concern himself with details of administration. In the vast majority of cases, it matters little who sits in the Attorney General's office. He usually is aware of departmental action only in a broad sense or if unusual circumstances require subordinates to appeal for his decision. In terms of the government's routine legal work, then, the office's authority is more theoretical than actual. The bulk of the department's work is routine and neither requires nor receives the attention of the Attorney General or other political appointees in the department's upper management levels.[168]

This is not to say routine decisions of subordinate officials are unimportant. Whether a U.S. Attorney chooses to vigorously prosecute fraud in defense contracting or whether he focuses on enforcement of drug and narcotic laws will establish the meaning of federal law within the community he serves.[169] Of course, his decisions must fit within the administration's or the Attorney General's general policy guidelines, which are, however, by nature broad and unspecific. Justice Department subordinates possess vast discretionary power in the handling of individual cases.[170]

Some divisions and offices within the department enjoy greater freedom from central supervision than others. Behind their relative autonomy stands the belief that certain law enforcement functions should be removed from the sphere of political influence. For example, the U.S. Parole Commission and the Foreign Claims Settlement Commission, though both formally located in the Justice Department, were established as independent agencies and are buffered from direct control.[171] Acting on the advice of Congress, the President appoints their principal officers to fixed terms, and they are not subject to the ordinary removal authority of the Attorney General or President. The FBI director, though under the statutory supervision of the Attorney General, also is appointed to a fixed term; he generally is thought to be immune from political interference.

There exist, in addition, offices in the department, which, though formally subject to the Attorney General's supervision and removal authority, by reason of their function enjoy a certain amount of autonomy. The offices of Pardon

Figure 2.3. **U.S. Department of Justice Organizational Chart**

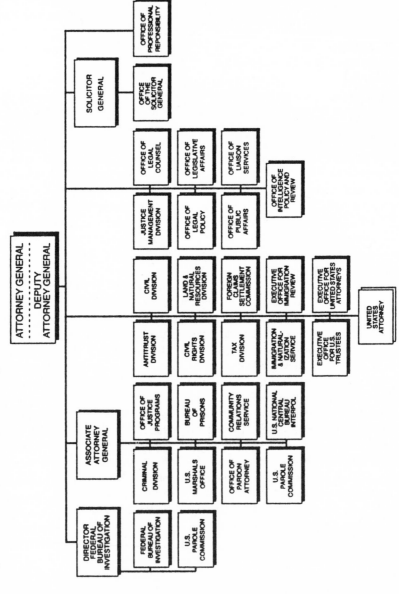

Source: Department of Justice Manual, 1988.

Figure 2.4. **The Justice Department, 1989. (a) 1989 Personnel Distribution. (b) 1989 Budget Distribution**

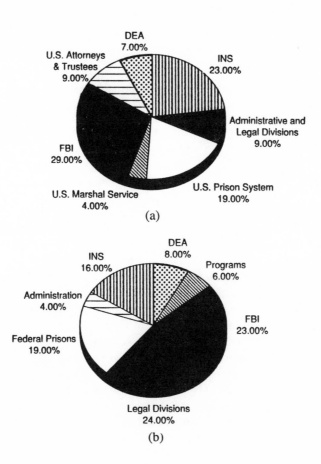

(a)

(b)

Source: Justice Management Division (June 24, 1989).

Attorney, Professional Responsibility, and Immigration Review all function with varying degrees of independence from direct political interference. A tradition of independence also has grown up around the Solicitor General's office, buffering it in its role as the federal government's chief representative to the Supreme Court.[172]

These exceptions are neither widespread nor absolute. It is one thing to say that under normal circumstances the Pardon Attorney or the Solicitor General is free to make independent judgments, but quite a different thing to say the Attorney General cannot intervene or reverse their decisions should he so choose. Nearly all of the department's statutory authority is vested directly in the Attorney General. Thus, the authority to intervene in the work of subordinates, quite apart from its prudence, is subject to few restraints. While routine legal work may receive little notice from the top, cases impinging on the administration's policy agenda will generally receive the attention of the Attorney General. Interventions occur with enough regularity that they usually occasion little controversy. As one career official in the Justice Department commented:

> A reversal by [political appointees in the department] may upset you—after all you might have spent several days or even weeks developing a position—but it is something you live with and expect. It's part of the job, that's where the authority exists. It happens in any large organization, and it happens frequently.[173]

Conclusion

The U.S. Attorney General's office has a long pedigree stretching back to medieval England. Although they share common roots, the British and American offices have developed in distinctly different directions. While the role of the former has remained that of an elite barrister, and the office has developed conventions protecting it from direct political interference, the U.S. office has developed into a major political policymaker. This difference ultimately results from the disparate constitutional settings surrounding the two offices. The constitutional theory undergirding British political institutions leaves relatively little room for the overt politicization of law or the government's legal administration. The U.S. separation of powers has of course led to politicization in ways that will be elaborated upon later.

The first Congress, unable to predict such an outcome, little heeded the political implications when it created the Attorney General's office in 1789. The Judiciary Act left the office weak and ill defined. Consequently, the actions and predispositions of early incumbents, and the course of major constitutional disputes such as the National Bank controversy and the Civil War, left lasting marks on the office's institutional nature. The creation of the Justice Department marked a watershed in the development of the Attorney General's office. Codifying its evolutionary nature, the 1870 act added several new functions and roles to the office and made it the head of the government's law machine. Various factors of unequal importance led to the tremendous growth the Justice Department has undergone since 1870: the transfer of functions from other federal agencies, the expansion of responsibilities as the size and complexity of the federal government grew, and the addition of new responsibilities as federal regulatory authority expanded. All these augmented the size and power of the department. Its expansion, together with changes in the constitutional setting of the office, paint a background for the recent controversy surrounding the political role of the Attorney General.

Notes

1. Hugh H.L. Bellot, "The Origin of the Attorney-General," *The Law Quarterly Review* 25 (1909), 403.

2. Sewell Key, "The Legal Work of the Federal Government," *Virginia Law Review* 166 (1938), 25.

3. James Hightower, "From Attornatus to the Department of Justice—An Historical Perspective," reprinted in U.S. Congress, Senate Committee on the Judiciary, Subcommittee on the Separation of Powers, *Removing Politics from the Administration of Justice*, 93rd Cong., 2d sess. (1974), 405–6; J. Ll. J. Edwards, *Law Officers of the Crown* (London: Sweet and Maxwell, 1969), 12–31.

4. Key, "The Legal Work of the Federal Government," 171–77.

5. Edwards, *Law Officers of the Crown*.

6. For a description of the DPP, see R. Jackson, *The Machinery of Justice in England*, 7th ed. (Cambridge: Cambridge University Press, 1977), 219–21.

7. Edwards, *Law Officers of the Crown*; see also J. MacDermott, *Protection from Power under English Law* (London: Stevens, 1957), 29–30.

8. For an account of these two cases see C. Ponting, *The Right to Know* (1985); and M. Turnbull, *The Spy Catcher* (London: NCCL, UK, 1985).

9. *The Sunday Times* (London), January 23, 1977, 16.

10. For an account of the Campbell case see McDermott, *Protection from Power*, 32; and Edwards, *Law Officers of the Crown*, 199–226.

11. G. Marshall, *Constitutional Conventions* (Oxford: Oxford University Press, 1984), 112–13.

12. Ibid.

13. Ibid.

14. Blackstone's discourse on mixed government is well known, see *Commentaries on the Laws of England*, vol. 2 (Facsimile ed. Chicago: University of Chicago Press, 1979), 413–15. The American theory of separation of powers is based on Montesquieu's analysis of the English constitution in his celebrated book *De l'Esprit des lois* (1748). That Montesquieu misunderstood English constitutional theory, however, is quite clear. See M.J.C. Vile, *Constitutionalism and the Separation of Powers* (Oxford: Oxford University Press, 1967). Not only did Montesquieu misconstrue the concept of mixed government into his notion that three specialized institutions should be coequal and separated. But he also misread Locke and Blackstone with regard to the judicial function. Locke distinguished between only two different government functions, the legislative and the executive. Judges perform part of the executive function in that they execute or apply the law. Nevertheless, natural justice requires judges be removed from direct political influence. As a lawyer, Blackstone further emphasized this notion of judicial impartiality. Montesquieu, however, misconstrued judicial impartiality into a wholly separate and distinct government function, the judicial function.

15. For a discussion of the difference between the theory of "mixed government" and the separation of powers, see Marshall, *Constitutional Theory* (Oxford: Clarendon Press, 1971), 100–3.

16. P. Atiyah, "Judicial-Legislative Relations in England," in Robert A. Katzmann (ed.), *Judges and Legislators: Toward Institutional Comity* (Washington, D.C.: Brookings, 1988), 129, 135.

17. Restrictions on the office's common-law authority were made by some colonial charters or statutes but this was the exception: see Key, "Legal Work of the Federal Government," 169. Such restrictions were usually resisted. When the Assembly of New York attempted to limit the office's prosecutorial powers by statute, the Attorney General

and Solicitor General of England objected, calling the effort "high encroachment" on the powers of Crown officers. See Homer Cummings and Carl McFarland, *Federal Justice* (New York: Macmillan, 1937), 13.

18. Cummings and McFarland, *Federal Justice*, 12.

19. Ibid., 13–14.

20. Key, "Legal Work of the Federal Government," 169.

21. Cummings and McFarland, *Federal Justice*, 9–10.

22. The first procurator was appointed in the state of New York in 1781, and others shortly thereafter. See *Journals of the Continental Congress, 1774–1789*, ed. Gaillard Hunt, vol. 14 (Washington: Library of Congress, 1912), 75.

23. Key, "Legal Work of the Federal Government," 173–74.

24. 1 U.S. Stat., 28; 1 U.S. Stat., 49; 1 U.S. Stat. (1789), 65.

25. 1 U.S. Stat., 73.

26. 1 U.S. Stat., 73, Sec. 35.

27. Huston, *The Department of Justice*, 9.

28. Easby-Smith, "Edmund Randolph—Trail Blazer," 419.

29. For a discussion of the operation of the district attorneys offices see John Heinberg, "Centralization in Federal Prosecution," *Missouri Law Review* 15 (1950), 244; North, *United States Attorney*; Eisenstein, *Counsel for the United States*.

30. Easby-Smith, "Edmund Randolph—Trail Blazer."

31. The first twenty-two Attorneys General treated the office as a part-time post, and all but Richard Rush kept their primary residence outside the capital. Huston, *The Department of Justice*, 11.

32. Leonard White, *The Federalists* (New York: New York University Press, 1948), 45.

33. Easby-Smith, "Edmund Randolph—Trail Blazer," 421.

34. Easby-Smith, "Edmund Randolph—Trail Blazer," 421–22.

35. Huston, *The Department of Justice*, 148.

36. White, *The Federalists*, 156.

37. For an analysis of the Attorney General's early functions under the Judiciary Act, see Charles Warren, "New Light on the Federal Judiciary Act of 1789," *Harvard Law Review* 37 (1923), 108, 109; Harold Relyea, "Circumstances Surrounding the Creation of the Office of Attorney General and the Justice Department," reprinted in *Removing Politics from the Administration of Justice: Hearings Before the Subcommittee on Separation of Powers of the Senate Committee on the Judiciary*, 93d Cong., 2d sess. (1974), 420.

38. Ibid.

39. Huston, *The Department of Justice*, 6.

40. Ibid., 11.

41. Hightower, "From Attornatus to the Department of Justice," 414–15.

42. *The Department of Justice*, 3.

43. Hightower, "From Attornatus to the Department of Justice," 415.

44. Huston, *The Department of Justice*, 19.

45. 26th Cong., 2d sess., H. Exec. Doc. 123, Serial 387.

46. Langeluttig, *The Department of Justice*, 6.

47. 1 *Opinions of the Attorney General of the United States* (hereafter, *Op. A.G.*) (1820), 335.

48. Quoted in Arthur Miller, "The Attorney General as the President's Lawyer," in Huston et al., *Roles of the Attorney General*, 51.

49. For an account of Jackson's purge of his cabinet and his actions in connection with the National Bank, see Robert Remini, *Andrew Jackson*, vol. 2: *The Course of American Freedom* (New York: Harper & Row, 1981).

50. For a discussion of the constitutional ramifications of Jackson's removal of cabi-

net officials, see Edward Corwin, *The President: Office and Powers*, (New York: New York University Press, 1957), 21–22 and 82–84; Louis Fisher, *Constitutional Conflicts* (Princeton, N.J.: Princeton University Press, 1985), 66–68.

51. Ibid.

52. Huston, *The Department of Justice*, 21–22.

53. Cummings and McFarland, *Federal Justice*, 130–40.

54. Langeluttig, *The Department of Justice*, 7.

55. 6 *Op. A.G.* (1853), 330, 354.

56. Cummings and McFarland, *Federal Justice*, 149–51.

57. Ibid., 152–54.

58. The Attorney General's salary was raised by Act of August 4, 1854: 10 U.S. Stat. L. 558; the Assistant Attorney General's position was created by Act of March 3, 1859: 12 U.S. Stat. L. 420.

59. 6 *Op. A.G.* (1854), 330.

60. Ibid., 333–41.

61. Ibid., 347–51.

62. For a discussion of the impact the Civil War had on the Attorney General's office, see Cummings and McFarland, *Federal Justice*, 191–229.

63. *Ex parte Merryman*, 17 Fed. Case No. 9 (1861), 487.

64. 10 *Op. A.G.* (1861), 74.

65. 67 U.S. (1862), 635.

66. See Cummings and McFarland, *Federal Justice*, 196, and 67 U.S. (1862), 635 and 639.

67. 10 *Op. A.G.* (1862), 382, 11 *Op. A.G.* (1864), 43.

68. 12 U.S. Stat. (1861), 257, 12 U.S. Stat. (1862), 589.

69. Cummings and McFarland, *Federal Justice*, 199–201.

70. Letter from Bates to A. Knapp, Sept. 16, 1863, quoted in Cummings and McFarland, *Federal Justice*, 204; see also Bates's private comments about military abuses in Beale (ed.), *Diary of Edward Bates* (New York: Faber, 1933), 350–52.

71. 11 *Op. A.G.* (1864), 215, 11 *Op. A.G.* (1865), 297.

72. Cummings and McFarland, *Federal Justice*, 201.

73. 71 (4 Wall.) U.S. (1866), 2.

74. Ibid., 6.

75. Huston, *The Department of Justice*, 26.

76. Ibid., 37.

77. See Sewell Key and Francis LeSourd, "The Struggle of the Attorney General to Retain His Powers," Manuscript 43–0846, Department of Justice Main Library.

78. See Key, "Legal Work of the Federal Government," 175; Huston, *The Department of Justice*, 8.

79. Letter from Randolph to Washington, December 26, 1791, reprinted in *American State Papers, 1789–1809*, vol. 1 (New York: Bureau of National Literature, 1834), 46.

80. Easby-Smith, *The Department of Justice*, 5–6.

81. Eighth annual message of President Madison, reprinted in James Richardson (ed.), *Messages and Papers of the President*, vol. 1 (New York: Bureau of National Literature, 1897), 577.

82. First annual message of President Jackson, reprinted in Richardson, *Messages and Papers of the President*, vol 3, 1016.

83. See Easby-Smith, *The Department of Justice*, 11; Key and LeSourd, "Struggle of the Attorney General," 8–11.

84. 4 U.S. Stat. (1830), 414.

85. Langeluttig, *The Department of Justice*, 5.

86. Act of July 4, 1836, c. 352, sec. 5, 5 Stat. L., 111.

87. Act of February 24, 1855, c. 122, sec. 2, 10 Stat. L., 612. This responsibility was transferred to the Assistant Attorney General in 1868.

88. Act of February 20, 1863, c. 44, sec. 3, 12 Stat. L., 656.

89. Act of July 28, 1866, c. 299, sec. 36, 14 Stat. L., 337.

90. Act of July 13, 1866, c. 184, sec. 64, Stat. L., 170; Act of July 25, 1866, c. 233, sec. 2, 14 Stat. L., 226; Act of March 3, 1891, c. 541, 26 Stat. L., 945.

91. Second annual message of President Jackson, reprinted in Richardson, *Messages and Papers*, vol. 2, 527.

92. First annual message of President Polk, reprinted in Richardson, *Messages and Papers*, vol. 4, 415.

93. For a discussion of Stuart's proposal, see Cummings and McFarland, *Federal Justice*, 148.

94. 6 *Op. A.G.* (1854), 330.

95. *Congressional Globe*, 33d Cong. 2d sess. (1854), 69–70, 95. The measure drew opposition from an unlikely source—former Attorney General John Crittenden—who thought the bill placed "too laborious" an administrative burden on the office.

96. *Congressional Globe*, 41st Cong., 2d sess. (1860), Pt. IV, 3035.

97. Cummings and McFarland, *Federal Justice*, 222–24.

98. *Congressional Globe*, 41st Cong., 2d sess. (1870), Pt. IV, 3036.

99. Act of June 22, 1870; 16 U.S. Stat., 162.

100. See Hightower, "From Attornatus to the Department of Justice," 418; Key, "Legal Work of the Federal Government," 182.

101. The administrative responsibilities that the 1870 act gave the Attorney General may ultimately have had a greater impact on the office than even the consolidation of litigating authority; see Daniel Meador, "The President, the Attorney General, and the Department of Justice," paper presented at the White Burkett Miller Center, University of Virginia, January 4, 1980, 10–13.

102. 28 S. Ct. (1893), 483, 491.

103. *McGrain v. Daugherty*, 273 U.S. (1927), 273.

104. *Annual Report A.G.* (1986), 1.

105. See Harold Seidman, *Politics, Position and Power: From the Positive to the Regulatory State*, 4th ed. (New York: Oxford University Press, 1986).

106. U.S. Congress, *Digest of Appropriations* (1872). Even this figure exaggerates its size, however, because it included miscellaneous expenditures of the federal courts and the budgets of legal offices which remained in the departments of Treasury, Navy and the Office of Internal Revenue. It also included the salary and expenses of the U.S. attorneys and marshals. If these items were removed the budget of the central Justice Department was only $57,000. This was an increase of only $8,000 over the budget of the Attorney General's office the year before when there was no department.

107. Figures for the Justice Department's budgets used in this chapter are taken from three sources: U.S. Congress, *Digest of Appropriations* (1790–1990); U.S. Congress, *Budget of the United States Government* (1955–1990); *United States Statistical Abstract* (1920–1990).

108. Ibid.

109. Robert Higgs, *Crisis and Leviathan: Critical Episodes in the Growth of American Government* (Oxford: Oxford University Press, 1987).

110. *Annual Report A.G.* (1872), 1–3. In addition, the department had employees in field offices of the U.S. district attorneys and U.S. marshals.

111. Cummings and McFarland, *Federal Justice*, 496–99.

112. See *Annual Report A.G.* (1872–1895).

113. Ibid.

114. *Annual Report A.G.* (1903).

115. Ibid., For a more detailed discussion of the actual duties of these and other officers in the department at this time see Easby-Smith, *The Department of Justice*, 26–35.

116. 32 U.S. Stat. (1903), 1031, 1062.

117. Easby-Smith, *The Department of Justice*, 25–30.

118. *Annual Report A.G.* (1907), 8–9.

119. Ibid.

120. During this period a seemingly inconsequential impediment to managing the department was overcome. In its frugality Congress had never provided a central office building for the new department. With the department's personnel scattered throughout Washington, day-to-day management was impossible, and the employees never developed an esprit de corps. Lawyers that had been formally transferred to Justice from other departments remained in their old offices and retained former loyalties. Finally, in 1905 Attorney General William Moody pleaded with Congress for funds for a central office complex:

> The Attorney General and all of his subordinates have been driven to the street to find refuge where they could. The department is now occupying seven rented buildings in different parts of the city. . . . None of the buildings is fireproof, and not one of them contains a vault. This condition is inconvenient, uneconomical, and humiliating. (*Annual Report A.G.* [1905], 4)

Moody's appeal convinced Congress, and money for a new building was appropriated, though construction was not completed until 1934.

121. *Annual Report A.G.* (1909).

122. See Frank Buckley, "The Department of Justice."

123. The Attorney General's Annual Report for 1920 was the first to include an organizational chart of the Justice Department.

124. A complete description of the statutory duties and authority of each of the Justice Department's divisions, agencies and offices can be found in *Department of Justice Manual* (New York: Harcourt & Javonovich, 1988), I–3.

125. U.S. Department of Justice, *Report of the A.G.'s Committee on Antitrust Laws* (Washington, D.C.: GPO, 1955), 1.

126. *Annual Report A.G* (1986), 109.

127. *Annual Report A.G.* (1986); *DOJ Manual*, I–3.

128. Ibid.

129. Ibid.

130. Ibid.

131. For a history of the Solicitor General's office, see Rex Lee, "Lawyering in the Supreme Court: The Role of the Solicitor General," *Supreme Court Historical Society Yearbook* (1985), 15; Charles Fahy, "The Office of the Solicitor General," *American Bar Association Journal* 28 (1942), 20; and Thomas Thatcher, "Genesis and Present Duties of the Office of Solicitor General," *American Bar Association Journal* 17 (1931), 519.

132. Act of June 22, 1870, ch. 150, sec. 2, 16 Stat., 162–63.

133. These regulations have been codified in 28 C.F.R., sec. 0.20 (1987).

134. For an account of the Solicitor General's functions, see Wade McCree, Jr., "The Solicitor General and His Client," *Washington University Law Quarterly* 59 (1981), 337; Erwin Griswold, "The Office of the Solicitor General—Representing the Interests of the United States Before the Supreme Court," *Missouri Law Review* 34 (1969), 527; "Government Litigation in the Supreme Court: The Roles of the Solicitor General," *Yale Law Journal* 78 (1969), 1442; and Michael McConnell, "The Rule of Law and the Role of the Solicitor General," Eric Schnapper, "Becket at the Bar—The Conflicting Obligations of

the Solicitor General," Richard Wilkins, "An Officer and an Advocate: The Role of the Solicitor General," *Loyola Los Angeles Law Review* 21 (1988), 1105–1271.

135. There are a few quasi-official histories written about the FBI: see Don Whitehead, *The FBI Story* (New York: Random House, 1956); Harry and Banoro Overstreet, *The FBI in Our Open Society* (New York: Norton, 1969). More critical histories are Max Lownthal, *The Federal Bureau of Investigation* (New York: William Sloan, 1950); Fred Cook, *The FBI Nobody Knows* (London: Macmillan, 1964).

136. For a good account of the Hoover FBI's independence from the rest of the Justice Department, see Navasky, *Kennedy Justice*.

137. Ibid., 7.

138. Data on departmental personnel and budgets was obtained from the Office of Justice Management, June 23, 1989.

139. See "Thornburgh and Sessions Clash over Congressional Meetings," *Washington Post*, March 11, 1989, A–5.

140. *Annual Report A.G* (1986); *DOJ Manual*, I–3.

141. Ibid.

142. See note 138 above.

143. *Annual Report A.G.* (1934).

144. *Annual Report A.G,* (1986); *DOJ Manual*, I–3.

145. Ibid.

146. See note 138 above.

147. *Annual Report A.G.* (1986); *DOJ Manual*, I–3.

148. The reorganization was carried out through statute 67 U.S. Stat., 636 (Reorg. Plan 4, 1953); *Annual Report A.G.* (1954).

149. *Annual Report A.G.* (1986); *DOJ Manual*, I–3.

150. Ibid.

151. Reorganizational efforts to depoliticize the department following Watergate, and the Reagan administration's repoliticization of it are discussed in detail in chapter 5.

152. *Annual Report A.G.* (1986); *DOJ Manual*, I–3.

153. See note 138 above.

154. *Annual Report A.G.* (1986); *DOJ Manual*, I–3.

155. Ibid.

156. Ibid.

157. *Annual Report A.G.* (1978), 1–2.

158. Ibid., 13.

159. For a discussion of the history of Justice Department's role in judicial administration and the Carter administration's efforts to increase it, see Meador, "Role of the Justice Department," *Annuals AAPSS* 462 (1982), 36, and Peter Fish, *The Politics of Federal Judicial Administration* (Princeton, N.J.: Princeton University Press, 1973).

160. *Annual Report A.G.* (1982), 1–3.

161. Examples of reports authored by OLP include: U.S. Department of Justice, *Report to the Attorney General: The Law of Pretrial Interrogation* (February 1986); *The Search and Seizure Exclusionary Rule* (February 1986); *Original Meaning Jurisprudence* (March 1987); *Wrong Turns on the Road to Judicial Activism* (September 1987); *Redefining Discrimination: "Disparate Impact" and the Institutionalization of Affirmative Action* (November 1987); and *Economic Liberties Protected by the Constitution* (March 1988). For a discussion of the Reagan administration's judicial selection procedures, see Sheldon Goldman, "Reaganizing the Judiciary," *Judicature* 68 (1985), 312; and Goldman, "Reagan's Judicial Legacy: Completing the Puzzle and Summing Up," *Judicature* 72 (1989), 318.

162. One career attorney who asked not to be identified wryly commented that OLP really stood for "the Office of Legal Propaganda."

163. Arthur Miller discusses this aspect of the office in "The Attorney General as the President's Lawyer," Huston et al., *Role of the Attorney General*, 47–49.

164. "The Department of Justice: Nowhere to Go but Up," *National Journal* (June 10, 1989), 1478.

165. Ibid.

166. See note 138 above.

167. It has long been recognized that executive branch agencies and departments are characterized by certain central features inherent in the nature of complex organizations. See Lewis Gawthorp, *Bureaucratic Behavior in the Executive Branch* (New York: Free Press, 1969); Chris Argyris, *Understanding Organizational Behavior* (Homewood, Ill.: Dorsey Press, 1960).

168. The only general study of bureaucratic behavior in the Justice Department is Horowitz, *The Jurocracy*. For studies of specific divisions in the department, see also Susan Olson, "Comparing Justice and Labor Department Lawyers: Ten Years of Occupational Safety and Health Litigation," *Law and Policy* 7 (1985), 287; Weaver, *Decision to Prosecute*; Eisenstein, *Counsel for the United States*; and W.E. Brigman, *The Office of the Solicitor General of the United States* (Ph.D. dis., University of North Carolina, 1966).

169. For an excellent discussion of strategies and tactics used by subordinates in the Justice Department to increase their autonomy and avoid central control, see Eisenstein, *Counsel for the United States*, 76–125.

170. Ibid.

171. See *DOJ Manual*, I-3.

172. 1 *Op. Office of Legal Counsel* (1977), 228. The Solicitor General's relationship to the Attorney General is discussed in more detail in chapter 4.

173. Interview with Jerry Jones, Deputy Assistant Attorney General, Civil Rights Division, Washington, D.C., August 21, 1988.

3

The Political Role of the Attorney General

The Attorney General plays a variety of roles in American government: administrator, legal counselor, law enforcement officer. This chapter focuses on the Attorney General's emergence as a major political actor and the policymaking role the office plays as the head of the government's law machine. In particular, it examines the office's power to influence policy flowing from the federal courts and its ability to shape administrative policymaking through control over government litigation.

From Judicial to Executive Branch

In addition to consolidating the government's legal authority, the Justice Department Act of 1870 marked the culmination of the Attorney General's evolution from a judicial to an executive branch institution. Neither the Constitution nor the Judiciary Act defined explicitly the Attorney General's relationship to the three branches of federal government. Caleb Cushing lamented in his 1854 opinion on the nature of the office, "the act establishing the Attorney General is wholly silent on this point."[1]

All of the evidence surrounding the office's creation and early operation, however, reveals that the Attorney General was originally perceived as a judicial, rather than executive, branch institution. It was established under an act creating the courts rather than one establishing executive departments. Indeed, in its original Senate-adopted form, the Judiciary Act even empowered the Supreme Court to appoint the Attorney General. The House of Representatives amended the bill to say only that "an Attorney General shall be appointed."[2] The change in terminology shifted the appointment power from the Supreme Court to the President but it did not necessarily affect the Attorney General's constitutional status.[3] Federal judges also are appointed by the President and confirmed by the Senate. It is likely the change in terminology merely reflected Congress's desire for uniformity in the appointment of major judicial officers.[4]

It is noteworthy that lawmakers perceived the Attorney General's role to be intricately connected to that of the courts. In 1790, Thomas Jefferson wrote of Edmund Randolph that he had been appointed "the Attorney General for the Supreme Court."[5] Early Attorneys General shared office space with the Supreme Court; and until 1870, their budgets were line items in federal court budgets according to congressional appropriations and budget documents.[6]

The early functions of the office also support the view that it was intended as a judicial post. Historian Harold Relyea noted that the Judiciary Act envisioned a Supreme Court barrister "cloaked in judicious impartiality."[7] Nor did the early Attorneys General perform duties related to executive prerogative, such as advising on judicial nominations and pardons or prosecutions. Until 1820, the office's heaviest responsibility was rendering judicial-type opinions on the constitutionality of proposed legislation. Even opinions rendered to the executive branch were expected to be impartial and judicial. William Wirt once refused to write an opinion on an issue he thought was a policy matter. "As my official duty is confined to the giving of my opinion on questions of law," he said, "I consider myself as having nothing to do with the settlement of fact."[8]

Early Attorneys General also had a peculiar relationship to the cabinet. Because the Attorney General administered no department or agency, the office was not a member of the cabinet by statutory right. Unlike other executive officers, whose rank in the line of succession to the presidency was established by statute, the Attorney General's rank was not defined until 1886.[9] Although early Attorneys General were invited to attend cabinet sessions, their role was regarded primarily as one of a legal, not a political advisor.[10] Contrasting his duties with those of other cabinet officers, Edward Bates said "the office I hold is not properly political, but strictly legal; and it is my duty, above all other ministers of State to uphold the Law and to resist all encroachments, from whatever quarter, of mere will and power."[11] Richard Fenno, in his classic study of the origin and development of the cabinet, summed up this unique position by noting that the Attorney General attended cabinet sessions not "by right" and "not in pursuance of any policy other than convenience and expediency."[12] So apolitical was the Attorney General's role that President John Quincy Adams instructed William Wirt not to resign his post during the transition between administrations. The Attorney General's "duties are different," Adams said, "the President has less connection with, and less responsibility for the performance of them."[13]

Despite the judicial trappings of the early Attorney General's office, the institution gradually became assimilated into the executive branch. Although custom and tradition, such as Jackson's dismissal of Berrien, brought about this transformation, it later was sanctioned by statute and Supreme Court opinion. The Attorney General's conventional inclusion in the cabinet brought him into the President's inner circle of political advisors.[14] New duties that began to accumulate in the office increasingly linked it with presidential authority. Older functions of a quasi-judicial character gradually were eliminated or transferred.

Wirt's decision to stop writing opinions for Congress, in particular, further cemented the office to the executive and separated it from the legislative branch. Congress still can obtain legal advice from the Attorney General through the roundabout method of requesting testimony, but the nature of the advice has changed. Modern-day Attorneys General appear before Congress "as protagonists of measures favored by the executive or as opponents of bills that do not meet with administration approval."[15] The office is no longer a neutral advisor but a partisan advocate.

In his 1854 opinion on the nature of the office, Cushing was the first to recognize its conversion into an executive branch institution.[16]

Congressional acquiescence came in 1870, when lawmakers created the Department of Justice. As the head of an executive branch department, the Attorney General's subordination to the President was codified. The 1870 act placed the office on the same statutory footing as other executive department heads. Judicial recognition followed in the 1887 case of *United States v. San Jacinto Tin Company*. In this case, the Supreme Court greatly expanded the Attorney General's powers by declaring that the office possessed the common law right to bring suit on behalf of the United States, even without specific statutory authorization from Congress. In dicta, however, the Court went on to note "that in all this the Attorney General serves as head of one of the Executive Departments, representing the authority of the President in the class of subjects within the domain of that department and under his control."[17]

The Court's dictum in *San Jacinto* aimed at ensuring that the Attorney General remained democratically accountable when exercising sweeping common law powers. A constitutional justification for locating the office within the executive branch came two years later in *In re Neagle* (1889).[18] In *Neagle*, the Supreme Court maintained that the "faithful execution clause" formed the foundation for Congress's creation of the executive departments.[19] Although the case did not deal specifically with the Attorney General or Justice Department, its implications were obvious. The *Neagle* rationale was applied directly to the Attorney General in *Ponzi v. Fessenden* (1922).[20] In *Ponzi*, the Court examined the constitutional basis for the Attorney General's control of government prosecutions and decided that it came from presidential delegation of that authority. Chief Justice Taft wrote: "The Attorney General is . . . the hand of the President in taking care that the laws of the United States in legal proceedings and in the prosecution of offenses, be faithfully executed."[21]

Cushing's opinion in 1854 and the Supreme Court's *Ponzi* decision in 1922 helped cement the Attorney General's constitutional status as an executive officer. The political implications of this status did not emerge until later, when other developments in U.S. politics greatly enhanced the value of legal policy. Meanwhile, a mystique surrounding the Attorney General's quasi-judicial role distinguished the office from other cabinet posts. The Attorney General became a paradox within the framework of U.S. government. It was an executive branch office reliant on the Article II power, yet assigned legal functions to be carried out independent of partisan political considerations.

The Attorney General as Politician

Since the appointment of Edmund Randolph, Presidents have appointed personal friends as Attorney General—individuals who were confidants as well as legal advisors. President John F. Kennedy appointed his brother Robert to the post in 1960.[22] President Richard M. Nixon selected his partner in private legal practice, John Mitchell. And President Ronald Reagan singled out his personal attorney, William French Smith, to be Attorney General in 1980 and his close friend Edwin Meese for the post in 1984.

As the Attorney General became associated with executive branch politics, however, the professional and political qualifications of individuals appointed to the office began to change. During the office's early years, Presidents usually nominated highly distinguished members of the bar to fill the post. Early Attorneys General such as Randolph, Wirt, and Cushing stood out among the most prominent members of the legal profession in their day. A high level of legal acumen was essential when the office was a one-man operation, and the Attorney General functioned primarily as a lawyer. The creation of the Justice Department, however, allowed the Attorney General to surround himself with talented and distinguished attorneys and the need for legal talent on his own part was diminished.

Modern Presidents generally select Attorneys General more on the basis of political and administrative skills rather than on the basis of professional expertise.[23] For example, Homer Cummings, appointed by President Franklin D. Roosevelt in 1933, was the former chairman of the Democratic National Committee. Frank Murphy, selected by Roosevelt in 1939, was a former Democratic Governor of Michigan. J. Howard McGrath, chosen by President Harry S. Truman in 1949, had served as a Senator from Rhode Island and chairman of the Democratic National Committee. President Dwight D. Eisenhower selected Herbert Brownell, a former chairman of the Republican National Committee and Eisenhower's campaign manager, to be the Attorney General in 1953. Robert Kennedy, elevated to the post in 1961, had worked as his brother John's campaign manager. John Mitchell, appointed in 1969, had managed Nixon's presidential campaign.[24]

In the wake of Watergate, both Gerald Ford and Jimmy Carter shied away from appointing highly partisan individuals to the office. Ford picked Edward Levi, a former dean of the University of Chicago School of Law. And Carter appointed a former federal judge, Griffin Bell. In an effort to codify this arrangement, in 1977 the Senate passed the Bentsen amendment, which flatly stated: "any individual who has played a leading partisan role in the election of a President shall not be appointed Attorney General or Deputy Attorney General." Although the House of Representatives narrowly defeated the Bentsen amendment, it nevertheless continues to serve as the Senate's semi-official policy regarding confirmation of Attorneys General.[25]

The Reagan administration challenged the unwritten policy by appointing two extremely partisan individuals to the post. William French Smith and Edwin Meese, both of whom had been active in Republican party politics, played prominent roles in Reagan's campaigns. Their close relationships with the President and their partisan backgrounds drew attacks from Democratic senators during Senate Judiciary Committee hearings. Nevertheless, both men eventually won confirmation from the Republican-controlled Senate.[26]

To observe that many modern Attorneys General have emerged from political or administrative backgrounds is not to challenge their legal expertise but to point out that other criteria have simply eclipsed professional qualifications. Attorneys General still are expected to be "learned in the law," though it is significant that this requirement was lifted from statute when the Attorney General's office was reconstituted under the 1870 act.[27] An incompetent or inexperienced lawyer still would not normally be nominated to the post, and if one were, he or she would run the risk of Senate rejection. Robert Kennedy was an exception to this rule because of his extraordinary relationship with the President. But even in his case, the *New York Times* attacked his record, noting:

> If Robert Kennedy was one of the outstanding lawyers of the country, a pre-eminent legal philosopher, a noted prosecutor or legal officer at the Federal or State level, the situation would have been different. But his experience . . . is surely insufficient to warrant his present appointment.[28]

In addition to friendship, political activity and administrative experience, modern-day Presidents have also focused on a nominee's ideology. The Attorney General is expected to be a member of the administration's team. Presidents rely on their Attorneys General to formulate and implement, not just react to, administration policy. The importance attached to ideology ultimately depends on the President's policy objectives, his views about the law and the role of the Justice Department.

As Attorneys General became increasingly associated with executive branch policymaking and administration, the Solicitor General office inherited some of its quasi-judicial aura. As the administrative role of the Solicitor General was diminished and the office became exclusively involved in litigation, it became increasingly identified with professional expertise and legal scholarship.[29] Partisanship is not irrelevant to the selection of a Solicitor General, and Presidents generally tend to appoint individuals who share their political views. It is requisite, however, that the Solicitor General, unlike the modern-day Attorney General, be a distinguished lawyer first and a partisan second. On at least two occasions since 1925, Presidents have even appointed Solicitors General from the opposite political party. William Mitchell, a Democrat, served during the Coolidge administration from 1925 to 1929. And Erwin Griswold, a Republican, was appointed by Democratic President Lyndon Johnson in 1967; he continued in office through the first term of the Nixon administration.

The Solicitor General's unique relationship to the Supreme Court also tends to attract an elite group of young attorneys to serve in the office. Assistants to the Solicitor General usually remain in the office for several years before taking positions as law school professors, clerks to Supreme Court Justices, or litigators for large private law firms. The rarefied tradition and history of the Solicitor General's office, as well as the continuity of its talented staff, give rise to a special *esprit de corps* in the office.[30]

In his book on Robert Kennedy's tenure,[31] journalist Victor Navasky characterizes the gulf that has developed between Attorneys General and Solicitors General, noting that "the Attorney General, any Attorney General, is advisor to the President, and the Solicitor General, any Solicitor General, is advisor to the Supreme Court."[32] Navasky perhaps overstates the point. The relationship between Kennedy and Archibald Cox was probably the most extreme ever to exist between an Attorney General and Solicitor General. Kennedy possessed none of the traditional qualifications for the Attorney General's office. He had never practiced law, never argued a case in court, never negotiated a legal settlement. He had graduated in the middle of his University of Virginia Law School class, and was, in Navasky's words, uninformed on "weighty issues of jurisprudence."[33]

Cox, on the other hand, had devoted his life to the law. He had served as student editor on the *Harvard Law Review*, he had been a clerk for Judge Learned Hand, and had served as an Assistant Solicitor General. At the time of his appointment, he had earned a reputation as a leading law professor at Harvard. The contrast between the two men and their approach to the law could not have been greater. Cox saw the law as having "a life of its own"; Kennedy regarded it merely as a "continuation of politics."[34]

Nevertheless, Navasky's portrait accurately depicts the trend in the two offices. A survey of the men who have served as Solicitors General since Cox's day further strengthens the point. Thurgood Marshall, appointed in 1965, had been a clerk for the Supreme Court and federal appeals court judge. Erwin Griswold, picked by Johnson in 1967, had served as Dean of Harvard Law School. Robert Bork, chosen by Nixon in 1973, had taught at Yale Law School. Wade McCree, Carter's appointee in 1977, graduated from Harvard and had been a judge in the federal appeals court. Rex Lee, appointed by Reagan in 1981, was the dean of Brigham Young University School of Law. Charles Fried, selected by Reagan in 1985, was a distinguished professor at Harvard Law School. And George Bush's Solicitor General, Kenneth Starr, has served as a clerk to Chief Justice Warren Burger and judge on the Court of Appeals in Washington, D.C.

The Solicitor General and the Myth of Independence

Because Attorneys General and Solicitors General come from different back-grounds, it is not surprising that friction can occur between their offices over government litigation. Whereas Attorneys General tend to focus on the political consequences of a given legal policy, Solicitors General tend to look ahead to the potential impact on the law or on the federal courts. The Solicitor General also enjoys greater autonomy from central direction and supervision than other offi-cers in the Justice Department. There are several practical reasons for this auton-omy: the highly distinguished nature of individuals appointed as Solicitors General, the belief that autonomy bolsters the Solicitor General's influence on the Court, and the view that the office is most valuable to an administration when it can offer unbiased advice. All of these factors play into what has come to be known as the office's "tradition of independence." Francis Biddle, who served as Solicitor General from 1940 to 1941, rendered an idealized view of this tradition when he wrote:

> The Solicitor General is responsible neither to the man who appointed him, nor to his immediate superior in the hierarchy of administration [the Attorney General] . . . his guide is only the ethic of his law profession framed in the ambience of his experience and judgement. . . . The Solicitor General has no master to serve except his country.[35]

The origin of this tradition, however, is not entirely clear. When the office was created by the Justice Department Act in 1870, it certainly was not intended to be independent, formally or otherwise, from the Attorney General or the President.[36] The section of the act that established the office explicitly defined its subordinate role: "There shall be in said Department an officer learned in the law, to assist the Attorney General in the performance of his duties, to be called the Solicitor General."[37]

Indeed, during the early years, the Solicitor General functioned as just such a general administrative assistant to the Attorney General.[38] The office gradually was relieved of nonlitigating functions; however, they were not entirely removed until the Deputy Attorney General's post was created in 1953. And although the Solicitor General made regular appearances in the Supreme Court, until about 1920, he shared that role with other officers in the department.[39]

Nevertheless, a myth of independence gradually emerged as the Solicitor General assumed more and more of the Attorney General's litigating functions. Thomas Thatcher, who served from 1930 to 1933, is credited with being the first Solicitor General to assert a role independent from the rest of the Justice Depart-ment. If Thatcher disagreed with the administration's legal position, he would sign the government's brief but disassociate the himself from its contents. He would do this by inserting a footnote or sentence to the effect that "the foregoing is presented as the position of the Internal Revenue Service," or the "Solicitor General does not fully subscribe to. . . ." This addendum clued in the justices to Thatcher's dissent.[40]

Perhaps the most controversial use of Thatcher's technique by a Solicitor General occurred during the Reagan administration in *Bob Jones University v. United States* (1982).[41] In 1972, the IRS began denying tax-exempt status to private universities that discriminated on the basis of race. Bob Jones University sued the IRS, claiming the policy violated the university's First Amendment right to the free exercise of religion and exceeded the IRS's statutory authority. In the lower courts, attorneys for the IRS and the Department of Justice successfully defended the new policy. In 1982, however, Bob Jones University filed a petition for certiorari with the Supreme Court. When the case went to the Solicitor General for review, Rex Lee, who had argued similar cases as an attorney for the Mormon Church, removed himself from the case. Deputy Solicitor General Lawrence Wallace sided with the IRS in what he thought was a routine tax case. The brief filed by Wallace "acquiesced" in granting certiorari, but opposed the university's petition on the merits.

Within days of the filing, White House Counselor Edwin Meese contacted Attorney General William French Smith to request a reversal of the government's position on the case. When the brief on merits was filed four months later, the Justice Department switched sides and supported Bob Jones University, leaving the IRS on its own.[42] As acting Solicitor General, Wallace was required to sign the department's brief even though it contradicted the position he had presented the Court months earlier. Wallace added a footnote on the first page of the brief disassociating himself from the main part of the administration's argument. The note read: "The acting-Solicitor General fully subscribes to the position set forth on question number two, only."[43] The Justices saw the red light and, by an eight-to-one margin, rejected the administration's argument and upheld the IRS's position.

The Bob Jones episode severely strained relations between the Solicitor General's office and political leaders in the Reagan Justice Department.[44] It was not, however, the first or last time that a Solicitor General conflicted with an Attorney General over how far government litigation should bend to accommodate administration policy. President Truman's Solicitor General, Philip Perlman, reportedly resigned because Attorney General James McGranery had asked him to settle in the politically explosive Dollar Line Steamship Case.[45] Similarly, President Eisenhower's Solicitor General, Simon Sobeloff, refused to argue the government's position against a challenge to a McCarthy-era organization called the Loyalty Review Board.[46] Archibald Cox is reported to have acted as a brake on the progressive civil rights stance favored by Robert Kennedy.[47] And Erwin Griswold declined to argue several national security and Vietnam-related cases for the Nixon administration.[48]

The majority of recent Solicitors General would agree that the office owes allegiance to the Supreme Court as well as to the executive. Robert Bork, for example, has said the "Court and its function under our Constitution are far more important than a Government victory in any given case."[49] Similarly, Charles Fried characterized the office as having a "responsibility to help guide the Court on the development of precedent in vital areas of the law."[50] The Court reciprocates this relationship. The Solicitor General provides accurate and complete representations and assistance in selecting meritorious cases; the Supreme Court extends to the Solicitor General special privileges and confidence that no other litigant enjoys.[51] This commonality of interest between the Solicitor General and Supreme Court led Professor Katheryn Werdagar to describe the Solicitor General as the Court's "ninth and a half Justice."[52]

The nature of this unique relationship is best illustrated when the Solicitor General "confesses error." Unlike private litigants whose role is purely adversarial, the Justice Department is expected to have a broader interest in the proper development of law and in the just disposition of cases. If the government wins a case in the lower courts on grounds that, after consideration, appear faulty or inequitable, the Solicitor General recommends that the Supreme Court overturn the lower court on appeal. In *Young v. United States* (1942), the Supreme Court declared: "The public trust reposed in the law enforcement officers of the Government requires that they be quick to confess error, when in their opinion, a miscarriage of justice may result from their remaining silent."[53]

Confession of error often places the Solicitor General in a delicate position. He must betray both the government lawyers who won the case in the lower courts and the judge whose decision the Solicitor General wants reversed.[54] The practice, however, underscores the relationship between the Solicitor General and Court. Confessing error, Archibald Cox said, "tests the strength of our belief that the office has a peculiar responsibility to the Court."[55] Cox took this responsibility so seriously that, in one antitrust suit, he amazed the Justices by arguing both sides of the case.[56]

Despite abundant anecdotal evidence, the only official statement of the Solicitor General's "tradition of independence" is a memorandum opinion from the Office of Legal Counsel to Attorney General Griffin Bell in 1977.[57] The memorandum was drafted at the height of the post-Watergate reform movement and followed on the heels of a controversial brief filed in *Tennessee Valley Authority v. Hill* (1976).[58] In this case, the Solicitor General had defended the Tennessee Valley Authority (TVA) against a suit brought under the Endangered Species Act. The suit asked the Court to stop construction of a TVA dam that threatened the breeding grounds of a tiny fish called the snail darter. Bell intended to use the case to make his maiden argument before the Supreme Court. However, environmental groups alerted President Carter's domestic policy advisor, Stewart Eizenstat, of the Justice Department's position. After much discussion between Carter, Eizenstat, and Bell, an addendum arguing for the protection of the fish was included in the government's brief.[59]

Furious over the administration's intervention, Bell asked the Office of Legal Counsel to prepare a memorandum outlining the Solicitor General's relationship to the President and Attorney General. The memorandum noted that while the office was subordinate to the Attorney General by statute, traditionally "the Solicitor General has enjoyed a marked degree of independence" in his role as litigator before the Supreme Court. Why? The "dual nature of the Attorney General's role as policy and legal advisor to the President" makes him vulnerable to political considerations. Said the memorandum:

> Very simply, an independent Solicitor General assists the President and the Attorney General in the discharge of their constitutional duty: concerned as they are with matters of policy, they are well served by a subordinate officer who is permitted to exercise independent and expert judgment essentially free from extensive involvement in policy matters that might, on occasion, cloud a clear vision of what the law requires.[60]

The Reagan administration was criticized for sacrificing the Solicitor General's tradition of independence in order to pursue its ideological agenda. In the first published book on the Solicitor General's office, Lincoln Caplan charged the Reagan administration with violating the office's independence and undermining its credibility with the Supreme Court. Under Reagan, Caplan argued, the Solicitor General became an "ideological mouthpiece for administration policy."[61] Caplan and other critics of the administration's litigating policies point to briefs filed in agenda cases such as: *Bob Jones*; *Thornburgh v. American College of Obstetricians* (1986), in which the government asked the Court to overturn its 1972 abortion decision;[62] *Wygant v. Jackson Board of Education* (1984), in which it argued that affirmative action programs violate the Fourteenth Amendment;[63] and *Wallace v. Jaffree* (1985), in which the government requested the Court to permit silent prayer in public schools.[64]

While it remains clear that the Reagan Justice Department acted out a more aggressive litigation strategy than previous administrations, claims that it somehow violated the office or changed its institutional standing are exaggerated. Just because some briefs were controversial does not mean they lacked professional merit. Robert Bork, for instance, has argued "there is nothing wrong with the Solicitor General having a view of what the law should be. Even though that differs from what the Court thinks it should be, or what the Court in the past has said it should be."[65]

Indeed, previous administrations also used government litigation to challenge the prevailing status of the law. The government's advocacy during the New Deal under Solicitors General Robert Jackson and Stanley Reed stands out in this regard.[66] Jackson and Reed continued to argue that Congress could delegate quasi-legislative authority even after the Supreme Court made clear its belief that such practices were unconstitutional.[67] Another example occurred during the Truman and Eisenhower administrations, when the Justice Department's intervention in early civil rights cases such as *Shelly v. Kraemer* (1948)[68] and *Brown v. Board of*

Education (1954),[69] challenged the separate-but-equal doctrine firmly established by the Supreme Court in *Plessy v. Ferguson* (1896).[70]

In fact, no evidence suggests that Justice Department advocacy under the Reagan administration violated any professional norms, or that the quality of the government's argumentation suffered.[71] Although the Reagan Justice Department reversed the government's legal position in a number of controversial areas of law, these reversals appear to have had little effect on the Solicitor General's institutional standing with the Court. Reagan's Solicitors General, Rex Lee and Charles Fried, enjoyed the highest overall rates of success in Supreme Court litigation for any administration since that of Calvin Coolidge.[72] Even in so-called agenda cases, the government's position attracted considerable support and sometimes even carried a majority of the Court.[73] Based on existing evidence, Caplan and other critics mischaracterized the Solicitor General's traditional role in order to make their arguments more attractive.[74] The office's independence was always within the context of statutory responsibility running from the Solicitor General to the Attorney General, and the Attorney General to the President.[75]

Here we arrive at the heart of the matter. Expectations for honesty and professionalism in government advocacy began with the Attorney General. The Solicitor General inherited these expectations along with the Attorney General's litigating role. They comprise a tradition that attaches itself to the function, not the office. The tradition does not demand political neutrality, only honesty and accuracy in representations.[76]

One indicator of the politicization of the Attorney General is the way controversy surrounding the intersection of law and politics has recently focused instead on the Solicitor General. The Solicitor General is, by statute, responsible to the Attorney General in the carrying out of all of his responsibilities. Rex Lee made this point clearly when he wrote that the Solicitor General has only one role: "it is assisting the attorney general, who has the statutory responsibility for all litigation on behalf of the United States, and who was arguing cases in the Supreme Court eight decades before there was a solicitor general of the United States."[77] The Bell Memorandum put it even more bluntly: "the short of the matter is that under the law the Attorney General, not the Solicitor General, has the power and the right to 'conduct and argue' the Government's case in any court of the United States."[78]

Aside from statutory accountability, the relationship between the Attorney General and Solicitor General is idiosyncratic and varies from one administration to the next. It hinges not only on informal understandings between the two individuals, but on the political and legal environment in which they operate.[79] As for tradition, Fried points out that "independence" has always meant the freedom to recommend legal positions to the President and Attorney General, not to determine alone what they should be. It "does not, and never has meant freedom from being directed on what the government's ultimate position should be in any case," he says.[80]

Fried undoubtedly has a correct understanding of the Solicitor General's functional, traditional relationship to the Attorney General. Indeed, giving the Solicitor General's office the final voice on government litigation would inevitably subject it to the political entanglements critics yearn to avoid. The Attorney General's authority to overrule the Solicitor General reinforces the latter's independence by removing the office from political pressure. As the Bell Memorandum concludes:

> The Solicitor General can and should enjoy independence in matters of legal judgment. He should be free to decide what the law is and what it requires. But if "law" does not provide a clear answer to the question . . . then the Solicitor General's independent and dispositive function may give way to the greater need for the Solicitor General to seek guidance on the policy question. Questions of policy are questions that can be effectively addressed by the Attorney General, a cabinet officer who participates directly in policy formation and who can go to the President for policy guidance when the case demands.[81]

Whenever the Attorney General overrules a decision by the Solicitor General, he does so only after carefully considering the costs. The Solicitor General's opinion regarding the law and the Supreme Court's willingness to accept a particular legal argument usually receive great weight. If, after evaluation, the Attorney General decides the government's position should differ, he has the authority, and usually he has had the will, to countermand his litigating assistant.[82] No Solicitor General has ever adopted a view to the contrary.[83]

Not even Francis Biddle challenged the Attorney General's authority to direct the government's position. Erwin Griswold and Wade McCree flatly denied the Solicitor General is "an ombudsman with a roving commission to do justice as he sees it."[84] Rather, Griswold said, "it is a political office, which the administration can, within limits, use to advance its policies."[85] Archibald Cox, Erwin Griswold, Robert Bork, Wade McCree, Rex Lee, and Charles Fried all have recounted instances when the Attorney General intervened to reverse their positions on cases.[86]

Focusing on the Attorney General's authority to reverse the Solicitor General makes it easy to forget the obvious, that such intervention usually is unnecessary. Not only are Solicitors General appointed with administration policy in mind, major cases do not simply pop up in the Solicitor General's office. Rather they arrive by way of one of the Justice Department's divisions, accompanied by explicit or implicit recommendations. The Solicitor General rarely intervenes unilaterally in a major policy case without knowing where the Attorney General and President stand.[87] The question of the Solicitor General needing political direction before filing a brief or being overruled by the Attorney General seldom arises. The administration's desired position, as Fried notes, "is simply in the air, one need not be beat over head with it."[88]

Empirical studies conducted by political scientists confirm that government litigation in the Supreme Court tends to conform to the ideological direction of the current administration. Karen O'Connor's study of the *amicus curiae* ("friend of the court") briefs filed during the Johnson, Nixon, Ford, and Carter administrations in cases involving personal liberties, civil equality, and criminal rights found that Griswold and McCree, under the Johnson and Carter administrations respectively, "took decidedly more pronounced 'pro-rights' positions" than did Bork or Griswold under Nixon and Ford. O'Connor could explain the disparities only by pointing to the policy preferences of the administrations in power.[89]

Jeffrey Segal, expanding on O'Connor's work, examined *amicus curiae* filings in the areas of civil liberties, civil rights, and economics between the 1953 and 1982.[90] Segal's study encompassed eight Solicitors General: Sobeloff, Rankin, Cox, Marshall, Griswold, Bork, McCree, and Lee. Segal found that Archibald Cox, during the Kennedy administration, "emerged as the most liberal, filing liberal briefs in seventy-seven percent of his cases." The Reagan administration's Rex Lee "was the most conservative, filing liberal briefs only 46.3 percent of the time." Moreover, Segal noted that adding economic cases to the study made Bork look more liberal than in O'Connor's study. This variance is noteworthy because Bork is a well-known apostle of the Chicago School of Law and Economics; the only possible explanation for his more liberal briefs is the moderate economic outlooks of the Nixon and Ford administrations.[91] Segal concludes that his study "strengthens the notion that solicitors general are responsive to the President they serve, and not their own policy preferences."[92]

A study conducted by Sidney Ulmer and David Williamson arrives at findings similar to Segal's. Ulmer and Williamson wrote that "patterns of *amicus* participation depend upon the political affiliation of the administration under which the solicitor general serves."[93] An even more recent study by Rebecca Salokar examines the Solicitor General's briefs in individual rights cases between 1959 and 1986.[94] Salokar concluded that the pattern of arguments made by Solicitors General in such cases was closely "reflective of the agenda of the administration they served."[95] Salokar's study also included empirical evidence on the rates of success of different Solicitors General in rights cases. She found little linkage between success rate and the quality of advocacy, but found that success varied with the degree of ideological congruence between the administration and the Court. She deduced that "winning and losing depends on whether the administration and the Court agree, in principle, on the goals and remedies that should be implemented."[96]

The above studies and empirical evidence highlight the uniform understanding among former Solicitors General that the office serves the current Attorney General and President. Recent assertions to the contrary, the notion that the office can be independent of either is without support in law or history. Chief Justice Burger put the matter in proper perspective when he said the Solicitor

General, like the Attorney General, is "the Government's advocate in the Supreme Court, not the Supreme Court's representative in the Department of Justice."[97]

The Attorney General and Judicial Policymaking

Studies linking government litigation to administration policy are important because they suggest the nature of the Attorney General's political role. The office's power over judicial policymaking makes it politically strategic. The Attorney General can exercise this influence in three ways: through the judicial selection process, through control of government litigation, and through the use of rhetoric to shape the legal-political environment.

The Attorney General and Judicial Selection

The most effective means by which an administration can influence judicial policymaking is through appointments to the courts.[98] Modern Presidents can no longer expect to fill the bench with personal friends or acquaintances. Instead they rely on their Attorneys General to find and prepare candidates for appointments. So far has the judicial selection process become the domain of the Attorney General that Professor Joel Grossman's classic 1965 study on judicial selection concluded that: "The choice of a federal judge is the Attorney General's to make—provided that he makes it within the framework of the relevant norms of behavior which operate on the selection process."[99]

"Relevant norms" include the constraints that operate on any administration's judicial selections: such as senatorial courtesy, the opinions of the American Bar Association (ABA) and other professional groups, or the need for minority representation on the federal bench.[100] In terms of executive discretion, Grossman's observation is entirely accurate. Although modern Presidents may occasionally involve themselves in particular appointments, the process usually is left entirely in the hands of the Attorney General.[101]

An administration's judicial selections can affect the federal bench either through quality or quantity.[102] How long an administration remains in office, the rate of retirement from the bench, and congressional decisions with respect to the number of federal judgeships all factor into the volume of appointments that administration makes. In terms of a percentage of the sitting judiciary, Franklin Roosevelt oversaw the appointment of 81 percent of all federal judges. Harry Truman appointed 47 percent, Dwight Eisenhower 56 percent, John Kennedy 33 percent, Lyndon Johnson 38 percent, Jimmy Carter 40 percent, and Ronald Reagan 47 percent.[103]

The size of the federal judiciary, however, rests largely outside the direct control of the President. The Justice Department can propose legislation to increase the number of judgeships, but the size of the lower federal judicial system traditionally has been linked to growth in its case load.[104] The character of individuals appointed to the bench, on the other hand, is within the Attorney General's domain. Professor David O'Brien has pointed out that, in developing a judicial selection strategy, most administrations attempt to balance four different factors: party patronage; race, ethnicity, or gender; professional qualifications; and ideology.[105] Different Attorneys General assign these factors different weights in the screening process.

Prior to 1932, most Presidents allowed their Attorneys General to forward nominations for lower court judgeships to the Senate after only perfunctory White House approval. The selection process inside the department, however, was neither regular nor systematic. For lower court appointments, the primary influence was senatorial courtesy.[106] Presidents worked closely with their Attorneys General on nominations to the Supreme Court, often appointing the Attorney General himself or other members of the administration.

Throughout the nineteenth century, the federal judiciary remained small enough that Attorneys General could personally oversee the selection process.[107] During Franklin Roosevelt's administration judicial selection was delegated to the staff, and the Attorney General began spending less time in the actual process. President Roosevelt also took a special interest in lower court appointments, using them to reward personal loyalty. According to O'Brien, Roosevelt frequently offered judgeships to friends or would make deals with Senators without consulting his Attorney General. This habit upset Justice Department officials, who thought it undermined any coherent selection strategy. In 1940, Solicitor General Francis Biddle wrote a letter to Attorney General Robert Jackson complaining that this "should not be [Roosevelt's] practice, and I cannot help feeling that he doesn't realize the immense importance to his whole program of these federal judges."[108]

During the Roosevelt and Truman administrations, White House involvement in lower court nominations remained informal and the Justice Department's screening was unsystematic. Personal interviews were rare and appointments were viewed primarily as instruments of patronage. In nominations to the Supreme Court, the Justice Department continued to take the leading role, canvassing the country for candidates and performing background checks. The White House continued to show greater interest in Supreme Court than lower court nominations; consequently, it worked closely with the Justice Department on filling high court vacancies.[109]

It was not until Eisenhower's administration that the judicial selection process inside the Justice Department became formalized. Attorney General Herbert Brownell delegated responsibility for nominations to Deputy Attorney General William Rogers. Judicial nominations continued to be seen primarily as acts of patronage. After twenty years of Democratic domination, Brownell wanted to elevate Republicans to the bench; by the end of the administration, the federal bench was roughly half Republicans.[110] Brownell and Rogers forged new links with the ABA and began utilizing its reports to evaluate potential candidates. By

Eisenhower's second term, all judicial candidates were subjected to routine FBI background checks and ABA evaluations. Personal interviews with candidates, especially to appellate level posts, were conducted but remained relatively uncommon. While the department continued to rely mainly on Republican Senators or local party officials for recruitment, it began compiling its own list of potential candidates, especially for circuit court nominations. Both Brownell and Rogers cultivated close ties to the Senate Judiciary Committee to avoid confirmation obstacles. With little interest or experience in the law, Eisenhower was happy to delegate judicial selections entirely to the Justice Department. He did little more than rubber-stamp the Attorney General's recommendations to all but Supreme Court positions.[111]

The systematic process that began under Eisenhower remained the norm through the Kennedy, Johnson, Nixon, and Ford administrations. Screening continued to be handled from the Deputy Attorney General's office. Although they emphasized different steps, each administration worked closely with the Senate and party leaders to identify candidates, with the FBI and ABA to investigate them, and with the Senate Judiciary Committee before and during confirmation.[112] Although Presidents would occasionally take an interest in a particular judgeship, there was little regular or formal White House involvement in lower court nominations.[113]

The Carter administration brought sweeping changes to judicial selection. President Carter and Griffin Bell pledged to "remove politics" from the process and to make appointments based "strictly on merit."[114] Despite this commitment, the administration's overriding priority was to diversify the federal bench by appointing more women and minorities. Bell ordered his Assistant Attorney General for Civil Rights, Drew Days III, to inventory qualified women and minority candidates. To further democratize the recruitment of judges, Bell urged the President to establish merit selection commissions charged with recommending nominees for federal judgeships.[115]

In 1977, the Carter administration created two merit selection commissions, the United States Circuit Judge Nominating Commission (by E.O. 11972) and the Committee on Selection of Federal Judicial Officers (by E.O. 11992). The Circuit Court Commission was broken into thirteen panels (one for each circuit except the First and Ninth Circuits, where there were two panels each), with eleven members each. The Committee on Judicial Officers was a seven-member body charged with finding nominees to all specialized federal courts such as the Court of Claims and Bankruptcy Courts. Bell also encouraged Senators to establish selection panels in their individual states. By 1980, district court panels were established in thirty states.[116]

The Justice Department forwarded the names of qualified women and minority candidates to the commissions or individual Senators to be considered alongside candidates drawn from other sources. The selection commissions decentralized the recruitment process. For the first time, responsibility for initial recruitment of federal judges was moved outside the Justice Department. In addition, the commissions significantly reduced the role of senatorial patronage in judicial nominations, especially to the circuit courts.[117]

Associate Attorney General Michael Egan took on primary responsibility for screening candidates during the Carter administration. After names arrived at the department from the selection commissions, an FBI report was obtained, and Justice officials performed a background screening. The list of individuals who survived the preliminary screening went to the Attorney General. Bell read each candidate's report; if he noticed irregularities, he called the candidate in for a personal interview. After the Justice Department settled on a name, it was forwarded to the ABA for a report, then to the White House for formal recommendation. Under Bell, the Justice Department also de-emphasized the role of the ABA. In an effort to obtain alternative professional evaluations, it mailed the names of potential nominees to the National Bar Association and other professional organizations representing minorities and women.[118]

The White House role in the selection of lower court judges became a subject of debate during the Carter administration. At one point in late 1978, an *ad hoc* committee was established in the White House to review the Justice Department's recommendations prior to submitting them to the President. Bell, angered by what he saw as a turf invasion, appealed to President Carter.[119] The committee was dissolved and Justice Department recommendations once again went directly to Carter for approval.[120]

By 1979, the merit selection commissions themselves also had attracted controversy.[121] There were reports that panels were applying litmus tests by asking potential judges to commit themselves on specific policy issues. The administration sometimes fueled the conflict by circumventing the commissions to get preferred candidates nominated. On one occasion, Senator Edward Kennedy of Massachusetts, Chairman of the Senate Judiciary Committee, made a deal with the administration to enable an aide, Steven Breyer, to be appointed to the First Circuit Court. When the nominating panel twice refused to return Breyer's name on a list of candidates, the administration simply added it and nominated him.[122]

During the Reagan administration, controversy over judicial selections reached new heights.[123] William French Smith recentralized judicial selection in the Justice Department. Bell's merit commissions were abolished, and Smith delegated recruitment and screening responsibility to the newly created Office of Legal Policy. Though OLP continued to rely for district court nominations on recommendations from Republican Senators and party officials, it developed its own list of nominees for appellate level courts.[124]

OLP introduced rigorous ideological screening to the selection process. All judicial candidates were asked to visit the department for extensive interviews. OLP compiled data banks of speeches, articles, and judicial opinions to better evaluate candidates' ideological compatibility with the administration's policy agenda. After OLP screening, names were forwarded to an intradepartmental working group that consisted of the Attorney General, Deputy Attorney General, and Assistant Attorney General for OLP. This group would further scrutinize candidates before making recommendations to the White House.[125]

The Reagan administration's emphasis on ideology put strains on its relations with the ABA. Previous administrations regularly sounded out an ABA committee for tentative ratings of leading candidates prior to settling on one. The reports could thus be used to guide the Justice Department during the final stages of selection. The introduction of merit panels during the Carter administration ended this process. Although they dissolved the merit selection commissions, Smith and Meese maintained the more formal relationship with the ABA, seeking ratings only after the administration had selected its nominee. The administration also abandoned the policy of working with the National Bar Association and with women's groups to obtain alternative ratings of candidates.[126]

However, the most important innovation to the judicial selection process made by the Reagan administration was institutionalizing a role for the White House Legal Counsel's office. The administration created the President's Committee on Judicial Selection. Chaired by Reagan's White House Legal Counsel, Fred Fielding, the committee also included the Justice Department working group, the Assistant to the President for Personnel, the Assistant to the President for Legislative Affairs, and the White House Chief of Staff.[127] The committee was responsible for reviewing names as they emerged from the Justice Department, before forwarding them to the President. Thus, it performed a final ideological screen, but it also weakened the Attorney General's control over judicial nominations.[128]

The impact of changes in the judicial selection process on the nature of the federal bench is represented in data on partisan appointments. Figure 3.1 depicts the percentage of judicial appointments received by members of the President's party during the last nine administrations. The evidence reflects greater emphasis on ideology and partisanship during the administrations of Franklin Roosevelt and Ronald Reagan: 97 and 95 percent of their respective judicial appointments went to members of their parties. Efforts to "depoliticize" the Justice Department and the judicial selection process following Watergate show up in the relatively low numbers of partisan appointments under the Ford and Carter administrations: 81 percent and 90 percent respectively.

The federal court hierarchy demands that a President appoint Supreme Court Justices if his administration has any hope of significantly influencing judicial policy. The pattern of Supreme Court vacancies is crucial to assessing trends in the political relationship between the judiciary and the executive. The Roosevelt administration had the most opportunity to influence the ideological makeup of the Supreme Court, making a total of nine appointments.[129] Between 1932 and 1968, Democratic administrations made seventeen of the twenty-three appointments to the Court.[130] Of the five appointments that Republican President Eisenhower made, two (William Brennan and Earl Warren) proved to be liberal jurists.[131] Since 1968, the tide has turned: Republicans have made ten appoint-

Figure 3.1. **Partisan Appointments to the Federal Courts by Administration, 1932–1988**

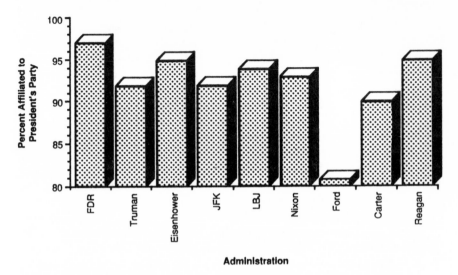

Administration

Source: David O'Brien, *Judicial Roulette* (New York: Priority Press, 1988), p. 37.

ments to the Court, six of them since 1982.[132] If we assume that Supreme Court Justices usually share the ideological perspective of the appointing administration, we would expect friction to have developed between the Justice Department and the Supreme Court during the Eisenhower, Nixon, Ford, and Reagan administrations, and generally harmonious relations to have existed during the Kennedy, Johnson, Carter, and Bush administrations. The impact that this pattern of political control of White House and appointments to the high court has had on the relationship between the Justice Department and the federal judiciary will be discussed in later chapters.

The Attorney General and Government Litigation

If judicial selection is the most effective method for an administration to influence judicial policymaking, then government litigation is the most direct. The Justice Department's singular relationship with the federal courts makes it an especially persuasive litigator; in the Supreme Court's, historically, it has been the most frequent and most successful litigator. The department participates in one-fourth to one-half of the cases on the Supreme Court docket. Figure 3.2 illustrates the frequency of government participation in the Court from 1925 to 1988.

The data indicate that Justice Department participation has kept pace with the growth in the Court's case load since the 1950s. During the 1988 Court term (the last year of the Reagan administration), the Justice Department participated in 38

Figure 3.2. **Justice Department Participation in Cases Docketed in the United States Supreme Court**

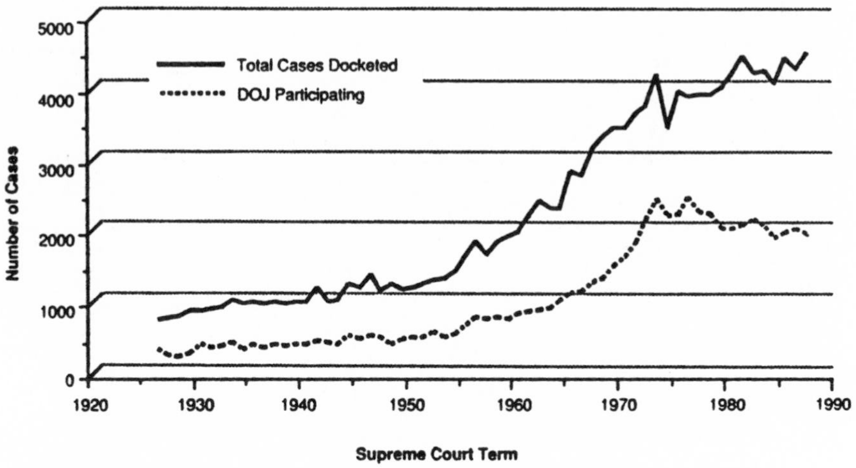

Source: Annual Report of the Solicitor General (1926–1989).

percent of all cases docketed.[133] The highest percentage of cases in which the Justice Department participated in a single term was just over 51 percent in 1976.

Of greater significance from the standpoint of influencing judicial policymaking is the department's rate of success. This can be measured in two ways: first, the ability to place issues before the Court via petitions for certiorari; second, the ability to win cases on the merits. Any strategy for influencing judicial policymaking must concern itself as much with agenda-setting as with the legal position it hopes to persuade the Court to adopt. Directing the issues the Court hears is not just prerequisite to a decision on the merits; it also serves as a fulcrum for focusing public attention on issues. The Justice Department's ability to persuade the Court to grant its petitions for certiorari is therefore very important. So great is the department's influence in setting the Court's agenda that Solicitor General Simon Sobeloff writes: "the power of the Supreme Court is limited to deciding the cases brought before it. It is the Attorney General who decides what the Supreme Court will decide—at least in the area of public issues."[134] Even if Sobeloff overdraws the point, it is no secret that the Justice Department serves a vital role in helping the Court screen petitions.[135] Not only does the Solicitor General filter government appeals from the lower courts, he also files briefs supporting or opposing review in cases in which the government is not directly involved. Figure 3.3 illustrates the success in all petitions for certiorari filed or supported by the Justice Department from 1925 to 1988.

The Supreme Court granted more than half of the petitions the Justice Department filed or supported for every term covered by the data except four (1933,

Figure 3.3. **Justice Department Success in Petitions for Certiorari in the Supreme Court, 1925–1988**

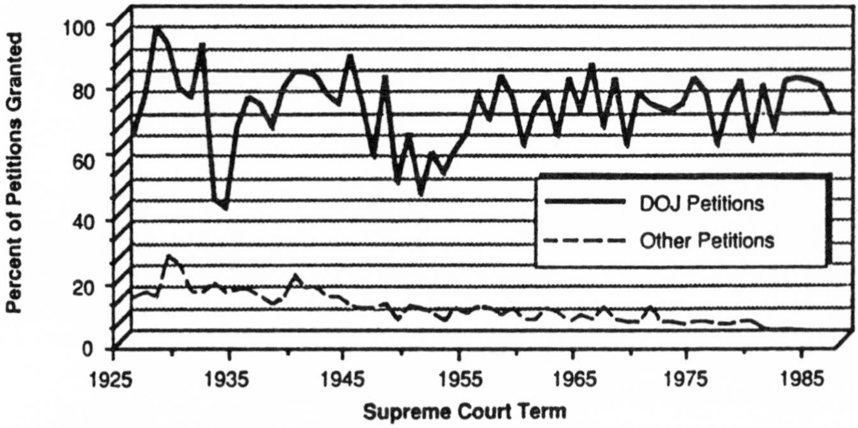

Percent of Petitions Granted

DOJ Petitions
Other Petitions

1925   1935   1945   1955   1965   1975   1985

Supreme Court Term

Source: Annual Report of the Solicitor General (1926–1989).

1934, 1949, and 1951). During three terms (1928, 1929, and 1932), its rate of success was above 90 percent. The department's average success rate for the entire period was just over 70 percent. In contrast, the Supreme Court granted over 20 percent of petitions filed by other litigants in two terms only (1929 and 1930); otherwise the average rate of success for such petitions was less than 19 percent.

While the Court's docket has mushroomed during the past forty years, the amount of time that Justices can spend hearing cases has not. The squeeze on Court time shows clearly in the declining percentage of cases accepted for review. The Justice Department's rate of success on petitions for certiorari, however, has not been eroded by the case load crisis. In fact, the constriction of the Court's time appears to have strengthened the department's position, as the Court is forced to rely increasingly on external cues, such as government support, when screening petitions.[136] Of course, persuading the Court to accept cases for review is only the first step; one must also win cases on the merits. The Justice Department enjoys victories in this area as well. Justice Department briefs have always been vested with special credibility because of their technical superiority and the department's traditional image as an honest broker.[137] This holds true for department briefs as party to a suit and as *amicus curiae*.

The Justice Department's role as *amicus curiae* is especially noteworthy because the Solicitor General enjoys greater discretion over this function than when the government is an actual party. When the department files a brief as an *amicus*, the government has neither a direct interest to protect nor an agency to represent. Such briefs are considered purely advisory and are intended to provide information or counsel to the Court as it considers the ramifications of the case on broader developments in the law.[138]

The Attorney General first appeared as *amicus curiae* in the Supreme Court in *Florida v. Georgia* (1854).[139] Prior to 1950, however, the use of *amicus* briefs was rare. As late as the Court's 1950 term, the Justice Department filed just one such brief.[140] Since then, however, the department has become more active as an *amicus* intervener. In 1988, the Justice Department filed *amicus* briefs in 41 (or 26 percent) of the 170 cases in which the Supreme Court heard arguments. On average since 1950, the Justice Department has participated as *amicus curiae* in 22 cases per term.[141]

Several scholars have analyzed success rates and types of cases in which the Justice Department appears as *amicus curiae*, and all have reached similar conclusions regarding the influence of the department's briefs. A comprehensive study by Jeffrey Segal of the 393 *amicus* briefs filed by the Justice Department between 1953 and 1982 revealed that the party supported by the department prevailed more than 77 percent of the time.[142] This extraordinary effectiveness leads some scholars to question the fairness of the department's intervention in private disputes. Professor Robert Scigliano, for instance, argues that the department's intervention in private disputes "smacks too much of partisanship: it subjects the Solicitor General to strong pressures from organizations and individual litigants."[143]

The Supreme Court's rules reflect the high esteem in which the Justice Department's *amicus* briefs are held. The Solicitor General has traditionally been exempt from the standard requirement that *amicus* participants obtain the consent of both parties, or receive special permission from the Court to intervene.[144] Moreover, the Justice Department often receives special invitations from federal courts to appear as *amicus curiae* in important cases, especially when questions of constitutional law are considered. In the 1957 Little Rock school desegregation case, for instance, the district court asked the Attorney General to appear as *amicus curiae* and authorized him to "submit pleadings, evidence, arguments, and briefs and to file a petition for injunctive relief to prevent obstructions to the carrying out of the court's orders."[145]

The Supreme Court also tends to display extraordinary deference to off-the-record factual assertions by the Justice Department. The Court's willingness to accept at face value factual statements of the Solicitor General, particularly regarding the operation or functions of government agencies or officers, is notorious among close observers of the Court. Similar statements made by ordinary litigants would not go unquestioned.[146]

The deference the Court shows Justice Department filings translates into an extraordinarily high degree of success. Figure 3.4 illustrates the Justice Department's success in cases decided by the Court between 1925 and 1988. During only two terms (1934 and 1935) did the department lose more than 50 percent of its cases. Conversely, during four terms (1939, 1953, 1981, 1983) the department won in excess of 80 percent of the cases in which it participated. For the entire period covered by the data, the Justice Department prevailed on average in nearly 69 percent of its cases.

Figure 3.4. **Justice Department Success in Cases Decided on Merits in the Supreme Court, 1925–1988**

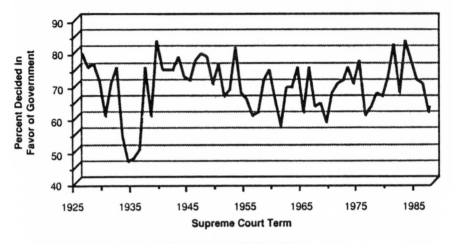

Source: Annual Report of the Solicitor General (1926–1989).

The Justice Department's institutional capital allows the Attorney General to influence the Supreme Court in a way no other litigant can. Issues that appear on the agenda of the Attorney General will, more often than not, be heard by the Supreme Court. Of the cases decided on the merits, the decision usually will support the position advanced by the Attorney General.

The Justice Department's institutional standing before the Court does not, however, guarantee success. Effectiveness of Justice Department litigation depends also on the competency of the advocacy and the respectability of its legal arguments. Administrations whose policy agenda conforms to the Court's jurisprudential posture are likely to taste victory; administrations whose agenda is out of sync with the Court can expect to suffer setbacks. Thus, the Justice Department's litigating success should be viewed in light of its opportunities to influence the Court's ideological composition through judicial appointments and its ability to lobby the Court in less direct ways.

The Attorney General and Rhetoric

While scholars have long been familiar with the Attorney General's role in judicial selection and litigation, his ability to influence the judiciary through rhetoric has gone relatively unnoticed. It is well known that judges, even when tenured for life, do not operate in a political vacuum. The Supreme Court, as Mr. Dooley noted, "follows th' iliction returns." Judges are conscious that judicial authority ultimately rests on the public perception of its legitimacy. As the most visible law enforcement officer in the country, the Attorney General can exert enormous pressure on the judiciary by appealing to the public and the legal profession in speeches or written word.

The Justice Department is the closest thing to a constituent the federal courts have. Moreover, courts must rely on the Justice Department to give political sanction to controversial decisions. Consequently, it is no wonder federal judges are especially sensitive to the attitudes of the Attorney General.[147] Although the Attorney General's rhetorical function is more difficult to quantify than litigation or judicial selection, it may be the best gauge of an Attorney General's political activism because few restraints operate on rhetoric. The nature and frequency of an Attorney General's public remarks are left entirely to his discretion. While the majority of the speeches of the Attorneys General are perfunctory, when they address controversial issues, their remarks receive extensive media coverage and are published in the nation's major legal journals.

Attorneys General have used their office as a platform from which to support or attack the Supreme Court. Following the Court's decision in *Brown v. Board of Education*, for example, Attorney General Brownell strongly supported the Court's decision in a series of public speeches.[148] Such support was especially critical in the South, where executive branch ambivalence would have further legitimized noncompliance tactics. Conversely, when the Court struck down major elements of Franklin Roosevelt's political program, Attorney General Homer Cummings publicly condemned the Justice's decisions and challenged their authority to interpret the Constitution.[149]

More recently, Attorney General Meese attacked the Court's "liberal jurisprudence" in a series of controversial speeches he delivered between 1986 and 1987. Meese not only attacked specific rulings but, like Cummings, he challenged the Court's role as final arbiter of the Constitution.[150] Whether Meese's remarks directly influenced Court decisions in the sense of prompting individual Justices to change their votes in specific cases is unlikely. Nevertheless, the strategy clearly succeeded in shifting the center of political-jurisprudential debate in the United States to the right. Meese's disputatious speeches continued to be discussed in the pages of the nation's most prestigious law publications well after he resigned.[151]

Such attention does not go unnoticed by the federal judiciary. In the future, liberal judges might find themselves more receptive to conservative arguments, or less sympathetic to liberal positions. Moreover, by provoking debate in the nation's top law schools, the Attorney General's remarks may significantly shape the views of future jurists. Terry Eastland, Assistant Attorney General for the Office of Public Affairs under Meese, sees this as the major impact of the speeches. In an interview, Eastland noted:

> The Attorney General's speeches were not necessarily calculated to change anyone's mind in particular. But rather we wanted to make conservative jurisprudence intellectually respectable again. I think we accomplished this. Con-

Figure 3.5. **Average Number of Speeches Made Annually by Attorneys General: By Administration**

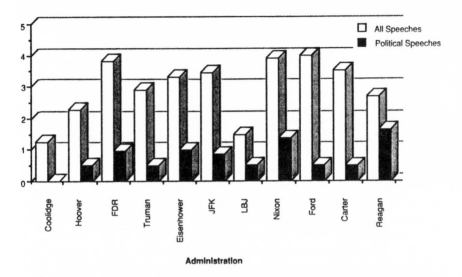

Source: As indexed by *An Index to Legal Periodicals* (New York: Wilson Co.).

servative legal think tanks have flourished, conservative scholars like Burger and Posner have found a new popularity, even Lawrence Tribe has included in the last edition of his book on constitutional law a section on original intent. This ultimately will change what type of decisions are made on the bench.[152]

In terms of rhetorical activism, modern Attorneys General vary considerably. Figure 3.5 contrasts the average number of speeches or articles published on an annual basis by Attorneys General for each administration beginning with Coolidge's and ending with Reagan's.

The data also show the average number of speeches dealing with substantive constitutional or jurisprudential issues. The author compiled this data after reviewing published speeches and determining the primary thrust of their content. Thus constrained by subjective analysis, the data nevertheless roughly portray trends in the Attorney General's rhetorical activism.

The Attorney General and Administrative Policymaking

In addition to influencing judicial policymaking, the Attorney General plays an important political role in the administrative arena. The office's ability to control federal litigation makes it an attractive instrument for regulating other administrative agencies and departments. The use of the office in modern presidential administrative strategies is discussed in detail in chapter 6. It is important at this juncture, however, to outline the nature of the Attorney General's control and the debate surrounding it.

The Struggle for Centralization

Since Edmund Randolph's day Attorneys General have struggled to centralize government litigating authority. The 1870 act appeared to accomplish this feat by giving the Attorney General sweeping authority. But enacting a statute was one thing, dislodging a power jealously guarded by other agencies and departments was quite another. Other agencies valued the right to litigate as part of their regulatory missions and attempts to remove it were regarded as hostile invasions on their turf.[153]

Instead of supporting the Attorney General in the scuffle, Congress actually undermined the centralizing reforms it had ordered.[154] Immediately after it passed the 1870 act centralizing legal authority, Congress set about making exceptions to it. In 1872, lawmakers granted independent litigating authority to the Interior and Post Office Departments.[155] When the Agriculture Department was created in 1889 and the Departments of Labor and Commerce in 1913, they also received independent litigating powers.[156]

Even more threatening to the central authority of the Attorney General, however, was the establishment of independent regulatory agencies, beginning with the Interstate Commerce Commission (ICC) in 1887.[157] The rationale behind the creation of independent agencies permanently altered assumptions about the department's role in controlling government legal work. Although the Interstate Commerce Act was silent on the issue of litigation, its implicit independence from the executive led the commission to assert the right to litigate for itself. From the beginning, it hired its own attorneys and litigated cases in the lower courts, though it cooperated with Justice Department attorneys in cases before the Supreme Court.[158]

In 1910, President Taft criticized the independent regulatory commissions and urged Congress to bring all government litigation under the explicit control of the Attorney General.[159] Congress did precisely the opposite. Instead of limiting the independent agency's litigating authority, lawmakers in 1920 enacted legislation explicitly authorizing the ICC to represent itself in the lower courts.[160] They followed this precedent by giving similar authority to the Securities and Exchange Commission and the National Labor Relations Board.[161] Given Congress's traditional mistrust of the President, its failure to live up to its promise under the 1870 act comes as no surprise.

Although Congress was ambivalent about centralizing litigating authority, the Attorney General found a sympathetic ear in the Supreme Court. As early as *The Gray Jacket* case in 1866, the Court had held that when the Attorney General represented the United States it would not hear opposing counsel from other government departments or agencies.[162] In the *Confiscation Cases* two years later, the Court extended the rule to government litigation in lower courts.[163]

The most important contribution made to the Attorney General's power came in the *San Jacinto* case.[164] When it was argued that the Attorney General's power to initiate proceedings extended only to cases specifically authorized by statute, the Court responded by recognizing the office's broad common law authority to initiate suits. By directing the office to represent the interests of the United States, the Court argued, Congress had implicitly vested it with plenary power to initiate suits to protect those interests. The Court justified its decision by appealing to the office's history. By using the title of Attorney General, it said, Congress undoubtedly "had reference to the similar office with the same designation existing under English law."[165] With this, the Court clothed the U.S. office with the same common law powers of its English predecessor, and bridged the gaps in its statutory authority.

In *Kern River Company v. United States* (1921), the Supreme Court further strengthened the Attorney General's grip over government litigation.[166] In this case, the Court refused to hear a suit brought by the Solicitor of the Navy. Unless expressly authorized to conduct litigation, the Court said, other departments should refer all cases to the Department of Justice which "is charged with the duty of determining when the United States shall sue, for what it shall sue, and that such suits shall be brought in appropriate cases."[167]

The federal courts have consistently supported the Justice Department's monopoly over government litigation, even against encroachment from independent regulatory agencies. In *Federal Trade Commission v. Guignon* (1968), for example, the Solicitor General refused to authorize a Federal Trade Commission (FTC) action to enforce an agency subpoena.[168] The FTC brought suit, arguing that its independent power to issue the subpoena implied independent power to sue for its enforcement. The Justice Department disagreed. Relying on *Kern River*, the Eighth Circuit Court of Appeals held that the presumption of Justice Department control over litigation, even involving independent agencies, could be rebutted only by "unambiguous evidence of express congressional intention" to the contrary.

The Supreme Court assisted in another aspect of the Attorney General's effort to secure control over executive branch legal work. In *Smith v. Jackson* (1918), it examined the authority of the Attorney General's official opinions.[169] Although the Judiciary Act required the office to write opinions for executive department heads, it remained silent regarding the officers' obligation to comply with them. Dispute arose as to whether the opinions were merely advisory or legally binding.[170] In 1893, Attorney General Richard Olney determined that they were enforceable until or unless a federal court ruled otherwise.[171] Olney's successors followed his example and the Supreme Court agreed with him in *Smith*.

As important as the Court has been, the President has been the Attorney General's strongest ally in the wrestle for government/legal authority. Centralized control of litigation provides the President a convenient handle on the bureaucracy, and Presidents since George Washington have supported the consolidation of government legal work. In the midst of the First World War, President Woodrow Wilson signed an executive order placing all nonmilitary legal offices, regardless of department or agency, under the Attorney General's direct supervision.[172] The sweeping language of the order left little doubt about the Attorney General's authority:

> All litigation in which the United States or any Department, executive bureau, agency or office thereof, are engaged shall be conducted under the supervision and control of the Department of Justice; and that any opinion or ruling by the Attorney General upon any question of law arising in any Department, executive bureau, agency or office shall be treated as binding upon all Departments, bureaus, agencies or offices therewith concerned.[173]

For the first time, the central authority envisaged by the 1870 act became reality. Wilson's directive, however, was issued pursuant to wartime powers under the Overman Act.[174] When the war ended, the statute and executive order were repealed, and centrifugal forces immediately reappeared.

In 1920, Congress granted independent litigating authority to the U.S. Shipping Board and the Veterans Bureau.[175] Six years later, the Bureau of Internal Revenue requested and received independent authority.[176] Attorney General John Sargent, in his 1928 report to Congress, warned that continued decentralizations of authority would result in confusion and added government expense. Of the more than 900 attorneys then employed by the federal government, Sargent estimated only 115 were under his supervision.[177] Moreover, he noted, at least nine different government departments or agencies over which the Attorney General had no control conducted litigation on their own.[178]

Not until the Great Depression of the early 1930s did Congress, seeking ways to save money, aid the Attorney General's centralization fight. The Economy Act of 1932 required the President to reorganize where possible to improve government efficiency.[179] Pursuant to this act, Franklin Roosevelt signed Executive Order 6166 in June 1933. The order, which is still in effect, requires that all claims brought by or against the United States be litigated by the Department of Justice, unless otherwise authorized specifically in statute. Thus, the Attorney General's control over government litigation was restored by administrative fiat. Shortly thereafter, Congress codified this control in 28 U.S.C. Sec. 516:

> Except as otherwise authorized by law, the conduct of litigation in which the United States, an agency, or officer thereof is a party, or is interested, and securing evidence thereof, is reserved to the officers of the Department of Justice, under the direction of the Attorney General.

It is important to note that under Roosevelt's Order and 28 U.S.C. Sec. 516 department heads retained control over their legal officers. Only the authority to litigate independently was stripped from them. With central control over government litigation secured, efforts to centralize legal counsel were abandoned after 1933. Individual agencies and departments could still hire their own staff attorneys, even though the lawyers no longer could litigate without approval from the Attorney General. The arrangement creates a peculiar division of authority in government legal administration. Litigation has become virtually the exclusive domain of the Justice Department; the role of agency lawyers is limited to counseling administrators on the legal ramifications of their programs.

Legal scholar Donald Horowitz has conducted the only systematic study of the division of legal functions between Justice and other government agencies. He describes it as a "division of labor and a divorce of function."[180] Agency attorneys draft regulations, advise officials, and represent their agencies before administrative tribunals. But when agencies are forced into court, they literally become clients of the Justice Department. In such cases, agency attorneys are supposed to cooperate with Justice by assembling background information such as facts and applicable laws. Justice lawyers, on the other hand, are expected to represent agency interests without "interfering with the policy prerogatives of (the) agency client."[181]

Justice's monopoly on government litigation went unchallenged until the 1970s, when Watergate era reforms threatened it.[182] Prior to then, statutes establishing or reauthorizing legal officers in various executive branch agencies used general terms that did not carve out exceptions to the Justice Department's control of litigation.[183] The only categorical exception was the litigating authority Congress had granted to independent regulatory agencies and commissions. These exceptions, however, arose from the larger conflict between Congress and the President over the regulatory bureaucracy, and did not represent an attempt to fragment the litigating power of the executive. Even independent agencies must receive "express" statutory authorization to carry out independent litigation, and none can represent themselves in the Supreme Court without Justice Department authorization.[184]

The current division of government legal labor is defended primarily on the grounds of efficiency and economy. Uniformity in government legal arguments has been achieved. Justice Department lawyers accumulate litigating expertise and become familiar with idiosyncratic preferences of particular courts or judges. They gain experience in arguing routine procedural defenses that shield agencies from judicial review. Because Justice attorneys are not obliged to advise agencies on policy, they are less constrained when it comes to offering an objective perspective and pursuing the most responsible litigating strategy. Because agencies were allowed to retain in-house counsels, some of the fears that thwarted earlier efforts to centralize litigation were allayed. In addition to sharing their respective agency's regulatory perspectives, in-house lawyers develop special expertise in substantive areas of regulatory law. Therefore they can offer their agencies expert advice which the generalists at Justice cannot.[185]

Its advantages notwithstanding, the current division of labor is not entirely satisfactory to Justice or agency lawyers. According to Horowitz, the division duplicates effort and sparks disputes over effectiveness. Agency attorneys complain they have to teach Justice Department lawyers the substantive law and facts in cases that go to trial. Justice Department attorneys, for their part, point to their courtroom expertise, saying it frees agencies from judicial interference that might result from decentralization.[186]

Implicit in the debate over who has the right to litigate is the assumption that agency and Justice attorneys litigate differently. This may not necessarily be so. If agency lawyers and Justice lawyers argue the same way, then questions of efficiency and effectiveness are redundant. A study by Susan Olson of litigation under the Occupational Safety and Health Act between 1971 and 1980 found only marginal differences between in-house Labor Department attorneys and Justice attorneys.[187] Olson found that the nature of the government's argument, as well as its rate of success, remained stable over the nine years. Roughly halfway through the study, litigating authority was transferred from the agency to the Justice Department. Olson's study, though limited in scope, suggests that centralized government litigation is no more efficient than decentralized. Increasingly, the debate over centralization has thus turned into one over political control.

Centralization and Policy Control

The contrast between the President's and the courts' support for centralization and Congress's opposition underscores what is really at stake in the debate. Centralization strengthens the President's ability to dictate policy orientation through government litigation. The Justice Department acts to control regulatory agencies that might otherwise advocate parochial positions regardless of the administration's political agenda. As Horowitz points out:

> It takes no special perspicacity on the part of a President to sense the propensity of agencies to gallop off in different directions and the concomitant difficulty of controlling them. The ability to locate responsibility in one place is a goal which has, and presumably will continue to have, great appeal in the White House. Centralized litigating authority is one of the few ready handles on the bureaucracy that a President possesses.[188]

Unlike most regulatory agencies, the Justice Department has no vested interest or industry to mollify, consequently it is less likely to resist unpopular presidential policies. When Nixon embarked on a program of policy impoundments during the early 1970s, for example, he had little difficulty inducing Justice to defend his legal position in court.[189] Had he been forced to rely on the attorneys for the agencies that his actions affected, he would doubtless have met with little enthusiasm. Thus, centralization is not only convenient but politically expedient for the President.

To be sure, from time to time the White House overrules positions favored by Justice Department attorneys. Like agency lawyers held captive by their industry–agency perspectives, Justice lawyers at times suffer from the legalistic myopia of the courtroom environment. On occasion, the White House forces hesitant Justice lawyers into postures they fear are too far out of line with the current courts. Nevertheless, the White House has vigilantly supported Justice's control over government litigation. Most Presidents apparently have found the department in tune with their political agenda or, at least, more susceptible to White House intervention.[190]

Centralization also yields important benefits to the judiciary. By screening agency litigation, the Justice Department can shield the courts from frivolous suits and interagency conflicts. The screening generally takes place in the Solicitor General's office.[191] Whenever the government loses a case in the lower courts, the Solicitor General reviews it for possible appeal. Given the large number of appealable cases that could be used to advance legal doctrine, only the best emerge from the Solicitor General's office. As a rule, the government does not appeal cases unless they meet at least three conditions: they have a strong factual background; they have the potential to make good law; and they represent an issue the court is open to address.[192]

The salutary effect of Justice Department screening on judicial dockets is clear. During the Supreme Court's 1985 term, the Solicitor General filed or supported petitions for certiorari in only 48 of the more than 665 government cases under review.[193] At no time since 1950 has the percentage of government petitions authorized exceeded 24 percent of the cases reviewed by the department.[194]

Not all unauthorized cases result from conflicts between the agencies and Justice. In many instances, the agencies may themselves have recommended against review. Nevertheless, conflict is present in a significant number of cases. Horowitz's study found disagreement in as many as 20 percent of applicable cases.[195] Even in cases when Justice authorizes an appeal, the department often compels the agency to pare back or accept compromise in its position; this occurs frequently enough to be a source of friction as well.

As a filter for government litigation, then, the Justice Department assists the courts. It forces agencies to compromise and ensures that appeals have "special and important reasons for seeking judicial review."[196] This task helps relieve the courts of a screening burden at a time when their dockets are burgeoning.

The President, Justice, and the courts win when government litigation is centralized. The losers are government agencies that deplore being held hostage to Justice Department representation.[197] In addition to raising questions of efficiency, agency heads complain that they cannot attract high-caliber attorneys, who are uninterested in posts that offer little or no courtroom experience. More important, they regard Justice's oversight powers as a threat to independent policymaking. On one hand, they argue that Justice lacks enforcement vigor and tends to sacrifice agency policy out of a conservative adherence to judicial precedent. On the other hand, they complain that Justice is an arm of the White House that will, at times, sacrifice law to promote ideology.[198]

Justice's screening also has its cost to the judiciary. Because interagency disputes arise from conflicting government interests, the question of who will resolve such conflicts has implications beyond questions of efficiency. The more power the Justice Department possesses in its role as gatekeeper to the courts, the less opportunity courts have to influence administrative policy. Centralized government litigation means the Attorney General or the White House resolves interagency disputes, regardless of whether they represent policy differences or bureaucratic turf battles. Decentralized litigation, on the other hand, would more frequently require the courts to settle such disputes.[199]

Yet it is Congress that has the least to gain and the most to lose from centralizing government litigation. It derives no direct benefit from centralization other than government economy. On the deficit side, it gives up influence over judicial policymaking because centralization eliminates the litigating power of "subgovernments." (Subgovernments are policymaking networks consisting of congressional committees, regulatory agencies, and industry or regulated interests.)[200]

Neither agencies nor congressional subcommittees working with agencies want the Justice Department looking over their shoulders and making decisions. "Fiefdoms have been created," Griffin Bell noted, "and the Justice Department's efforts to ensure uniformity in government litigating postures can constitute a real threat to them."[201] Thus it is not surprising that Congress has supported centralizing government litigation only during periods of fiscal crisis. Once the economic pressure subsides, lawmakers usually revert to supporting a more centrifugal system of litigation.

The point is that centralizing government litigation has important policy implications in a system of separated powers. Centralization shifts policymaking authority away from Congress and the judiciary, and shifts it toward the White House.[202] For the judiciary, the loss of policymaking opportunities that would otherwise arise from exposure to interagency conflicts is more than offset by the department's assistance in controlling its docket. For Congress, however, the advantages are less clear. Centralization also affects the policymaking calculus within the executive branch, reducing the role of regulatory agencies and facilitating White House control of the bureaucracy. In this light, Congress's ambivalence to central control is understandable, particularly during periods of heightened interbranch conflict. In a 1975 study, Professor John Davis aptly characterized the struggle over centralization when he wrote that it was a history characterized by:

A continuing effort by Attorneys General to centralize responsibility for all government litigation in Justice, a continuing effort by many agencies to escape from that control with respect to civil litigation, and a practice by Congress of accepting the positions of the Attorney General in principle and then cutting them to pieces by exceptions.[203]

Conclusion

The transformation of the Attorney General from a judicial to an executive branch institution profoundly altered normative views of the office. From a legal officer charged with political duties, the Attorney General increasingly became viewed as a political officer charged with legal duties. This change not only led to the expansion of the office's political functions, but also to the appointment of a different type of incumbent. More and more modern-day Attorneys General have come to the office as politicians and administrators rather than lawyers or legal scholars.

As the Solicitor General gradually assumed the role of chief government barrister in the Supreme Court, the office inherited some of the quasi-judicial aura formerly attached to the Attorney General in that role. The Solicitor General's tradition of independence, however, must be kept in proper perspective. Unlike the Attorney General, the Solicitor General has no independent statutory or common law authority to represent government interests in court. The office depends entirely on the Attorney General for its standing. Indeed, nearly all Justice Department authority is vested by statute in the Attorney General. Therefore, questions regarding political control of government litigation must seek answers in the accountability and independence of the Attorney General.

One thing is clear: the modern Attorney General is a major actor in American politics and influences policy in a variety of ways. Through the office's role in judicial nominations and government litigation, and through use of the office as a rhetorical platform, the Attorney General can exert tremendous influence over judicial policymaking. Moreover, the office's check on agency litigation puts it in a strategic position to control bureaucratic policymaking. Different Attorneys General have exercised these powers differently; the remaining chapters explore how and why.

Notes

1. 6 *Op. A.G.* (1954), 326, 340.
2. U.S. Library of Congress, *Journal of First Session of the Senate* (1820), 34–42.
3. The records are silent about what prompted the wording change, but its consequences seem to have been understood by members of Congress. See Warren, "New Light on the Federal Judiciary Act of 1789," 109.
4. See Hightower, "From Attornatus to the Department of Justice," 405 (hereafter cited as Ervin Hearings).
5. Quoted in Cummings and McFarland, *Federal Justice*, 1.
6. U.S. Congress, *Digest of Appropriations* (1790–1873). Congress originally made no office provisions for the Attorney General. Because of the Attorney General's close responsibility to the Court, Randolph was given a room in the Supreme Court's quarters. See Easby-Smith, *The Department of Justice*, 423.
7. "Circumstances Surrounding the Creation of the Office of Attorney General and the Department of Justice," in Ervin Hearings, 420.

8. Ibid., 421.

9. 2 U.S. Stat. L., 1.

10. Although Randolph had been invited to attend cabinet meetings as early as 1791, the Attorney General was not considered a regular member. The duty of the office, said one early study, was to "impart legal counsel" not political advice. See Henry Learned, "The Attorney General and the Cabinet," *Political Science Quarterly* 24 (1909), 444.

11. Miller, "The Attorney General as the President's Lawyer," in Huston et al., 51.

12. Richard Fenno, *The President's Cabinet* (Cambridge: Harvard University Press, 1959), 17.

13. Cummings and McFarland, *Federal Justice*, 53.

14. Learned, "Attorney General and the Cabinet."

15. Huston, *The Department of Justice*, 53.

16. Although the office continued to perform functions of a "quasi-judicial" nature, Cushing said, "a sense of subordination has come to exist . . . with regard to the directory power of the President." In the absence of specific statutory language to the contrary, he concluded, constitutional authority to control the Attorney General's discretionary function must "reside with the President, who has the power to appoint and remove, and whose duty it is to take care that the laws be faithfully executed." See 6 *Op. A.G.* (1854), 326, 332–33, 340–41.

17. 125 U.S. (1887), 747.

18. 135 U.S. (1889), 1.

19. U.S. Constitution, art. II, sec. 3.

20. 258 U.S. (1922), 254.

21. Ibid., 262.

22. Anticipating criticism, Kennedy joked that he would announce the appointment "some morning about 2:00 A.M., look up and down the street, and, if there's no one there, I'll whisper, it's Bobby." Arthur Schlesinger, *Robert Kennedy and His Times* (London: Andre Deutsch Ltd., 1978), 233.

23. For a discussion of the office's transformation from legal scholar to politician and administrator, see Victor Navasky, "The Politics of Justice," *New York Times Magazine* (May 5, 1974), 18; "The Attorney General as Scholar, Not Enforcer," *New York Times Magazine* (September 7, 1975), 13.

24. Ibid.

25. The Bentsen amendment was raised as an objection to Edwin Meese's nomination and in connection with other appointments to the Justice Department. In 1984 Senator Max Bacus introduced similar legislation, see 130 *Congressional Record* S2020. For a full discussion of the Judiciary Committee's commitment to it, see comments of Senator Howard Metzenbaum in Senate Judiciary Committee, *Hearings on the Nomination of Edwin Meese III to be Attorney General*, 98th Cong., 2d. sess. (1984), 6.

26. Ibid.

27. A few recent Attorneys General have had distinguished professional backgrounds. In addition to Edward Levi and Griffin Bell, Ramsey Clark, who was appointed by President Johnson in 1967, was a former director of the American Judicature Society and President of the Federal Bar Association. Nicholas Katzenbach, appointed by Johnson in 1965, was a professor of law at both Chicago and Yale. But despite these noteworthy cases, a distinguished legal career is clearly no longer the prerequisite that it was prior to 1870.

28. *New York Times*, December 29, 1960, A–21.

29. Robert Stern summed up the relationship between the Attorney General and the Solicitor General by noting: "The Attorney General is the chief law officer of the Government, but he is primarily an administrator, policy maker and Presidential adviser. The

Solicitor General, on the other hand, may not unfairly be described as the highest Government official who acts primarily as a lawyer." See Stern, "The Solicitor General's Office and Administrative Agency Litigation," *ABA Journal* 46 (1960), 154.

30. Ibid., 155.

31. Navasky, *Kennedy Justice.*

32. Ibid., 280.

33. Ibid.

34. Ibid., 281.

35. Biddle, *In Brief Authority* (Garden City: Doubleday & Co., 1962), 97.

36. For a general discussion of this point, see Charles Fahy, "The Office of Solicitor General," 28 *ABA Journal* (1942), 20. Like the Attorney General, the Solicitor General's office is rooted in English history. Historically, the term "solicitor" in England applied to a class of individuals that acted as attorneys' assistants. Holdsworth tells us that in 1589 solicitors were defined as persons, " 'being learned in the Laws, and informed of their Masters Cause, do inform and instruct the Counsellors in the same.' " They were agents of the attorney or his client. It was not until 1750 that solicitors were recognized as attorneys and became a new class of practitioners before the bar. See William Holdsworth, *History of English Law VI* (London: Little, Brown, 1922),440–49. Likewise, the British Solicitor General functions as a general assistant or agent of the Attorney General, and has no specialized litigating function like its American counterpart. It undoubtedly was this conception of the office that Congress intended to establish under the 1870 act. Thus, the formal or statutory relationship between the Attorney General and the Solicitor General is the same in the United States as in Britain. Former Solicitor General Rex Lee writes: "the significant similarity is that on both sides of the Atlantic, the attorney general was and is the nation's chief legal officer, and the Office of the Solicitor General was created (solely) to assist him in that task." See Lee, "Lawyering in the Supreme Court," 15.

37. 16 U.S. Stat. sec. 2 (1870), 162.

38. For a discussion of the functions of the early office see Thomas Thatcher, "Genesis and Present Duties of Office of Solicitor General," 17 *ABA Journal* 519 (1931), and Fahy, "The Office of Solicitor General."

39. Lee, "Lawyering in the Supreme Court," 19–22.

40. See Ronald Chamberlain, "Mixing Politics and Justice: The Office of Solicitor General," *Journal of Law and Politics* 4 (1987), 379.

41. 461 U.S. (1983), 595.

42. For an account of the department's shift in position in *Bob Jones*, see Caplan, *The Tenth Justice*, 51–64.

43. See Brief for United States, *Bob Jones University v. U.S.*, no. 81–3 (1981), 1.

44. Wallace was subsequently removed from other civil rights cases and in 1983 was replaced as Deputy Solicitor General by a political appointee, Paul Bator. More importantly the case raised controversy about the independence of the Solicitor General. See Caplan, *The Tenth Justice*, 58–64.

45. For an account of this case, see Navasky, *Kennedy Justice*, 294.

46. The case involved was *Peters v. Hobby*, 349 U.S. (1954), 331, a discussion of which is in Joseph Rauh, "Nonconfrontation in Security Cases," *Virginia Law Review* 45 (1959), 1175, 1178. Soboloff's reasons for refusing to represent the government are outlined in "Memorandum for the Attorney General from the Solicitor General Re: *Peters v. Hobby*," January 14, 1955.

47. See Navasky, *Kennedy Justice*, 295–98.

48. Caplan, *The Tenth Justice*, 34.

49. Bork, "The Problems and Pleasures of Being Solicitor General," *Antitrust Law Journal* 42 (1973), 701, 705.

50. Interview with Charles Fried, Salzburg, Austria, August 20, 1987.

51. For a discussion of this reciprocal relationship see Joshua Schwartz, "Two Perspectives on the Solicitor General's Independence," *Loyola of Los Angeles Law Review* 21 (1988), 1119, 1143.

52. Werdegar, "The Solicitor General and Administrative Due Process: A Quarter Century of Advocacy," *George Washington Law Review* 36 (1968), 481, 482.

53. 315 U.S. (1942), 257, 258.

54. Judge Learned Hand is quoted as complaining that: "it's bad enough to have the Supreme Court reverse you, but I will be damned if I will be reversed by some Solicitor General." Caplan, *The Tenth Justice*, 9–10.

55. Ibid., 10.

56. *United States v. St. Regis Paper Co.*. Cox's performance in the case is discussed in Navasky, *Kennedy Justice*, 295.

57. "Memorandum Opinion for the Attorney General Re: Role of the Solicitor General," 1 *Op. Office of Legal Counsel* (1977), 228 (hereafter cited as Bell Memorandum).

58. 437 U.S. (1978), 153.

59. The episode is discussed in Bell and Ostrow, *Taking Care of the Law*, 42–45.

60. *Bell Memorandum*, 223.

61. J. Price, "What Price Advocacy," *New York Times*, October 25, 1987, 13. (Book Review of Caplan, *The Tenth Justice*.)

62. 476 U.S. (1986), 747.

63. 476 U.S. (1986), 267.

64. 472 U.S. (1985), 38.

65. See Chamberlain, "Mixing Politics and Justice," 425.

66. See William K. Gardner, "Government Attorney," *Columbia Law Review* 55 (1955), 438.

67. The positions taken by the New Deal Solicitors General were consistently rejected by the Court. Reed and Jackson had the worst success records of any Solicitors General over the last sixty years (see Figure 3.4). Despite this, both Jackson and Reed went on to be appointed to the Supreme Court and served distinguished careers.

68. 334 U.S. (1948), 1.

69. 347 U.S. (1954), 483.

70. 163 U.S. (1896), 537.

71. See Burt Neuborne, "In Lukewarm Defense of Charles Fried," *Manhattan Law*, October 20–26, 1987, 37; Wilkins, "An Officer and an Advocate," 1167; and Chamberlain, "Mixing Politics and Justice."

72. See Figure 3.4.

73. Chamberlain, "Mixing Politics and Justice," 425–426.

74. See Louis Fisher, "Is the Tenth Justice an Executive or a Judicial Agent? Caplan's Tenth Justice," *Law and Social Inquiry* (1990), 601.

75. Caplan, *The Tenth Justice*, 64.

76. See Fisher, "Is the Solicitor General An Executive or a Judicial Agent;" McConnell, "The Rule of Law and the Role of the Solicitor General," 1105; Chamberlain, "Mixing Politics and Justice."

77. Lee, "Lawyering in the Supreme Court," 23.

78. Bell Memorandum, 229.

79. Stern, "The Solicitor General's Office."

80. Interview with Charles Fried, Salzburg, Austria, August 22, 1987.

81. Bell Memorandum, 235–36.

82. Wilkins, "Officer and Advocate," 1186.

83. Bell Memorandum, 229.

84. Griswold, "The Office of Solicitor General," 527; and McCree, "The Solicitor General and His Client," 337, 346.

85. U.S. Congress, House Committee on the Judiciary, *Hearings on the Solicitor General's Office*, 100th Cong., 1st sess. (1987), 45.

86. See Chamberlain, "Mixing Politics and Justice," 413–19.

87. "Interview with Charles Fried," *Washington Lawyer*, May 1987, 48.

88. Interview with Fried, Salzburg, Austria, August 22, 1987.

89. See O'Connor, "The Amicus Curiae Role of the United States Solicitor General in Supreme Court Litigation," *Judicature* 66 (1982), 6.

90. Segal, "Amicus Curiae Briefs by the Solicitor General During the Warren and Burger Courts," *Western Political Science Quarterly* 41 (1988), 135.

91. Conversely Segal found that Lee, serving under the economically conservative Reagan administration, was much more conservative in these cases.

92. Segal, "Amicus Curiae Briefs by the Solicitor General," 138.

93. Ulmer and Williamson, "The Solicitor General of the United States as Amicus Curiae in the U.S. Supreme Court, 1969–1983 Terms," paper presented at the American Political Science Association Annual Meeting at New Orleans, Louisiana, 1985.

94. Rebecca M. Salokar, "The Solicitor General and Individual Rights: Supreme Court Cases, 1959–1986," paper presented at the Annual Meeting of the Law and Society Association, Berkeley, California, 1990.

95. Ibid., 23.

96. Ibid.

97. Warren Burger, "Wade McCree," *Loyola Los Angeles Law Review* 21 (1988), 1051, 1052.

98. The literature on the political implications of judicial appointments is extensive—see, e.g., John Schmidhauser, *Judges and Justices: The Federal Appellate Judiciary* (Boston: Little, Brown, 1979), and Henry Abraham, *Justices and Presidents: A Political History of Appointments to the Supreme Court* (Oxford University Press, 1974). For an account of two recent administration's strategies to influence judicial policy through judicial selection, see James Simon, *In His Own Image: The Supreme Court in Richard Nixon's America* (New York: David McKay, 1973); and Herman Schwartz, *Packing the Courts: The Conservative Campaign to Rewrite the Constitution* (New York: Scribners, 1988).

99. Grossman, *Lawyers and Judges: The ABA and the Politics of Judicial Selection* (New York: Wiley, 1965), 25.

100. For a general account of the judicial selection process, see Howard Ball, *Courts and Politics: The Federal Judicial System* (Englewood Cliffs, N.J.: Prentice Hall, 1987), 174–227.

101. See David O'Brien, *Judicial Roulette: Report of the Twentieth Century Task Force on Judicial Selection* (New York: Priority Press, 1988), 49–50.

102. Ibid., 29–48.

103. Figures supplied by the Administrative Office of the U.S. Courts, October 23, 1988.

104. For a discussion of the growth of federal courts and the judiciary, see David Clark, "Adjudication to Administration: A Statistical Analysis of Federal District Courts in the Twentieth Century," *Southern California Law Review* 55 (1981), 65.

105. O'Brien, *Judicial Roulette*.

106. See Burke Shartel, "Federal Judges—Appointment, Supervision and Removal," *Michigan Law Review* 28 (1930), 485.

107. Ibid.

108. O'Brien, *Judicial Roulette*, 50–51.

109. Ibid.

110. See John Gottschall, "Eisenhower's Judicial Legacy," *Legal Studies Forum* 9 (1875) 251; and William Rogers, "Judicial Appointments in the Eisenhower Administration," *Judicature* 41 (1957), 38.

111. Ibid.

112. O'Brien, *Judicial Roulette*, 52–58.

113. Johnson, in particular, followed Roosevelt's practice of using nominations as instruments of personal power. See N. McFeeley, *Appointment of Judges: The Johnson Presidency* (Austin: University of Texas Press, 1987).

114. These pledges are reported in "The Merit System vs. Patronage," *Wall Street Journal*, February 28, 1977, 14.

115. See Gary Fowler, "Judicial Selection under Reagan and Carter: A Comparison of Their Initial Recommendation Procedures," *Judicature* 67 (1984), 266.

116. For a more detailed account of the creation of the merit commissions see Michael J. Egan, Associate Attorney General during the Carter administration, "Carter's Merit Selection," *Trial* 13 (1977), 45.

117. For a discussion of the operation of the merit selection commissions see Judith Parris, "Merit Selection of Federal Judges," Library of Congress, Congressional Research Service, December 20, 1979; Alan Neff, *The United States District Judge Nominating Commissions: Their Members, Procedures and Candidates* (Chicago: American Judicature Society, 1981); Larry Berkson and Susan Carbon, *The United States Circuit Judge Nominating Commission: Its Members, Procedures and Candidates* (Chicago: American Judicature Society, 1980); Elliot Slotnick, "The U.S. Judge Nominating Commission," *Law and Society Quarterly* 1 (1979), 465; J. Rosenbaum, "Implementing Federal Merit Selection," *Judicature* 61 (1977), 125.

118. For a discussion of the procedure inside the Justice Department during the Carter administration, see U.S. Congress, Senate Committee on the Judiciary, *Hearings on the Selection and Confirmation of Federal Judges*, Pt. 1, 96th Cong., 1st sess. (1980), 15.

119. Telephone interview with Griffin Bell, August 22, 1988.

120. For a general account of the controversy see Bell and Ostrow, *Taking Care of the Law*, 40–42.

121. See note 116 above.

122. For an account of the Breyer nomination, see *Congressional Record–Senate*, December 9, 1980, 32998–33012.

123. See U.S. Congress, Senate Committee on the Judiciary, *Hearings on Judicial Selection and the Reagan Administration*, 100th Cong., 2d sess. (1988).

124. For a discussion of the changes made by the Reagan administration see Fowler, "Judicial Selection Under Reagan and Carter," and Sheldon Goldman, "Reagan's Judicial Appointments at Mid-term: Shaping the Bench in His Own Image," *Judicature* 66 (1983), 335 and "Reagan's Judicial Legacy," 318; Memorandum from the Office of Legal Policy, "Myths and Realities—Reagan Administration Judicial Selection," May 17, 1988.

125. O'Brien, "Reagan's Judges."

126. See Philip Lacovara, "The Wrong Way to Pick Judges," *New York Times*, October 3, 1986, A–35; and O'Brien, "Reagan's Judges," 67–71.

127. See Goldman, "Reagan's Judicial Appointments at Mid-Term."

128. Interviews with Deborah Owen, Assistant White House Legal Counsel, July 15, 1988; and Sherie Marshall, Assistant White House Legal Counsel, August 21, 1988.

129. Harlan Fiske Stone, Hugo Black, Stanley Reed, Felix Frankfurter, William O. Douglas, Frank Murphy, James Byrnes, Robert Jackson, and Wiley Rutledge.

130. Truman appointed Frederick Vinson, Harold Burton, Thomas Clark, and Sherman Minton; Kennedy appointed Byron White and Arthur Goldberg; Johnson appointed Abe Fortas and Thurgood Marshall.

131. The other three appointees were John Harlan, Charles Whittaker, and Potter Stewart.

132. Nixon appointed Warren Burger, Harry Blackmun, Lewis Powell, and William Rehnquist; Ford appointed John Paul Stevens; Reagan appointed Sandra Day O'Connor, Antonin Scalia, and Anthony Kennedy; Bush, thus far, has appointed David Souter and Clarence Thomas.

133. Because the Justice Department stopped printing the statistics regarding government litigation in the Supreme Court after 1986, the data for 1987–1988 were obtained from Virginia Bowling, Case Management Section, Office of the Solicitor General office, June 13, 1990.

134. Sobeloff, "The Law Business of the United States," *Oregon Law Review* 34 (1955), 145.

135. For more detailed discussion of this point see "Government Litigation in the Supreme Court," 1442; and Chamberlain, "Mixing Politics and Justice," 386–99.

136. For further discussion of cue theory and government participation, see David Rohde and Harold Spaeth, *Supreme Court Decision-Making* (San Francisco: Freeman, 1976), 176.

137. See Schnapper, "Becket at the Bar," 1187; Wilkins, "Officer and Advocate"; Schwartz, "Solicitor General's Independence."

138. Probably the best general discussion of the Justice Department's *amicus curiae* participation in the Supreme Court is found in Samuel Krislov, "The Role of the Attorney General as Amicus Curiae," in Huston et al., *Roles of the Attorney General*, 71.

139. 58 U.S. (17 How.) (1854), 478.

140. *Annual Report A.G.* (1951).

141. Between 1950 and 1988 the department filed more than 836 *amicus* briefs in the Court. *Annual Report A.G. 1951–1989* (statistics on Supreme Court litigation are not included in the printed reports for 1986 on, but are included in the reports transmitted to Congress, available through the Office of Solicitor General).

142. Segal, "Amicus Curiae Briefs."

143. Scigliano, *The Supreme Court and the Presidency* (New York: Free Press, 1971), 180.

144. For a discussion of the Court's preferential treatment of the Justice Department, see O'Connor, "The Amicus Curiae Role of the United States Solicitor General in the Supreme Court Litigation"; Krislov, "The Role of the Attorney General as Amicus Curiae," in Huston et al., *Roles of the Attorney General*; and William Brigman, "The Office of the Solicitor General of the United States," Ph.D. diss., University of North Carolina at Chapel Hill (1966).

145. *Aaron v. Cooper*, 156 F. Supp. (D.C. Ark. 1957), 220.

146. Schwartz, "Solicitor General's Independence," 1143.

147. See David O'Brien, *Storm Center: The Supreme Court in American Politics*, 2d ed. (New York: Norton, 1990), 346.

148. See Brownell, "The United States Supreme Court: Symbol of Just Government," *ABA Journal* 42 (1956), 1032; "Protecting Civil Rights," *Chicago Bar Record* 39 (1957), 55; and "Lawyers and a Government of Law," *Record* 13 (1958), 188.

149. See Cummings, "The American Constitutional Method," *ABA Journal* 22 (1936), 24; and "The Nature of the Amending Process," *George Washington Law Review* 6 (1938), 247. Also see the discussion in chapter 5.

150. See Meese, "Our Constitutional Design: The Implications for its Interpretation," *Marquette Law Review* 70 (1987), 381; "Towards a Jurisprudence of Original Intent," *Harvard Journal of Law & Public Policy* 11 (1988), 5; "The Supreme Court: Bulwark of a Limited Constitution," *South Texas Law Review* 27 (1986), 455. See also the discussion in chapter 5.

151. See the discussion in chapter 5. See also Debra Cassens Moss, "The Policy and Rhetoric of Ed Meese," *ABA Journal* 64; February 1987; and a special symposium on the controversy that surrounded Mr. Meese's speeches in *Tulane Law Review* 61 (1987), 979 et seq.

152. Interview with Terry Eastland, Washington, D.C., August 22, 1988.

153. Key, "The Legal Work of the Federal Government," 166.

154. Congress unwittingly provided a basis for resistance to the Attorney General by failing to repeal the old statutes creating departmental solicitors and legal counsels offices. As long as the originating statutes remained in force they could continue to claim independent legal authority. Department heads, anxious to retain control over department lawyers and litigating authority, supported these claims. Consequently, the Solicitor of the Treasury, Commissioner of Internal Revenue, and the Solicitors for the Departments of State and the Navy continued to insist that they retained full and absolute control over legal work and litigation that fell within their departments. As early as 1872 the Attorney General asked Congress to repeal the organic statutes of the department solicitors and clarify their accountability. A bill to "Facilitate the Conduct of Law Business Arising in the Executive Departments," was introduced in Congress in 1873, but it fell victim to strong opposition from other department heads. Williams renewed his plea in 1873. While department Solicitors "are nominally subjected to the control of this Department," he said, "they are attached to and exclusively perform duties assigned to them by the heads of other Departments. Obviously, this is an arrangement which not only creates a divided jurisdiction, but produces confusion in the transaction of the public business." Congress, however, ignored his advice. See *Annual Report A.G.* (1872), 16, and *Annual Report A.G.* (1873), 18.

155. 16 Stat., 432, and 17 U.S. Stat., 284. Although given the title of Assistant Attorneys General, these officers were not appointed or removable by the Attorney General and they performed such duties exclusively as were assigned by the heads of their departments. At the request of Attorney General McReynolds in 1914 they were formally reestablished as Solicitors in their respective departments. See *Annual Report A.G.* (1913), 6.

156. The proliferation of departmental solicitors and their insistence on maintaining independent legal authority led Attorney General Olney to author a long opinion on the subject in 1894, see 20 *Op. A.G.*, 714.

157. 16 Stat., 162.

158. See Griffin Bell, "The Attorney General: The Federal Government's Chief Lawyer and Litigator, or One Among Many," *Fordham Law Review* 46 (1978), 1054–1055.

159. "Special Message of the President of the United States on Interstate Commerce and Antitrust Laws and Federal Incorporation," 61st Cong., 2d sess. H. Doc. 484 (1910), 5.

160. 41 Stat., 92 (Transportation Act of 1920, ch. 250, sec. 3).

161. 48 Stat., 885 (Securities and Exchange Act of 1934, ch. 404, sec. 4); 49 Stat., 451 (Act of July 5, 1935, ch. 372, sec. 3).

162. 72 U.S. (1866), 370.

163. 7 Wall (74 U.S.) (1868), 454.

164. 125 U.S. (1887), 747.

165. Ibid., 750.

166. 257 U.S. (1921), 147.

167. Ibid., 198.

168. 390 F.2d (8th Cir. 1968), 323.

169. 246 U.S. (1918), 388.

170. See *The Department of Justice*, 147–155.

171. 20 *Op. A.G.*, 97.

172. Executive Order 2877 (1918); 32 *Op. A.G.*, 276.

173. Ibid.

174. 40 U.S. Stat. (1918), 556.

175. 41 Stat., 990 (Act of June 5, 1920, ch. 250); and 42 Stat., 147 (Act of August 9, 1921, ch. 57).

176. 44 Stat., 126 (Act of February 26, 1926, ch. 27).

177. *Annual Report A.G.* (1928), 1–2.

178. Ibid.

179. 47 U.S. Stat. (1932), 413.

180. Horowitz, *The Jurocracy*, 5.

181. See the comments of Griffin Bell, quoted in Susan Olson, "Challenges to the Gatekeeper: The Debate over Federal Litigating Authority," *Judicature* 68 (1984), 73.

182. These efforts are discussed in chapter 6.

183. Horowitz, *The Jurocracy*, 6, 23.

184. For a discussion of the Justice Department's authority to control litigation in the Supreme Court, see "The Solicitor General and Intragovernmental Conflict," *Michigan Law Review* 76 (1977), 324.

185. See Olson, "Challenges to the Gatekeeper," 78–83.

186. Ibid.

187. Olson, "Comparing Justice and Labor Department Lawyers," 287.

188. Horowitz, *The Jurocracy*, 107.

189. Ibid.

190. Ibid., 104.

191. For a discussion of this process, see Robert Stern, "The Solicitor General's Office and Administrative Agency Litigation," 154.

192. See "The Solicitor General and Intragovernmental Conflict" and "Government Litigation in the Supreme Court," 1475.

193. *Annual Report A.G.* (1986), 3.

194. See Figure 6.1 and the accompanying text.

195. Horowitz, *The Jurocracy*, 50.

196. The first official statement of principles that guides the Solicitor General in the selection of cases in which certiorari is sought was in *Annual Report A.G.* (1938), 35–36.

197. The principal source of information about Justice–Agency conflicts are government hearings and reports. See, e.g., U.S. Congress, Senate Committee on Governmental Affairs, *Study on Federal Regulation: Regulatory Organization*, vol. 5. 95th Cong., 2d. sess. (1977), 54–67; U.S. Judicial Conference of the District of Columbia Circuit, *Proceedings of the 40th Annual Judicial Conference*, 85 *F.R.D.* 155, 164–68; and Senate Committee on the Judiciary, *Department of Justice Authorization and Oversight Hearings*, 96th Cong., 2d sess. (1981), 379–520, 815–908, 1191–1238.

198. Olson, "Challenges to the Gatekeeper," 80–82.

199. "The Solicitor General and Intragovernmental Conflict."

200. See Randall Ripley and Grace Franklin, *Congress, the Bureaucracy, and Public Policy* (Homewood, Ill.: Dorsey Press, 1987).

201. Bell, "The Attorney General," 1049, 1058.

202. Horowitz, *The Jurocracy*, 103–16.

203. Davis, *Department of Justice Control of Agency Litigation* (Washington, D.C.: Administrative Conference of the U.S., 1975), 17.

4

The Attorney General and the Separation of Powers

The mixture of law and politics in the government's legal office is awkward in any system of constitutional government. Constitutions are meant to limit politics by the rule of law. What the rule of law means, however, is ultimately determined by the same constellation of political forces it attempts to limit. Law and politics in such systems are not easily distinguishable, and government legal officers must divide their loyalty between "the law" and the political interests of their elected masters in the executive or legislative branches.

This holds equally true for states with unwritten constitutional traditions and those with written documents. Legal decisions by British judges are by nature just as "political" as those made by their American counterparts.[1] Nevertheless, law in the United States has become more politicized than in Britain, at least in the sense that public policy is made more frequently in the courts.[2] This difference stems not from a written as opposed to unwritten constitutional tradition, but from the number of fragmentations in sovereign authority.[3]

In Britain, the government *is* the executive, both in a figurative and literal sense. When one speaks of "the government," one refers to the executive Cabinet. The fusion of officeholding has provided the executive with sufficient control of the legislature to secure the passage of whatever legislation it wishes. This, coupled with the doctrine of parliamentary sovereignty, necessarily leads to a reduced political role for British courts. As British legal scholar Patrick Atiyah points out, "there is no such thing as an unconstitutional statute in British law, and even though the courts can declare executive action to be unlawful, such action can easily be legalized for the future."[4] The judiciary, and hence the government's legal counsel, is more professional and less political in Britain precisely because the executive and legislature have little reason to intervene in their functioning.

By creating rival political institutions, the separation of powers and federalism implicitly transform "the law" into a weapon in institutional struggles over control of public policy. Policy disputes between the three branches or between the different levels of government become legal/constitutional conflicts acted out in the judicial arena. The result is the strikingly common use by courts in the United States of judicial review powers.[5] The courts are able to assert the remarkable power of being "infallible" because they are "final."[6]

The legalization of political conflict that results from the separation of powers complicates the role of the U.S. Attorney General beyond the simple loyalty split inherent in constitutional government itself. The office's statutory and common law charge to represent the "legal interests of the United States" presupposes the sovereign is a single entity, or at least of a single will, when in fact, it comprises a multiplicity of wills split among three branches. Although today the Attorney General is seen primarily as the President's lawyer, his functions give him a special relationship to the judiciary and he also retains clear obligations to congressional statute.[7]

The built-in schizophrenia of the Attorney General's office is most manifest during separation of powers litigation. When the three branches disagree over constitutional principles, what defines the interests of the "United States"? Cases such as *United States v. Nixon* (1974), *United States v. House of Representatives* (1983), and *United States v. United States District Court* (1972), illustrate the problem.[8] As with other areas of constitutional adjudication, appeals to the text of the Constitution merely provide a point for analytical departure, not specific answers. The ambiguous language of the Constitution conjured up to support one branch's claims over another is less conclusive than rhetorical. The "faithful execution clause"[9] or the "necessary and proper clause"[10] are not self-interpreting; assertions about their meaning, implied or overt, usually flow from the policy preferences of one branch or another. Law professors Arthur Miller and Jeffery Bowman have argued that because the "United States" is merely a theoretical construct and can have no interest independent of its constituent parts, the Justice Department should not utilize the term during separation of powers litigation.[11] In such cases, the term only breeds confusion regarding the interests of the parties involved. A preferable styling of such cases might be: "Special Prosecutor v. President" or "President v. Congress."

Style is, of course, less important than ascertaining who it is the Justice Department represents during interbranch legal conflicts. So long as this is clear, it matters little whether one refers to the Justice Department's side as the "United States" or "counsel for the President." The "United States" clearly enjoys special privileges under federal rules of procedure.[12] However, if it is acknowledged that the Justice Department employs the title during separation of powers litigation to represent the narrower interests of the executive only, then similar privileges could be extended to counsel representing other government branches or agencies as well.

The crucial question, then, centers on the relationship of the Attorney General and Department of Justice to the three branches of government. To what degree does the President control them, and what are the implications of that control? The answer comes in two parts. The first emerges from the more traditional separation of powers analysis that focuses on presidential power to appoint and remove subordinate officials. This can be called the organizational chart approach; under which branch does the Attorney General and Department of Justice fall? This organizational chart analysis, which to this point has dominated discussions involving the role of the Justice Department, is taken up in this chapter. It follows the evolution of legal authority over the administrative bureaucracy with specific reference to presidential control of the Justice Department and its principal officers.

A different type of analysis provides the second part of the answer. It focuses less on organizational charts and more on governmental functions. In this functional, or power, analysis, the role and nature of administrative discretion is at issue. This approach to the separation of powers grew out of the more complex institutional relationships that have emerged in twentieth-century American government. How these new relationships have changed the Justice Department's role is discussed in chapters 5 and 6.

Presidential Removal Authority and Control of the Executive Branch Bureaucracy

From America's beginnings as an independent nation, partisan rhetoric has clouded the legal relationship between the bureaucracy and three branches of the federal government. It is useful, therefore, to distinguish at the outset between what is true in constitutional theory and what has become true in practice and convention.

The American theory of separation of powers borrows most heavily from Montesquieu's famous *De l'Esprit des lois,* published in 1748. James Madison, in the forty-seventh *Federalist,* calls Montesquieu the "authority" and "oracle who is always consulted and cited on the subject."[13] Although Montesquieu derived his theory from analyzing the English constitution, his framework for political institutions differs radically from Britain's. In contrast to Locke's theory of mixed government, Montesquieu developed a tripartite system of separate government functions and institutions. Unlike Locke and Blackstone, he argued that judges and executive ministers performed conceptually distinct roles. He recognized three functions of government—legislative, executive, and judicial—and he envisioned three branches or institutions of government. He contended that separating government functions and vesting them in equal and independent institutions protects liberty.[14]

Early American experience with the pure Montesquieuian division of powers left a bitter taste. Under the Articles of Confederation, states experimented with the strict separation he recommended. Instead of preserving liberty, the theory proved to be a prescription for legislative tyranny. State legislatures not only assumed executive powers, they even began carrying out criminal trials in their chambers. Once unlimited lawmaking powers were vested in legislatures, there was no way to prevent them from usurping functions and powers of other branches.[15] Consequently, the framers of the Constitution wished to alter Montesquieu's theory. While they retained the general tripartite framework of institutions, they modified the strict division of functions to allow some overlap.

Constitutional provisions blending some government functions between institutions became known collectively as "checks and balances."[16] By granting each branch "partial agency in" or "control over" the acts of the other two, James Madison said, each retained the power to defend itself from intrusions by the others.[17] The framers justified the checks and balances as necessary to protect and implement the general separation of powers established by the document. Not only did the system empower each branch to defend itself against attacks from the others, it locked the three together, forcing them to cooperate. In an often quoted concurring opinion, Justice Robert H. Jackson noted: "the Constitution diffuses power the better to secure liberty"; it also predicts that "practice will integrate the dispersed powers into a workable government." The Constitution, he continued, requires "interdependence and reciprocity" as well as "separateness and autonomy."[18]

From the time of the Constitution's ratification, debate has been waged as to whether the separation of powers requires a "hermetic sealing off" of the three branches of government outside of the express checks and balances.[19] Even the Supreme Court has vacillated between a "formalistic" view demanding the strict separation of "three unitary, airtight departments," and a "functionalistic" view that allows greater flexibility and blending of functions between departments.[20] Nowhere is the Court's ambivalence more apparent than in its decisions regarding control of the administrative bureaucracy. Under the traditional "organizational chart" approach to the separation of powers, the crucible comes in cases over the removal of subordinate officers; power to remove is seen as power to control.

When the issue initially surfaced in American politics, the Supreme Court ruled that removal authority was inherent in appointment authority; the latter gave rise to the former. Under the Constitution, principal officers of the United States must be appointed by the President with the advice and consent of the Senate. Congress may, however, "vest the appointment of such inferior Officers, as they think proper, in the President alone, in the Courts of Law, or in the Heads of the Departments."[21] In an early case, *Ex Parte Hennen* (1839), the Court was asked to decide whether Congress could grant the judiciary the power to appoint and remove court clerks. Answering in the affirmative, the Court said "the appointing power was . . . intended to be exercised by the department of government to which the officer to be appointed most appropriately belonged."[22] Because the courts needed to control the judicial function, the power to appoint and remove court clerks rightfully belonged to them.

The *Hennen* model, however, applied only to "inferior" officers.[23] Whether or not Congress could remove principal officers confirmed by the Senate had yet to be resolved. The issue began to smolder when President Jackson purged his cabinet during the National Bank controversy in 1833. Justifying his action, Jackson cited a decision made by the First Congress in response to debate over the removal of executive department chiefs. Originally proposed by James Madison, bills establishing the departments of War, State, and Treasury provided for secretaries appointed by the President with the Senate's advice and consent, but "removable by the President" alone. Some in Congress objected, saying removal power should be vested jointly in the President and Congress. Madison countered by pointing out that such a restriction would dilute presidential authority to control the operation of the executive branch.

At the heart of the debate was whether the separation of powers implicitly gave the President unilateral authority to remove executive officials. If it did, the statutory language was redundant; if it did not, could Congress unilaterally grant removal authority? In the end, a compromise was struck. The changed statutes did not grant the President removal power, but merely implied it. The new language ordered the second in command of each department to take charge whenever the "Secretary shall be removed from office."[24] The resolve to treat the President's removal authority implicitly rather than head-on is known as the "Decision of 1789." Jackson construed Congress's compromise as a license to remove any officer performing an executive function.[25]

Congress disagreed with Jackson's broad view of presidential power resulting from his interpretation of the Decision of 1789. The Senate, evenly split between Democrats and National Republicans, passed a resolution censuring his actions:

> Resolved, That the President, in the late Executive proceedings in relation to the public revenue, has assumed upon himself authority and power not conferred by the Constitution and the laws, but in derogation of both.[26]

Jackson responded with his famous letter of protest, in which he argued that the Constitution vested federal executive power in the President alone; he alone is "responsible for the entire action of the executive department."[27]

Jackson could afford a confrontation with the Senate without fear of serious congressional reprisals; his party held a solid majority in the House. When Martin Van Buren became President and Jacksonian Democrats consolidated their power in the Senate in 1836, the controversy quickly faded.[28]

Contention over congressional power to effect the removal of cabinet officers erupted again during Andrew Johnson's presidency. Johnson engaged in a bitter battle with the Unionist majority in Congress, as he faced a frontal challenge to presidential removal authority. In an effort to protect cabinet critics of Johnson's Reconstruction policies, Congress passed the Tenure of Office Act in 1867.[29] The act provided that secretaries of State, Treasury, War, Navy, and Interior, the Postmaster General and the Attorney General holding office during the term of the President who appointed them were "subject to removal by and with the advice and consent of the Senate." Despite the law, Johnson fired his Secretary of War, Edwin Stanton, in hopes the confrontation would force the courts to resolve the matter once and for all. Instead, the affair became fodder for congressional impeachment proceedings against Johnson. Johnson survived impeachment by a single vote in the Senate, but was forced to reappoint Stanton.[30] Grant's election in 1869 brought a normalization of relations between the White House and Congress, and the Tenure of Office Act was repealed in 1887.[31]

The nationalization of political power during the Progressive Era and New Deal created massive new federal regulatory authority and generated new conflict over removal power. Congress was unwilling simply to hand control of the regulatory bureaucracy over to the White House. When it established regulatory agencies such as the Interstate Commerce Commission and Federal Trade Commission, Congress protected principal officers from presidential removal by providing for fixed terms and allowing removal "for good cause" only.[32]

The independent commission innovation was driven not just by interbranch suspicion, but by the emergence of a new school of thought in the science of public administration. This new school rejected older patronage models of staffing the bureaucracy in favor of new ones that emphasized merit and neutral expertise.[33] The emphasis on "scientific" or "expert" government went hand in hand with the nationalization of policymaking and calmed traditional antipathy toward large government. Gradually, an administrative lore accumulated granting independent commissions a peculiar hybrid status that included "quasi-judicial" and "quasi-legislative" powers.[34]

Against the backdrop of these major changes in political and theoretical views of the administrative bureaucracy, the Supreme Court was forced to address directly the removal power issue. In *Myers v. United States* (1926), President Woodrow Wilson removed a postmaster prior to the expiration of his four-year term.[35] The postmaster brought suit based on tenure provisions in the statute creating his office that required the advice and consent of Congress for removal. Writing for the Court, Chief Justice Taft clearly enunciated the traditional separation of powers doctrine. Under the Constitution, Taft said, only the President could wield executive power, and he alone was charged to "take care that the Laws be faithfully executed." As the power to control officers who execute the law is necessary to perform this function, the President's power to unilaterally remove such officers must be preserved. To hold otherwise, Taft continued, would paralyze the presidency "in case of political or other differences with the Senate or Congress."[36]

Taft's motives in the *Myers* opinion were transparent. As a former President, he was sympathetic to arguments for maintaining the unity of the executive.[37] In upholding the President's plenary removal authority, however, Taft shifted the analytical approach previously used by the Court to decide removal power cases. Although he did not abandon the appointment clause mode of analysis entirely, he relied primarily on the implicit logic of the separation of powers to justify his opinion. For Taft, the separation of powers erected three monolithic departments of government. In performing discretionary duties, executive branch officers were appendages of the President himself. The notion that they could operate independently was akin to suggesting that the hand could operate without the head.[38]

Taft's opinion left only a narrow exception to the President's plenary control over all civil officers. Congress could continue to vest the appointment and removal of "inferior officers" outside presidential control. But inferior officers could not be members of the policymaking echelons of government. Hence, the exception served limited political value. Although *Myers* did not deal directly with the new hybrid regulatory commissions, the implications of Taft's opinion were clear. In dissents, Justices Holmes, Brandeis, and McReynolds pointed out that the Court's opinion prevented Congress from protecting any major civil government officer from the President's political control.[39] As a consequence, the Court reconsidered *Myers* just nine years later.

In *Humphrey's Executor v. United States* (1935), President Roosevelt fired a member of the Federal Trade Commission because of a disagreement over federal trade policy.[40] The commissioner, William E. Humphrey, brought suit against the government, arguing that the Federal Trade Commission Act prohibited removal for any reason other than malfeasance in office. In rendering its decision, the Supreme Court once again relied on the broad theory of the separation of powers rather than the appointment clause specifically to analyze removal authority. This time, however, the Court focused on a second issue: whether the "necessary and proper" clause allowed Congress to create independent commissions at all. The crucial question for the *Humphrey's* Court was not whether the President had absolute removal power over executive officials, but whether Congress could establish governmental bodies independent of the three branches. If so, Congress could limit presidential removal authority over such officers.

Writing for the majority, Justice George Sutherland argued that, in passing the Federal Trade Commission Act, Congress intended to establish an agency with a function separate and distinct from the executive. The FTC was charged with enforcing "no policy except the policy of the law. Its duties are neither political nor executive but predominantly quasi-judicial and quasi-legislative."[41] Thus, he said, an FTC commissioner's role was distinct from that of other executive branch officers such as the postmaster. The latter is "merely one of the units of the executive department and hence inherently subject to the exclusive and illimitable power of removal by the chief executive, whose subordinate and aid he is." The FTC, on the other hand, "cannot in any proper sense be characterized as an arm or an eye of the executive." FTC commissioners "perform their duties without executive leave, and in contemplation of the statute must be free from executive control." Sutherland concluded:

> It (is) plain under the Constitution that illimitable power of removal is not possessed by the President in respect of officers of the character of those just

named. The authority of Congress, in creating quasi-legislative or quasi-judicial agencies, to require them to act in discharge of their duties independently of executive control, cannot be well doubted; and that authority includes, as an appropriate incident, power to fix the period during which they shall continue, and to forbid their removal except for cause in the meantime.[42]

Sutherland's opinion preserved the removal power corollary, but in so doing sacrificed the classical separation of powers theory. To maintain the facade of a unitary executive, the Court "conjured up a fourth branch of government, floating independently" and completely untethered by the Constitution.[43] The Constitution recognizes no "quasi" powers. Moreover, the Court's opinion gave no indication of what other government functions might belong to this new fourth branch. The determination of whether an agency was purely executive in nature or a part of the new quasi hinterland could proceed only from a subjective analysis of its creation and function.

The Court reaffirmed its modification of the separation of powers in *Wiener v. United States* (1958).[44] In *Wiener*, the Court was asked to determine the institutional nature of the War Claims Commission, an agency set up to adjudicate claims against the government arising from the Second World War. According to the Court, the commission's functions were of an "intrinsically judicial character" and not "purely executive." Writing for the Court, Justice Felix Frankfurter said:

> The Court has (drawn) a sharp line of cleavage between officials who were part of the Executive establishment and were thus removable by virtue of the President's constitutional powers, and those who are members of a body to exercise its judgment without leave or hindrance of any other official or any department of the government, as to whom a power of removal exists only if Congress may fairly be said to have conferred it. This sharp differentiation derives from the difference in functions between those who are part of the Executive establishment and those whose tasks require absolute freedom from Executive interference.[45]

While the Court's creation of a fourth branch accomplished its immediate purpose—protecting independent regulatory commissions from presidential political control—it could not be squared with the traditional theory of separation of powers. By creating a new branch, the Court admitted that the classical theory no longer accommodated the political reality of an expanded federal government. Indeed, in *FTC v. Ruberoid Co.* (1952), Justice Jackson wrote: "The mere retreat to the qualifying 'quasi' is implicit with confession that all recognized classifications have broken down, and 'quasi' is a smooth cover which we draw over our confusion as we might use a counterpane to conceal a disordered bed."[46]

Constitutional scholars such as Edward Corwin criticized the Court's *Myers–Humphrey's* line of decisions. The truth, Corwin said in 1957, is that "Justice Sutherland's dicta are quite as extreme in one direction as some of Chief Justice Taft's dicta were in the opposite direction; and especially does he provoke wonderment by his assertion that a member of the Federal Trade Commission 'occupies no place in the executive department.' " If this is the case, Corwin asked, "Where is he? In the legislative department; or is he, forsooth, in the uncomfortable halfway situation of Mahomet's coffin, suspended 'twixt Heaven and Earth?"[47]

Corwin urged the Court to preserve the existing tripartite governmental framework. All nonjudicial agencies established to carry out the law, he said, could be nothing other than executive under the Constitution. A distinction, however, could be made between executive functions that require presidential control and those that do not.[48] Corwin's view is similar to the Lockean concept of a political and a nonpolitical executive. Had it been adopted by the Court, it would have provided a theoretical basis for giving executive branch officers, such as the Attorney General, conventional or statutory independence from direct presidential control.

The Supreme Court was not insensitive to such criticisms. In chiseling out exceptions to the traditional tripartite separation of powers, it acted cautiously and attempted to limit the reach of the fourth branch. In *Buckley v. Valeo* (1976), for instance, the Court upheld Congress's authority to vest quasi-executive powers in the Federal Elections Commission (FEC), but refused to permit Congress to appoint its members.[49] Under the original act, four of six FEC commissioners were supposed to be appointed by Congress and the remaining two by the President. After analyzing the commission's function, however, the Court concluded that FEC commissioners were principal officers, not inferior ones, and must be appointed by the President. This decision was premised on the FEC's statutory power to conduct civil litigation. Litigating functions, the Court said, "may be discharged only by persons who are 'Officers of the United States' within the language" of the Constitution. Thus, while Congress could create independent agencies, it could not ignore the requirements of the Appointments Clause.[50] The Court's decision forced Congress in 1976 to amend the act and vest the appointment of all six commissioners in the President.

In *INS v. Chadha* (1983), the Supreme Court reaffirmed the traditional theory's prohibition of mixing governmental functions other than those specifically authorized by the checks and balances.[51] In striking down legislative vetoes as a congressional "intrusion into the executive function," Chief Justice Burger wrote, "the Constitution sought to divide the delegated powers of the Federal Government into three defined categories, Legislative, Executive, and Judicial." Congress cannot exercise an executive function without "violating that division." Thus, once Congress delegates discretionary authority to an executive branch official (in this case the Attorney General), "Congress must abide by its delegation of authority until that delegation is legislatively altered or revoked."[52]

In *Bowsher v. Synar* (1986), the Supreme Court again confirmed the President's absolute removal power over officers performing "core" executive functions.[53] In *Bowsher*, it concluded that the Gramm–Rudman–Hollings Balanced Budget Act violated the separation of powers because it vested in the

Comptroller General, an official removable by Congress, a core executive function.[54] Under the act, the Comptroller General was authorized to tell the President what fixed-percentage cuts must be made in federal spending if deficit reduction guidelines were not met. Writing for the Court, Burger gave the clearest description of the classical separation of powers theory since *Myers*. Even "a cursory examination of the Constitution reveals the influence of Montesquieu's thesis," Burger noted.[55] Contrasting *Bowsher* with *Humphrey's*, Burger drew a sharp distinction between officers performing quasi functions and those performing purely executive functions. He wrote:

> Congress cannot reserve for itself the power of removal of an officer charged with the execution of the laws except by impeachment. To permit the execution of the laws to be vested in an officer answerable only to Congress would, in practical terms, reserve in Congress control over the execution of the laws. As the District Court observed, "Once an officer is appointed, it is only the authority that can remove him, and not the authority that appointed him, that he must fear and, in the performance of his functions, obey." The structure of the Constitution does not permit Congress to execute the laws; it follows that Congress cannot grant to an officer under its control what it does not possess.[56]

Despite these efforts to limit the reach of *Humphrey's*, the Court had deviated significantly from the traditional separation of powers theory. The implications of its decision for other government agencies and offices could not readily be ignored. If the FTC and FEC could be upheld as nonexecutive agencies, what certainty existed that other departments and agencies, previously considered executive, might not also be removed from presidential control? The Court's distinction between core and quasi functions was intellectually murky. Even Justice Sutherland admitted to a "field of doubt" in the Court's distinction between *Myers* and *Humphrey's*.[57]

Political Scandals and Political Control

Against this legal/constitutional setting, controversy regarding political control of the Justice Department arose in the 1960s. There had been earlier scandals involving control of the Justice Department, but prior to the 1960s such scandals usually revolved around corruption and misuse, not ideological influence. The Justice Department's unique role as prosecutor of federal criminal law necessarily sets it in the middle of any scandal involving political graft or corruption. When such scandals involve the President or his administration, the department's prosecutorial role can severely strain its loyalty. A series of scandals during the Wilson and Harding administrations prompted the first serious efforts to limit presidential control over the Justice Department. The troubles began in 1919, when Attorney General A. Mitchell Palmer ordered the so-called Palmer Raids in response to a spate of letter bombs sent by left-wing extremists.[58] In what historian Luther Huston called "the most bizarre performance by any Attorney General," Palmer used the Justice Department to conduct a massive campaign against various left-wing political organizations.[59] In a four-month period, the department investigated more than 60,000 individuals, more than 5,000 of whom eventually were arrested or deported. The arrests were carried out in a draconian fashion with complete disregard for process rights and statutory controls.

Palmer was widely criticized for the raids. The episode prompted investigations by Congress and by an independent group of legal scholars including such prominent figures as Felix Frankfurter, Ernst Freund, and Roscoe Pound.[60] The report published by this latter group concluded that the department's actions were "utterly illegal" and struck "at the foundations of American free institutions."[61] Despite the controversy, Palmer survived in office and served for the remainder of the Wilson administration.

In 1921, the incoming administration of Warren G. Harding replaced Palmer with Harry M. Daugherty. Daugherty proved even more controversial than his predecessor. Initially, calls to remove Daugherty stemmed from his involvement in the Teapot Dome scandal. He allegedly failed to investigate or prosecute people involved in bribing Interior Secretary Albert Fall in connection with the government's oil reserve leasing program.[62] Although a House Judiciary Committee investigation exonerated Daugherty, suspicions about his complicity continued.

When Daugherty was implicated in a second scandal, this time involving illegal trafficking of pardons and liquor permits, doubts about his role in Teapot Dome reignited. A Senate Select Committee on Investigation of the Attorney General was established.[63] During the committee hearings, Assistant Attorney General John Crim recommended that principal officers in the Justice Department as well as U.S. Attorneys be removed from partisan politics and direct presidential control.[64] Although Crim's recommendations were never acted on, Congress eventually passed legislation creating a special prosecutor's office to further investigate Daugherty. The investigations by Congress and the Special Prosecutor forced the Attorney General to resign; both he and Fall were later prosecuted on fraud and conspiracy charges. Fall was sentenced to prison, but the case against Daugherty was dismissed after two trials resulted in hung juries. The Teapot Dome scandal became entwined in the partisan debate surrounding the 1924 and 1928 elections. Democratic critics claimed it was part of a larger cover-up of widespread corruption and misconduct in the Harding and Coolidge administrations; supporters of Coolidge argued that the controversy was calculated to embarrass the Republican party and the incumbent administration.[65]

In early 1952, the Justice Department found itself in the midst of yet another scandal. President Truman's Attorney General, James Howard McGrath, and an Assistant Attorney General, Lamar Caudle, stood accused of tax fraud. Congress called for an independent investigation into the affairs of both men and eventually pressured Truman to appoint a special prosecutor.[66] Caudle was convicted of fraud and conspiracy. McGrath escaped prosecution but was forced to resign. His successor, James McGranery, also recommended that Congress remove the U.S. Attorneys and other subordinate Justice Department officials from partisan politics and make them part of the civil service.[67] Although Congress again failed to act on this recommendation, McGranery unilaterally instituted reforms aimed at recruiting new attorneys into the department on the "basis of merit and ability and not politics or cronyism."[68]

However, the most notorious political scandal in the history of the Justice Department was Watergate. No institution, outside of the presidency itself, was so badly damaged by the episode. During a two-and-a-half-year period between 1972 and 1975, the Justice Department went through five Attorneys General, six Deputy Attorneys General, and two Special Prosecutors.[69] The scandal reached its nadir in late 1973, when President Nixon fired Attorney General Elliot Richardson for refusing to dismiss the Watergate Special Prosecutor. Although the President's legal authority to fire the Attorney General was never seriously challenged, the controversy surrounding Richardson's removal illustrates the conflicting norms surrounding the Justice Department and its accountability to the President.[70]

The Watergate Special Prosecutor, Archibald Cox, had been appointed in 1973 to investigate allegations that high-ranking officials in the Nixon administration were involved in illegal activities. His appointment ensued after revelations that an earlier investigation by Justice Department personnel had resulted in a cover-up of administration wrongdoing.[71] Specifically, Congress learned in 1972 that John Dean, Counsel to the President, had arranged with Attorney General John Mitchell and Assistant Attorney General Henry Petersen for White House staff depositions to be taken outside the presence of the Grand Jury investigating the Watergate break-in. With information from Petersen, Dean had been able to anticipate the FBI's leads and coach witnesses in advance. FBI Director L. Patrick Gray also destroyed sensitive Watergate-related documents to keep them from falling into investigators' hands. As the investigation progressed, the President and Dean continued to use Petersen as a conduit for information, effectively preventing an independent investigation of the White House from ever getting off the ground.[72]

After the Justice Department's involvement in the initial cover-up was made public, Attorney General Mitchell and his successor, Richard Kleindienst, were forced to resign. Both were later prosecuted on conspiracy charges. Congress was pressing for an independent investigation in 1973, when Nixon appointed Elliot Richardson to become the Attorney General. At the time, the Special Prosecutor's office was technically part of the Justice Department and legally responsible to the Attorney General. Cox was assured at the time of his appointment, however, that he would be able to conduct an investigation without political interference. During his own Senate confirmation hearings, Richardson vowed to the Judiciary Committee he would stand by the promise made to Cox.

When Cox sought to obtain papers and tape recordings of White House conversations, however, his requests were denied.[73] The Special Prosecutor filed suit in district court, where he obtained a subpoena from Judge John Sirica. Lawyers for the President appealed, but the Court of Appeals affirmed Judge Sirica's order.[74] Instead of complying with the subpoena, Nixon ordered Richardson to dismiss Cox, precipitating what has come to be known as the "Saturday Night Massacre." Richardson resigned rather than carry out Nixon's order. Deputy Attorney General William Ruckelshaus also refused to dismiss Cox; he was fired. Finally, the department's third-ranking official, Solicitor General Robert Bork, obeyed the President's order.[75]

The Saturday Night Massacre severely eroded Nixon's political support in Congress. He was eventually forced to appoint another Special Prosecutor, Leon Jaworski, who was able to prosecute the case to its conclusion and on appeal to the Supreme Court, Jaworski asked for enforcement of the original subpoena.[76] Attorneys for Nixon countered that the separation of powers precluded judicial intervention. Their argument was twofold: first, that the President could invoke executive privilege to withhold the tapes; and, second, that the Special Prosecutor lacked the standing to bring the suit. Prosecution, they argued, was inherently an executive function, and those who exercised the function were responsible to the President. The case therefore represented an intraexecutive dispute in which the courts could not properly intervene.

The *Nixon* case has become synonymous with Supreme Court recognition of the constitutional concept of executive privilege. For the first time, the Court agreed that the separation of powers provided limited protection from disclosure of confidential conversations and discussions between the President and his advisors.[77] However, the Court's conclusion with regard to the second contention, though less heralded, is more important in terms of presidential control of the Justice Department. The Court agreed that the powers of the Special Prosecutor were executive in nature and thus subject to presidential control. The nature of this control, however, was limited. Because the Special Prosecutor was a subordinate of the Attorney General, and statutory authority to conduct prosecution was specifically vested in the chief officer of the Justice Department, the President's control of the Special Prosecutor could be exercised only indirectly via his authority to remove the Attorney General. In this case, the Attorney General had issued a regulation limiting his own authority, expressly delegating to the Special Prosecutor power to conduct the Watergate investigation and limiting removal except for "extraordinary improprieties."[78] It was "theoretically possible for the Attorney General to amend or revoke the regulation defining the Special Prosecutor's authority," the Court said, "but he has not done so. So long as this regulation is extant it has the force of law."[79]

The Court in *Nixon* thus upheld the President's power to control government prosecution. For the President to exercise control over Jaworski, however, he would have had to use the same method as with Cox: order the Attorney General to dismiss him. Both the Court and Nixon knew another Saturday Night Massacre would be politically infeasible. Congress had already initiated impeachment proceedings; the firing of another Special Prosecutor would only seal Nixon's fate. In *Nixon*, then, the Court succeeded in preserving presidential authority and protecting the Special Prosecutor's investigation. Significantly, the compromise was brought about not by the law but by the threat of impeachment.

Watergate and other scandals illustrate the difficulties that arise in any discussion about political control of the Justice Department. The term "politics" in American parlance is often used to connote more than one meaning: politics as ideology and politics as government corruption. The tendency to equate corruption and graft with "politics" is rooted deeply in the antistatist nature of American political culture.[80] This holds especially true for scandals involving the Justice Department, which, because of the legal nature of its functions, is supposed to retain a stance of impartiality and apoliticism.[81]

Confusion between the positive and the pejorative meanings of "politics," however, clouds the legitimate role of presidential ideology in the making of legal policy. It is one thing to say the President should not be allowed to obstruct criminal investigations of his own administration; it is quite another to deny him any influence over government legal policy. Nixon's intervention into the Watergate investigation was a clear example of impropriety on the part of the White House. Not all examples might be so clear-cut; motives in other cases will not be so transparent. The problem is that it is next to impossible to erect legal obstacles that prevent partisan corruption and cronyism that do not also effect political influence of a proper kind.

One popular solution proposed in the wake of Watergate was to distinguish between White House influence in setting broad policies from its intervention in individual cases.[82] This presumes that government legal policy can properly be influenced by the President's ideology, but that politics should play no part in how particular cases are handled. While the distinction between interventions on a policy level versus an individual case level may serve as a general rule of thumb in regulating White House–Justice Department relations, it is not discriminating enough to tell the difference between proper and improper influences. Good reasons may often exist for White House intervention in particular cases.

Two examples illustrate the difficulty faced by any *a priori* effort to distinguish between proper and improper political influence. The first occurred in early 1971, when the Justice Department was preparing to file a major antitrust suit against the conglomerate International Telephone and Telegraph. The Johnson administration initiated the action, and it was ongoing when the Nixon administration came to power. The day the suit was to be filed, Attorney General Kleindienst received a phone call from President Nixon instructing him to hold off. Kleindienst called the Antitrust Division and arranged for the suit to be settled out of court. Nixon's intervention in the ITT affair may merely have reflected his interest in changing federal antitrust policy. This was a major issue during the 1968 campaign, and Nixon promised to ease antitrust controls. Kleindienst later learned, however, that ITT promised to contribute $400,000 to Nixon's reelection campaign in exchange for an out-of-court settlement.[83]

Nixon's intervention in the ITT case contrasts with President Carter's in the *Bakke* case in 1978. In *Regents of the University of California v. Bakke*, the Court was asked to decide whether race conscious quotas in an admissions program at the University of California violated Title VI of the Civil Rights Act of 1964 and the Equal Protection clause of the Fourteenth Amendment.[84] Intervening in the case as *amicus curiae*, the government's position was bound to have great influence on the Court. Solicitor General Wade McCree originally drafted a brief taking the position that any race conscious treatment within the context of a voluntary program was unconstitutional. After learning of the Solicitor General's position, Joseph Califano, Carter's Secretary of Health, Education and Welfare, and Vice President Walter Mondale appealed to the President to modify the Justice Department's position. Carter, who was strongly committed to affirmative action, instructed Attorney General Bell to order McCree to rewrite the brief. After some protest, McCree did. The government's eventual position was softer on affirmative action, arguing only that numerical quotas, not racial preferences, were objectionable.[85] The department's brief no doubt was influential in shaping the Court's decision, which, not surprisingly, took a similar view on quotas.

In both examples, the White House intervened to change department policy. Just because Nixon's encroachment in the ITT case may have been inappropriate does not mean the President is not entitled to some say about enforcement of antitrust laws. Similarly, Carter's mediation in an affirmative action case was not necessarily improper or undesirable. This difficulty in distinguishing between proper and improper political influences became the major stumbling block for efforts to reform the post-Watergate Justice Department.

Constitutional Problems with Institutional Reform

The Watergate episode merits attention not only for its political drama, but for its long-term institutional impact on the Attorney General and Department of Justice. Following Nixon's resignation, Congress held hearings to find ways to guard against future political abuse of the Justice Department. The hearings, held by Senator Sam Ervin's Subcommittee on the Separation of Powers, provide the most comprehensive account of the Justice Department and its functions to date.[86] The Ervin Committee considered two types of proposals. The first called for radical surgery: removing the Justice Department entirely from presidential control and reestablishing it as an independent agency. The second was more limited, aiming only to remove certain kinds of prosecutions from presidential control. Scholars criticized both types of proposed reform, but a variation of the latter was eventually accepted and codified by the statutory creation of the independent counsel's office in 1978.

Senator Ervin personally proposed to create an "independent Justice Department" by limiting the President's removal power over the Attorney General.[87] Under his plan, the Attorney General would continue to be appointed by the President, but would serve a six-year term subject to removal "for good cause" only. Ervin defended Congress's authority to sever the Justice Department from the executive branch by pointing out that all of its authority "flows from acts of Congress." There "can be little doubt," he said, "that what Congress gives, Congress can take away."[88]

To support his argument, Ervin cited the Court's decision in *McGrain v. Daugherty* (1927).[89] The *McGrain* case arose from the Senate investigation of Attorney General Daugherty during the Teapot Dome scandal. In the process of the Senate's own investigation into the affair, its legal authority to subpoena witnesses was challenged. Upholding Congress's authority to investigate the Justice Department, the Supreme Court in *McGrain* said, "the functions of the Department of Justice, the powers and duties of the Attorney General and the duties of his assistants, are all subject to regulation by congressional legislation."[90]

Senator Ervin's reliance on *McGrain* to support congressional creation of an independent Justice Department, however, was highly problematic. First, *McGrain* enabled Congress to investigate the Justice Department in connection with its oversight and legislating functions. Investigation and oversight of an executive department is not the same as wholesale transfer of its duties. Second, even if one did interpret *McGrain* as giving Congress power to disestablish the Justice Department, the question of whether core executive functions could be vested in an office outside presidential control remained. Simply because Congress is authorized to dismember the Justice Department does not necessarily imply it can reestablish it as an independent agency.[91]

With respect to the latter issue, the Court's earlier decisions regarding presidential removal power are important. The Supreme Court defined the department's functions as executive in nature in the *Ponzi* line of cases. Thus, most legal scholars were convinced that under the Court's decisions in *Myers* and *Humphrey's*, Congress was prevented from separating the Justice Department or major portions thereof from presidential control. Of the seventeen witnesses appearing before the Ervin Committee, fourteen testified that the Senator's plan violated the separation of powers in this respect.[92]

It is nevertheless curious why more attention was not focused on the Attorney General's origin as a judicial branch institution. Using the *Humphrey's* line of analysis, examining the functions of an office is not alone sufficient to establish its institutional accountability. Not only was the distinction between "quasi" and "core" functions ambiguous, the Court indicated that functional analysis should proceed only after an inquiry into Congress's intent when creating the office. The Court premised its own decision in *Humphrey's* on the fact that Congress had intended to make a new kind of governmental agency that was independent of presidential power. It is not difficult to see how a similar conclusion could have been reached with respect to the Attorney General based on the office's origin as a judicial post. Nevertheless, this possibility was overlooked; a strict functional analysis led most experts to reject the Ervin plan.[93]

In addition to constitutional objections, the Ervin plan drew fire on prudential grounds. Critics asked: Even if it were constitutionally permissible, would it be desirable to have federal law enforcement removed from democratic control? The question loomed particularly large in light of a growing critique of "sub-system governments" and "agency capture" by special interests. A period of policy stagnation during the 1970s led to a major change in normative theories of public administration. Older theories favoring "neutral competency" began giving way to new ones emphasizing government responsiveness and accountability.[94]

The neutral bureaucracy came under siege from several different quarters. New interest group liberals saw independent regulatory commissions as overly responsive to the desires of the industries they regulated. Conservatives saw them as antidemocratic bastions for bureaucratic opposition to presidential policy. Public administrators, for their part, saw them as a source of bureaucratic drift and policy unresponsiveness. Consequently, despite the abuses of Watergate, many believed the last thing American government needed was another powerful bureaucracy that was removed from democratic control.[95]

The notion that the administration of law could be made apolitical simply by removing it from presidential control was also criticized for relying on an unsophisticated and outmoded jurisprudence.[96] The title of the Ervin hearings, "Removing Politics from the Administration of Justice," echoed the old formalistic view that law and politics could be neatly separated. The Ervin Committee's Special Counsel, Arthur Miller, urged this law school approach to the Justice Department. Miller, a professor at Harvard Law School, had in 1968 authored a study on the Attorney General's relationship to the President in which he argued that the Attorney General's role would remain controversial so long as the "polar opposite forces . . . law and politics" were allowed to "collide" in the office.[97]

At the time, Miller's view of the law no longer found acceptance anywhere but in the nation's law schools. More "critical" or "realistic" theories of jurisprudence emerging during the first half of the twentieth century undermined the analytical wall that formerly had separated law and policy. Modern theories of jurisprudence increasingly emphasized the extralegal forces that shape judicial decision making, especially when it came to constitutional adjudication.[98] Testifying before the committee, Burke Marshall, for instance, argued that Ervin's proposal was based on the faulty premise that a view of "the law" could be formulated and enforced independent of policy considerations. The "Justice Department cannot simply operate in a policy vacuum," Marshall said; "you can't remove politics from politics."[99]

The "law school" approach to government legal administration was particularly ill suited to the committee's purpose of erecting safeguards against Watergate or Teapot Dome–style abuses. These scandals were not about politics as ideology, but about corruption and cronyism. The recognition of both proper and improper political influences in White House relations with the Justice Department led many to reject the Ervin plan as too radical. A distinction must be made, Elliot Richardson said, between "the proper role of the political process in the shaping of legal policies and the perversion of the legal process by political pressures."[100]

The more moderate reform proposal considered by the Ervin Committee did eventually find its way into the statute books. As matters stood before, whenever allegations of executive branch misconduct arose, the executive faced the awkward task of investigating and prosecuting itself. The conflict of interest inherent in Justice Department prosecutions of administration officials seemed the inescapable result of the unitary branch corollary to the traditional separation of powers theory. Nevertheless, many legal scholars thought a narrow exception in the case of executive branch prosecutions might be justified. Constitutional scholar Raoul Berger, for instance, argued that "to insist that the President must investigate and prosecute himself . . . is plainly unreasonable. The power of appointment and the separation of powers were not designed to obstruct justice."[101]

The statutory establishment of a permanent Special Prosecutor's office of the type appointed during the Watergate prosecution emerged as the most acceptable means of providing a regularized method for investigating misconduct by administration officials. Over a period of five years, beginning with the Ervin hearings during the 93d Congress and continuing until the 95th Congress, various proposals for such an office were examined.[102] Finally, a permanent independent counsel's office was established under the 1978 Ethics in Government Act.[103] The act requires that the Attorney General conduct a preliminary investigation whenever he receives substantive information or allegations that high-ranking administration officials have violated the law. If, after preliminary review, the Attorney General determines there are "reasonable grounds to believe that further investigation or prosecution is warranted," the act directs him to apply to a special division of the District of Columbia Court of Appeals for appointment of an independent counsel.[104]

An Attorney General can remove an independent counsel, once he is appointed, only for "good cause." In addition, the office possesses "full power and independent authority" to investigate and prosecute inside the boundaries of jurisdiction established by the special division of the court. When a matter is assigned to an independent counsel, the Justice Department must cease all related investigations and provide the office with any requested assistance and support. In effect, once appointed, independent counsels become "mini-Attorneys General limited only by their grant of jurisdiction."[105]

By restricting the independent counsel's function and leaving the decision to initiate an investigation in the hands of the Attorney General, Congress hoped to avoid the constitutional objections that more radical restructuring proposals encountered. Nevertheless, by vesting the power to appoint independent counsels in the courts and by restricting presidential removal authority, the act clearly deviated from the Supreme Court's previous pronouncements on the prosecutorial power and presidential control.

The Justice Department originally opposed creation of the independent counsel's office. During hearings in 1976, Harold Tyler, Deputy Attorney General during the Ford administration, argued that divesting "the Attorney General of prosecutorial jurisdiction and restrict(ing) the President's power of removal" represented a clear violation of the separation of powers.[106] However, the Carter administration's commitment to restoring confidence in federal law enforcement led to a reversal of the department's position. During 1978 hearings on the Ethics in Government Bill, Assistant Attorney General John Harmon testified that the department no longer had "objections to the manner in which the appointment process is initiated, the method of judicial appointment, or the restrictions placed on the Executive's power of removal." Though recognizing that the prosecutorial function generally could not be removed from presidential control, Harmon said, "on balance, we think that the extraordinary circumstances which would warrant a resort to the special prosecutor would also justify him the measure of independence provided."[107] Based on this support, the Ethics in Government Act was passed by Congress and signed by President Carter in 1978.

Since its enactment, the Ethics in Government Act has been reauthorized twice, in 1982 and 1987. Independent counsels have been appointed to investigate officials in both Democratic and Republican administrations.[108] Under the Reagan administration, the Justice Department again reversed its view regarding the constitutionality of the act. In 1982, Attorney General William French Smith and Associate Attorney General Rudolph Giuliani appeared before Congress to urge repeal of the independent counsel provisions, insisting they "institutionalized distrust in the Justice Department" and were "constitutionally flawed."[109] Though promising to comply with the act, Smith vowed to challenge it in an appropriate case in the future.[110]

By 1987, the Justice Department had readied itself for a court challenge to the independent counsel provisions. Even though he signed reextension legislation that year, President Reagan said he believed the provisions were unconstitutional. Shortly thereafter, Assistant Attorney General Charles Cooper said flatly that the department was looking for an "appropriate challenge" to ask the Court to overturn the law.[111]

The Independent Counsel's Office: An Exception or a New Rule?

During the Carter and Reagan administrations, independent counsels were appointed on at least nine occasions. The first two cases involved alleged violations of federal narcotics law by President Carter's White House Chief of Staff, Hamilton Jordan, and the head of Carter's presidential campaign committee, Timothy Kraft. Of the other seven cases, five involved charges of corruption or misuse of office against officials in the Reagan administration. They included Secretary of Labor Raymond Donovan and White House Assistants Michael Deaver and Lyn

Nofziger. And, on two occasions, independent counsels were appointed to investigate the business dealings of Attorney General Edwin Meese.[112]

During these investigations, the operations of the independent counsel's office proved relatively uncontroversial. Indeed, in at least three instances, the targets of the investigations requested the special counsel's appointment.[113] However, the remaining two occasions when independent counsels were appointed are analytically distinct. The first involved the investigation of Oliver North, Richard Secord, and John Poindexter in connection with the Iran-Contra scandal.[114] The second involved the prosecution of Assistant Attorney General Theodore Olson for his role in obstructing Congress's investigation of the Environmental Protection Agency, and the role of the Justice Department during the Superfund scandal of 1982.[115]

These cases are analytically interesting because they emerge not from corruption or ethical misconduct, but from policy disputes between Congress and the executive. Both resulted in criminal charges against individual officers; both embodied disputes about executive authority to effect policies disapproved by Congress. In Iran-Contra, the policy was aid to the Nicaraguan Contras; in the Superfund scandal, the policy was environmental deregulation. Chapter 6 returns to the policy implications of these cases. However, the Superfund scandal merits attention here because of the Court's decision in *Morrison v. Olson* (1988) and its implications for the President's constitutional removal authority.[116]

The *Morrison* case surfaced in 1982, when Congress began investigating the EPA's enforcement of the Superfund Law.[117] At the time, Theodore Olson was the Assistant Attorney General in charge of the Office of Legal Counsel and played the key role in the administration's decision to withhold Superfund enforcement documents from Congress. Lawmakers eventually issued a contempt citation against EPA Administrator Anne Burford; the controversy was resolved only after a lawsuit and White House intervention to assure congressional access to the information.[118] After the initial conflict between the EPA and Congress was resolved, however, Olson acted to obstruct a congressional investigation into the Justice Department's role in counseling EPA to withhold information. In 1985, the House Judiciary Committee asked the Attorney General to seek appointment of an independent counsel to investigate whether Justice Department officials had perjured themselves or otherwise acted illegally to obstruct Congress.[119]

Independent Counsel Alexis Morrison was appointed in 1986 to investigate Olson and other members of the Justice Department.[120] A year later, Olson filed a suit challenging the constitutionality of the independent counsel law. The district court in Washington, D.C., upheld the act but, in 1988, a divided Court of Appeals reversed.[121] On appeal to the Supreme Court, the Department of Justice entered the case and filed an *amicus curiae* brief in support of Olson's challenge.[122]

The department's brief in *Morrison v. Olson* (1988) argued that the Ethics in Government Act was unconstitutional in at least two respects: First, the act violated the Appointments Clause by allowing the court to appoint a principal officer; second, it intruded on the President's authority by vesting a core executive function in an officer removed from Oval Office control. During oral argument, Solicitor General Fried said the act "strips the President of a purely executive function—criminal prosecution—and gives that function to a wholly untethered official."[123]

Given the factual background of the case, the wisdom of the Justice Department's intervention was highly questionable. The case clearly presented a conflict of interest for the department because the appellees were Justice Department officials. Moreover, the department's argument that prosecution could not be removed from presidential control amounted not only to saying that the executive should be free to prosecute the executive, but that the Justice Department should be left to investigate and prosecute itself. Finally, at the heart of the case was an interbranch dispute between Congress and the executive.[124] If ever there was a need for prosecutorial independence, *Morrison* appeared to be it.

In this light, the Supreme Court's seven-to-one decision upholding the act might have been expected.[125] Nevertheless, given the Court's formalistic approach to the separation of powers and its stated support for presidential authority in recent cases such as *Buckley*, *Chadha*, and *Bowsher*, its decision in *Morrison* was an aberration. The only changes to the Court since the *Bowsher* case were the elevation of William Rehnquist to Chief Justice and the ascension of Antonin Scalia and Anthony Kennedy to the high bench. All three were thought to be strong advocates of presidential power. The Court's decision limiting presidential removal power over a purely executive function in *Morrison* was something of a surprise.

Writing for the majority, Chief Justice Rehnquist departed fundamentally from the Court's previous doctrine regarding presidential power over administrative functionaries. Rather than assert that independent counsels performed "quasi-executive" or "quasi-judicial" roles, which would have brought the office under the umbrella of *Humphrey's*, Rehnquist completely broke with the previous argument that the President possessed illimitable removal authority over purely executive officers. Instead, he concluded that some functionaries, though executive in nature, need not be directly controlled by the President.[126]

Before turning to this point, however, Rehnquist had to respond to the objection that the office's method of appointment violated the Appointments Clause. Allowing that the "line between 'inferior' and 'principal' officers is one that is far from clear," he said, the independent counsel "clearly falls on the 'inferior officer' side of that line" as it performs no major policymaking functions.[127] This conclusion was startling in the context of the Court's opinion in *Buckley*, which had held that inferior officers could not control litigation (albeit civil litigation, in that case). Rehnquist's summary of what constituted an inferior officer did not completely dismiss the matter; the more fundamental question of whether Congress could restrict the President's removal authority over an officer who performed core executive functions lingered.

The obvious avenue open to the Court was simply to conclude that the independent counsel performed "quasi" functions. The problem was, historically, the Court had viewed prosecution as exclusively executive. As recently as *Nixon*, it had decided that the Constitution confers on the executive the "exclusive authority and absolute discretion to prosecute a case."[128] Even more recently, in *Heckler v. Chaney* (1985), the Court held that "the decision of a prosecutor in the Executive Branch not to indict [is] a decision which has long been regarded as the special province of the Executive Branch, in as much as it is the Executive who is charged by the Constitution to take Care that the Laws be faithfully executed."[129]

Still, the Court might have carved out a narrow exception for occasions when the executive was prosecuting itself. The canons of prosecutorial ethics or the need to avoid a conflict of interest could have justified such an exclusion. An exception might also have been lodged in the inherent logic of the separation of powers as a system established to prevent the abuse of power. A mechanism aimed at an obvious source of abuse certainly could have been inferred from the doctrine itself.

The Court, however, refused to back down from its stand that prosecution was an exclusive executive function. Rather, Rehnquist wrote, "there is no real dispute that the functions performed by the independent counsel are executive." Nevertheless, he said, no constitutional prohibition exists to vesting such powers in an office that "is to some degree 'independent' and free from executive supervision."[130]

Rehnquist asserted that the Court never intended to establish a fourth category of governmental function. The use of the "quasi-legislative" and "quasi-judicial" classifications, he said, merely "reflected our judgment that it was not essential to the President's proper execution of his Article II powers that these agencies be headed by individuals who were removable at will." This was not to suggest that functional analysis is irrelevant, but only that "the real question is whether the removal restrictions are of such a nature that they impede the President's ability to perform his constitutional duty." When seen in this light, Rehnquist said, there is no reason to believe that the President's "need to control the exercise of that [the independent counsel's] discretion is so central to the functioning of the Executive Branch as to require as a matter of constitutional law that the counsel be terminable at the will of the President."[131] What about the *Myers–Humphrey's* line of cases? Rehnquist noted:

> We undoubtedly did rely on the terms "quasi-legislative" and "quasi-judicial" to distinguish the officials involved in *Humphrey's Executor* and *Wiener* from those in *Myers*, but our present considered view is that the determination of whether the Constitution allows Congress to impose a "good cause"-type restriction on the President's power to remove an official cannot turn on whether or not that official is classified as "purely executive." The analysis

contained in our removal cases is designed not to define rigid categories of those officials who may or may not be removed at will by the President, but to ensure that Congress does not interfere with the President's exercise of the "executive power" and his constitutionally appointed duty.[132]

Thus the Court returned to the traditional tripartite classification of governmental functions. A distinction between quasi and ordinary executive functions, the Court admitted, was untenable.[133] By breaking the traditional nexus between constitutional function and removal authority, the Court implicitly recognized a bifurcated executive power: one that is essential to carrying out the President's constitutional obligations, and one that can be exercised independent of the President's political control.

Despite this radical departure from its previous separation of powers analysis, the *Morrison* Court stressed the limits of its holding by pointing out the unique circumstances involving the independent counsel. Not only were conflict-of-interest considerations inherent in the office's function, the office was of limited tenure and jurisdiction and lacked significant policymaking or administrative authority. The Court thereby implied that executive branch officials performing broader functions, such as the Attorney General, could not be severed so easily from presidential control.[134]

As Justice Scalia noted in his dissent, for the first time the Court fragmented control over core executive functions. It did so via a "totality of circumstances mode of analysis" that provided no rule for future cases other than what a majority of the Court decides would "impede" the President from performing his constitutional obligations.[135] In a very real sense, then, the Court reopened the Pandora's box regarding presidential control of administrative agencies. If the Court can decide that the functions of the independent counsel, though purely executive, are not central enough to the President's constitutional power that they need be under his control, nothing prevents it from doing the same with other executive branch offices or agencies, including the Attorney General and the Department of Justice. The line, moreover, between political and nonpolitical executive functions is even more difficult to draw than the one between executive and quasi functions.

In *Morrison*, the Court severely weakened the constitutional barriers originally raised against the establishment of an independent Justice Department. With the bond severed between function and removal authority, the Court wiped clean a slate. Whether *Morrison* remains an exception to the general rule or becomes the basis for a new set of executive officers remains to be seen.

Conclusion

The political role played by the government's legal office ultimately depends on the political-constitutional environment in which it operates. Divided sovereignty in the American system leads to a peculiar set of conflicts over the law and control of the administrative bureaucracy. The Justice Department's role in both arenas makes it particularly valuable and therefore a vulnerable target for interbranch conflict.

Such disputes have traditionally arisen out of sparring matches between the President and Congress over constitutional appointment and removal authority. The classical separation of powers theory that divided government into three unitary branches reserved enormous power for the President to oversee the operation of government. Application of this theory reached its zenith in Chief Justice Taft's dicta in *Myers*: All principal officers of government, with the exception of judges and members of Congress, were subject to the President's exclusive and illimitable removal authority.

The relative weakness of the federal government prior to the twentieth century led to few challenges to the President's extraordinary power under this traditional view. Only during periods of fundamental political realignment, such as the periods of Jacksonian Democracy or the Civil War, were interbranch conflicts intense and protracted enough for presidential authority to be threatened seriously. As the federal government moved from positive to plenary authority following the jolts of the Progressive Era and the New Deal, however, the political realities of this theory forced its reformulation. In *Humphrey's*, the Court effectively allowed Congress to draw an entirely new branch into the federal government's organizational scheme. In the spirit of the period, the new branch was theoretically free to make decisions based on expertise and would be uninfluenced by politics.

The fourth branch always served as a sore point for constitutional purists. By the late 1960s, it also suffered increasing attacks from political quarters. Consequently, Congress ceased to add to the size of the fourth branch, and the Supreme Court began to back away from its constitutional recognition of hybrid functions and agencies. The Court's conclusions regarding presidential appointment and removal authority in *Nixon*, *Buckley*, and *Bowsher*, quite apart from their implications for the separation of powers, mark that retreat.

As part of the administrative bureaucracy, the Justice Department cannot escape the consequences of changes that occur in separation of powers theory and law. The Attorney General's transformation from a judicial to an executive branch institution, and the Court's early recognition of that change in *San Jancinto*, *Ponzi*, and *McGrain*, brought it and other principal officers in the department under presidential control. The department's prosecutorial function, however, has always been problematic during periods of political scandal or misconduct by the administration. The establishment of the special counsel's office created a mechanism to solve the conflict of interest inherent in having the executive prosecute itself. Importantly, however, the Court's opinion in *Morrison* may have consequences far beyond the limited question of an effective means of prosecuting executive branch misconduct and may contain the seeds of an executive law enforcement function entirely independent of the President.

Notes

1. Nearly all commentators in Britain agree that judges should avoid making "political decisions" whenever possible. However, no one seriously suggests that law and politics can be completely separated or that judges never make policy. Rather it is usually seen as a question of degree. See Alan Paterson, *The Law Lords* (Toronto: University of Toronto Press, 1982), chap. 7; Lord Roskill, "The Lords: Reactionaries or Reformers?" *Current Legal Problems* 37 (1984), 247; Ronald Dworkin, "Political Judges and the Rule of Law," *Proceedings of the British Academy* 64 (1978), 259.

2. The literature on the political role of the Supreme Court in the United States is extensive. Perhaps the best early discussions are Robert Dahl, "Decision-Making in a Democracy: The Supreme Court as a National Policy-Maker," *Journal of Public Law* 6 (1957), 279; Alexander Bickel, *The Least Dangerous Branch: The Supreme Court at the Bar of Politics* (New York: Bobbs-Merrill, 1962); Raoul Berger, *Government by Judiciary* (Boston: Harvard University Press, 1977). More recent literature focuses not on whether judges should make political decisions but how and when they should; see Donald Horowitz, *The Courts and Social Policy* (Washington, D.C.: Brookings, 1977); Gerhard Casper, "The Supreme Court and National Policy Making," *American Political Science Review* 70 (1976), 50; Stephen Wasby, "Arrogation of Power or Accountability: Judicial Imperialism Revisited," *Judicature* 65 (1981), 209; Bradley Cannon, "Defining the Dimensions of Judicial Activism," *Judicature* 66 (1983); Richard Posner, *The Federal Courts: Crisis and Reform* (Harvard University Press, 1985); and Ronald Dworkin, *Law's Empire* (London: Fontana Press, 1986).

3. For a discussion of this argument, see Patrick Atiyah, "Judicial-Legislative Relations in England," in Robert A. Katzmann (ed.), *Judges and Legislators: Toward Institutional Comity* (Washington, D.C.: Brookings, 1988). See also Patrick Atiyah and Robert Summers, *Form and Substance in Anglo-American Law: A Comparative Study in Legal Reasoning, Legal Theory and Legal Institutions* (Oxford: Oxford University Press, 1987).

4. Atiyah, "Judicial-Legislative Relations in England," in Katzmann (ed.), *Judges and Legislators* 134–35.

5. The judicialization of U.S. politics is discussed in detail in the next chapters. Briefly, however, the separation of powers creates a system that frustrates political closure. Groups or parties who lose in the electoral process can continue to pursue their policy agenda, and upset that of the electoral victors, by shifting the battle to other arenas such as the courts or the bureaucracy. See Paul Bator, "Legalistic Constitutionalism and Our Ineffective Government," in Jeremy Rabkin and L. Gordon Crovitz (eds.), *The Fettered Presidency* (Washington, D.C.: AEI, 1989), 265.

6. This power was claimed by Justice Jackson in his concurring opinion in *Brown v. Allen*, 344 U.S. (1953), 443, 540.

7. A discussion of these conflicting roles is found in Robert Palmer, "The Confrontation of the Legislative and Executive Branches: An Examination of the Constitutional Balance of Powers and the Role of the Attorney General," *Pepperdine Law Review* 11 (1984), 349.

8. 418 U.S. (1974), 683; 556 F. Supp. (D.D.C. 1983), 150; 407 U.S. (1972), 297.

9. U.S. Const. art. II, sec. 3.

10. U.S. Const., art I., sec. 8, cl. 18.

11. "Presidential Attacks on the Constitutionality of Federal Statutes: A Separation of Powers Problem," *Ohio State Law Journal* 40 (1979), 51.

12. For a discussion of the special privileges enjoyed by the United States before the Supreme Court, see Samuel Krislov, "The Role of the Attorney General as Amicus Curiae," in Huston et al., *Roles of the Attorney General.*

13. Madison, *The Federalist*, ed. Max Beloff (Oxford: Blackwell, 1948), 246.

14. Montesquieu, *De l'Esprit des lois* (The Spirit of Laws), Book 11.

15. For a discussion of the influence of the colonial experience in shaping the American separation of powers, see Edward Corwin, "Progress of Constitutional Theory," *American Historical Review* 30 (1925), 511; and L. Wright, "The Origins of the Separation of Powers in America," *Economica* 13 (1933), 169.

16. Malcolm Sharp, "The Classical American Doctrine of the Separation of Powers," *University of Chicago Law Review* 2 (1935), 385.

17. *The Federalist*, 253.

18. *Youngstown Co. v. Sawyer*, 343 U.S. (1952), 579, 635.

19. *Buckley v. Valeo*, 424 U.S. (1976), 1, 121.

20. For a discussion of the Supreme Court's use of these two analytical approaches, see Harold Bruff, "Special Prosecutor Case a Balancing Act," *Legal Times*, July 4, 1988, 15.

21. U.S. Const., art. II, sec. 2.

22. 38 U.S. (1835), 225, 258.

23. For a discussion of the application of the *Hennen* precedent, see Arthur Larson, "Has the President an Inherent Power of Removal of his Non-Executive Appointees?" *Tennessee Law Review* 16 (1940), 259, 271–272.

24. The House debate in 1789 on removal of the heads of the three executive departments appears in U.S. Library of Congress, *Annals of the First Congress*, 368–96, 455–615. A discussion of the events surrounding the Decision of 1789 is found in Corwin, *The President*, 86.

25. Corwin, *The President*, 82–84.

26. U.S. Congress, *Senate Journal*, 24th Cong., 2d sess. (1824), 123–124.

27. J. Richardson (ed.), *Messages and Papers of the Presidents*, vol. 3, 1288–1312.

28. Robert Remini, *Andrew Jackson*, vol. 2: *The Course of American Freedom* (New York: Harper & Row, 1981); Leonard White, *The Jacksonians* (New York: Harper & Row, 1954), 317–21; E. McKinley Erikson, "The Federal Civil Service under President Jackson," *Mississippi Valley Historical Review* 13 (1927), 517.

29. 14 Stat. (1867), 430.

30. Lately Thomas, *The First President Johnson* (New York: Free Press, 1968), 484–618; Harold Hyman, "Johnson, Stanton, and Grant: A Reconsideration of the Army's Role in the Events Leading to Impeachment," *American Historical Review* 66 (1960), 85.

31. Louis Fisher, "Grover Cleveland Against the Senate," *Congressional Studies* 7 (1979), 11.

32. H. Seidman, *Politics, Position and Power*, 260–80.

33. The classic statements of this school of thought in public administration are Woodrow Wilson, "The Study of Administration," *Political Science Quarterly* 2 (1887), 197; and James Landis, *The Administrative Process* (New Haven: Yale University Press, 1938).

34. Elizabeth Sanders, "The Presidency and the Bureaucratic State," in Michael Nelson (ed.), *The Presidency and the Political System*, 2d ed. (Washington, D.C.: CQ Press, 1988), 379.

35. 272 U.S. (1926), 52.

36. Ibid., 163–64.

37. While President, Taft strongly objected to the Interstate Commerce Commission, which he believed was "usurping" presidential authority. See U.S. Congress, House of Representatives, *Special Message of the President on the Interstate Commerce and Antitrust Laws and Federal Incorporation*, H. Doc. 484, 61st Cong., 2d. sess. (1910), 5.

38. See Edward Corwin, "Tenure of Office and the Removal Power under the Consti-

tution," *Columbia Law Review* 27 (1927), 353; and Arthur Larson, "Has the President an Inherent Power of Removal?"

39. 272 U.S., 52, 177, 181.
40. 259 U.S. (1935), 602.
41. Ibid., 627–29.
42. Ibid.
43. Louis Fisher, *Constitutional Conflicts between Congress and the President* (Princeton, N.J.: Princeton University Press, 1985), 79.
44. 357 U.S. (1958), 349.
45. Ibid., 355.
46. 343 U.S. (1952), 470, 487–88.
47. Corwin, *The President*, 93.
48. Ibid., 278–379.
49. 424 U.S. (1976), 1.
50. Ibid., 134–43.
51. 462 U.S. (1983), 919.
52. Ibid., 936–42.
53. 478 U.S. (1986), 714.
54. 99 U.S. Stat. (1985), 1038.
55. Ibid., 719–21.
56. Ibid.
57. 295 U.S., 602, 632.
58. An account of the "Palmer Raids" may be found in Stanley Cohen, *A. Mitchell Palmer: Politician* (New York: DaCapo, 1972).
59. Luther Huston, "History of the Office of Attorney General," in Huston et al., *Roles of the Attorney General*, 13.
60. U.S. Congress, House Committee on Rules, *Attorney General A. Mitchell Palmer on Charges Against the Justice Department by Louis Post and Others*, 66th Cong., 2d sess. (1920); R.G. Brown, Z. Chafee, *Report Upon the Illegal Practices of the United States Department of Justice* (Washington, D.C.: National Popular Government League, 1920).
61. Ibid., 4–5.
62. Contemporary accounts of scandals besieging the Justice Department at this time are John Goodwin, *What Happens When Organized Genius is Applied to Government* (Washington, D.C.: Hammond, 1924); and Harry M. Daugherty, *The Inside Story of the Harding Tragedy* (New York: Churchill, 1932). A more recent account is Burl Noggle, *Teapot Dome: Oil and Politics in the 1920's* (Baton Rouge: Louisiana State University Press, 1962).
63. U.S. Congress, Senate, *Hearings Before the Select Committee on Investigation of the Attorney General*, 68th Cong., 1st sess. (1924).
64. Ibid., 2565–90.
65. Noggle, *Teapot Dome: Oil and Politics*, and Goodwin, *Organized Genius*.
66. *Congressional Record*, January 18, 1952, A260; January 23, 1952, A350; February 4, 1952, A609.
67. U.S. Congress, House Committee on the Judiciary, *Hearings on Investigation of the Department of Justice*, 82d Cong., 2d sess. (1952–1953).
68. See Richard Ehlke, "Proposals for Reform of the Justice Department," reprinted in U.S. Congress, Subcommittee on Separation of Powers, Senate Committee on the Judiciary, *Hearings on Removing Politics from the Administration of Justice*, 93d Cong., 2d. sess. (1974), 443 (hereafter cited as Ervin Hearings).
69. The Attorneys General were: John Mitchell, Richard Kleindienst, Elliot Richard-

son, William Saxbe, and Edward Levi. The Deputy Attorneys General were Richard Kleindienst, Ralph Erickson, Joseph Sneed, William Ruckelshaus, Laurence Silberman, and Harold Tyler, Jr. The Special Prosecutors were Archibald Cox and Leon Jaworski.

70. Watergate generated an extraordinary amount of literature on the accountability of the Attorney General and Justice Department. Unfortunately, much of it was colored by the fiercely partisan spirit of the period. The best discussions from this period are in the Ervin Hearings; National Association of Attorneys General, *Selection of the Attorney General of the United States*, a report of the Committee on the Office of U.S. Attorney General (1974); American Bar Association, *Preventing Improper Influence on Federal Law Enforcement Agencies*, a report of the Special Committee to Study Federal Law Enforcement (1976); "Removing Politics From the Justice Department: Constitutional Problems with Institutional Reform," *New York University Law Review* 60 (1975), 366.

71. Leon Jaworski, *The Right and the Power: The Prosecution of Watergate* (Houston, Tex.: Gulf Publishing Company, 1976).

72. U.S. Congress, House of Representatives, *Impeachment of Richard Nixon*, H. Rep. 1305, 93d Cong., 2d sess. (1974), 57.

73. Ibid. See also Richardson, *The Creative Balance* 1–152; and Kleindienst, *Justice*. Richardson's commitment to the Senate on allowing an independent investigation is found in U.S. Congress, Senate Committee on the Judiciary, *Hearings on the Nomination of Elliot L. Richardson to Be Attorney General of the United States*, 93d Cong., 1st sess. (1973), 24.

74. *Nixon v. Sirica*, 487 F. 2d 700 (D.C. Cir. 1973), affirming 360 F. Supp. 1 (D.D.C. 1973).

75. See Jaworski, *The Right and the Power*; and Kleindienst, *Justice*, 73. Bork's dismissal of Cox came back to haunt him when his role in the episode became a major issue in the Senate refusal to confirm his nomination to the Supreme Court in 1987. See U.S. Congress, Senate Judiciary Committee, *Nomination of Robert H. Bork to be an Associate Justice of the United States Supreme Court*, 100th Cong., 1st sess. (1987), 65–70.

76. *United States v. Nixon*, 418 U.S. (1974), 683.

77. The history of "executive privilege" and the judicial precedents are discussed in Archibald Cox, "Executive Privilege," *University of Pennsylvania Law Review* 122 (1974), 1383; and Raoul Berger, *Executive Privilege* (Boston: Harvard University Press, 1974). However, that protection was not absolute and must be weighed against the constitutional powers and requirements of the other two branches. In the instant case the Court said "the President's generalized assertion of privilege must yield to the demonstrated, specific need for evidence in a pending criminal trial," 418 U.S. (1974), 683, 704–12.

78. This issue was litigated separately in *Nader v. Bork*, 366 F. Supp. 104 (D.D.C. 1973). The district court held that:

> As an appointee of the Attorney General, Watergate Special Prosecutor served subject to congressional rather than presidential control, and Congress had power to directly limit the circumstances under which he could be discharged. . . .
>
> Though in absence of limitations issued by Congress, Attorney General would have authority to fire at any time and for any reason Special Prosecutor appointed by him, Department of Justice regulation issued by the Attorney General and limiting his own authority with respect to discharge had the force and effect of law and was binding on him. . . .
>
> In light of Justice Department regulation providing that Watergate Special Prosecutor would not be removed except for extraordinary improprieties, discharge on ground that the Special Prosecutor was insisting on compliance with a court order which was no longer subject to further judicial review was illegal. . . .
>
> Order revoking Justice Department regulation providing that the Watergate Special Prosecutor could not be discharged . . . was arbitrary and unreasonable and could not retroactively

validate the prior discharge of the Special Prosecutor. . . . Actions of administrative agencies in revoking their regulations must be neither arbitrary nor unreasonable.

79. 418 U.S., 683, 692–96.

80. The antistatist nature of American culture and its impact on the general view of politics is thoroughly exposed in classics such as Richard Hofstadter, *The American Political Tradition* (New York: Random House, 1973); Daniel Boorstin, *The Genius of American Politics* (Chicago: University of Chicago Press, 1953); Charles and Mary Beard, *The American Spirit* (New York: Scribners, 1943).

81. The use of the term "politics" to describe episodes of corruption or scandal is prevalent in literature on the Justice Department and Attorney General's office, especially during this period. The Ervin Hearings, which considered reform of the Justice Department in the wake of the Watergate scandal, for instance, was entitled "Removing politics from the Administration of Justice." See also Ralph Fine, "The Politics of Justice," *American Bar Association Journal* 59 (1973), 102; Mitchel Rogovin, "Reorganizing Politics out of the Department of Justice," *American Bar Association Journal* 64 (1978), 885; J. Griffith, "Putting Politics in its Place at the Justice Department," *Fortune*, October 1973, 228, or Navasky, "The Politics of Justice," 18.

82. For a discussion of this proposal see Daniel Meador, "The President, The Attorney General and the Department of Justice," 79–105.

83. Kleindienst, *Justice*, 90–109; and J.Ll.J. Edwards, "The Integrity of Criminal Prosecutions—Watergate Echoes Beyond the Shores of the United States," in P. Glazebook (ed.), *Reshaping the Criminal Law* (London: Stevens & Sons, 1978), 364.

84. 438 U.S. (1978), 265.

85. Bell and Ostrow, *Taking Care of the Law*, 28–32.

86. Ervin Hearings.

87. S. 2803, 93d Cong., 2d sess. (1974).

88. Ervin Hearings, 3.

89. 273 U.S. (1927), 135.

90. Ibid., 178.

91. See "Removing Politics from the Department of Justice: Constitutional Problems with Institutional Reform," *New York University Law Review* 50 (1975), 366.

92. See statements of Ramsey Clark, Archibald Cox, Alan Cranston, Lloyd Cutler, Robert Dixon, Arthur Goldberg, Charles Goodell, Nicholas deB. Katzenbach, Richard Kleindienst, Burke Marshall, J. Lee Rankin, Mitchell Rogovin, Whitney Seymour Jr., and Theodore Sorenson in Ervin Hearings.

93. Only a few scholars have recognized the fact that the Attorney General began as a judicial rather than an executive office, and usually this has been only in passing. There has been no critical analysis of the institutional implications of the office's beginnings. See Meador, "The President and the Attorney General," 5; Arnold Relyea, "Circumstances Surrounding the Creation of the Office of the Attorney General," reprinted in Ervin Hearings, 420; and Henry Warren, "New Light on the Federal Judiciary Act of 1789," *Harvard Law Review* 37 (1923), 108, 109.

94. On the changing attitudes in public administration during the 1960s and 1970s, see Douglas Cater, *Power in Washington* (New York: Random House, 1964); J. Lieper Freeman, *The Political Process* (New York: Random House, 1965); Roger H. Davidson, "Breaking Up Those 'Cozy Triangles': An Impossible Dream?" in Susan Welch and John Peters (eds.), *Legislative Reform and Public Policy* (New York: Praeger, 1977); E. Lewis, *American Politics in a Bureaucratic Age* (Framingham, MA: Winthrop Pub., 1977); Paul Quirk, *Industrial Influence in Federal Regulatory Agencies* (Princeton, N.J.: Princeton University Press, 1981); Robert Rabin, "Federal Regulation in Historical Perspective," *Stanford Law Review* 38 (1986), 1278.

95. Ervin Hearings; see especially the statements of Arthur Goldburg, 57; Burke Marshall, 113; Nicholas deB. Katzenbach, 150.

96. Ibid., see especially the testimonies of Archibald Cox, 202; Burke Marshall, 115–17.

97. Miller, "The Attorney General as President's Lawyer," in Huston et al., *Roles of the Attorney General*, 51.

98. These shifts in American jurisprudence are traced in Morton J. Horowitz, "The Conservative Tradition in the Writing of American Legal History," *American Journal of Legal History* 17 (1973), 280; G. Edward White, *Patterns of American Legal Thought* (Oxford: Oxford University Press, 1978), 18.

99. Ervin Hearings, 119–20.

100. Richardson, *The Creative Balance*, 27.

101. In "The Prosecutor," *New York Times* (November 7, 1973), section A (magazine).

102. Senate Committee on Governmental Operations, *Hearings on S. 495: Watergate Reorganization and Reform Act*, 94th Cong., 1st sess. (1977); House Subcommittee on Criminal Justice, *Hearings on H.R. 14476 Provisions for a Special Prosecutor*, 94th Cong., 2d sess. (1976); House Committee on the Judiciary, *Special Prosecutor Legislation: Hearings on H.R. 2835*, 95th Cong., 1st sess. (1977); Senate Committee on Governmental Affairs, *Public Officials Integrity Act: Hearings on S. 555*, 95th Cong., 1st sess. (1977).

103. 92 Stat. (1978), 1867; as amended 96 Stat. (1983), 2039; 101 Stat. (1987), 1293. For a history of the Special Prosecutor's office, see Terry Eastland, *Ethics, Politics and the Independent Counsel: Executive Power, Executive Vice* (Washington, D.C.: National Legal Center, 1989).

104. Sections 592–93.

105. Statement of Deputy Attorney General Harold Tyler, in *Hearings on Watergate Reform Act, 1977*, 7–8.

106. Ibid., 29–31.

107. *Hearings on Public Officials Integrity Act*, 1978, 8.

108. For a discussion of the use of the office since 1978, see Eastland, *Ethics Politics and the Independent Counsel*. A more concise discussion is also found in Mark Bertozzi, "Separating Politics from the Administration of Justice," *Judicature* 67 (1984), 486, and "The Special Counsel Law," *Congressional Quarterly*, December 19, 1987, 3166.

109. U.S. Congress, Senate Committee on the Judiciary, *Hearings on Ethics in Government Act Amendments*, 97th Cong., 2d sess. (1982), 24.

110. Letter from William French Smith to Michael Davidson (April 17, 1981) reprinted in U.S. Congress, Subcommittee on Oversight of Government Management of Senate Committee on Governmental Affairs, *Special Prosecutor Provisions of Ethics in Government Act*, 97th Cong., 1st sess. (1981), 249–50.

111. See, "Congress Moves to Amend Special Counsel Law," *Legal Times*, January 12, 1987, 4.

112. See U.S. Congress, House Committee on the Judiciary, *Independent Counsel Amendment Act of 1987*, H. Rept. 316, 100th Cong., 1st sess. (1987), 14.

113. Ibid., the three were Raymond Donovan, Lyn Nofziger, and Edwin Meese.

114. U.S. Congress, *Report of the Congressional Committees Investigating the Iran-Contra Affair* (New York: Random House, 1988).

115. U.S. Congress, House Committee on Energy and Commerce, *Investigation of the EPA: Report on Abuses in the Superfund Program*, Committee Print No. 99-AA, 98th Cong., 2d sess. (1984); House Judiciary Committee, *Report on Investigation of the Role of the Department of Justice in the Withholding of EPA Documents*, H. Rept. 99–435, 98th Cong., 1st sess. (1985).

116. 108 S. Ct. (1986), 2597.

117. Comprehensive Response, Compensation and Liability Act of 1980, Pub. L. No. 96–510.

118. Ibid.

119. *Report on Role of Justice Department in Withholding Documents*, 229. In addition to Theodore Olson, the report also criticized Charles Schmults, Deputy Attorney General, and Carol Dinkins, Assistant Attorney General for the Lands and Natural Resources Division.

120. See *Report of A.G. Regarding Allegations Against Department Officials in U.S. House Judiciary Committee Report 22, 45* (April 10, 1986), filed in No. 86–1 (CADC) (A.G. Rep.); and *Order of the Appointment of Special Counsel James McKay*, Div. No. 86–1 (CADC Special Division, April 23, 1986).

121. *In re Sealed Case*, 665 F. Supp., (D.D.C., 1987), 56; 838 F.2d (D.C. Cir., 1988), 476.

122. See brief for the United States (No. 87–1279) in *Morrison v. Olson*, 108 S. Ct. (1988), 2597.

123. For an account of the Solicitor General's oral arguments before the Court see "Counsel Law's Constitutionality Argued," *Washington Post*, April 27, 1988, A–5.

124. See chapter 6.

125. Justice Scalia dissented and Justice Kennedy did not participate.

126. 108 S.Ct. 2597, 2616–20.

127. Ibid., 2608–9.

128. 418 U.S., 683, 693.

129. 470 U.S. (1985), 821, 832.

130. 108 S. Ct., 2597, 2619.

131. Ibid., 2618–19.

132. Ibid.

133. Ibid., footnote 28 in Court's opinion.

134. An argument that the Court's decision should be construed narrowly is found in Bruff, "Special Prosecutor Case a Balancing Act."

135. 108 S. Ct. 2597, 2641. For a similarly negative appraisal regarding the constitutionality and prudence of the Court's decision, see Eastland, *Ethics, Politics and the Independent Counsel*.

5

The New American Political System and the Judicialization of Politics

The paralysis that characterized American politics during the 1970s and 1980s generated new interest in the separation of powers. Whereas traditional analysis focused on constitutional conflicts between Congress and the President, recent studies have concentrated increasingly on the role of the courts. This shift reflects fundamental changes in the American political system. The 1960s witnessed a period of extraordinary growth in national political power. Compared to earlier periods of growth, that decade saw far greater centralization of political policymaking and an institutionalization of ideological conflict. While the effect of these changes on individual institutions such as the presidency or the Congress has been discussed in scholarly research, their impact on the judiciary, the bureaucracy, and on interbranch relations generally has not yet been fully appreciated or understood.

Much of the recent controversy surrounding the Justice Department and legal policy relates to the emergence of a "new system politics" and how it has altered public policymaking in America. A conspicuous gap exists between traditional literature on the Justice Department and the new debate about the department's political role. Whereas traditional controversies centered on presidential removal power, especially during periods of crisis or political scandal, recent arguments tend to focus on the Justice Department's routine litigating and law enforcement functions. The remainder of this book examines these recent changes in American politics and their impact on the Department of Justice.

The New American Political System

During the 1970s and 1980s a new American political system emerged. Anthony King's edited volume titled *The New American Political System* appeared more than a decade ago and is now published in a second version.[1] William Lunch's

The Nationalization of American Politics, a more integrated analysis of the changed nature of the federal government, is now several years old as well.[2] What these and other political scholars describe is how, in postwar America, political power has grown increasingly nationalized, while simultaneously, our central political institutions have lost the ability to act in a coherent and decisive fashion.

The old institutions appear as familiar landmarks on the horizon, but the way they operate has changed fundamentally. Congressional power has been decentralized: old committee functions have moved to subcommittees; the seniority system has been diluted; and the size and power of congressional staff have increased enormously. Power in the new Congress is fragmented and atomized. Staffers increasingly influence policy by drafting intricate, complex legislation and committee reports. With the erosion of seniority, junior members have more influence and prestige. Subcommittee chairs can dominate "issue networks" that propel them to national prominence and attract interest group financing for campaigns that have become more personalized as local party organizations have collapsed. In short, for members of the new Congress, the incentives all favor entrepreneurship, fragmentation, and independence, while discouraging party discipline, consensus building, and submission to presidential leadership.[3]

Party organizations lost even greater ground in relation to the presidency during this period. The McGovern–Fraser Commission was the coup de grâce in a gradual erosion of control over selection of presidential candidates. Personalization of presidential campaigns coincided with an explosion in presidential responsibility. Presidents assumed responsibility over all aspects of American domestic and foreign policy, becoming "all things to all men," as one British commentator put it.[4] The expansion in answerability, of course, came precisely as Congress's cohesiveness and susceptibility to presidential leadership or party discipline began to decline.

These changes fostered the view held by an increasing number of Presidents of both parties that the presidency should be plebiscitary in nature; its mandate and appeal to a national constituency should sweep aside political opposition from whatever quarter, especially Congress.[5] Once in the White House, Presidents moved to centralize control over the administrative bureaucracy and strip it from congressional control. The size and power of White House staff have expanded substantially at the expense of the cabinet and sub-cabinet; the bureaucracy in general has become subject to increasingly sophisticated budgetary and personnel screening measures centered in the White House.[6]

The erosion of party government further exacerbated centrifugal forces in American politics. It drove even deeper the wedge between Congress and the executive by institutionalizing partisan conflict. Republican candidates have captured the White House; Democrats have retained an electoral lock on Congress. Campaign finance laws that overwhelmingly favor incumbents entrench partisan camps. Neither party finds the current electoral situation so objectionable that it is willing to jeopardize its institutional stronghold in a gamble on reform.[7] As a consequence, ordinary partisan policy disputes now have an even greater chance of escalating into constitutional conflicts over the powers of the two branches, each trying to bolster its authority to control future policy.

Although always a political institution, in the new system the Supreme Court has evolved into a more active and unpredictable source of political innovation. During most of its history the Supreme Court has partnered the other two branches in extending federal power over state and local government. Its most controversial decisions historically have upheld federal authority or struck down state laws. Rarely did the Court clash with Congress or the President. When it did—during the New Deal, for instance—it generally was forced to retreat. Today's Court, by contrast, has assumed a more independent political role vis-à-vis the other branches.[8]

By opening the floodgates to political litigation, the Warren Court did more than just encourage interest groups to use the judicial forum for policy change; it significantly enhanced the judiciary's political independence. In making itself accessible to powerful new interest group constituencies, the Court decoupled itself from the political agenda of the other branches.[9] With support from clientele groups, the Court now can more readily engage in political clashes with other branches without fear of institutional reprisals such as court packing or statutory overrides. Groups that benefit from the new role of the judiciary are able to mobilize political support whenever judicial autonomy appears threatened.[10]

The new "political class" in America also differs greatly from the old. Politics in the United States used to be pragmatically based: largely void of deep ideological convictions and conflicts, it was seen primarily as a struggle between competing groups over the distribution of material resources. This materialist, group-based view of American politics was shared by political theorists on the left and right: by those who admired the system, such as Truman and Dahl, and those who deplored its results, such as Schattschnieder and Lowi.[11] So thoroughgoing was the assumption of a materialistic basis of American politics that, by 1960, Daniel Bell even proclaimed the "end of ideology."[12]

Bell could not have foreseen the Washington of today: a city of ideologues who hope to see their principles made into public policy.[13] In both major parties, "principled" factions play increasingly large, if not dominant roles. Applicants for even lower-level bureaucratic posts in the Carter and Reagan administrations had to prove they were "true believers." A proliferation of new, ideologically based interest groups on the left as well as the right drive policy decisions. Ralph Nader's impact on the left may have come first, but the Moral Majority and Richard Viguerie made up for lost time on the right in the 1980s.

Whether or not they are sincere, people who see politics as a calling rather than a profession often place dysfunctional demands on the system. When deeply held personal beliefs are perceived to be at stake, flexibility is lost and policy give-and-take becomes impossible. Policy demands become rigid and are magnified into "rights" or absolute culture claims; pragmatic compromises are equated with betraying "the cause." Losers are much less likely to accept the legitimacy of election outcomes and wait quietly for the next round of voting.[14] The repercussions of these changes in American politics have left the system less able to resolve important policy issues. National politics used to be fought out in the voting booth every four years, with clearly identified partisan camps competing for control of policymaking institutions. The electoral arena produced clear winners and losers. The winners gained a chance to implement their policy agenda, centered around a set of materialistic claims; the losers, playing the role of the loyal opposition, waited for the next election. Today, however, national politics is a series of guerrilla-style confrontations, where the terms "winner" and "loser" have almost lost their meaning.[15] Entrenched in their respective institutions, partisans continue to struggle for control of policy long after the election is over. Each side tries to erode the other's institutional power, and ideological conflict spills over into other arenas, such as the courts and the bureaucracy. Political scientists Benjamin Ginsberg and Martin Shefter recently described this shifting of political struggle as America's entry into a "post-electoral era."[16]

The implications of postelectoral politics for the Justice Department are profound. The regularization of institutional conflict, especially over the control of the administrative bureaucracy, and the legalization of policy disputes thoroughly politicizes the day-to-day environment of the Justice Department. The separation of powers and the unique character of the Supreme Court power of judicial review have always left America's legal establishment susceptible to politicization during periods of constitutional conflict or crisis. The difference is that constitutional conflicts used to be limited to periods of extraordinary political development and transformation, periods of critical realignments. In the new American political system, they have become regularized and routine, merely the pursuit of politics by other means.[17]

The Justice Department's intimate relationship with the federal judiciary and its control of government litigation place it at a strategic juncture in the new system politics. The remainder of this chapter focuses on department changes resulting from judicialization of larger and larger areas of public policy. Chapter 6 examines the Justice Department's part in executive-congressional relations and the new-style separation of powers conflict in the administrative arena.

The Executive-Judicial Branch Alliance

Franklin D. Roosevelt's administration hinted at a new role for the Justice Department. Faced by a Supreme Court whose jurisprudence spurned the political transformations envisaged by the New Deal, Attorney General Homer Cummings utilized Justice Department resources to launch an all-out assault on the judicial branch. He and Assistant Attorney General Robert Jackson advanced a plan to expand the Supreme Court from nine to fifteen members.[18] Cummings

billed the court-packing proposal as a measure to promote efficiency, but clearly
it was an overt attempt to mute Court resistance to the administration's agenda.[19]
As Cummings admitted in Senate testimony, "we are facing not a constitutional
but a judicial crisis . . . (in which) the deciding vote of one or two judges has
nullified the will of Congress, has overruled the approval of the President . . . and
has run counter to the sentiment of the country."[20]

The extremity of the court-packing proposal points up the administration's
failure to influence the judiciary through more conventional means. Justice Department efforts to defend administration policies through litigation had collapsed. During Cummings's first three years in office, the Supreme Court
invalidated more than thirteen major pieces of legislation at the heart of the
administration's political program.[21] Judicial opposition to the administration
was so broad based that between 1934 and 1936, the Justice Department, for the
only time in history, lost more cases than it won before the Supreme Court.[22] To
minimize the department's judicial defeats, Cummings added a disclaimer to his
report to Congress in 1937:

> In view of the fact that many cases are taken by the Government to (the)
> Court, or their taking is acquiesced in, merely to settle questions of public
> interest and importance, the Government attains an appropriate degree of suc-
> cess if the ratio of cases won to those lost is about equal.[23]

In an attempt to coax the judiciary into cooperating, Cummings launched a
series of public speeches attacking the Court's jurisprudence. The timing of his
speeches coincided closely with Court decisions striking down the administration's legislative program. In May 1935, the Court handed down a wave of
opinions invalidating the Railway Pension Act, National Industrial Recovery Act,
and Frazier-Lemke Act.[24] Cummings responded with a broadside to the Court at the
annual meeting of the American Bar Association. In his speech, the Attorney General reminded the Court it "does not operate in a legalistic vacuum . . . on the
contrary, it is part and parcel of an organic process of government." The Court's
constitutional interpretations have never been considered absolute; indeed, "the
absolute theory of one and only one rational construction of the Constitution
renders impossible any proper understanding of the nature of our American
constitutional method and the functions of the Supreme Court."[25]

Criticized by the press for using his office as a "bully-pulpit," Cummings
defended his remarks, arguing that, "far from being unfair to the Court" they
were "an important and valid aid in acquainting them (the Justices) with some of
the weighty factors which should properly enter into the process of decision."[26]
Despite Cummings's attempt to "acquaint" the Supreme Court with administration views of the Constitution and role of the judiciary, it continued to strike
down New Deal legislation. In early 1936, it invalidated the Agricultural Adjustment Act, Guffrey Coal Act, and Municipal Bankruptcy Act.[27]

Convinced the administration could wait no longer for the retirement of conservative Justices, the Attorney General sent the court-packing bill to Congress in early February 1937. In a national radio speech defending the plan, Cummings said the judiciary "is but a coordinate branch of Government. It is entitled to no higher position than either the legislative or the executive. If the Constitution is to remain a living document and the law is to serve the needs of a vital and growing nation, it is essential that new blood be infused into our judiciary."[28]

It is unlikely the court-packing bill ever would have passed Congress. Popular resentment of the measure and a general anxiety that FDR had gone too far in challenging traditional institutional structures led to electoral rebuff of Democratic candidates during the 1938 midterm election. Fortunately for the administration, however, the Court was the first to blink in the standoff. In March 1937, it handed down decisions in *West Coast Hotel v. Parrish*[29] and *NLRB v. Laughlin Steel Company*,[30] upholding key elements of the New Deal. Shortly thereafter, Justice Willis Van Devanter, one of the "Four Horsemen" who consistently opposed the Roosevelt administration, retired. Once Hugo Black replaced Van Devanter, a majority on the Supreme Court began to defer to executive branch policies. The crisis was over.

The New Deal introduced a paradigmatic shift in American politics, greatly broadening the scope of federal authority and realigning electoral politics for more than a generation in its wake. It also ushered in a new era for the Department of Justice and Attorney General. Following Cummings's assault on the Court, the Attorney General increasingly became viewed as a partisan advocate of presidential policy. The department's closer relationship to the White House was formalized with the Office of Legal Counsel, established in 1935 and given responsibility for "assisting the Attorney General in his role as legal advisor to the President and the executive branch."[31] Important shifts occurred also in the normative conceptions of the Attorney General's office. In contrast to early Attorneys General who saw themselves playing quasi-judicial roles, Robert Jackson, who served between 1940 and 1941, referred to his role as one of a "partisan advocate" exempt from the "judicial judgment" required of federal judges.[32]

Above all the New Deal forged a practical political alliance between the federal judiciary and the executive branch. Models of strong presidential leadership fit comfortably with a judiciary that narrowed the sphere of its constitutional power and deferred to the elected branches. Roosevelt and Truman appointed the next thirteen Justices to the Supreme Court; all embraced the New Deal jurisprudence that political liberalism could best be advanced by judicial deference to presidential policy direction.[33] Looking back on this period, Supreme Court scholar Alexander Bickel wrote, "far from entering new claims to judicial supremacy, the Court seemed at times to forget even its independence."[34] Political scholars Benjamin Ginsberg and Mark Silverstein are more blunt, calling the New Deal judiciary "an essentially second-line branch of government, subservient to executive politics."[35]

The story of the Warren Court's transformation of New Deal jurisprudence into an engine for judicial activism is familiar.[36] The Court systematically loosened the rules of standing and justiciability, while simultaneously expanding the types of judicial remedies available to political litigants.[37] Linked to the post–New Deal scrapping of judicially made rules in favor of more open-ended "balancing of interests" jurisprudence, the Court moved beyond merely supporting government action: it began requiring the government to act in a variety of new policy areas such as school desegregation, reapportionment, criminal justice, First Amendment protection, and abortion.[38] Although the Burger and Rehnquist Courts exercised judicial power differently than the Warren Court, neither revamped post–New Deal open-ended jurisprudence or closed avenues to political litigants.[39] New Justices, of both liberal and conservative stripe, appear to have accepted the idea that whatever else a decision may settle, leaving the door open to future litigation is wise. Rather than proving a temporary phenomenon of Earl Warren's tenure as Chief Justice, the Supreme Court's independent political role has become institutionalized.[40]

Less well known is the Justice Department's role in the development of the new judicial politics, and the consequences of that role for the alliance that emerged between the executive and judicial branches. The executive branch originally supported—even drove—the Supreme Court in its new political role. As long as the ideological direction of the judiciary harmonized, or at least did not conflict with the policy agenda of the executive, the Attorney General welcomed judicial activism of the Warren Court variety. The Justice Department pursued in the courts social policy objectives not readily obtainable in Congress. By this means, Presidents could effect liberal reforms in areas such as civil rights and criminal justice with a minimum expenditure of political capital. An added benefit was the ability to deflect criticism onto the Court.

The Justice Department's expanded use of *amicus curiae* briefs during this period reflects the executive's use of the Supreme Court as a back door for its political agenda. Figure 5.1 clearly traces the explosion in government use of *amicus* briefs since 1950.

As recently as 1950, the Justice Department filed only a single *amicus* brief. Since 1980, it has filed on average more than thirty-nine briefs per term. The Justice Department has employed *amicus* briefs to advocate positions on political issues as diverse as desegregation, reapportionment, the exclusionary rule, school prayer, and abortion. As noted earlier, these briefs carry extraordinary weight with the Court, and the Justice Department enjoys great success as *amicus*.

By urging the Court to plunge into political litigation, the Justice Department helped encourage the growth of a new judicial lobby industry. From traditional coalitions such as the National Association for the Advancement of Colored People (NAACP) and the American Civil Liberties Union (ACLU) to new partnerships such as the Washington Legal Foundation and National Resources De-

Figure 5.1. **Justice Department *Amicus* Participation in Supreme Court, 1950–1988**

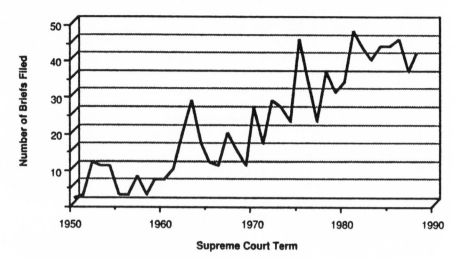

Source: *Annual Report of the Solicitor General* (1926–1989).

fense Council, interest groups on the left and right have come to see the courts as the institutions best able to serve their interests.[41] By expanding their stock of political prescriptives, the courts have delivered to these groups political benefits previously available only through the executive and legislative branches.[42] In return, the judiciary has gained a new, independent source of political support. Able to rely on interest groups during policy clashes with the other branches, the judiciary is now in a better position to sustain a political stance separate from the other branches.[43]

The development of a more independent judicial politics explains why recent Republican administrations have been frustrated with the federal judiciary and have felt compelled to use the Justice Department as an instrument against it. The Nixon and Reagan administrations faced a sitting judiciary whose ideological outlook not only differed from their own, but could also bring greater political clout to bear in conflicts with the executive.

The Alliance and Civil Rights

The modified political relationship between the executive and judicial branches and its impact on the Justice Department are most manifest in the area of civil rights. The department's entrance into the modern civil rights debate was precipitated politically by the Truman administration. With Truman's Fair Deal in electoral trouble, the administration sought a strategy that would net black votes in the important swing states of the North without jeopardizing white Democratic support in the South. Judicializing the civil rights struggle presented the perfect solution.

In 1947 Truman's Presidential Committee to Study Civil Rights recommended using the Justice Department to promote civil rights reform more aggressively.[44] Only three months earlier, the NAACP had tried to enlist Justice Department support in a series of restrictive covenant cases, but neither Attorney General Tom Clark nor Solicitor General Philip Perlman was interested. In light of the administration's deteriorating electoral situation and the Civil Rights Committee recommendation, Clark changed his mind.[45]

After conferring with Truman, Clark ordered the Justice Department to file a brief supporting the NAACP position in *Shelly v. Kraemer* (1948).[46] This was the first time the United States entered a civil rights case between private litigants. The brief, arguing for the broad elimination of all racial discrimination, was a piece of advocacy that dropped all pretense of being objective. Philip Elman, the Deputy Solicitor General who handled civil rights cases between 1944 and 1961, recalls:

> Truman's Gallup poll ratings at the time were very low; it looked as though whoever was going to run against him in 1948, probably Dewey, would beat him badly. Tom Clark was Attorney General, and both he and Perlman (the Solicitor General) were political animals, very much aware of the Negro vote. . . . I don't know exactly what happened. Probably Tom Clark made the decision after checking with Truman. In any event, I was told by Perlman, on extremely short notice, to start drafting an *amicus* brief in *Shelly v. Kraemer*. . . . The brief we wrote contained a lot of high-blown rhetoric about liberty and equality and so on . . . but also letters from various government agencies and departments. It was not an ordinary brief. It was a statement of national policy. We were showing the flag; we were expressing an authoritative, forthright position that all government officials would be bound by.[47]

The thrust of the government's argument was that restrictive covenants, though private acts of discrimination, were unenforceable by government officials, including the courts. To add weight to the argument, both the Solicitor General and Attorney General signed the brief. The Supreme Court decided the cases unanimously in favor of the government's position.[48]

In the four years following *Shelly*, the Justice Department aligned itself with the NAACP in at least four more major civil rights cases. In each, the Court supported the department's pro-rights stance.[49] Of greatest interest as far as Justice was concerned was the brief in *Henderson v. United States* (1950). The case challenged an Interstate Commerce Commission ruling that upheld segregation on trains in interstate transit. In the lower court, the Justice Department successfully argued the case on behalf of the ICC. On appeal to the Supreme Court, it switched sides. Lawyers for the ICC argued alone in favor of "separate but equal." The Justice Department not only confessed error with respect to the lower court's decision in the ICC case but, for the first time, it asked the Supreme Court to overrule *Plessy v. Ferguson*[50] on Fourteenth Amendment grounds. The Supreme Court, though unprepared to touch on the constitutional issue, invalidated the railroad's practice on the statutory grounds suggested by the department.

The Justice Department's partnership with the federal courts on civil rights continued during the Eisenhower administration. Although Attorney General Brownell has received credit for pushing the administration against Eisenhower's will into support of the civil rights movement, some more recent scholars have suggested that Eisenhower played a larger hidden-hand role than early accounts detected.[51] One recent study avers that, by depicting Brownell as a maverick, Eisenhower was able to use his Attorney General as a lightning rod for what were really his own civil rights policies. In this way, Eisenhower was able to reap political accolades in the North for civil rights reforms, as well as to disassociate himself from those reforms to maintain Southern congressional support for other elements of his program.[52]

Whatever the impetus, the Eisenhower Justice Department filed the key brief in the seminal civil rights case, *Brown v. Board of Education* (1954); the administration appointed Earl Warren and William Brennan, the staunchest supporters of civil rights on the Court; the Justice Department pushed the 1957 and 1960 Civil Rights Acts through Congress; and Eisenhower sent federal troops into the South to implement judicial integration orders. Clearly, the administration, with or without Eisenhower's personal stamp, was committed to the civil rights reform agenda that the Supreme Court had embarked upon.

The Justice Department originally entered *Brown v. Board of Education* in 1952 during the Truman administration.[53] The department's brief, signed by Attorney General McGranery, argued flatly that *Plessy* should be overturned. More important, it offered the Court a way out of a sticky remedial dilemma. Although a majority on the 1952 Court wished to rule segregation unconstitutional, the same majority did not exist for providing the constitutional remedy—immediate integration—favored by the NAACP.[54] Southern opposition would have regarded an order requiring immediate integration as an open invitation to mass noncompliance, making it impossible to enforce. What the Court needed was a way to recognize the constitutional principle of desegregation while splitting it from the argument for immediate relief.

One illustration of the incestuous relationship between the Justice Department and the Supreme Court was Philip Elman's status as a law clerk and close friend of Justice Frankfurter prior to becoming Deputy Solicitor General. Elman says that throughout the civil rights cases, Frankfurter kept him apprised of Court dynamics and offered advice about how to sway individual Justices in particular cases.[55] Relying on Elman's inside information, the government's brief in *Brown* joined the NAACP in arguing for a reversal of *Plessy*, but abandoned the NAACP's position on relief. Instead the government suggested that district courts be given a "reasonable period of time" to implement the decision: in other words, "with all deliberate speed." Assistant Attorney General Lee Rankin first used the phrase during oral arguments in the *Brown* case.[56]

The purely political nature of the Supreme Court–Justice Department alliance is illustrated by the fact that attorneys arguing the government's case in *Brown* considered their own brief to be legally flawed. Elman said the government's position "was entirely unprincipled, it was just plain wrong as a matter of constitutional law, to suggest that someone whose personal constitutional rights were being violated should be denied relief."[57] The Justice Department adopted its position out of pure pragmatism: it knew neither Jackson nor Frankfurter would vote for an outcome that required the Court to order immediate relief. The Solicitor General's office was "simply counting votes," Elman said.[58]

Unable to reach an immediate decision in *Brown*, the Court scheduled it for reargument the following year. Between its first hearing in 1952 and its reargument in 1954, Eisenhower was elected President, Brownell was appointed Attorney General, and Earl Warren became the Chief Justice. Warren's role in forging a unanimous Court in the *Brown* decision is well documented.[59] Of perhaps equal value was Brownell's decision to file a second *amicus* brief. When the Court set the case for reargument, it issued a special invitation to the Attorney General to file a brief and present oral argument.

The Eisenhower administration split on whether to continue support for the Court's civil rights innovations.[60] Inside the Justice Department, Assistant Attorney General Lee Rankin and the career attorneys in the Solicitor General's office contended that an invitation from the Court could not be refused. Deputy Attorney General William Rogers, on the other hand, maintained that an invitation could be declined. Refusing to file another brief would be diplomatic silence, he argued. Leaving the Court to decide the issue based on the law would spare the administration entanglement in a controversy sure to erode congressional support.[61]

After discussions with Eisenhower, Brownell directed the Solicitor General to file a second brief. It is unclear how much arm-twisting Brownell performed on the President.[62] In letters to Governor Byrnes of South Carolina, Eisenhower depicted himself as a Chief Executive whose hands were tied:

> I have been compelled to turn over to the Attorney General and his associates full responsibility in the matter. He and I agreed that his brief would reflect the conviction of the Department of Justice as to the legal aspects of the case . . . it is clear that the Attorney General had to act according to his own conviction and understanding.[63]

The department's second brief limited itself to specific points the Court asked it to address and did not formally restate a position on overruling *Plessy*. With the title of "supplemental brief," however, the second document implicitly endorsed the same arguments made in 1952. When asked his opinion on *Plessy*, Lee Rankin, who argued the case for the Justice Department, informed the Court that the government supported "the position previously taken by the United States."[64]

The Court unanimously opined that separate is unequal, overturning *Plessy*, and permanently changing race relations in the United States. It scheduled another hearing for argument on the remediation issue for the following term. In its third brief, the Justice Department restated its position—one rejected by all other parties but adopted by the Court—for flexibility in setting down a timetable for desegregation. The Justice Department's three briefs were crucial to the outcome of *Brown*. Between them, they offered a remedial compromise that allowed the Court to decide the constitutional issue of segregation. They also provided a clear statement of political support endorsed by a Democratic and a Republican administration.

Opponents of the Court's *Brown* decision criticized Brownell's actions. The *Times-Dispatch* of Richmond, Virginia, for example, characterized the decision as the "Warren–Brownell coup."[65] For his part, Brownell reaffirmed political support for the Court in a series of speeches. In an address to the American Bar Association entitled "The Supreme Court: Symbol of Orderly, Stable and Just Government," Brownell said that as "national umpire of all great legal controversies the Court was bound on occasion to make unpopular decisions." However, he described attacks on the Court's institutional integrity as "unfair, irresponsible and uninformed . . . anyone who tears the Court down does as much harm as tearing down the Congress, the executive branch, and for that matter all the government."[66]

In the decade after 1954, the Warren Court formed an active partnership with the Justice Department in further expanding the rights enunciated in *Brown*. In a 1968 study Robert Dixon thoroughly documents the Justice Department's alliance with the Court in revolutionizing civil rights policies nationwide. Dixon concludes: "Within the governmental framework concerned with civil rights the attorney general and his Department of Justice have been dominant, if not all-important."[67]

During Eisenhower's second term, the Justice Department filed *amicus* briefs in four desegregation cases in Arkansas (including the Little Rock controversy that precipitated the confrontation with Governor Orval Faubus); three in Tennessee; seven in Louisiana; and one in New York.[68] Then in 1957, the department embarked on a legislative campaign to codify strides in its legal strategy. It became the driving force behind both the 1957 and 1960 Civil Rights Acts.[69]

The 1957 act is particularly noteworthy because the Justice Department received major new powers from it, and because Brownell went to extraordinary lengths to strengthen the measure.[70] Originally, the Justice Department drafted four civil rights bills: the first created the Civil Rights Commission; the second established the Civil Rights Division in the Justice Department; the third granted the department new authority to bring suits enforcing voting rights; and the fourth gave the department injunctive authority to protect other undefined civil rights.

The first two bills aroused minimal argument. The second two, especially the measure giving the Attorney General broad authority to initiate public school desegregation suits, were controversial. Conservative legal scholars such as Alexander Bickel attacked the Justice Department proposal. Bickel expressed concern that:

> The Attorney General would gain and share with the courts, at his option, powers entirely free of the imprecise safeguards implicit in our reliance on private litigating initiative. It would be the Attorney General, in the exercise of a discretion for whose control no machinery exists or is easily conceived, who would chose to make existing rules of constitutional law effective.[71]

Although the Attorney General later received nearly identical authority under the 1964 Civil Rights Act, Eisenhower was unwilling to support the Brownell quest for such authority in 1956. Consequently, the White House cleared the first two bills for submission to Congress but rejected the latter two.[72]

According to historian John Anderson, Brownell transmitted the first two bills openly to Congress. He then arranged privately for the second two to be introduced separately and then later to have them consolidated in committee along with the administration's bills.[73] In this devious way, Brownell hoped to obtain the strong enforcement powers he wanted in a bill with Eisenhower's name on it. Brownell's attempted coup backfired, however, nearly defeating the entire civil rights package. When Congress began debating the consolidated proposals, Eisenhower withdrew his support from the controversial bill. Without the President's backing, the measure was doomed to go down to defeat by southern opposition.

Senate Majority Leader Lyndon Johnson was key in crafting a compromise.[74] The bill Congress eventually passed in 1957 retained provisions for the Civil Rights Commission and Civil Rights Division within Justice, and authorized voting rights litigation. Absent were the provisions for injunctive power in discrimination cases. Anderson thus concludes his account of the episode: "In his astonishingly bold tactics, Brownell had deliberately jeopardized his own office to get this set of powerful bills introduced; it appeared that he had, as a Cabinet member, overstepped the line that divided initiative from insubordination."[75]

Recent scholarship challenges Anderson's analysis. Political historian Richard Ellis writes, one should be careful "not to exaggerate the differences between Eisenhower and Brownell." The evidence does not support the claim that Brownell acted on his own to "slyly defy Eisenhower's wishes." Instead, "Eisenhower and Brownell were in close agreement" on all of the Justice Department's recommendation except the final provision. Even there, Eisenhower authorized Brownell to seek the authority because the President "knew how deeply

(Brownell) felt about it."[76] When the administration's bill became controversial Eisenhower did not abandon his policy or his Attorney General. Instead, "Eisenhower was faced with a tradeoff between using Brownell as a lightning rod and getting civil rights legislation through Congress." According to Ellis, Eisenhower shifted public responsibility to his Attorney General to preserve his personal popularity and obtain policies substantially his own.[77]

Whether the administration's civil rights policies reflected Eisenhower's or Brownell's beliefs, the Attorney General bore the brunt of southern anger. Characteristic was a *Times-Dispatch* editorial heralding Brownell's resignation in 1957:

> No tears are being shed for the retirement of Herbert Brownell, Jr., as Attorney General. The frightful mess the South, and the country, are in is probably as much his responsibility as that of any living man. . . . It was Brownell who journeyed to California in 1953 to confer with Earl Warren before that worthy was named Chief Justice of the United States. It was Brownell who pressed the government's case in the integration suits before Chief Justice Warren, and told the nine justices that it was their "duty" to rule out segregation in the public schools. It was Brownell who either drafted or sponsored the unspeakable "civil rights" bill, as originally introduced in Congress, and who convinced President Eisenhower that it was a mild and moderate piece of legislation. And finally, it was Brownell who had Eisenhower's ear throughout the Little Rock affair, and who is generally credited with persuading the President that Governor Faubus should be put in his place with bayonets.[78]

Clearly, Brownell was central in the elaboration of the administration's civil rights policies. Yet Eisenhower could have overruled his Attorney General at any point; he chose not to. Moreover, the administration's policies changed little after Brownell resigned. Under William Rogers, the Justice Department continued to file *amicus* briefs supporting desegregation and began to file voting rights actions pursuant to new authority under the 1957 act. Rogers pushed through Congress the 1960 Civil Rights Act expanding Justice Department authority in voting rights cases, reestablishing the Civil Rights Commission, and empowering the Justice Department to bring criminal charges against individuals willfully obstructing federal court orders. This final provision clearly was aimed at avoiding future Little Rocks.[79]

During the administration of John F. Kennedy, the activist partnership between the Department of Justice and the Supreme Court in civil rights expanded still further. Kennedy committed his administration to a broad civil rights agenda during the presidential campaign. While black votes aided in Kennedy's election, once in office he realized southern congressional support was necessary for a governing coalition. He was therefore reluctant to make civil rights an integral part of his legislative agenda. Instead, like Eisenhower and Truman, Kennedy left his administration's civil rights policy almost exclusively to the Department of Justice.[80]

As Attorney General, Robert Kennedy demonstrated his support for civil rights almost from the outset. He chose a Georgia reapportionment case, *Gray v. Sanders* (1963), to make the Attorney General's traditional maiden appearance before the Supreme Court.[81] He delivered his first public speech as Attorney General in Georgia, the heart of the Old South; the title was "Civil Rights and Respect for the Law." In the speech, Kennedy defended the Supreme Court's desegregation decisions and touted Justice Department's efforts to implement them.[82]

The Kennedy Justice Department intensified voting rights litigation under the 1957 act, filing forty-five cases in the first three years in contrast to the ten cases entered during the last three years of the Eisenhower administration.[83] The department also stepped up intervention in desegregation suits as *amicus curiae*. Moreover, in many highly controversial cases such as the New Orleans school crisis of 1961, the integration of the University of Mississippi in 1962, and the Alabama school emergency in 1963, the Justice Department, though appearing in court as *amicus*, acted as the primary party in the litigation.[84]

The Kennedy Justice Department used *amicus curiae* briefs to advocate broad policy objectives in other civil rights areas as well. The department filed briefs supporting Supreme Court decisions that banned discrimination in public facilities, interstate commerce, private facilities accommodating the public, and in laws dealing with sexual and matrimonial relations between races.[85] Perhaps the best-known examples of the Justice Department's willingness to push the judiciary further into the "political thicket," as Justice Frankfurter referred to it, were its briefs in *Baker v. Carr* (1962) and *Reynolds v. Sims* (1964) urging the Court to intervene in the reapportionment fray.[86]

The Justice Department's intervention in the reapportionment cases was even more crucial than it had been in *Brown*. Unlike desegregation, reapportionment had no momentum and no real constituency. Even the Court was severely divided over the issue. The liberal majority not only had to overrule its recent opinion in *Colegrove v. Green* (1946),[87] it also had to confront Justice Frankfurter, who had been the intellectual force behind *Brown*, but who was violently opposed to the Court's intervention in reapportionment. The fact that Archibald Cox, whose own jurisprudence was similar to Frankfurter's, argued the government's position, clearly aided Justices in the middle who had to answer Frankfurter's concerns about politicizing the Court. In addition to Frankfurter, the Justice Department's mediation was vital in persuading at least two members of the Court—Potter Stewart and Tom Clark—to join the majority.[88]

Navasky makes the point that government intervention in the reapportionment cases mattered in a broad psychological way, making the cases more palatable to the Court and indicating political support for an idea whose time had come.[89] Even Cox, who initially resisted the department's "one man, one vote" position, later acknowledged the pivotal nature of the government's role. In a memorandum to Robert Kennedy, Cox wrote: "It is no exaggeration to recognize among

Figure 5.2. **Desegregation Cases Filed or Supported by the Department of Justice, 1959–1968**

Fiscal Year	United States as Party	United States as Amicus
1959	0	1
1961	2	5
1963	7	4
1964	3	5
1965	9	2
1966	5	8
1967	56	0
1968	20	5

Source: Annual Report of the Attorney General (1968), 109.

ourselves that we played the most important role in *Baker v. Carr*, and our brief and argument may even have determined the result."[90]

The unusually high level of *amicus* activity by the Justice Department during the 1962 and 1963 Court terms (see Figure 5.1) stems directly from its interventions in reapportionment and civil rights cases. Ten of the nineteen *amicus* briefs filed in 1962 and fifteen of the twenty-five filed in 1963 involved race discrimination or legislative reapportionment cases.[91] That the Justice Department's "pro-rights" position prevailed in every case, often after the Court had solicited a brief, illustrates how close the alliance between the Court and Justice Department had become during the period.

The Kennedy Justice Department also moved to codify its new civil rights role by pushing legislation that would give it statutory authority to bring suit as a direct party in discrimination cases. Indeed, the dramatic decline in *amicus* filings beginning with the Supreme Court's 1964 term is the result of the Justice Department receiving that authority under the 1964 Civil Rights Act.[92] The act, drafted under the direction of Attorney General Kennedy, vested massive new authority in the department. Of its ten titles, six gave new authority to the Attorney General.[93] By giving the department the power to initiate discrimination suits rather than merely react as *amicus*, the 1964 act greatly increased the department's ability to forge civil rights policy through litigation.[94] The increasing number and changing nature of desegregation suits that the Justice Department filed before and after passage of the act demonstrate its impact on the department's civil rights role (see Figure 5.2).

The Kennedy–Johnson Justice Department also pushed through Congress the Voting Rights Act of 1965.[95] This act, in effect, made the Attorney General an election supervisor for most southern states by allowing him to suspend any law or practice used to determine voting eligibility, and requiring states covered by the act to clear changes in voting practices. It allowed the Attorney General extraordinary policing power over political turf traditionally controlled by state and local governments.[96] Together, the 1964 and 1965 acts represented congressional recognition of what had become obvious both to advocates and opponents of the civil rights movement: the Attorney General, in partnership with the judiciary, had become the nation's chief civil rights policymaker.

Throughout the 1950s and 1960s, the federal judiciary reciprocated its relationship with the Justice Department by recognizing and expanding federal authority to litigate policy issues. In the New Orleans school desegregation cases, for example, the district court invited the department to file a brief or "initiate such further proceedings as may be appropriate." The case had already been decided on its merits, and all that remained was the question of remedial enforcement of the court's injunction. When attorneys for the state objected that *amicus* interveners are normally restricted to presenting advisory briefs, not allowed to request orders or initiate other types of proceedings, the judge responded:

> It is said that the government has no interest. Of course, it has no proprietary or financial interest to protect. . . . But that does not mean that the Justice Department of the United States can have nothing to do with the administration of justice or that it must remain indifferent when the judgments of federal courts are sought to be subverted by state action. . . . The absence of specific statutory authority is of itself no obstacle.[97]

The Fourth Circuit Court of Appeals went even further in *Simkins v. Moses Cone Memorial Hospital* (1963).[98] This case dealt with a challenge to a federal hospital finance law that contained a separate-but-equal provision. The Justice Department filed an *amicus* brief supporting the challenge and attacking the constitutionality of the statute. When defendants objected to the Justice Department's abdication, the court said the Attorney General had plenary control over the government's position in *amicus* filings, even to the point of attacking the constitutionality of the federal government's own statutes.

In *United States v. Cox* (1965), the Fifth Circuit Court of Appeals upheld the Attorney General's absolute discretion in prosecution of federal criminal laws. The appeals court vacated a contempt citation issued by Judge Harold Cox of the district court in Mississippi against Attorney General Katzenbach for refusing to return Grand Jury indictments against civil rights protesters. In rejecting Judge Cox's argument that the Justice Department must prosecute Grand Jury indictments, the Appeals Court said: "It follows as an incident of the separation of powers, that the courts are not to interfere with the free exercise of the discretionary powers of the attorneys of the United States in their control over criminal prosecutions."[99]

When the Attorney General's authority to bring discrimination suits against private parties under Title II of the 1964 Civil Rights Act was challenged, the Supreme Court upheld the act in two landmark cases: *Heart of Atlanta Motel v.*

United States (1964) and *Katzenbach v. McClung* (1964).[100] To do so, however, the Court had to construct a bizarre interpretation of the commerce clause. In *Katzenbach*, the Justice Department brought suit against a small restaurant called Ollie's Barbecue to force desegregation of its facilities. When attorneys for the restaurant argued that it served only local residents and was not involved in interstate commerce, the Justice Department argued, and the Court agreed, that enterprises supplied by interstate commerce were themselves subject to federal regulation.

The Collapse of the Executive-Judicial Alliance

Conservatives eventually began to complain about the alliance between the judiciary and Justice Department. As this occurred, criticism of an "activist" Supreme Court spread quickly to include censure of a "politicized" Attorney General. Robert Kennedy and Nicholas Katzenbach, in particular, were accused of using their offices to further a liberal agenda.[101] As long as the policymaking activities of the executive-judicial alliance focused on the area of civil rights, the brunt of Justice Department criticism came mainly from the South. By the mid-1960s, however, the Justice Department's partnership with the Warren Court began to expand into other areas of social policy. As it did, conservative hostility spread. When Ramsey Clark became Attorney General in 1967, conservative consternation with the Justice Department finally congealed.

Clark inherited the office at a time when antiwar demonstrations and violent social protests were leading to cries for tough law-and-order policies.[102] Despite mounting public pressures, Clark continued to support the criminal justice initiatives by the Warren Court in cases such as *Mapp v. Ohio* (1961),[103] *Gideon v. Wainwright* (1963),[104] *Escobedo v. Illinois* (1964),[105] and *Miranda v. Arizona* (1966).[106] The Justice Department actively supported the Court's criminal justice reforms through its rhetoric and legislative proposals it sent to Congress. As head of the Justice Department's Criminal Division, Clark had initiated the 1964 Criminal Justice Act and 1966 Bail Reform Act. The acts limited the use of bail to detain indigent defendants, restricted the use of preventive pretrial detention, and provided federal funds for legal representation of indigents. Despite public concern over the growing crime rate, Attorney General Clark argued against the imposition of the death penalty, saying the federal government should emphasize "rehabilitation" and the "social causes of crime" rather than punishment.[107]

By 1968, public fears of crime and violence had reached an apex.[108] President Johnson supported the Omnibus Crime Control and Safe Street Act of 1968, a catch-all piece of legislation in an attempt to appease the growing demand for action. Among the act's most controversial provisions were those authorizing the FBI to wiretap without a warrant and allowing federal prosecutors to use evidence obtained in violation of *Miranda*.[109] Attorney General Clark publicly opposed these measures; even after the act's passage, he refused to allow the department to take advantage of the authority it granted.[110]

Administration critics characterized Clark as being "soft on crime," a charge that seemed to gather substance from his decision not to prosecute the Chicago Eight, who led protests at the 1968 Democratic Convention.[111] The law-and-order issue finally gave conservatives a morally acceptable platform from which to attack Justice Department activism. In Congress, there were calls for Clark's ouster and for legislation to remove the Justice Department from presidential control.[112] The administration's legal policies received a vote of no confidence in the form of the Senate's refusal to confirm Abe Fortas to replace Warren as Chief Justice. Clark's unpopularity, Johnson's waning influence as a lame-duck President, and Fortas's close association with the "liberal jurisprudence" of the Warren Court all contributed to his defeat.[113]

At the Republican National Convention in 1968, presidential candidate Richard Nixon pledged to "appoint a new Attorney General to restore order and respect for law . . . and judicial restraint in our federal courts."[114] Nixon's pledge revealed how thoroughly politicized the view of the Attorney General and Justice Department had become. For the first time in its history, partisan control of the Justice Department had become a campaign issue. Also, the first scholarly study of the Attorney General's political functions, *Roles of the Attorney General*, was published the same year by the conservative think tank, American Enterprise Institute.[115]

Richard Nixon's election in 1968 was a watershed in the political relationship between the legal bureaucracy and the federal judiciary. A bond previously marked by shared goals and common interests became marred increasingly by distrust and conflict. As a presidential candidate, Nixon had criticized the Supreme Court's activism and pledged to work for a more "restrained" role for the federal courts. The appointment of his campaign manager, John Mitchell, as Attorney General marked his commitment to honor that promise.[116]

Mitchell's view that the Justice Department was a partisan instrument for pursuing presidential policies became immediately apparent when he announced that the government would reinstate charges against the Chicago Eight. Although the prosecutions themselves were insignificant, the change in policy served as a powerful political statement that the powers of federal law enforcement had changed hands.[117] Within a matter of months, Mitchell also announced that the Justice Department would reverse its policy and begin using its authority under the controversial wiretapping and criminal prosecution provisions of the 1968 Omnibus Crime Control Act.[118] Then in July 1969, the Justice Department sent to Congress a proposal to amend the 1966 Bail Reform Act to allow pretrial detention.[119]

In civil rights too, the department's legal policy shifted.[120] Nixon had built his electoral strategy around capturing the South for the Republican Party. The political calculus of using the courts to pursue the White House's civil rights agenda was reversed. By using the courts Nixon could deliver on his implicit promise to southern conservatives to slow down the pace of civil rights reform, without alienating the moderate element of the Republican coalition by directly opposing racial equity.[121]

During debate over the extension of the 1965 Voting Rights Act, the Justice Department lobbied to lift mandatory preclearance requirements.[122] In litigation before the Supreme Court, Justice Department attorneys challenged judicial authority to impose remedial busing. In the landmark case of *Swann v. Charlotte Mecklenburg Board of Education* (1971), the government for the first time filed an *amicus* brief supporting a local school district and opposing court authority to force integration.[123] The Supreme Court, however, rejected the Justice Department's arguments and upheld the lower court order which required busing in areas where a history of *de jure* segregation existed.

Failing to convert the Supreme Court with its legal arguments, the administration pursued a strategy of nonenforcement. In *Alexander v. Holmes* (1969) the Justice Department switched its support away from black petitioners and instead argued in support of the Mississippi school district petition to defer court-ordered desegregation.[124] When the Supreme Court rejected its argument and ordered immediate desegregation, the Justice Department refused to implement the Court's decision and instead continued to file briefs in other cases asking for implementation delays.[125] The department's switch in the Mississippi case and similar desegregation cases sparked a revolt by career civil rights attorneys. One-fourth of the attorneys in the Civil Rights Division resigned during the first six months of 1970 and all but nine of the seventy-four nonsupervisory attorneys in the division signed a letter to Mitchell protesting the administration's "disregard for clear judicial mandates."[126]

As the administration's frustration with the Court mounted it became increasingly apparent that the Court had new weapons available to it to combat nonenforcement strategies. In *Adams v. Richardson* (1973) the NAACP brought suit against the administration for noncompliance with Title VI of the 1964 Civil Rights Act, which required suspension of federal funds to school districts not showing progress in dismantling segregation.[127] Relying on cases such as *Cox*, the Justice Department argued that law enforcement decisions fell into the "realm of non-reviewable executive discretion." The Court of Appeals for the District of Columbia, however, disagreed. Paring back the authority that judicial opinions had recently expanded, the court labeled the executive's claim of absolute discretion "untenable" and the administration's nonenforcement policy a clear "dereliction of duty reviewable in the courts."[128]

With the aid of the new public law interest groups and a Democratic Congress, the judiciary was able to blunt efforts to retether it to executive branch policy direction. In addition to resisting the administration's civil rights agenda, the Court handed it losses in other major cases. In the *Pentagon Papers* case, the Supreme Court rejected the executive branch's assertion of unreviewable discretion over national security.[129] In the *Keith* case, the Court cited the Fourth Amendment to reject the department's authority under the 1968 Omnibus Crime

Control Act to perform wiretaps without warrants.[130] Furthermore, in a series of separation of powers decisions, the Court restricted presidential veto authority,[131] executive branch impoundment powers,[132] limited claims to executive privilege, and restricted presidential control of the special prosecutor.[133]

Frustrated by the Court's resistance, Attorney General Mitchell launched a rhetorical assault on the judiciary.[134] In a series of speeches he attacked the Warren Court's jurisprudence and called for greater restraint. Addressing the American Bar Association, he admonished judges that "restraint is precisely the quality that most distinguishes a great judge." If judges, who are not elected, he said, "step beyond judgment and substitute their will for the people's will—as expressed through the other branches—then we revert to some form of government other than democracy."[135]

By the early 1970s, conservatives had begun pointing to interest groups as a prime source of the judiciary's new independence.[136] Mitchell's speeches lashed out at these groups also. The judiciary, he said, "can and does work in either direction, those who may be enchanted with the Supreme Court as an instrument of change today would have opposed its actions yesterday and may oppose them again tomorrow." The new breed of public law activists, he argued,

> do violence to our plan of government itself. When it comes to the judiciary, they hope to use it as, in President Roosevelt's words, a "third house of Congress"—but a house not responsible to the people. Such a superlegislature might accomplish short-term results. But when will is thus substituted for judgment, neither the champions of the right nor of the left can benefit for long. What had seemed to be a sophisticated exploitation of the machinery of government would, in reality, turn the clock back hundreds of years to a day when the law was what the King said it was.[137]

The widening schism between the judiciary and the administration was further illustrated by the administration's heightened emphasis placed on ideology in judicial selections. The administration invested more time than any previous one in screening lower court appointments. Deputy Attorney General Richard Kleindienst personally headed up the selection process.[138] Through the appointment of "strict constructionists" to the Supreme Court, the administration planned to sow the seeds for a judicial counter-revolution.[139] During President Nixon's first term, two vacancies opened on the Court. Warren Burger's appointment to replace Chief Justice Warren won easy confirmation. But the nominations of conservative Clement Haynesworth and Harold Carswell to fill the seat vacated by Fortas were seen by lawmakers and interest groups as a direct challenge to the Court's independence. Both Haynesworth and Carswell were critical of Warren Court jurisprudence. Organized labor and civil rights groups united to defeat their nominations and the administration was compelled to appoint Harry Blackmun, a political moderate, instead.[140]

The fact that the Nixon administration was able to make four appointments to

the Supreme Court (including the Chief Justice) without winning judicial deference to its policy agenda illustrates how fundamental the change to the executive-judicial relationship had been.[141] The Nixon administration also realized the
impact of the new judicial politics on the Justice Department and legal
policymaking bureaucracy. The tradition of the Attorney General as a quasi-
judicial legal advisor had evaporated; in its place was a powerful policymaking
post. Presidential candidates saw the Attorney General's office as one of the
election spoils which was to be used for partisan gain.

Nixon's campaign pledges, the Justice Department's reversal of law enforcement policies, and Mitchell's rhetorical attack on Supreme Court jurisprudence
reflect the new understanding of the Justice Department's role. Complaints by
opponents of the Nixon administration about politicization of Justice sounded
only like the familiar protestations of the party out of power. No less a figure
than William Rehnquist, an Assistant Attorney General at the time, defended the
new partisanship at Justice. In a 1970 speech titled "The Old Order Changeth,"
Rehnquist said, "the basic charge made by the 'outs,' as I understand it, is that
the 'ins'—the Republicans under Attorney General Mitchell—have 'politicized'
the Department of Justice." There is truth to the charge, he said, continuing:

> That there should not have been considerable changes in the department's
> policies, would be unthinkable under any meaningful system of two-party
> government. I am sure that the policies of law enforcement, just as other types
> of governmental policies, are generally cyclical in nature, and your generation,
> if not mine, will undoubtedly live to witness departures from the policies of the
> present administration of the Department of Justice, and doubtless departures
> from those departures. Each of us retains his right to freely criticize, oppose,
> and vote at every opportunity against policies or changes of policy of which he
> does not approve. But it is a denial of the fundamental assumptions of govern-
> ment to suggest that John Mitchell ought not to have been a different Attorney
> General than was Ramsey Clark.[142]

Depoliticizing Justice

Watergate forced the nation to reexamine the new political role assumed by the
Justice Department in American government. Without the scandal, the new
norms of partisanship might have been firmly established. The department's
involvement in Watergate, however, led many to agree with former Justice Goldberg, who said bluntly: "Justice and politics do not mix and should not mix."[143]

Congressional response to Watergate primarily took the form of proposals for
structural changes and increased oversight of the Justice Department and its
activities.[144] The FBI, in particular, became the focus of heightened congressional scrutiny after revelations that it secretly wiretapped administration ene-
mies.[145] While constitutional concerns blocked radical reforms of the sort
advanced by Senator Ervin, others, less radical, were instituted. In addition to

Congress's establishment of the Independent Prosecutor's Office and the Senate's passage of the Bentsen amendment, the executive embarked on its own series of reforms.

President Ford pledged to appoint an Attorney General on the basis of professional qualifications and to avoid individuals that were partisan activists.[146] In naming Edward Levi, he promoted the first legal scholar to the office since Harlan Stone had been selected by President Hoover in the wake of the Teapot Dome scandal. The impact of Levi's appointment on normative views of the office cannot be underestimated.[147] Even the British publication *The Economist* commented, saying that it symbolized renewed commitment to a nonpartisan Justice Department and to treating it "differently from other Cabinet departments."[148]

Before accepting the appointment, Levi reached an understanding with President Ford about the "independent role" he thought the Attorney General should play. In particular, Levi promised to resign if the President ever ordered him to not prosecute a case he deemed worthy.[149] Levi stated in his first address as Attorney General that the "law is not an instrument of partisan purpose and it is not an instrument to be used in ways that are careless of the higher values."[150] He later reiterated his resolve to root out partisan politics. "There is no half-heartedness in our efforts to achieve and maintain a Department of the highest professional competence, free of partisan purpose," he said.[151]

Levi prohibited Justice Department personnel from participating in the 1976 presidential campaign or other high-level partisan activities, and he issued strict new investigative guidelines. In 1975, he created the Office of Professional Responsibility to investigate and prosecute allegations of misconduct by Justice Department personnel. He also tried to limit partisan influence over the appointment of judges by insisting judges be selected on the basis of merit and professional competence.[152] With the exception of John Paul Stevens's appointment to the Supreme Court in 1975, Levi had virtually a free hand in judicial nominations. As a result, 21 percent of the administration's district court posts went to Democrats, the highest percentage of judgeships ever granted members of the opposition party.[153]

At the same time as he de-emphasized the Justice Department's partisan role, Levi played up its role as a "ministry of justice," a reference to European institutions responsible for judicial administration.[154] Levi was a prominent presence at the Pound Conference on judicial administration and, in 1976, he appointed a special committee, chaired by Solicitor General Bork, to follow up on the conference's recommendations.[155] In addition, Levi established a new Federal Justice Research Fund to find ways to improve judicial administration and efficiency.[156]

Despite his determination to reestablish integrity and impartiality in the Justice Department, however, Levi did not contemplate insulating it from presidential policy direction.[157] For Levi, the two were separate and distinct considerations. "Independence," in his mind, meant not that the Attorney General should make policy choices in a vacuum but only that unethical or improper influences should be eliminated. He insisted on drawing the "distinction between partisanship—the manipulation of law enforcement for political advantage—and the interaction of law and policy."[158]

Consequently, Levi had no qualms about White House ideology influencing law enforcement decisions. The department's policies, especially in controversial areas such as criminal justice and civil rights, continued to adhere to the tenor of the administration's policy agenda. Above all, Levi's views led him to oppose post-Watergate efforts to institutionally restructure the department and separate it entirely from the President's control.[159] Instead, he insisted that increased congressional oversight and "a morality of appropriate behavior" were all that were needed to restore the integrity of the Justice Department. Moral behavior—an "even-handed approach"—would deter corruption and misconduct while still permitting government law enforcement policies to be informed by the proper "governmental processes which govern the United States."[160]

The Carter administration was less sanguine about the salutary effect of appointing moral individuals to head the Justice Department. During the campaign, Jimmy Carter promised to make "as far as constitutionally possible, an independent Department of Justice."[161] The promise reflected idealism common in the rhetoric of the time and appealed to post-Watergate America. But it was blind to changes that had occurred in the American political system and their implications for the Justice Department. A significant number of political policy areas had become judicialized by 1976; a pledge to insulate the Justice Department from White House control was tantamount to erasing the most effective means of exerting presidential influence in those areas.

Griffin Bell's nomination as Attorney General in 1977 made clear the nature of the new judicial politics and their impact on the Department of Justice. A former federal judge with a distinguished professional career, Bell should have achieved easy confirmation by a Senate controlled by the President's own party. Bell's civil rights record and conservative views on the federal judiciary, however, focused nationwide debate on his nomination.

Confirmation hearings of Attorneys General used to be perfunctory events. Prior to 1952, Attorneys General were confirmed by the Judiciary Committee in executive session with little or no formal testimony.[162] Not until Robert Kennedy's nomination in 1960 did a special-interest group appear at a confirmation hearing. [163] It was not until after Watergate, during the confirmation hearings of Richard Kleindienst in 1972, that a group opposed confirmation.[164] At Levi's confirmation hearing, five groups testified, four adversely.[165]

In the first-ever televised hearings, Bell's nomination drew fire from the political left and right. More than two dozen interest groups testified; twenty-one opposed him.[166] Groups on the left felt betrayed because Carter had not nominated a more liberal Attorney General. The NAACP, the National Conference of Black Lawyers and the Black Economic Development Conference testified against Bell based on the judge's civil rights record.[167] A group called Citizens for Class Action Lawsuits and the National Lawyers Guild opposed confirmation based on Bell's "judicial philosophy."[168] As a district court judge, Bell had questioned the constitutionality of class-action suits and spoken out against the expansion of judicial remedies.[169] He thus presented a significant threat to the new judicial politics, which relied on interest group litigation to effect broad policy goals. The problem, Bell later remarked, was that "I thought too many were trying to solve political problems by judicializing them."[170] Some republicans wishing to portray themselves as civil rights champions also saw it as politically opportune to attack Bell. An unlikely coalition between left-wing judicial action groups and moderate Republican Senators, then, comprised the opposition.[171] In the end, Bell was confirmed by a 75 to 21 vote split along partisan and ideological lines. Democrats and conservative Republicans voted for him; moderate Republicans voted against him. Ironically, while adverse testimony to Bell came primarily from liberal interest groups, Senate Democrats found partisan ties strong enough to support the administration's nomination. Republicans split on the nomination along ideological lines. Thus, the Judiciary Committee vote on Bell had all ten Democrats supporting nomination, while three of the five Republicans voted against it. All three voting against were from the GOP's moderate wing—Charles Mathias (Maryland), John Chafee (Rhode Island), and John Heinz (Pennsylvania)—while the two Republicans supporting nomination were both conservative southerners—Strom Thurmond (S. Carolina) and William Scott (Virginia).[172]

The strongest sign of controversy over the new institutional role of the Justice Department was the intervention in the Bell hearings of Common Cause, a widely respected watchdog group that promotes ethics in government. Members argued that the Attorney General should not only cease partisan activities, he "should stop being a political advisor to the President." The "free and unchecked flow of political advice and pressure between the department and the White House must be checked," the group contended.[173]

Once in office, however, Bell allayed concerns expressed by Common Cause and others who wanted to see the Justice Department further insulated from White House politics. Reiterating Carter's campaign promise, Bell pledged to make the department "a neutral zone in government where decisions will be made on the merits free of political interference or influence."[174] Bell made several institutional changes aimed at "depoliticizing" its operations. In 1977, he asked the Office of Legal Counsel to draft a memo outlining the Solicitor General's "traditional independence."[175] The following year, he established a set of "mutually agreed procedures" to channel and limit contact between White House and Justice Department personnel.[176] Bell's experience as a federal judge, moreover, instilled in him particular interest in developing the department's role in judicial administration. In 1977, he established the Office for Improvements in the Administration of Justice (OIAJ). Under Assistant Attorney General Daniel Meador, OIAJ sent several legislative proposals to Congress aimed at improving federal judicial administration. In 1979, Meador's office also proposed a major reorganization of the Department of Justice that envisioned the creation of a new Secretary of Justice to insulate the department's political from its nonpolitical functions.[177]

The most drastic reform initiated by Bell, however, was the creation of the merit selection commissions for judicial nominations. Whether the merit panels actually removed or merely shifted political influence in the judicial selection process has been widely debated,[178] and Bell now concedes he was "disappointed with the politics attending the creation and operation of several of the panels."[179] Meador, who was in charge of establishing the panels, also admits "the White House intervened much too heavily in the entire selection process; they saw appointments primarily in terms of patronage."[180] Though successful in elevating record numbers of women and minorities to the bench, Carter's appointments were just as partisan as those of previous administrations. According to studies by political scientist Sheldon Goldman, the Carter administration appointed the lowest percentage (82 percent) of Democrats to circuit courts, but the number of "party activists" it appointed exceeded every previous administration. Of its district court appointments 92 percent went to Democrats.[181] Nevertheless, the merit commissions set an important precedent toward professionalizing the selection process and removing it from direct political control.[182]

Bell's effort to remove politics from other aspects of the department's work also proved problematic. As discussed earlier, the Justice Department's positions in the *Bakke* and *TVA* cases were both modified after White House intervention. In yet another episode, Bell was pressured to change a legal opinion regarding the use of funds under the Comprehensive Employment Training Act to support programs at church-owned schools. When Carter's Domestic Policy Advisor, Stewart Eizenstat, received wind of the legal dispute, he suggested that Bell should have any opinion on the subject before issuing it. Angered by Eizenstat's attempt to oversee the Attorney General's opinion-writing function, Bell shot Carter a memorandum reminding him of his pledge to keep the department "free of political interference." Bell wrote:

> There is nothing inconsistent with my concept of an independent Attorney General for you to overrule my decision, even on a question of law. However, the notion . . . that I should have given you the opportunity to direct what my legal opinion should be flies in the face of all that we have been trying to do since coming to Washington to rebuild the Department of Justice.[183]

The controversies that sprang up around these isolated incidents of White House intervention nevertheless illustrate the effectiveness of post-Watergate reforms in changing the norms and conventions of the Justice Department. White House politics, as the *Bakke*, *TVA*, and CETA cases illustrate, had not completely disappeared from decision making at the Justice Department. But the scope of influence was significantly reduced. The Justice Department became less vital to White House policymaking strategy and it was "no longer perceived to be on the front lines in enacting the administration's political agenda."[184]

Ford and Carter themselves made possible whatever depoliticization of Justice took place in the wake of Watergate. Both Presidents belonged to the moderate wings of their respective parties, and both were committed to giving the Justice Department greater autonomy. Moreover, both were in office when America's changing international role and its stagflation-ridden economy were absorbing presidential energy. The domestic policy goals of the Ford and Carter White Houses were generally more modest, pragmatic, and less oriented to legal-political issues involving the judiciary.

The activities of the federal courts during the late 1970s also made possible a less politicized atmosphere at the Justice Department. Without reducing the scope of judicial power, the Burger Court entered a period of retrenchment. The focus of judicial politics began to shift away from older policy concerns, such as civil rights and criminal justice, to new ones, such as life-style issues and economic, environmental, and consumer regulation. With the exception of a few highly visible social issues (abortion, for one), recognition of the role of courts in these new policy areas was just beginning to emerge. Recognition of the political implications of new trends in administrative law was particularly late in coming.

On most fronts, the Ford and Carter administrations felt comfortable with policies emanating from the bench. With fewer sources of friction between the executive's policy agenda and the judiciary, the Justice Department served less strategic value to the White House.

The Reagan Administration

Ronald Reagan's election in 1980 ended the new-found comity between the executive and judiciary. The Reagan administration was the first to be elected from the far right of the modern Republican party. Its policy agenda emphasized free-market liberalism and the return of social policy to local control. Renewed appreciation for the role of the federal courts was the basis of much of its policy agenda. As a candidate, Ronald Reagan criticized judicial "intrusions into the political process" and pledged to restore restraint to the federal bench.[185]

During the early 1980s, there was a sense in Washington, D.C. that the Reagan administration was on the brink of ushering in the judicial counterrevolution that never quite materialized during the Nixon years.[186] The administration—especially people appointed to Justice Department positions—possessed a thoroughly politicized view of the law and a sense of mission about how it might be utilized for political reform. Many of the department's political appointees regarded themselves as the vanguard of a new conservative legal movement. It was, said one, "an exciting time to be in Washington and to be involved in remaking the law."[187]

In the context of this view of law and the judicial process, it is not surprising that the Reagan administration dismantled post-Watergate reforms of the Justice Department, calling them "misguided over-reactions"[188] or "deliberate efforts to strip from the executive the means of restoring balance to the federal courts."[189] Reagan's first Attorney General, William French Smith, made clear from the outset that he envisioned the Justice Department would play "an active role in effecting the principles upon which Ronald Reagan campaigned."[190] In speeches, Smith criticized the department's earlier encouragement of judicial activism. "In recent decades, at the behest of private litigants and even the executive branch, federal courts have engaged in judicial policy-making . . . and intervened in areas properly and constitutionally belonging to the other branches," he contended.[191] To restore the proper relationship between the judiciary and other branches, the Reagan Justice Department would:

> . . . support the selection and appointment of federal judges who recognize the limits of judicial power and the virtues of judicial restraint. We will review our litigation efforts across the board and bring our concern about judicial restraint to bear in deciding what cases to bring and what appeals to prosecute. The arguments lawyers from the department will make in court—whether as plaintiff, defendant, or *amicus*—will consistently reflect an awareness of the vital importance of judicial restraint in our democratic system and an effort to secure its implementation.[192]

During his first year in office, Smith dissolved the merit selection commissions and reasserted the Justice Department's centralized role in the recruitment and screening of judicial nominees. Centered in the newly formed Office of Legal Policy, the administration's selection process relied on personal interviews and extensive investigations of candidates' written work to ensure ideological compatibility.[193] Consequently, according to studies by Goldman, less than 3 percent of the administration's appointments went to non-Republicans. The administration appointed a higher percentage of partisan activists to the lower courts than any other in modern history.[194]

The politicization of Justice Department policy became immediately evident in civil rights litigation. After inquiry by the White House, Smith reversed the Solicitor General's position in the *Bob Jones* case, and the Justice Department wound up attacking the legal position it had successfully urged on the courts since 1970. A similar reversal of policy occurred in *Washington v. Seattle School District* (1982).[195] In this case, voters in the state of Washington had passed an initiative that prohibited local school districts from adopting voluntary busing programs. The department originally entered the case during the Carter administration, when it filed an *amicus* brief in the Ninth Circuit Court of Appeals supporting the school district's challenge to the state law. When Washington appealed to the Supreme Court in 1980, attorneys for the Justice Department filed a brief arguing against granting certiorari. When the case came up for argument in 1982, however, the Reagan administration switched sides. At the behest of the White House, Smith directed the Solicitor General to reverse the Justice Department's position and file a brief supporting the state. The Supreme Court, which called attention to the government's flip-flop in a footnote, rejected the department's argument and upheld the lower court.

The department's clash with the Court on affirmative action marked the most disputatious alteration to civil rights policy. Under Assistant Attorney General William Bradford Reynolds, the Civil Rights Division adopted a "color-blind" approach to the enforcement of civil rights laws.[196] Reynolds was referring to Justice Harlan's famous dissent in *Plessy*: "our Constitution is color-blind, and neither knows nor tolerates classes among its citizens."[197] What it meant to the Civil Rights Division during the Reagan administration was an absolute principle of nondiscrimination, inimical to the race-conscious remedies prescribed by the federal courts and supported by the federal government since the 1960s.

The implications of this approach to discrimination cases became clear in the 1984 case, *Firefighters Local Union v. Stotts*. Before the lawsuit, the fire district had been forced to lay off workers. Under its force reduction plan, white firefighters with seniority lost their jobs ahead of minorities hired more recently under a court-ordered affirmative action program. The white firefighters brought suit, claiming reverse discrimination. The Justice Department filed an *amicus* brief in which it argued that all race conscious remedies violated the Fourteenth Amendment and Title VII of the 1964 Civil Rights Act.[198] Although the Supreme Court agreed that remedies must be balanced against considerations such as bona fide seniority systems, the Civil Rights Division interpreted the Court's decision expansively. Relying on dicta in *Stotts*, the Civil Rights Division asserted that all race conscious reliefs had been invalidated by the Court. It subsequently initiated fifty-one separate suits asking lower courts to set aside affirmative action orders that the department previously had been party in obtaining.[199]

Solicitor General Fried, charged with defending the Justice Department's interpretation of *Stotts* when cases began filtering up to the Supreme Court, openly doubted the wisdom of the policy change. All the Civil Rights Division accomplished by acting so abruptly, he said, "is to scare the Court away from the moderate direction in which it was beginning to move on quotas."[200] Indeed, in the following term the Supreme Court handed down four major decisions explicitly rebuffing the department's position and giving clear support to affirmative action remedies.[201]

Shifts in other areas of Justice Department litigation policies also generated controversy during Reagan's first term. The department adopted a more lenient approach to the enforcement of merger and antitrust laws.[202] In *Oregon v. Elstad* (1985), the department argued that the *Miranda* standards should be loosened.[203] In *United States v. Leon* (1984), it asked the Supreme Court to back away from the exclusionary rule enunciated in *Mapp*.[204] And in *Akron v. Akron Center for Reproductive Health* (1983), the department asked the Court to narrow the abortion right enunciated in *Roe v. Wade* (1973).[205]

At the end of Reagan's first term, Smith resigned the Attorney General's post and Edwin Meese was named to succeed him. Meese's appointment aggravated the rift between the Justice Department and Supreme Court and further polarized a conflict brewing inside the Reagan administration itself over the direction of legal policy.[206] Ronald Reagan's electoral coalition was based on a union between moderate or "establishment" Republicans on the one hand, and the New Right or "movement conservatives" on the other. In the parlance of Beltway politics, the two elements of the coalition were "statists" and "true believers."[207] Their allied rejection of President Carter's policies was sufficient to catapult Reagan into office but, once he was in power, the marriage of these two disparate groups became increasingly fragile.

The split inside the administration manifested itself in the differences between the first and second-term Attorneys General. Smith had graduated from Harvard Law School and served as a partner in a large Los Angeles firm. A major figure in the California Republican establishment whose politics were tuned to the traditional center-right, he was not, in short, cut from revolutionary cloth. His leadership of the Justice Department reflected his statist perspective. Though willing to promote judicial restraint and push the Court in areas of traditional conservative concern, such as criminal justice and antitrust law, he was less willing to move aggressively on the New Right's social agenda, particularly in areas such as abortion and school prayer. During Smith's tenure, Justice Department policy changes in the latter realm usually resulted from White House intervention, not internal initiative.[208]

Smith angered the New Right in 1982 when he attacked conservative proposals for constitutional amendments to overturn Supreme Court decisions on school prayer and abortion.[209] That same year, when *Akron* came before the Court, the Justice Department's *amicus* brief, though asking the Court to enhance state regulatory authority over abortion, explicitly refused to ask the Court to overturn *Roe*.[210] Even in civil rights, Smith was often placed in the position of acquiescing to rather than engineering Justice Department policy changes. In both *Bob Jones* and the *Seattle* busing cases, for instance, White House Counselor Edwin Meese intervened to persuade the Justice Department to switch positions.

By the end of the first term, Attorney General Smith and Solicitor General Rex Lee were under siege from the left and the right. Movement conservatives characterized them as "detached" and "disinterested"; liberals labeled them too "activist."[211] After the department intervened in *Akron*, for example, the *New York Times* printed a column entitled "No Friend of the Court." It described the department's brief as nothing more than a "political tract to appease the disgruntled right wing."[212] On the other hand, James McClellan, editor of the New Right legal journal *Benchmark*, wrote that the Justice Department's position represented "orthodox liberalism" and "slavish submission" to precedent. McClellan criticized the department's litigation policies as overly moderate and called for Lee's resignation as Solicitor General. The Justice Department, he said, "has repeatedly taken positions that are directly at odds with the President's program, and has regularly advanced points of law that are calculated to preserve intact existing case law and the doctrines of the Supreme Court."[213]

The controversy surrounding the Justice Department at the time of Smith's resignation in 1984 reflected not just the department's aggressive advocacy of Reagan administration policy but also the struggle within the administration for ideological control over that policy. Smith had no qualms about his role as the administration's advocate in the courts; his view of what the administration stood for simply conflicted with that of the New Right.

Edwin Meese, on the other hand, embodied the spirit of movement conservatism; during the first term he had become the "guardian of the administration's ideological soul."[214] Unlike Smith, Meese had spent most of his career in the public sector. A former district prosecutor, he was appointed Governor Reagan's legal affairs secretary in 1967 and, two years later, became Reagan's executive assistant. In 1980, Meese headed Reagan's presidential campaign and subsequently became Reagan's chief domestic policy advisor during the first term.

Not surprisingly, Meese's nomination as Attorney General aroused public furor. The post-Watergate reforms had been erected to prevent individuals like Edwin Meese from becoming Attorney General.[215] His confirmation hearings were particularly contentious. More than thirty-three special-interest groups appeared at the confirmation hearings, twenty-seven of which opposed Meese's appointment.[216] Although concerns were raised about Meese's business dealings, it was clear throughout the proceedings that his politics were the real issue. In opening the hearings before the Senate Judiciary Committee, Senator Joseph Biden said, "the question relating to your [Meese's] confirmation is not merely whether you are . . . free of conflict of interest, but whether you are willing to enforce all the laws and the Constitution even though you might have philosophical disagreements with them."[217] Ironically, Democrats on the committee criticized Meese instead of Smith for policy changes in the Justice Department during the first term. Meese was asked repeatedly about his involvement in the *Bob Jones* and the *Seattle* school busing cases, and about White House involvement in reversing the government's decision on affirmative action.[218]

Edwin Meese's tenure as Attorney General proved even more controversial than his appointment and confirmation. Eventually forced from office in 1988, Meese's actions as Attorney General left lingering questions about the Justice Department and its political role. Three years earlier, after taking the oath of office, Meese had explained his view of the Justice Department's relationship to the White House by saying:

> This Department will be fiercely independent in accurately interpreting and upholding the law. But this is not inconsistent with conscientiously and vigorously implementing the President's philosophy, which is the mainstream of today's American political thinking.[219]

With Meese as Attorney General, the Justice Department increasingly came under the influence of New Right groups such as the Heritage Foundation, Federalist Society, and Washington Legal Foundation.[220] In terms of conservative access to the Justice Department, said James McClellan, "the difference between Smith and Meese was like night and day."[221] The increased influence which New Right groups exercised was seen both in the Department's policies and its staffing. Meese energized the leadership of the department with New Right activists and stepped up efforts to "credentialize" young New Right lawyers, placing them in key policymaking positions in the department. Charles Cooper headed up the Office of Legal Counsel, Steven Markman the Office of Legal Policy, John Bolton the Office of Legislative Affairs, Douglas Ginsburg the Antitrust Division, Terry Eastland the Office of Public Affairs, and Steven Calabrisi, David McIntosh, and Kenneth Cribb were Special Assistants.

The rising influence of the New Right inside the Justice Department further exacerbated friction between the Reagan administration and the federal judiciary.[222] Justice Department briefs stepped up the attack on race conscious remedies and other forms of affirmative action.[223] The department also launched an aggressive assault on Supreme Court decisions in social policy areas at the heart of the New Right's agenda. During the second term, for instance, the department filed *amicus* briefs in: *Wallace v. Jaffree* (1985), asking the Court to allow a "moment of silence" (or silent prayer) in public schools;[224] *Bethel School District v. Fraser* (1986), asking the Court to allow restrictions on First Amendment rights of students;[225] and *Thornburgh v. American College of Obst. & Gyn.* (1986) and *Webster v. Reproductive Health Services* (1989), asking the Supreme Court to overturn *Roe*.[226] The increased use and more intense tone of *amicus* advocacy in disputatious social policy cases aroused fresh conflict regarding the Solicitor General's role. Charles Fried came under increasing fire for being too deferential to the administration's policy agenda and for not fulfilling the Solicitor's putative role as the "Tenth Justice."[227]

The administration's efforts to reshape the judiciary through appointments also intensified during the second term. Goldman's studies, for example, indicate that ABA ratings of nominees declined drastically under Meese while the number of party activists increased sharply.[228] After Democrats recaptured the Senate in 1986, the administration had a much harder time winning confirmations. After experiencing no losses during the first term, the administration suffered its first rejection, Jefferson Sessions, in the second term. Another nominee, Daniel Mannion, was narrowly confirmed by a single vote, and several others encountered stiff opposition.[229] In Supreme Court nominations, the ideological drive of the second term was even more evident.[230] During the first term, the Senate unanimously approved Sandra Day O'Connor's appointment to the bench.[231] O'Connor, though a solid conservative, was by no means the choice of the New Right. The Moral Majority and the National Right to Life Committee opposed her confirmation because, as an Arizona legislator, she backed a family planning bill. Instead, O'Connor's nomination fulfilled Reagan's campaign promise to appoint the first woman to the Court. Although she clearly reflected Smith's commitment to judicial restraint, her appointment served symbolic rather than ideological purposes.[232]

The administration's second term appointments to the Supreme Court proved much more controversial. The elevation of William Rehnquist to Chief Justice in 1986 was preceded by fierce Senate debate ending in a sixty-five to thirty-three vote on the Senate floor.[233] Ever since Richard Nixon appointed him in 1972, Rehnquist was the Court's most conservative member and a strong champion of executive power. The creation of a "Rehnquist Court" was heralded as a coup by conservatives and viewed by others as a blow to the Court's independence.[234]

Antonin Scalia's nomination in 1986 to fill the seat vacated by Rehnquist would have drawn more fire had it not occurred in tandem with Rehnquist's.[235] Scalia, a former University of Chicago law professor, was young, intensely conservative, and (as demonstrated by his dissent in *Olson*) a strong supporter of executive power. His elevation to the Court gave Rehnquist an intellectually powerful ally and formed the nucleus of the Court's new conservative majority.[236]

Supporters of the Court's independence, however, struck back in 1987 when the administration tried to fill the seat of retiring Justice Lewis Powell. Two stunning defeats ensued from the nominations of Robert Bork and then Douglas Ginsburg. The political spectacle surrounding Bork's nomination stands as a unique incident in the Court's two-hundred-year history.[237] As a former Solicitor General, law professor at Yale, and Federal Appeals Court judge, Bork's professional credentials were impeccable. That he was nevertheless denied confirmation, in an overtly political campaign, indicates how divisive the administration's legal policies were, and how effectively the Court's interest-group allies could be in rebutting threats to its independence.

The Bork confirmation hearings became the focus of extensive opinion polling and were broadcast live by all three major television networks. More than two hundred groups campaigned for or against the nomination, spending record amounts of money. People for the American Way alone spent over $2 million in media advertising against Bork, while the National Conservative Political Action Committee spent over $1 million supporting him.[238] The intense lobbying even prompted a bill in Congress to require future financial disclosures by judicial lobby groups.[239]

With the nomination cast as a referendum on the integrity and independence of the Supreme Court, Bork became the symbol for the administration's legal policy agenda pursued during the previous seven years. A host of liberal interest groups armed with massive reports on Bork's positions argued against his confirmation. The ABA review committee rendered a split recommendation on his qualifications. And well-known moderate Republicans such as Philip Kurland of the Chicago Law School and William Coleman, a member of Ford's cabinet, testified against Bork.[240] The nomination was reported unfavorably by the Judiciary Committee and was defeated on the Senate floor by a 58 to 42 margin.[241] Republican Senator Arlen Specter, Bork's most ardent inquisitor during the hearings, and five other moderate Republicans abandoned the administration's nominee.[242]

Following Bork's defeat, the administration nominated Douglas Ginsburg, a Bork protégé and favorite of Meese's. Ginsburg, however, was forced to withdraw his name after only ten days, when he disclosed he had used marijuana as a young law professor at Harvard. Finally, the administration's third nominee, Anthony Kennedy, netted unanimous confirmation from the Senate.[243] Appointed by Gerald Ford to the Ninth Circuit Court of Appeals, Kennedy was championed by moderates in the administration. Though politically conservative, he was viewed as a legal technician rather than a judicial philosopher and thus a less risky choice.[244] Ironically, after the Bork affair, Kennedy even found favor with some New Right conservatives in the Senate who earlier had threatened to vote against the administration if it nominated a moderate. As one Republican staff member on the Judiciary Committee explained:

> What you get with Kennedy is predictability. Bork espoused conservative theories of constitutional adjudication, but his intellectual rigidity might take you off in all kinds of directions. You don't know where he might end up. . . . You don't get that with Kennedy. You get someone who is conservative in result not method.[245]

Jurisprudence and Rhetoric

The Bork defeat signaled the high-water mark in the New Right's war on the judiciary. The following year, Meese was forced to resign and the administration appointed a more moderate Republican, Richard Thornburgh, to head the Justice Department. What Meese accomplished as Attorney General, however, should not be underestimated. His rhetorical attack on the Supreme Court initiated a debate that may yet be the Reagan administration's most lasting legacy.[246]

In addresses between 1985 and 1987, Meese launched the most direct attack on the judiciary ever by an Attorney General.[247] The Supreme Court's decisions in *Mapp v. Ohio* and *Miranda*, for instance, Meese said, were "problem children of the law" that "find their origin in the Court rather than the Constitution."[248] In *Roe*, the Court had "abandoned the doctrines of federalism and separation of powers," confusing the Justice's own "moral inclinations with the Constitution."[249] In *Garcia v. San Antonio*, which required states to comply with federal minimum wage laws, Meese said the Court "simply struck federalism right out of the Constitution, or would have done so, if the Supreme Court's constitutional decisions were final and irrevocable."[250]

Meese pinpointed the doctrine of incorporation as the source of the Court's wrong turns in constitutional adjudication. He said the doctrine, however, was symptomatic of a more fundamental problem, which was, in his opinion, that the

Court had simply adopted jurisprudence rooted in interest group politics rather than the Constitution. Supported by the public law interest groups, the Court had judicialized ever-larger areas of public policy. Its opinions, Meese's said, had become:

> mere policy choices rather than articulations of constitutional principle. The voting blocks and the arguments all reveal a greater allegiance to what the Court thinks constitutes sound public policy rather than a deference to what the Constitution, its text and intention, may demand.[251]

Judicial restraint alone, however, could not correct the problems created by the Court's activism. Herein lay the difference between the New Deal effort at court-curbing and the dilemma facing conservative administrations after the Warren–Burger Court era. Earlier periods of activism had been marked by courts acting negatively to strike down legislation. The traditional conservative canons of adjudication which urged the judiciary to avoid political issues and adhere to precedent thus acted as a prophylactic to further negations of majoritarian policy. The modern activist role of the Supreme Court, however, obligated the federal government to act in a number of areas, restricting the room available for the other branches to make policy and entrenching an ongoing role for the courts. A call for the traditional notion of restraint was equivalent to abandoning these areas of policy to judicial control. If conservatives limited themselves to maintaining the status quo, then judicial restraint would be transformed into an instrument for establishing liberal policy and expanding judicial power, especially during an era when conservatives had no hope of controlling the legislative branch.[252]

What conservatives needed was a constitutional jurisprudence with a fixed point of reference, one more specific and value laden than vague notions of "restraint" or "strict construction." Edwin Meese offered precisely such a jurisprudence when he suggested a return to "original intent." In a speech to the American Bar Association in 1985, Meese said the federal judiciary should "serve as the bulwark of a limited Constitution." The only way to fulfill this role was to "resist any political effort to depart from the literal provisions of the Constitution. The standard of interpretation applied by the judiciary must focus on the text and the drafters' original intent," he said.[253]

Three months later, in a speech at Tulane University, Meese stepped up his attack on the Court by calling into question its role as the final arbiter of the Constitution.[254] He began by making a simple distinction between the Constitution and constitutional law.[255] While a decision of the Supreme Court has the character of law, he said, "it does not establish a supreme law of the land that is binding on all persons and parts of government henceforth and forever." The other branches of government are not bound by decisions with which they disagree. The Supreme Court, he argued, "is not the only interpreter of the Constitution. Each of the three coordinate branches of government created and empowered by the Constitution has a duty to interpret the Constitution in the performance of its official functions."[256]

Of course, it was not an original argument that the separation of powers freed the executive from obligations to "the law." Previous advocates of this theory included Jefferson, Jackson, Lincoln, Roosevelt, and Nixon. Indeed, to substantiate his argument, Meese cited speeches by Lincoln assailing the *Dred Scott* decision. To update the argument, however, Meese also criticized the Supreme Court's dicta in *Cooper v. Aaron* (1958), in which it characterized its own interpretations of the Constitution as establishing the "supreme law of the land."[257] This pronouncement, he said, assumes the Constitution is merely "what the judges say it is." By the very logic of its jurisprudence, the Court is "at war with the Constitution, at war with the basic principles of democratic government, and at war with the very meaning of the rule of law."[258]

Reaction to the Attorney General's speeches arrived quickly. New Right groups were elated. Paul Kamenar of the Washington Legal Foundation said Meese had "engaged the country in a healthy debate on the proper role of the judiciary in our democratic society."[259] Bruce Fein of the Heritage Foundation weighed in, saying "Meese's genius as Attorney General was to force the liberal legal establishment to defend assumptions about judicial power that have been accepted by default."[260] James McClellan added, "Meese is the first Attorney General to recognize that judges had usurped the Constitution in order to impose their own moral judgments on society . . . his actions to reverse this trend should be applauded."[261]

On the left, Ira Glasser of the American Civil Liberties Union accused Meese of conducting "a campaign against the rule of law . . . his statements are part of a strategy that is hostile to the Bill of Rights and hostile to the courts enforcing it."[262] Nan Aaron of the Alliance for Justice called Meese's use of his office as a "bully pulpit" to attack the Court "an unfortunate throw-back to a period most of us hoped was long gone."[263] Former Attorney General Ramsey Clark said Meese's views "cannot be acceptable to any person who aspires to live under constitutional government."[264] The *Washington Post* editorialized that his remarks were "an invitation to constitutional chaos and an expression of contempt for the federal judiciary."[265]

Reaction to Meese's attacks also reflected the split in the conservative coalition itself. Philip Kurland argued that the "intent of the authors, assuming it can be ascertained, has never been the exclusive tool for construction." The call for such a jurisprudence "simply replaced 'strict construction' as the rallying cry for those who want a revamping of constitutional law to bring it into closer conformity to their own political philosophy."[266] And Rex Lee, though agreeing with Meese that other branches may respond to the Court's opinions, criticized the notion that each branch interprets the Constitution for its own governmental purposes: "A constitutional system requires that the final authority to say what the Constitution means be vested somewhere. For several reasons that responsibility rests with the courts," he said. That "is where the Founding Fathers intended it to be . . . and any other view would profoundly distort the separation of powers."[267]

Lee attributed Meese's statements to an "over-zealous speech writer." Indeed, Meese did not foresee how inflammatory his remarks would appear to those accustomed to the new political role of the federal courts. The Attorney General's speechwriter, Terry Eastland, said Meese "simply did not grasp the nature of the assault we were making on the new judicial politics."[268] Meese himself admitted he was "surprised" by the reaction, "I thought what I was saying was self-evident," he later said.[269] Nevertheless, the strategy behind the speeches paid off for conservatives. According to Geoffrey Stone of the University of Chicago Law School, what they accomplished was to:

> move our expectations far to the right, so that a Supreme Court decision which from any prior standard is highly conservative might today be considered liberal because it doesn't go all the way to Meese's direction. . . . Meese has actually converted absurd and radical propositions into the center of legitimate debate.[270]

Indeed, a decade ago, attacks on the doctrine of incorporation or arguments that the Court should overturn landmark precedents in wholesale fashion would have been considered frivolous. The fact that the propositions now attract debate in the most prestigious legal journals marks no small step. Meese recognized the success of his campaign. In a speech to the Heritage Foundation, he noted:

> I think this is the first time in many years that the justices of the Supreme Court have felt compelled to defend their actions. I believe this is a good thing because it is much better for the public to see what is behind the arrogation of power by some members of the Court, and to have it laid out in front of them. That way a knowledgeable public will demand that we restore the balance that is inherent in a true separation of powers.[271]

Even more indicative of Meese's accomplishment, perhaps, is the response his criticisms drew from sitting Justices of the Supreme Court. Replies from Stevens, Marshall, and Brennan reveal the Court's continuing sensitivity to the opinions of the Attorney General.[272] Justice Brennan's rebuttal was the most passionate. In a speech at Georgetown University, he said:

> While proponents of this facile historicism justify it as a depoliticization of the judiciary, the political underpinnings of such a choice should not escape notice. . . . (It) is a choice no less political than any other; it expresses antipathy to claims of the minority to rights against the majority. Those who would restrict claims of right to the values of 1789 specifically articulated in the

Constitution turn a blind eye to social progress and eschew adaptation of overarching principles of changes of social circumstance.[273]

Subtle arguments about "judicial restraint" or "strict construction" cannot prevail, Brennan said. The proposition that all matters of political policy should be resolved by the majoritarian process violates the very notion of constitutional government. It is the purpose of the Constitution, he continued, "to declare certain values transcendent . . . the majoritarian process cannot be expected to rectify claims of minority rights that arise as a response to the outcomes of that very majoritarian process."[274] Nevertheless, the Constitution is not a blank slate. Instead, Brennan said, it makes substantive value choices regarding fundamental principles of "human dignity." These are not static; "each generation has the choice to overrule or add to the fundamental principles enunciated by the Framers." He concluded:

> Current Justices read the Constitution in the only way that we can: as twentieth century Americans. . . . Interpretation must account for the transformative purpose of the text. Our Constitution was not intended to preserve a preexisting society but to make a new one, to put in place new principles that the prior political community had not sufficiently recognized.[275]

Conclusion

Brennan's "human dignity" and Meese's "original intent" stand at either end of a growing gap in American jurisprudence that has accompanied the new judicial politics and the judicialization of ever larger areas of public policy. The fact that the Attorney General and sitting Supreme Court Justices carried on the debate illustrates the institutional consequences of these developments.

The judicialization of politics in America has several causes, some historical and cultural, others institutional. During this century, the federal courts assumed greater policymaking authority as politics became nationalized and the federal government assumed new roles. The Progressive Era and the New Deal redefined the role of the judiciary just as much as the roles of Congress and the President. It was the Warren Court's transformation of the judicial process, however, that allowed the judiciary to free itself from the political agenda of the elected branches. Contemporary controversies surrounding the Supreme Court's role in American government are merely a reflection of these changes. This is why debate about constitutional jurisprudence has shifted increasingly from questions about federalism, to protection of individual rights and, more recently, to the separation of powers.

Because the Justice Department occupies the strategic middle ground between the judiciary and the elected branches, these changes affected it dramatically. As the nationalization of politics transformed the federal courts into policymaking arenas, normative views of the Attorney General's office began to change. An office once thought of primarily as a "legal" instituition gradually became thought of as a major political one. During the New Deal, the Roosevelt Administration declared war on the conservative ideology that dominated the Supreme Court. The Justice Department became the principal weapon in the fight to limit judicial policymaking. But in the wake of the Roosevelt administration, with the New Deal Democrats dominating the Court, the legislative branch loomed as the primary obstacle to liberal reforms. During the 1950s and 1960s, the Justice Department began to encourage a more active role for the judiciary hoping to obtain liberal policy objectives in areas such as civil rights and civil liberties.

The consequences of the executive branch's instrumental use of judicial power, however, became apparent when the Nixon administration attempted to use it to effect a more conservative policy agenda. This is why there was controversy about the role of the Nixon Justice Department even before the Watergate scandal. While the confrontational atmosphere between the Justice Department and the federal courts came to a temporary halt after Watergate, it returned with a vengeance under Reagan. By the time the Reagan administration came to office, the conflict had also taken on a new dimension. Justice Department clashes with the courts were being acted out not only in the constitutional law arena; as a result of electoral dealignment and entrenchment of divided government, they began to spill over into administrative law as well. Thus, during the 1980s the Justice Department not only found itself at the center of policy disputes between the executive and the judiciary, it also increasingly was thrust into disputes between executive branch agencies and Congress.

Notes

1. Anthony King (ed.), *The New American Political System* (Washington, D.C.: AEI, 1978); *The New American Political System*, 2d ed. (Washington, D.C.: AEI, 1990).

2. William Lunch, *The Nationalization of American Politics* (Los Angeles: University of California Press, 1987). See also Burdett Loomis, *The New American Politician* (New York: Basic Books, 1988); John Chubb and Paul Peterson (eds.), *The New Direction in American Politics* (Washington, D.C.: Brookings Institution, 1985).

3. On the new Congress see Thomas Mann and Norman Ornstein (eds.), *The New Congress* (Washington, D.C.: AEI, 1981); Norman Ornstein, "The Two Congresses and How They Have Changed," in Ornstein (ed.), *The Role of the Legislature in Western Democracies* (Washington, D.C.: AEI, 1981); Michael Foley, *The New Senate* (New Haven, Conn.: Yale University Press, 1980); James Sundquist, *The Decline and Resurgence of Congress* (Washington, D.C.: Brookings Institution, 1981); David Mayhew, *Congress: The Electoral Connection* (New Haven, Conn.: Yale University Press, 1974); Richard Fenno, *Home Style: House Members in Their Districts* (Boston: Little, Brown, 1978); Michael Malbin, *Unelected Representatives* (New York: Basic Books, 1980); Samuel Patterson, "The Semi-Sovereign Congress," in King (ed.), *The New American Political System*, 125; Lawrence Dodd and Bruce Oppenheimer, *Congress Reconsidered* (New York: Praeger, 1977).

4. Godfrey Hodgson, *All Things to All Men: The False Promise of the American Presidency* (New York: Doubleday, 1980).

5. On the new presidency see Aaron Wildavsky, "The Past and Future Presidency,"

The Public Interest (Fall 1975): 56; Fred Greenstein, "Change and Continuity in the Modern Presidency," in King (ed.), *The New American Political System*, 45; Hugh Heclo, "Issue Networks and the Executive Establishment," in King, *The New American Political System*, 87; Hugh Heclo and Lester Salamon, *The Illusion of Presidential Government* (Boulder, Colo.: Westview, 1982); Theodore Lowi, *The Personal President: Power Invested, Promise Unfulfilled* (Ithaca N.Y.: Cornell University Press, 1985); James Pfiffner, "White House Staff versus the Cabinet: Centripetal and Centrifugal Roles," *Presidential Studies Quarterly* 16 (1986): 666; Samuel Kernell, *Going Public: New Strategies of Presidential Leadership* (Washington, D.C.: Congressional Quarterly Press, 1986); Aaron Wildavsky, *The New Politics of the Budgetary Process* (Boston: Little Brown, 1988), and "The Two Presidencies," in Aaron Wildavsky (ed.), *Perspectives on the Presidency* (Boston: Little Brown, 1975), 448; Richard Neustadt, *Presidential Power* (New York: Macmillan, 1980); Larry Berman, *The New American Presidency* (Boston: Little Brown, 1987).

6. On new patterns of presidential relations with the bureaucracy, see Richard Waterman, *Presidential Influence and the Administrative State* (Knoxville: Tennessee University Press, 1989); Terry Moe, "The Politicized Presidency," in Chubb and Peterson, *The New Direction in American Politics*; Richard Nathan, *The Administrative Presidency* (New York: Wiley, 1983); Lester Salamon, "The Presidency and Domestic Policy Formulation," in Heclo and Salamon, *The Illusion of Presidential Government*; and G. Calvin Mackenzie, *The Politics of Presidential Appointments* (New York: Free Press, 1980).

7. Benjamin Ginsberg and Alan Stone (eds.), *Do Elections Matter?* (Armonk, N.Y.: M.E. Sharpe, 1986); A. James Reichley (ed.), *Elections American Style* (Washington, D.C.: Brookings Institution, 1987); Walter Dean Burnham, *The Current Crisis in American Politics* (New York: Oxford University Press, 1982); Michael Malbin (ed.), *Money and Politics in the United States: Financing Elections in the 1980s* (Washington, D.C.: AEI, 1984), and *Parties, Interest Groups, and Campaign Finance Laws* (Washington, D.C.: AEI, 1980).

8. See Casper, "The Supreme Court and National Policy Making," and Mark Silverstein and Benjamin Ginsberg, "The Supreme Court and the New Politics of Judicial Power," *Political Science Quarterly* 102 (1987), 371.

9. Silverstein and Ginsberg, "The New Politics of Judicial Power."

10. Ibid.

11. This materialistic group-based view of politics is often called the "Madisonian system." David Truman, *Governmental Process* (New York: Knopf, 1951); Robert Dahl, *Who Governs?* (New Haven, Conn.: Yale University Press, 1961), have supported the pluralist tradition. Theodore Lowi, *The End of Liberalism* (New York: Norton, 1969), and E. E. Schattschneider, *The Semi-Sovereign People* (New York: Holt, Rinehart and Winston, 1960), on the other hand, have argued for greater centralization.

12. Daniel Bell, *The End of Ideology* (New York: Free Press, 1960).

13. Loomis, *The New American Politician.*

14. This argument is drawn primarily from Lunch, *The Nationalization of American Politics.* But evidence that ideological rigidity is an increasingly significant factor in American politics can also be found in Gillian Peele, *Revival and Reaction: The Right in Contemporary America* (Oxford: Clarendon Press, 1984); and Byron Shafer, "The New Cultural Politics," *Political Science* 18 (1985), 221.

15. On the shift from electoral to institutional style politics generally, see Ginsberg and Shefter, *Politics By Other Means*; John Chubb and Paul Peterson (eds.), *Can the Government Govern* (Washington, D.C.: Brookings, 1989), and *The New Direction in American Politics*; L. Gordon Crovitz and Jeremy Rabkin, *The Fettered Presidency* (Washington, D.C.: AEI, 1989); Ginsberg and Stone, *Do Elections Matter?*

16. Ginsberg and Shefter, *Politics By Other Means*, 1.

17. Ibid.

18. The size of the Court had been changed on six previously occasions, but the political calculation for change had never been so obvious. Previous changes occurred in 1799, from 6 to 5 members; 1802, from 5 to 6; 1837, from 6 to 7; 1863, from 7 to 10; 1866 from 10 to 8; and 1869, from 8 to 9. For a discussion of the Court's size, see U.S. Congress, Senate Committee on the Judiciary, *Hearings on Reorganization of the Federal Judiciary*, 75th Cong., 1st sess. (1937).

19. A good discussion of the court-packing episode is in Abraham, *Justices and Presidents*, 195–98. A more complete account is Leonard Baker, *Back to the Back: The Duel Between FDR and the Supreme Court* (New York: Macmillan, 1967).

20. *Hearings on Reorganization of the Federal Judiciary*, 9.

21. *Booth v. United States*, 291 U.S. (1934), 339; *Lynch v. United States*, 292 U.S. (1934), 571; *Panama Ref. Co. v. Ryan*, 293 U.S. (1935); *Perry v. United States* 294 U.S. (1935), 330; *R.R. Retirement Brd. v. Alton R.R.*, 295 U.S. (1935), 330; *Hopkins v. Cleary*, 296 U.S. (1935), 315; *Schechter Poultry Co. v. United States*, 295 U.S. (1935), 495; *United States v. Constantine*, 296 U.S. (1935), 287; *Rickert Rice Mills v. Fontenot*, 297 U.S. (1936), 110; *Aston v. Cameron*, 298 U.S. (1936), 513; *Carter v. Carter Coal*, 298 U.S. (1936), 238; *Butler v. United States*, 297 U.S. (1936), 1.

22. The government won 46 percent of the cases decided on the merits in 1934, 47 percent in 1936, and 50 percent in 1936. *Annual Report A.G.* (1937), 32.

23. Ibid., 33.

24. *Panama Ref. Co. v. United States*, 293 U.S., 388 and *R.R. Retirement Brd. v. Alton*, 295 U.S., 330.

25. *ABA Journal* 22 (1936), 24, 27.

26. Ibid., 28.

27. *Butler v. United States*, 297 U.S., 1; *Carter v. Carter Coal Co.*, 298 U.S., 238; and *Louisville Bank v. Radford*, 295 U.S., 555.

28. *Congressional Record* February 15, 1937, A217.

29. 300 U.S. (1937), 379.

30. 301 U.S. (1937), 1.

31. *Annual Report A.G.* (1936), 24.

32. The remark was made during oral argument in *Youngstown Co. v. Sawyer*, 343 U.S. (1952), 589 and reported by Arthur Miller, in "The Attorney General as the President's Lawyer," in Huston et al., *Roles of the Attorney General*.

33. The thirteen Justices were: Hugo Black (1937–1971), Stanley Reed (1938–1957), Felix Frankfurter (1939–1962), William O. Douglas (1939–1975), Frank Murphy (1940–1949), James Byrnes (1941–1942), Robert Jackson (1941–1954), Wiley Rutledge (1943–1949), Harlan Fisk Stone (1941–1946), Harold Burton (1945–1958), Thomas Clark (1949–1967), Sherman Minton (1949–1956), and Fredrick Vinson (1946–1953).

34. Bickel, *The Supreme Court and the Idea of Progress* (New Haven, Conn.: Yale University Press, 1978), 5.

35. Silverstein and Ginsberg, "The New Politics of Judicial Power."

36. See Martin Shapiro, "The Supreme Court: From Warren to Burger," in King (ed.), *The New American Political System*.

37. The two major judicial barriers to court policymaking were the "political question" doctrine and the rules governing standing. These underwent a radical transformation in a series of cases in the 1960s. The political question doctrine was transformed in *Baker v. Carr*, 369 U.S. (1962), 186 and *Powell v. McCormack*, 395 U.S. (1969), 486. While the rules governing standing were completely revamped in cases like *Flast v. Cohen*, 392 U.S. (1968), 83 and *In Association of Data Processing Services Org. v. Camp* 397 U.S. (1970), 150. For a general review of these and other changes in standing, see David

Currie, "Misunderstanding Standing," *Supreme Court Review* (1981): 41; Karen Orren, "Standing to Sue: Interest Group Conflicts in the Federal Courts," *American Political Science Review* 70 (1976), 723.

38. There are several discussions of the inflation of the Court's political power by the Warren Court; some of the classic descriptions are in Berger, *Government by Judiciary*; Bickel, *The Supreme Court and the Idea of Progress*; and Nathan Glazer, "The Imperial Judiciary," *The Public Interest* (Fall 1975): 106.

39. See Shapiro, "The Supreme Court: From Warren to Burger," in King (ed.), *The New American Political System*, 179.

40. See Vincent Blasi, "The Rootless Activism of the Burger Court," in Blasi (ed.), *The Burger Court: The Counter Revolution That Wasn't* (New Haven, Conn.: Yale University Press, 1983).

41. For a discussion of the growth of interest group litigation since the 1950s see Richard Cortner, "Strategies and Tactics of Litigants in Constitutional Cases," *Journal of Public Law* 17 (1968), 287; Lucius Barker, "Third Parties in Litigation: A Systematic View of the Judicial Function," *Journal of Politics* 29 (1967), 41; Susan Olson, "The Political Evolution of Interest Group Litigation," in J. Gambitta (ed.), *Governing Through the Courts* (Beverly Hills: Sage & Palmer, 1981); Karen O'Connor and Lee Epstein, "The Rise of Conservative Interest Group Litigation," *Journal of Politics* 45 (1983), 479; and Gregory Caldeira and James Wright, "Organized Interests and Agenda Setting in the Supreme Court," *American Political Science Review* 82 (1988), 1109.

42. Jeremy Rabkin, *Judicial Compulsions* (New York: Basic Books, 1989).

43. Silverstein and Ginsberg, "The New Politics of Judicial Power."

44. Report of the President's Committee on Civil Rights, *To Secure These Rights* (1947).

45. For general background to the restrictive covenant cases, see Clement E. Vose, *Caucasians Only* (Berkeley and Los Angeles: University of California Press, 1959). On the political environment attending the Justice Department's decision to intervene in civil rights cases, see John T. Elliff, "The United States Department of Justice and Individual Rights, 1937–1962" (Ph.D. diss., Harvard University, 1967), 208–75.

46. 334 U.S. (1948), 1.

47. Philip Elman, "The Solicitor General's Office, Justice Frankfurter, and Civil Rights Litigation, 1946–1960: An Oral History," *Harvard Law Review* 100 (1987), 817, 818.

48. For an account of the Truman Justice Department's civil rights role generally, see Henry Putzel, "Federal Civil Rights Enforcement: A Current Appraisal," *University of Pennsylvania Law Review* 99 (1951), 439.

49. *Takahashi v. Fish and Game Commission*, 334 U.S. (1948), 410; *Henderson v. United States*, 339 U.S. (1950), 816; *Sweatt v. Painter*, 339 U.S. (1950), 629; and *McLaurin v. Oklahoma*, 339 U.S. (1950), 637.

50. 163 U.S. (1896), 537.

51. On the recent academic rehabilitation of Eisenhower, see Kenneth Thompson, *The Eisenhower Presidency* (Lanham, Md.: University Press of America, 1984); Fred Greenstein, *The Hidden-Hand Presidency: Eisenhower as Leader* (New York: Basic Books, 1982). Examples of earlier accounts which tended to give Brownell sole credit for the administration's civil rights policies includes John Anderson, *Eisenhower, Brownell, and the Congress: The Tangled Origins of the Civil Rights Bill* (University of Alabama Press, 1964); James Sundquist, *Politics and Policy: The Eisenhower, Kennedy, and Johnson Years* (Washington, D.C.: Brookings, 1968), 226–29; and Richard Schlundt, "Civil Rights Policies in the Eisenhower Years" (Ph.D. diss., Rice University, 1973).

52. See Richard Ellis, "Limits of the Lightning Rod: Eisenhower, Brownell, Southern

Whites, and Civil Rights," presented at the 1989 meeting of the Western Political Science Association, Salt Lake City.

53. 349 U.S. (1955), 294. The best history of the *Brown* case and other class-action civil rights strategies during this period is Richard Kluger, *Simple Justice* (New York: Random House, 1977).

54. See James Hutchinson, "Unanimity and Desegregation: Decision-making in the Supreme Court," *Georgetown Law Journal* 68 (1979), 1; and Kluger, *Simple Justice*, 588–91.

55. Elman, "The Solicitor General and Civil Rights."

56. The phrase was actually quoted from an early antitrust suit: *Virginia v. West Virginia*, 222 U.S. (1918), 17, 29.

57. Elman, "The Solicitor General and Civil Rights," 827–29.

58. Compare Elman's account of the debate on strategy and tactics with R. Kennedy, "A Reply to Philip Elman," *Harvard Law Review* 100 (1987), 1938.

59. See the account of Warren's law clerk, G. Edward White, *Earl Warren: A Public Life* (New York: Oxford University Press, 1982); and Hutchinson, "Unanimity and Desegregation: Decision-making in the Supreme Court."

60. An excellent account of the divisions within the administration over civil rights generally is Michael S. Mayer, "Eisenhower's Conditional Crusade: The Eisenhower Administration and Civil Rights," (Ph.D. diss., Princeton University, 1984).

61. Elman, "The Solicitor General and Civil Rights," 833–34.

62. Compare Elliff, "The Department of Justice and Individual Rights," 410–30, to Ellis, "Limits of the Lightning Rod."

63. Letter from President Dwight D. Eisenhower to Governor James F. Byrnes, December 1, 1953. On Eisenhower's personal views regarding the emerging civil rights struggle, see James Duram, *A Moderate among Extremists: Dwight D. Eisenhower and the School Desegregation Crisis* (Chicago: Nelson-Hall, 1981).

64. Elman, "The Solicitor General and Civil Rights," 835–36.

65. July 30, 1957, A–14; and August 3, 1957, A–6.

66. Reprinted in *ABA Journal* 43 (1957), 595. See also H. Brownell, "Protecting Civil Rights," speech delivered before the Chicago Bar Association, November 1957, reprinted in *Chicago Bar Record* 39 (1957), 55; and "Lawyers and a Government of Law," *Record* 13 (1958), 188.

67. R. Dixon, "The Attorney General and Civil Rights," in Huston et al., *Roles of the Attorney General*, 151.

68. *Cooper v. Aaron*, 358 U.S. (1958), 1; *Faubus v. United States*, 254 F. 2d 797 (8th Cir. 1957); *Jackson v. Kuhn*, 249 F. 2d 209 (8th Cir. 1958); *Brewer v. Hoxie School Dist.*, 236 F. 2d 91 (8th Cir. 1956); *Kasper v. Brittain*, 245 F. 2d 92 (6th Cir. 1957); *Bullock v. United States*, 265 F. 2d 683 (6th Cir. 1959); *Kasper v. United States*, 265 F. 2d 683 (6th Cir. 1959); and *Taylor v. Board of Education*, 294 F. 2d 36 (2nd Cir. 1960).

69. 71 Stat. (1957), 634, and 74 Stat. (1960), 86.

70. The story of the enactment of the 1957 act and Brownell's involvement is detailed in Anderson, *Eisenhower, Brownell and Congress*, and Sundquist, *Politics and Policy*.

71. A. Bickel, "The Decade of School Desegregation: Progress and Prospects," *Columbia Law Review* 64 (1964), 193, 220.

72. Dwight D. Eisenhower, *Waging Peace: 1956–1961* (Garden City, N.Y.: Doubleday, 1965), 153–60; Duram, *A Moderate Among Extremists*, 125–35.

73. Anderson, *Eisenhower, Brownell and Congress*, 29–31.

74. Mayer, "Eisenhower's Conditional Crusade," 440–60.

75. Anderson, *Eisenhower, Brownell and Congress*, 43.

76. Ellis, "Limits of the Lightning Rod," 43–44.

77. Ibid., 48.

78. October 10, 1957, A–16.

79. On Eisenhower's support of the Justice Department's civil rights policies generally, see W. Bragg Ewald, Jr., *Eisenhower the President: Crucial Days, 1951–1960* (Englewood Cliffs, N.J.: Prentice-Hall, 1981). On Rogers's continued support of civil rights, see Elliff, "The Department of Justice and Individual Rights," 546–640. See also William Rogers, "The Problem of School Segregation: A Serious Challenge to Americans," speech reprinted in *ABA Journal* 45 (1959), 23, and "Desegregation: The Citizens Responsibility," *Cornell Law Quarterly* 56 (1960), 488.

80. For general discussion of the Kennedy administration's civil rights strategies and performance see Burke Marshall, *Federalism and Civil Rights* (New York: Columbia University Press, 1964); Harold Flemming, "The Federal Executive and Civil Rights," *Daedalus*, (Fall 1965); Heywood Burns, "The Federal Executive and Civil Rights," in Leon Friedman (ed.), *Southern Justice* (New York: Pantheon, 1965); Donald Francis Sullivan, "The Civil Rights Programs of the Kennedy Administration: A Political Analysis" (Ph.D. diss., University of Oklahoma, 1965).

81. 372 U.S. (1963), 368.

82. Robert Kennedy: "Civil Rights and the South," reprinted in *North Carolina Law Review* 42 (1963), 1.

83. *Annual Report A.G.* (1964), 30–33. A general discussion of the increased enforcement of civil rights under Kennedy is in Elliff, "The Department of Justice and Civil Rights," 644–739; and Kluger, *Simple Justice*, 754–55.

84. *Bush v. New Orleans Parish School Brd.*, 191 F. Supp. 871 (E.D. La. 1961); *Meredith v. Fair*, 305 F. 2d. 343 (5th Cir. 1962); and *United States v. Barnett*, 330 F. 2d. 369 (5th Cir. 1963). For a discussion of the department's role, see Dixon, "The Attorney General and Civil Rights," in Huston, et al., *Roles of the Attorney General*, 136.

85. For a discussion of the department's expanded use of the *amicus* brief during this period, see Samuel Krislov, "The Attorney General as Amicus Curiae," in Huston, et al., *Roles of the Attorney General*; and Robert Dixon, "Discrimination, Desegregation and Government Initiative," in Donald King and Charles Quick (eds.), *Legal Aspects of the Civil Rights Movement* (Detroit: Wayne State University, 1965).

86. 369 U.S. (1962), 186; 377 U.S. (1964), 533.

87. 328 U.S. (1946), 549.

88. See Robert McKay, *Reapportionment: The Law and Politics of Equal Representation* (New York: Twentieth Century Fund, 1965); and Robert Dixon, *Democratic Representation: Reapportionment in Law and Politics* (Oxford: Oxford University Press, 1968).

89. Victor Navasky make this point in *Kennedy Justice*, 299.

90. Memorandum from Solicitor General Archibald Cox to Attorney General Robert Kennedy, "Should the United States File a Brief Amicus Curiae in the Legislative Reapportionment Cases," August 21, 1963.

91. During the 1962 term the *amicus* briefs filed in civil rights cases were *Baker v. Carr*, 369 U.S., 186; *Avent v. North Carolina*, 373 U.S., 375; *Lombard v. Louisiana*, 373 U.S., 267; *Gober v. Birmingham*, 373 U.S., 374; *Shuttlesworth v. Birmingham*, 373 U.S., 262; *Peterson v. Greenville*, 373 U.S., 244; *Gray v. Sanders*, 372 U.S., 368; *Colorado Com. v. Continental Air Lines*, 372 U.S., 714; *Green v. Continental Air Lines*, 372 U.S., 714; and *Gross v. Brd.*, 373 U.S., 683. During the 1963 term the cases were *Griffin v. Maryland*, 378 U.S., 130; *Barr v. Columbia*, 378 U.S., 146; *Bovie v. Columbia*, 378 U.S., 347; *Bell v. Maryland*, 378 U.S., 226; *Robinson v. Florida*, 378 U.S., 153; *WMCA v. Lomenzo*, 377 U.S., 633; *Wesberry v. Sanders*, 376 U.S., 1; *Reynolds v. Sims*, 377 U.S., 533; *Maryland Com. v. Tawes*, 377 U.S., 656; *Anderson v. Martin*, 375 U.S., 399; *Davis v. Mann*, 377 U.S., 678; *Roman v. Sincock*, 377 U.S., 695; *Lucas v. Colorado*, 377 U.S.,

713; *Griffin v. Brd. of Ed.*, 377 U.S., 218; *Calhoun v. Latimer*, 377 U.S., 263.

92. 78 Stat. (1964), 241.

93. Titles giving authority to the Attorney General are: Titles I, II, III, IV, VIII, IX. For a discussion of the authority see Dixon, "The Attorney General and Civil Rights," in Huston et al., *Roles of the Attorney General*, 144–49.

94. For a discussion of the 1964 act and the authority vested in the Justice Department, see *Annual Report A.G.* (1964), 175.

95. 79 Stat. (1965), 437.

96. The regulatory role that the preclearance requirement gave the department forced it into a closer relationship with the federal courts over civil rights, a role that was later resisted by the department under conservative administrations. See Howard Ball, Dale Krane, and Thomas Lauth, *Compromised Compliance: Justice Department Implementation of Section 5 of the 1965 Voting Rights Act* (Westport, Conn.: Greenwoood Press, 1982).

97. 191 F. Supp. (D.C. La., 1961), 871, 877–78.

98. 323 F.2d. 959 (4th Cir. 1963).

99. 342 F.2d. (5th Cir., 1965), 167, 171. The Attorney General's broad prosecutorial discretion was also upheld in *Powell v. Katzenbach*, 123 U.S. App. D.C. (1965), 120; and *Moses v. Katzenbach*, 342 F.2d (D.C. Cir. 1965), 931.

100. 379 U.S. (1964), 241; and 379 U.S., (1964), 294.

101. Various charges of politicizing the Justice Department under Kennedy, Katzenbach, and Clark are discussed in Richard Harris, *Justice: The Crisis of Law, Order and Freedom in America* (London: Bodley Head, 1970), 11–80; and Schlesinger, *Robert Kennedy*, Ch. 17, "The Politics of Justice."

102. See Richard Harris, *The Fear of Crime* (New York: Praeger, 1969).

103. 367 U.S. (1961), 643.

104. 372 U.S. (1963), 335.

105. 378 U.S. (1964), 478.

106. 384 U.S. (1966), 436.

107. Clark's law-and-order views are discussed in Harris, *The Fear of Crime*; and Charles Fritchey, "Watch on the Attorney General," *Harper's Magazine*, November 1967.

108. Theodore H. White, *The Making of the President, 1968* (New York: Doubleday, 1969).

109. Ibid. See also Dana Bullen, "Clark Urges Abolition of Death Penalty," *Washington D.C. Evening Star*, July 2, 1968, A–2; "Clark Hits Back At Critics," *Washington D.C. Evening Star*, August 23, 1968, A–15.

110. Harris, *The Fear of Crime*, 97.

111. See Jason Epstein, *The Great Conspiracy Trial* (London: Faber, 1970).

112. *Congressional Record*, November 14, 1967, 32471; May 2, 1968, S11659; September 4, 1968, H25547; and September 27, 1968, H28688.

113. Bruce Murphy, *Fortas: The Rise and Ruin of a Supreme Court Justice* (New York: Morrow, 1988); and O'Brien, *Storm Center*, 121–26.

114. Nixon's speech is printed in *Congressional Record* 1968, S25547.

115. See Huston, et al., *Roles of the Attorney General*.

116. See Simon, *In His Own Image*. On John Mitchell's "repoliticization of the Justice Department," see Harris, *Justice*.

117. Harris, *Justice*, 63–70, 179–86.

118. Ibid., 128–39. See also Mitchell's speeches defending the policy change, "Violence in America and the Right to Dissent," *Tennessee Law Review* 37 (1969), 129; and "Remarks on Eavesdropping," *Kentucky State Bar Journal* 35 (1971), 26.

119. See Mitchell's defense of the administration's proposal, "Bail Reform and the

Constitutionality of Pretrial Detention," in *Virginia Law Review* 55 (1969), 1223; and "In Quest of Speedy Justice," *Judicature* 55 (1971), 139.

120. On the shift during the Nixon administration, see Leon Panetta and Peter Gall, *Bring Us Together, The Nixon Team and the Civil Rights Retreat* (Philadelphia: J.B. Lippincott, 1971); Abner J. Mikva, *Report of the Lawyer's Review Committee to Study the Department of Justice*, (1971).

121. Theodore H. White, *The Making of the President, 1968* (New York: Doubleday, 1969); and J. Nealon, "Civil Rights and Politics in the Department of Justice," *Fordham Law Review* 46 (1978), 1049.

122. The administration's efforts are discussed in Ball, et al., *Compromised Compliance*, 110.

123. 402 U.S. (1971), 1.

124. 396 U.S. (1969), 19.

125. The department claimed it lacked sufficient resources to seek desegregation under *Alexander: Washington Star*, January 15, 1970, A-1. But in *Carter v. West Feliciana School Brd.* 396 U.S. (1970), 290 and *Harris v. Yazoo City Municipal Separate School Dist.* (5th Cir. 1970), it asked the courts to give local school officials further delays in implementing desegregation plans.

126. See P.J. Greenberg, "Revolt at Justice," *The Washington Monthly*, vol. 1, no. 11, December 1969, 32; Clawson, "Justice Department Resignations," *Washington Post*, October 21, 1970, A–3; and "Problems at Justice," *National Journal* 33 (1970), 1188.

127. 480 F.2d (1973), 1159.

128. Ibid., 1163.

129. *New York Times v. United States*, 403 U.S. (1971), 713.

130. *United States v. United States District Court*, 407 U.S. (1972), 297.

131. *Kennedy v. Sampson*, 511 F.2d (D.C. Cir. 1974), 430. The Solicitor General refused to appeal this issue to the Supreme Court; see Arthur Keeffe, "The Solicitor General Pocket Vetoes the Pocket Veto," *ABA Journal* 61 (1975), 755.

132. *Train v. City of New York*, 420 U.S. (1975), 35.

133. *Nixon v. United States*, 418 U.S. (1974), 683.

134. For a discussion of the Court's general rejection of the administration's legal agenda, see Peter Quint, "The Separation of Powers under Nixon: Reflections on Constitutional Liberties and the Rule of Law," *Duke Law Journal* 1, (1981).

135. "Not Will But Judgment," printed in *ABA Journal* 57 (1971), 1185. See also "The Duty to Decide," *Catholic Law* 18 (1972), 2.

136. See William Landes and Richard Posner, "The Independent Judiciary in an Interest-Group Perspective," *Journal of Law and Economics* 18 (1975), 875.

137. Ibid., 1186.

138. O'Brien, *Judicial Roulette*, 55–56.

139. See Simon, *In His Own Image*; and Blasi (ed.), *The Counter-Revolution That Wasn't.*

140. An encapsulated account of the Haynesworth–Carswell nominations is found in O'Brien, *Judicial Roulette*, 55–56.

141. The four were: Warren Burger (1969–1986); Harry Blackmun (1970-); Lewis Powell (1972–1986); and William Rehnquist (1972–).

142. *Arizona Law Review* 12 (1970), 251, 259.

143. U.S. Congress, Senate Subcommittee on the Separation of Powers, *Hearings on Removing Politics from the Administration of Justice*, 93d Cong., 2d sess. (1974), 32.

144.For a discussion of post-Watergate legislation involving the Justice Department, see Benjamin Civiletti, "Post Watergate Legislation in Retrospective," *South West Law Journal* 34 (1981), 1043.

145. U.S. Congress, Senate Select Committee on Intelligence, *Intelligence Activities and the Rights of Americans*, 94th Cong., 2d. sess. (1976). For a capsulated account see "Domestic Spying Abuses Said to Cover 40 Years," *Washington Post*, April 24, 1976.

146. See Lawrence Meyer, "Levi: Liberal with a Taste For Restraint," *Washington Post*, February 9, 1975, A–3; and Ronald Carr, "Mr. Levi at Justice," *University of Chicago Law Review* 52 (1985), 300.

147. On this point see Navasky, "The Attorney General as Scholar."

148. "Justice Department Gets a Just Man," *The Economist*, January 25, 1975, 45.

149. U.S. Congress, Senate Committee on the Judiciary, *Hearings on the Nomination of Edward H. Levi to be Attorney General*, 94th Cong., 1st sess. (1975), 50–52.

150. "Remarks of Edward H. Levi at His Swearing in as Attorney General of the United States," *Weekly Compendium of Presidential Documents* 11 (Feb. 7, 1975), 164.

151. Levi, "A New Approach to Justice," *Pennsylvania Bar Quarterly* (1975), 404, 405.

152. For a more detailed discussion of Levi's efforts, see Howard Ball, "Confronting Institutional Schizophrenia: The Effort to De-Politicize the U.S. Department of Justice, 1974–1976," (paper presented at the President Ford Conference, Hofstra University, April 7, 1989); and Carr, "Levi at Justice."

153. O'Brien, *Judicial Roulette*, 57–58.

154. See Edward Levi, "The Justice Department: Some Thoughts on its Future," *Illinois Bar Journal* (1975), 216; and Daniel Meador, "Role of the Justice Department."

155. Meador, "Role of the Justice Department," 140–42.

156. See *Annual Report A.G.* (1977), 13.

157. Ball, "Institutional Schizophrenia."

158. Carr, "Levi at Justice," 312.

159. Ball, "Institutional Schizophrenia," 18–21.

160. Senate Committee on the Judiciary, *Levi Confirmation Hearings*, 6, 22.

161. Bell and Ostrow, *Taking Care of the Law*, 27.

162. Prior to 1952, in this century the nomination of just two Attorneys General had become the subject of open confirmation hearings: John Sargent, in 1925, and Frank Murphy (at his request) in 1939. In both instances the hearings were brief and held only because allegations of personal corruption or misconduct had surfaced.

163. U.S. Congress, Senate Committee on the Judiciary, *Hearings on the Nomination of Robert F. Kennedy to Be Attorney General*, 87th Cong., 1st sess. (1961).

164. U.S. Congress, Senate Committee on the Judiciary, *Hearings on the Nomination of Richard Kleindienst to Be Attorney General*, 92nd Cong., 2d sess. (1972).

165. U.S. Congress, Senate Committee on the Judiciary, *Hearings on the Nomination of Edward H. Levi*.

166. U.S. Congress, Senate Committee on the Judiciary, *Hearings on the Nomination of Griffin H. Bell to Be Attorney General*, 95th Cong., 1st sess. (1977).

167. Ibid., 149.

168. Ibid., 447.

169. In an address delivered at the meeting of the Pound Conference Follow-Up Task Force, Bell urged the abolition of class-action suits as a significant damage sanction. 70 *F.R.D.* (1976), 83. See also Bell's concurring opinions in *Miller v. Mackey*, 515 F. 2d. (5th Cir. 1975), 241, 243; and *Pettway v. American Pipe Co.*, 494 F. 2d. (5th Cir. 1974), 211, 267 in which Bell attacks class-action suits and the trend toward expanding judicial remedies.

170. Telephone interview with Griffin Bell, August 22, 1988.

171. Bell's own account of the debate together with recommendations for how future confirmation hearings can be depoliticized are in Bell and Ostrow, *Taking Care of the Law*, 63–71.

172. Senate Committee on the Judiciary, *Bell Hearings*, 611–612.

173. Ibid., 351.

174. Bell and Ostrow, *Taking Care of the Law*, 27.

175. "Memorandum Regarding the Role of the Solicitor General," September 29, 1977. Printed as "Memorandum 77–56," in *Opinions of the Office of Legal Counsel* 1 (1977), 228.

176. Bell outlined the procedures in an address to department lawyers on September 6, 1978. For a discussion of the procedures see Meador, "The President, the Attorney General and the Department of Justice," 56–60.

177. Ibid., and Meador, "An Effective Judiciary," 142–46.

178. See Fowler, "Judicial Selection," 265; John Gotschall, "Carter's Judicial Appointments: The Influence of Merit Selection and Affirmative Action," *Judicature* 67 (1983), 165; Alan Neff, "Breaking with Tradition: A Study of the U.S. District Court Nominating Commissions," *Judicature* 64 (1981), 257; and Parris, "Merit Selection of Federal Judges."

179. Interview with Bell, August 22, 1988.

180. Interview with Daniel Meador, Charlottesville, Virginia, July 7, 1988.

181. Of the Carter administration's judicial appointment 22 percent went to women and 21 percent went to racial or ethnic minorities. See Goldman, "Reagan's Judicial Appointments at Mid-Term," 334.

182. See Griffin Bell, "Merit Selection and the Future," address before the Mecklenburg County Bar Association, Charlotte, North Carolina, April 12, 1988.

183. Bell and Ostrow, *Taking Care of the Law*, 28.

184. Interview with Daniel Meador, July 7, 1988.

185. See *Congressional Record*, July 31, 1980, 20616–37.

186. For a discussion and defense of the Reagan Justice Department's policies, see Terry Eastland, "Reagan Justice: Curbing Excess, Strengthening the Rule of Law," *Policy Review* (Fall 1988), 16.

187. Interview with Stephen J. Markman, Washington, D.C., June 7, 1988.

188. Interview with Edwin Meese, Washington, D.C., August 20, 1988.

189. Interview with Stephen Markman, June 7, 1988.

190. J. Bonafede, "Smith Moves to Shed His Image as an Invisible Attorney General," *National Journal*, March 6, 1982, 415.

191. "Federal Courts Have Gone Beyond Their Abilities," *Judges Journal* 21 (Winter 1982), 3.

192. "Urging Judicial Restraint," *ABA Journal* 68 (January 1982), 59.

193. For discussion of the administration's judicial selection process, see Stephen J. Markman, "The Judicial Selection Process in the Reagan Administration," testimony presented to the Senate Committee on the Judiciary on February 2, 1988, later published by the Office of Legal Policy (1988). For a critical account see Goldman, "Reaganizing the Judiciary," 312; and Schwartz, *Packing the Court*.

194. Goldman, "Reagan's Judicial Legacy," 318.

195. 458 U.S. (1982), 457.

196. See William Bradford Reynolds, "The Civil Rights Establishment is All Wrong," *Human Rights* (Spring 1984), 34; and "The Reagan Administration and Civil Rights: Winning the War Against Discrimination," *University of Illinois Law Review* (1986), 1001.

197. *Plessy v. Ferguson*, 163 U.S. (1896), 537, 559 (Justice Harlan dissenting).

198. 467 U.S. (1984), 561.

199. For a discussion of the department's actions in the wake of the *Stotts* decision see Joel Selig, "The Reagan Justice Department and Civil Rights: What Went Wrong," *Uni-*

versity of Illinois Law Review (1985), 785, 821–29; and Reynolds's response in "Winning the War Against Discrimination," 1014–21.

200. Interview with Charles Fried, Salzburg, Austria, August 20, 1987.

201. *Sheet Metal Workers v. E.E.O.C.*, 106 S.Ct. (1986), 3019; *Local 93 v. City of Cleveland*, 106 S.Ct. (1986), 3036; *Wygant v. Jackson Brd. of Ed.*, 106 S.Ct. (1986), 3320; and *Johnson v. Santa Clara County*, 106 S.Ct. (1986). For a summary of the Court's opinions and the common view that they represented a clear rejection of the administration's position in *Stotts*, see George Church, "A Solid Yes to Affirmative Action," *Time* (July 14, 1986). Fried's analysis that the Court was willing to move slowly on limiting affirmative action, but was scared away by the administration's effort to force it into full retreat on civil rights appeared to be vindicated when the Court in two cases in 1989, *Richmond v. Croson*, 109 S.Ct. (1989), 706; and *Martin v. Wilks*, 109 S.Ct. (1989), 2180, proved willing to pare back its protection of affirmative action. See Joan Biskupic, "Groups Look to Capitol Hill for Help on Civil Rights," *Congressional Quarterly* (June, 17, 1989), 1479.

202. See Nadine Cohodas, "Reagan Seeks Relaxation of Antitrust Laws," *Congressional Quarterly* (February 1, 1986), 187. For a comprehensive analysis of how antitrust enforcement changed under the Reagan administration, see Government Accounting Office, *Report to the Chairman, Committee on the Judiciary, House of Representatives: Justice Department Changes in Antitrust Enforcement   Policies and Activities* (GAO/GGD–91–2 Justice Department, 1991).

203. 470 U.S. (1985), 298.

204. 468 U.S. (1984), 897.

205. 462 U.S. (1983), 416.

206. For a general discussion of the administration's growing conflict with the Court, see Elder Witt, "Reagan vs. Court: A Continuing Crusade," *Congressional Quarterly* (July 20, 1985), 1463; and "Reagan Crusade Before the Court Unprecedented in Intensity," *Congressional Quarterly* (March 15, 1986), 616.

207. David Stockman's book *The Triumph of Politics* (New York: Harper and Row, 1986) gives perhaps the best general account of the internal warfare that took place between the two camps within the administration. On its impact in the Justice Department, litigation policy in particular, see Caplan, *The Tenth Justice*.

208. See Bonafede, "Smith Moves to Shed Image," 415.

209. See letter from William French Smith to Senator Strom Thurmond, Chair Senate Committee on the Judiciary, May 6, 1982. On the conservative reaction, see "Smith Questions Moves to Limit Courts," *National Journal* (May 15, 1982), 878.

210. During oral arguments in *Akron* the Solicitor General explicitly denied that the department was seeking to overturn the Court's 1973 *Roe* opinion. See John A. Jenkins, "The Solicitor General's Winning Ways," *American Bar Association Journal* 69 (1983), 734. For conservatives' attack on the department's position, see James McClellan, "A Lawyer Looks at Rex Lee," *Benchmark* 1 (1984).

211. Bonafede, "Smith Moves to Shed Image."

212. *Times*, August 4, 1982, A–22.

213. McClellan, "A Lawyer Looks at Rex Lee," 4–5.

214. Burt Solomon, "Meese Sets Ambitious Agenda that Challenges Fundamental Legal Beliefs," *National Journal* (November 23, 1985), 2640.

215. On Meese's appointment as a challenge to reforms of the office, see Phil Gailey, "Politics and the Attorney General," *New York Times*, April 21, 1985, A–50; Stewart Taylor, "Ties of Attorney General to Chief," *New York Times*, January 30, 1984, A- 14.

216. Because a Special Prosecutor was appointed to investigate Meese's business dealings there were two separate sets of confirmation hearings a year apart. U.S. Con-

gress, Senate Committee on the Judiciary, *Hearings on Edwin Meese to be Attorney General*, 98th Cong., 2d sess. (1984) and 99th Congress, 1st sess. (1985).

217. Senate Committee on the Judiciary, *Meese Hearings* (1984), 2–3.

218. Ibid.

219. Solomon, "Meese Set Ambitious Agenda"; and Al Kamen, "Meese Partially Achieved Conservative Goals," *Washington Post*, July 6, 1988, A–6. On the independent counsel's investigation see *Report of Independent Counsel In Re Edwin Meese III* (U.S. Court of Appeals for the District of Columbia Court, Division for the Purpose of Appointing Special Counsels, 1989); and Lou Cannon and Bill McAllister, "Meese Announces Resignation, Says Probe 'Vindicated Him,' " *Washington Post*, July 6, 1988, A–1. The quotation is from Inaugural Speech by Edwin Meese, United States Department of Justice, Washington, D.C., February 25, 1981.

220. See O'Brien, "Reagan's Most Enduring Legacy," 60.

221. Interview with James McClellan, Washington, D.C., August 19, 1988.

222. Elder Witt, "Reagan's Arguments Rebuffed by High Court," *Congressional Quarterly* (July 12, 1986), 1576.

223. See notes 206–8 and accompanying text.

224. 472 U.S. (1985), 38.

225. 478 U.S. (1986), 675.

226. 476 U.S. (1986), 747, and 109 S.Ct. (1989), 3040.

227. See Caplan, *The Tenth Justice*.

228. Sheldon Goldman, "Second Term Appointments at Midway," *Judicature* 70 (1987), 324, 329; see also O'Brien, "Reagan's Most Enduring Legacy," 81–83.

229. Schwartz, *Packing the Courts*; O'Brien, "Reagan's Most Enduring Legacy," 71–75.

230. Schwartz, *Packing the Courts*, 74–149.

231. U.S. Congress, Senate Committee on the Judiciary, *Hearings on the Nomination of Judge Sandra Day O'Connor to Serve as an Associate Justice of the Supreme Court*, 97th Cong., 1st sess. (1981).

232. For a New Right analysis critical of O'Connor's nomination see Grover Reese III, "Questions for Supreme Court Nominees: Excluding the Constitution," *Georgia Law Review* 17 (1983), 913.

233. U.S. Congress, Senate Committee on the Judiciary, *Hearings on the Nomination of Justice William H. Rehnquist to Be Chief Justice of the Supreme Court*, 99th Cong., 2d sess. (1986).

234. O'Brien, "Reagan's Most Enduring Legacy," 87–88.

235. U.S. Congress, Senate Committee on the Judiciary, *Hearings on the Nomination of Justice Antonin Scalia to Be Associate Justice of the Supreme Court*, 99th Cong., 2d sess. (1986).

236. In addition to Scalia's opinions, his intense conservatism is seen in his articles such as "The Disease as Cure," *Washington University Law Quarterly* (1979), 147; and "The Doctrine of Standing as an Element of Separation of Powers," in Mark Cannon and David O'Brien, *View from the Bench* (Chatham, N.J.: Chatham House, 1985), 200.

237. U.S. Congress, Senate Committee on the Judiciary, *Hearings on the Nomination of Judge Robert H. Bork to Be Associate Justice of the Supreme Court*, 100th Cong., 1st sess. (1987). The best account about the extraordinary nature of the Bork nomination controversy is Ethan Bonner, *Battle for Justice: How the Bork Nomination Shook America* (N.Y.: Norton, 1989). For Bork's own account, see Robert H. Bork, *The Tempting of America* (New York: Free Press, 1990).

238. See Richard Berke, "Bork as a Bonanza," *New York Times*, September 11, 1987, A–32.

239. Legislation was introduced by Representative E. Thomas Coleman (R-Mo.). For

discussion see "Judicial Lobby Legislation," *Congressional Quarterly* October 24, 1987, 2643.

240. The official reasons for Bork's rejection are in U.S. Congress, Senate Committee on the Judiciary, *Report on the Nomination of Robert H. Bork to be an Associate Justice of the Supreme Court (together with minority views)*, 100th Cong., 1st sess. (1987).

241. Bork's chances at confirmation were further hobbled by confusion in the administration over strategy. White House officials portrayed Bork as a "centrist" jurist to make him more acceptable to moderate Republicans. The Justice Department emphasized his conservative jurisprudence in an attempt to make the nomination a referendum on their efforts to reverse the post–Warren era politics of the Court. Bork himself also gave an unprecedented performance before the Judiciary Committee. He appeared cavalier, and in testimony lasting more than five days, discussed his judicial philosophy in great detail, giving assurances on how he might vote on particular issues. His performance violated a norm existing since 1925, when Harlan F. Stone first appeared as a witness during his confirmation hearings, that Supreme Court nominees should refuse to discuss specific cases or issues. See O'Brien, "Reagan's Most Enduring Legacy," 90–94.

242. The others were John Chafee (R.I.), Bob Packwood (Ore.), Robert Stafford (Vt.), Lowell Weicker (Conn.), John Warner (Va.).

243. For discussion of Ginsburg's nomination and withdrawal, see Kenneth Karpay, "In Search of Judge Ginsburg," *Legal Times*, November 2, 1987, and "Questions Linger as Ginsburg Returns to Circuit," *Legal Times*, November 16, 1987.

244. See Paul Marcotte, "Bork to Ginsburg to Kennedy," *American Bar Association Journal* 1 (1988), 15; and Gerald F. Uelman, "A Jurist to Fit Powell's Shoes," *Los Angeles Times*, November 22, 1987, Pt. 2, 23.

245. Interview with Terry Wooten, Minority Chief Counsel, July 22, 1988.

246. For an excellent discussion of the politicization, see Randy Barnett, "Judicial Conservativism vs. A Principled Judicial Activism," *Harvard Journal of Law & Public Policy* 10 (1987), 273.

247. See Moss, "The Policy and Rhetoric of Ed Meese," 64.

248. Edwin Meese, "Promoting Truth in the Court Room," printed in *Vanderbilt Law Review* (1987), 271, 272.

249. "Conservative Movement and the Reagan Revolution," address delivered before the Conservative Political Action Committee Conference, February 19, 1987, Washington, D.C.

250. "Remarks at the Detroit College of Law Commencement Ceremonies," printed in *Detroit College Law Review* (1986), 1161, 1167.

251. Meese, "Toward a Jurisprudence of Original Intent," address before the Federalist Society, January 30, 1987, Washington, D.C. Printed in *Harvard Journal of Law & Public Policy* 11 (1987), 5.

252. For discussion of the new conservative critique of judicial restraint, see Richard Posner, *The Federal Courts* (Cambridge, Mass.: Harvard University Press, 1985), 198–222; Stephen Macedo, *The New Right v. The Constitution* (New York: Basic Books, 1986); and Henry Aranson, "Judicial Control of the Political Branches: Public Purpose and Public Law," *Cato Journal* 4 (1985), 719.

253. "The Supreme Court of the United States: Bulwark of a Limited Constitution," printed in *South Texas Law Review* 27 (Fall 1986), 455, 464.

254. "The Law of the Constitution," printed in *Tulane Law Review* 61 (1987), 979.

255. Ibid., 981.

256. Ibid., 985.

257. 358 U.S. (1958), 1, 18.

258. Meese, "The Law of the Constitution," 987.

259. Moss, "Rhetoric of Ed Meese," 66.

260. Interview with Bruce Fein, August 19, 1988, Washington, D.C.

261. Interview with James McClellan, August 19, 1988, Washington, D.C.

262. Moss, "The Rhetoric of Ed Meese," 65.

263. Interview with Nan Aaron, August 20, 1988, Washington, D.C.

264. Clark, "Enduring Constitutional Issues," *Tulane Law Review* 61 (1987), 1093.

265. November 13, 1986, A–21.

266. Kurland, "Judicial Review Revisited: Original Intent and the Common Will," *Cincinnati Law Review* 55 (1987), 733, 735.

267. Lee, "The Provinces of Constitutional Interpretation," *Tulane Law Review* 61 (1987), 1009, 1014–15.

268. Interview with Terry Eastland, August 22, 1988, Washington, D.C.

269. Interview with Edwin Meese, August 20, 1988, Washington, D.C.

270. Moss, "The Rhetoric of Ed Meese," 65.

271. "Constitutionalizing the Reagan Revolution," delivered June 16, 1986, before the Heritage Foundation, Washington, D.C.

272. See John P. Stevens, "The Supreme Court of the United States: Reflections after a Summer Recess," *South Texas Law Review* 27 (1986), 447; see especially 451–53; Thurgood Marshall, "Unprecedential Analysis and Original Intent," *William & Mary Law Review* 27 (1986), 925; and William Brennan, "The Constitution of the United States: Contemporary Ratification," *South Texas Law Review* 27 (1986), 433.

273. Ibid., 436.

274. Ibid. Compare Meese's reply "The Battle for the Constitution: The Attorney General Replies to His Critics," *Policy Review* 35 (1987), 32.

275. Ibid., 437–38.

6

The Department of Justice and Administrative Law

In addition to changing the relationship between the department of Justice and the courts, the new system politics also changed the department's relationship to Congress. In particular, the department became more involved in administrative policymaking and administrative law as congressional-executive branch conflict became more frequent and regularized.

Between 1940 and 1968 Congress was the most politically conservative branch of the federal government. Due to the seniority system and the centralized leadership structure it was dominated by southern Democrats like Russell Long, Wilbur Mills, Sam Rayburn, Jaime Whitten, and Sam Ervin. Consequently, during this period Presidents often bypassed Congress and went through the courts to achieve liberal policy objectives. Congress largely acquiesced, or was dragged along, in the liberalization of American social policy as a result of the White House–Warren Court alliance during the 1950s and 1960s. The major civil rights legislation of the 1960s, for instance, was enacted after Congress was presented a *fait accompli* by the courts and the executive. In any event, the social reforms of the Warren and Burger Court era came primarily at the expense of state and local policymaking authority, not congressional power. Cases like *Brown*, *Baker*, *Gideon*, and *Roe* may have liberalized policy, but they nationalized it as well, and thereby indirectly expanded congressional authority.[1]

Following the tumultuous riots at the 1968 Democratic convention, however, congressional Democrats initiated a series of reforms that by the early 1970s had severely weakened central control in Congress.[2] The erosion of the seniority system and, in particular, the shifting of power to subcommittees, not only atomized policymaking in Congress; but at a more ephemeral level these changes, along with erosion of the Democratic electoral base in the South, removed southern conservatives from power in Congress. During the 1970s and 1980s, Congress was dominated increasingly by a younger, more liberal brand of Democrat. Thus while Democratic control of Congress continued uninterrupted (with the exception of Republican control of the Senate from 1981 to 1986), the ideological content of congressional policy changed during this period.[3]

This change, when linked to conservative domination of the White House and the new political independence of the judiciary, produced a new kind of separation of powers conflict in the administrative arena. Conservative Presidents, unable to rely on Congress or the judiciary to enact their policy agenda, instead turned to administrative strategies of policymaking. Congress, for its part, retaliated by placing detailed statutory controls on administrative discretion and increasing its oversight of the bureaucracy. The judiciary has been dragged into the conflict by Congress which seeks to enlarge the court's watchdog over administrative agencies on the one hand, and by the executive which seeks to use them to blunt congressional attempts to "micro-manage" policy on the other.

Because most sitting judges were appointed by Democratic administrations, the federal courts during the 1970s and into the early 1980s remained more responsive to the policy direction of Congress than the President. Consequently a shift in the policymaking balance between the three branches occurred. The courts, which earlier allied themselves with the executive, increasingly began to ally themselves with Congress and against presidential efforts to politicize the administrative bureaucracy. This development further exacerbated the institutional friction that had developed between the executive and judicial branches.

Conservative scholars have attacked the judiciary's role in the new administrative law. Their indictment is a familiar one. Since 1970, they argue, the federal courts have fettered democratic control of the administrative bureaucracy by judicializing the administrative rule-making process, demanding agency "synopticism," issuing complex remedies, and by recognizing nontraditional rights.[4] But the main focus of their critique is the institutional implications of these developments. The judiciary is painted as the culprit and the presidency as the victim. Courts, conspiring with liberal congressional subcommittees and special-interest groups, have emasculated the presidency and usurped its authority over the administrative bureaucracy.

Current trends in administrative law are described by these scholars as "judicial compulsions" leading to a "fettered presidency,"[5] as "iron rectangles" stripping the President of control of administration,[6] and "judicial arrogance" triumphing over the executive.[7] The enfeebling of the presidency results in policy stagnation and bureaucratic drift. The prescription for solving these problems is judicial deference to the executive and energetic control of the administrative bureaucracy by the White House: administrative policymaking should be centralized, the President should be contentious in the selection of judges, and the administration should utilize government litigation aggressively.

While the conservative critique describes an institutional shift in power, however, it does not offer institutional explanations for why this shift has occurred. Instead, judges are painted as being obsessed with the "virtues" of the legal process or "unsympathetic" to the problems and concerns of administrators. Usually the analysis gives way to a thoroughgoing realism in which judges are viewed first and foremost as political actors and judicial intervention is ideologically motivated. Liberal judges are advancing proregulatory interests and staying conservative, deregulatory interests. Thus, while the debate is conducted in the language of institutions, the dynamic is political and ideological. The courts, dominated by liberal judges, have disabled conservative policies favored by the elected executive.[8]

By ignoring the changing institutional relationship between Congress and the executive, however, conservatives have mischaracterized the nature of the new administrative law conflicts and offered prescriptions which will only exacerbate the conditions giving rise to such conflicts. The judiciary has become more involved in the administrative process precisely because Presidents have utilized administrative rather than legislative strategies of policymaking. By setting itself up as a competitor with Congress rather than a partner, the executive has undermined what traditionally served as the most potent obstacle to judicial policymaking, what Alexander Bickel called "the counter-majoritarian difficulty."[9] Judicial intervention into administrative decision making can be justified only as a means of ensuring compliance with constitutional or statutory duties of administrative officials. Conservatives have ignored this point and instead sought to justify a plebiscitary view of the presidency with few if any checks on its power.

Recent developments in administrative law and the debate surrounding them have important implications for the Department of Justice. The department has been utilized as a weapon in the administrative presidency strategy to control bureaucratic policymaking. The recent emphasis on ideological control of the department is due as much to the new conflict between the White House and Congress over administrative policy as to that between the White House and the courts over a variety of Constitutional rights issues. The remainder of this chapter examines recent developments in administrative law, the controversy surrounding them, and how they impact the role of the Justice Department.

Conflict or Subservience?

If judicial intrusion into administrative policymaking has increased in recent years, then it is hardly surprising that we would find that tension has grown between administrators and the courts. The mere existence of frustrations, however, does not necessarily lead to the conclusion that courts have usurped authority or acted improperly. Some constructive tension is expected to exist between courts and administrators.[10]

Courts are expected to perform a variety of duties that will at times frustrate administrators. Judges must ensure that government officials do not violate constitutional rights, ignore clear legislative commands, or act in an arbitrary or capricious manner.[11] Individual administrators will, at times, believe that individual judges or courts are overzealous in performing these tasks. Likewise, judges will make mistakes and occasionally allow personal biases to cloud judicial opinion. Judges are no more infallible than legislators or administrators; on occasion they are bound to err. While the particulars of judicial review in a constitutional system might be argued, the concept that courts are obliged to hold government administrators to statutory duty cannot really be disputed. The question then is not if the federal judiciary has intruded in administrative policymaking, but whether it has done so improperly. This normative question about institutional responsibility is much more complex than merely asking whether liberal judges should be allowed to thwart specific policy objectives of the President.

Although administrative agencies are involved in every stage of the policymaking process, their primary function is to execute legislative policy or "the law."[12] However, most political analysts have given up the traditional view that execution or implementation of law is unimportant and have instead pointed to administrative discretion as a major source of policy innovation.[13] Administrative discretion can even be used to thwart legislative policies.[14] Administrative discretion exists for two reasons: First, as a matter of theory, discretion allows administrators flexibility to implement legislative policy goals more effectively. Second, discretion exists for the practical reason that Congress simply cannot legislate in detail on every policy matter.

The scope and power of federal administrative discretion grew as the federal government assumed new functions and roles.[15] For instance, when Congress enacted laws prohibiting monopolies or cartels in restraint of trade, it gave the Department of Justice the power to decide when a particular merger or corporate takeover has that effect and when or who should be prosecuted.[16] The conflict in administrative law in the new American political system is now clear. As the national government assumed broader, more extensive regulatory responsibilities throughout the twentieth century, Congress was forced to delegate larger and larger amounts of discretion to executive branch administrators. Congress's natural institutional interest in separating the bureaucracy from presidential control has intensified as a result of partisan and ideological dealignment and the resulting division of government since 1968. Presidents, on the other hand, have simultaneously sought to centralize control over administrative discretion as a way of bypassing a Congress that will not support their policy agenda.[17]

What controls exist on administrative discretion? One thing is clear, Congress can limit presidential power over administrative agents by drafting detailed laws and making their duties purely ministerial. This principle, first recognized in *Marbury v. Madison* (1803),[18] was firmly established by the Supreme Court in the 1838 case *Kendall v. United States*.[19] In *Kendall,* the Post Office Department owed money to a former employee named Stokes. When President Jackson ordered Post Office officials to withhold payment, Stokes appealed to Congress, which passed a special act ordering payment. When the Post Office still refused, Stokes brought suit and the district court issued a *mandamus* requiring payment. In affirming the district court's order, the Supreme Court said:

> Certain political duties imposed upon many officers in the executive departments, the discharge of which is under the direction of the President. But it would be an alarming doctrine that Congress cannot impose upon any executive officer any duty they may think proper, which is not repugnant to any rights secured and protected by the Constitution; and in such cases, the duty and responsibility grow out of and are subject to the control of law, and not to the direction of the President.[20]

In this case the Court recognized that Congress may give administrators a practical independence from presidential control by specifying in elaborate detail their duties and the methods to be followed in performing them. As important as this control is, however, it does not respond to the question of controlling administrators performing in their nonministerial capacities. After all, discretion exists largely because Congress cannot legislate in detail.

A more useful check on administrative discretion is judicial review. The parameters for judicial review of administrative action are set out in only a few of the authorizing statutes of administrative agencies. Usually this judicial review is governed by the generic provisions of the Administrative Procedures Act (APA) of 1946. These provisions, however, are written in vague language; for instance, they require that agency decisions be grounded "on the record" or that they not be "arbitrary and capricious." Using the APA's ambiguity as a shield for administrative action, the federal courts traditionally were reluctant to review administrative decision making without express congressional authorization. Since the late 1960s, however, the judiciary has become less reticent in intervening in the administrative process. Turning the ambiguity of the APA into a source of authority, rather than an obstacle to review, courts have intervened to make the administrative process more formal, more open, more on the record, and consequently less receptive to presidential control.[21]

Here is where the expansion in administrative discretion, the regularization of institutional conflict between Congress and President, and the more independent nature of the judiciary all come together. Some judges, defending the court's oversight role as a response to the demise of the "non-delegation doctrine," have heralded these developments as a new era of "constructive partnership" between courts and administrative agencies.[22] Critics of the judiciary, on the other hand, have portrayed the courts as acting unilaterally to usurp executive power.

Although this criticism may accurately apply to the actions of particular judges or courts, it is problematic if applied more generally. To begin, we must question why the description of developments in administrative law, dealing with statutory review, is so dissimilar to developments in constitutional law, where disputes between Congress and the President over the power to control administrative personnel are involved. We might expect that courts suspicious of presidential power in one area of law would act similarly in another. It would be strange indeed if the judiciary usurped executive authority in administrative law disputes but consistently deferred to presidential power in constitutional power disputes.

Yet this would have to be the case if we accepted the critics' argument. According to a leading study by Michael Genovese, the Supreme Court held presidential orders invalid only eight times between 1956 and 1975, the period during which presidential power sustained its greatest growth.[23] More to the point, with the exception of the independent prosecutor issue, every recent separation of powers dispute regarding control of administration—*Buckley*, *Chadha*, and *Bowsher*—was decided in favor of the executive. The Supreme Court in recent years has usually adhered to a formalistic approach to the separation of powers which posits a unitary executive under presidential control and has blunted congressional efforts to expand oversight of the bureaucracy.[24]

Not only have the courts generally protected the President's constitutional power, but they have also been deferential to the executive's policy direction. As noted earlier, the extraordinary success rate of the Solicitor General's office has remained high throughout the 1970s and 1980s.[25] Even in highly politicized areas of law such as civil rights, many of the Court's most controversial decisions came at the prompting of the Justice Department.[26] The recent friction that has developed between the Court and the Justice Department in civil rights has occurred in cases where the department changed legal position from one administration to the next.[27] Thus, the problem is not judicial deference to executive direction per se, but rather what the judiciary does when the executive changes policy direction.

The gulf between what allegedly is taking place in the administrative law arena and what appears to be happening in other areas of law is important. If the argument is that the judiciary has fettered presidential leadership through judicializing policy, then the analysis certainly fails at the constitutional law level. Here, the judiciary has not only deferred to the presidency, but may even be guilty of allowing the executive to stifle democratic policy by accepting the Justice Department's instrumental arguments about the separation of powers. In the legislative veto and Gramm–Rudman cases especially, the Justice Department advanced formalistic, even arcane, views of the separation of powers in order to thwart executive-legislative compromises which facilitated democratic policymaking.[28] The executive's opportunistic use of the courts has been noted even by conservative supporters of the presidency such as Paul Bator:

> My complaint about the executive branch is that it feels free to use (legal) weapons and rules when they serve its parochial interests; it has recently participated extensively in undoing, delaying, or complicating the solution of problems through government.[29]

Leaving aside the executive's instrumental use of law, a second problem arising from the conservative critique is an embarrassing gap between its descriptive claims and its empirical support in case law. The failure to account for recent Supreme Court decisions is particularly troubling. Arguments are often presented in terms of "general theories about emerging trends" in the lower courts rather than analysis of doctrinal development or analysis of actual cases decided by the Supreme Court.[30] Yet, there is no shortage of cases illustrating that courts are sympathetic, even overly deferential, to the exercise of discretion by administrators. Here is where the failure to focus on Supreme Court opinions is most egregious. It is true that administrative law is initially set by lower courts. However, while lower court decisions tell us about the actions of particular judges or courts, focusing on isolated examples of judicial excesses in lower courts, cases noteworthy because they are exceptional, they do not yield institutional-level conclusions. Analysis of trends between the executive and judicial branches must be grounded in the doctrines enunciated at the Supreme Court level.

An examination of recent Supreme Court decisions in administrative law indicates that rather than usurping authority, the Court has displayed extraordinary deference to administrators and the presidency during the last two decades. Although a thorough examination of the Court's jurisprudence in this area is beyond the scope of this book, the point can be made by even a cursory review of recent cases in three important areas: agency rulemaking; agency interpretations of statute; and review of agency enforcement decisions.

The standard for procedural review of agency rulemaking was established by the Supreme Court in *Mathews v. Eldridge* (1976).[31] In *Eldridge* the Court upheld agency refusal to give social security recipients a right to a hearing prior to termination of social security benefits. The Court established a balancing test which explicitly recognized fiscal and administrative constraints as major factors in determining how far agencies had to go to accommodate procedural claims under the APA. In this case the right of a hearing prior to termination of benefits was viewed as an unreasonable burden on agency resources. Since 1976, the Supreme Court has consistently rejected calls for further expansion of administrative due process rights and even relaxed some of the requirements imposed under earlier decisions.[32]

The Supreme Court further restricted judicial review of agency rulemaking in *Vermont Yankee Nuclear Power v. United States Nuclear Regulatory Commission* (1978). In *Vermont Yankee* the Court chastised lower courts for fashioning common law procedural requirements beyond those required by the APA.[33] Although it did not resolve questions about the amount of deference due agencies under the APA, the decision nevertheless prohibits lower courts from constructing extrastatutory restraints on rulemaking. With this threat to administrative rulemaking removed, courts have become largely a passive force in the rulemaking process. The recent expansion in rulemaking requirements for agencies have come from executive orders requiring review by the Office of Management and Budget (OMB), not judicial decisions.[34]

In what is undoubtedly the most important administrative law case in recent years, the Court also placed major restrictions on lower court review of agencies' interpretations of their statutory duty. In *Chevron v. Natural Resources Council*[35] the Court unanimously upheld an Environmental Protection Agency (EPA) interpretation of the 1970 Clean Air Act, even though it agreed with the lower court that the "purpose of the act" would be better served under a different definition. The Court said that in the absence of clear evidence to the contrary, "reasonable" interpretations of statute by the agency should be controlling: "If the statute is silent or ambiguous with respect to the specific issue, the question for the court is whether the agency's answer is based on a permissible construction of the statute."[36]

Although *Chevron* left open the question of what constitutes statutory ambiguity, it clearly prohibited lower courts from constructing their own *de novo* interpretations of statute. Moreover, it rejected the argument that agencies must choose "the best" rule, insisting instead that they adopt a "reasonable" rule. Here the Court recognized that more than one reading of a statute is permissible and ideological considerations may legitimately influence the interpretation adopted.[37] Applauding the Court's decision, Kenneth Starr, Solicitor General for the Bush administration, remarked that it removes "the most obvious avenue for (lower) courts seeking to avoid deference to a particular agency interpretation."[38]

Taken together, the standards of review established by *Eldridge, Vermont Yankee*, and *Chevron* constitute a potent bar to lower court intrusions into administrative decision making. Only one major decision in recent years, *Motor Vehicle Manufacturers v. State Farm* (1983), seems to run counter to the Court's deferential posture.[39] In *State Farm* the Court prohibited an agency from rescinding a regulation it had previously adopted—the requirement that automobile manufacturers install passive restraint systems—until it compiled a reasonable record supporting its policy change. The apparent contradiction between *State Farm* and the Court's other opinions, especially *Chevron*, led some to criticize the Supreme Court as wanting to "pick and choose" when it wishes to defer.[40]

A closer reading of the Court's decision in *State Farm* will reveal why the Court did not reject the standard established in *Chevron*. In fact, it was implicitly upheld by the Court's conclusion that agencies could adopt more than one approach to their statutory obligations as long as they acted reasonably. What the Court rejected was the idea that repealing a rule was the same as making a decision to not issue a rule in the first instance. Traditionally courts have recognized nearly absolute discretion for administrators to decide whether to initiate enforcement actions. The Court merely distinguished the active step an agency takes in repealing a rule from the inaction of not issuing a rule. The burden placed on agencies to defend rule repeals, however, is still no greater than when they make rules.

The Supreme Court also recently reaffirmed its broad standard of deference to agency inaction. In *Heckler v. Chaney* (1985) inmates on death row sued the Food and Drug Administration (FDA) to prevent drugs from being used in executions by lethal injection.[41] The suit charged that the use of the drugs in human executions violated the "misbranding" and "new drug" provisions of the Food, Drug and Cosmetic Act.[42] The FDA claimed that it had "inherent discretion" to refuse to act unless there was "a serious threat to public health or a blatant scheme to defraud," and neither condition was present. In overturning the lower court, the Supreme Court agreed with the FDA. Unless "the substantive statute has provided guidelines for the agency to follow in exercising its enforcement powers," the Court said, an "agency's decision not to take enforcement action should be presumed immune from judicial review."[43]

The Court's traditional recognition of broad prosecutorial discretion and the equivalent administrative decision to not initiate enforcement action recognized in *Chaney* flow from its long-standing concern about intrusion into the executive's constitutional authority.[44] The Supreme Court's commitment to comity in such cases is clear and unambiguous.

Despite the Court's general deference to the executive, there are a growing number of cases in which Congress has embedded in statutes "private rights of action," detailed enforcement criteria, or agency-forcing provisions which aim at limiting executive discretion. These have been utilized by the courts to intervene in the administrative process. These types of provisions have been objected to on prudential and constitutional grounds. Constitutional objections are discussed in detail later. However, prudential objections raised to Congress's use of the courts to "micro-manage" policy are interesting because nearly everyone, including Congress itself, agrees that Congress should avoid playing the role of administrator. Congressman James Florio, for instance, recently wrote: "Congress is poorly suited institutionally for the task of detailed rulemaking and program administration." It is overtly political, does not possess substantive expertise, moves slowly and lacks flexibility. Given its institutional limitations, Florio said, "the interest of the public is best served by Congress' customary reluctance to immerse itself in the details of implementation."[45]

So why has Congress increasingly relied on such devices? Florio notes that it has been "provoked into assuming this new regulatory role" as a result of administrative agencies "abdicating statutory duty."[46] It is statutory abdication, for example, that led to the D.C. Circuit Court's decision in *Adams v. Richardson*.[47] Broad "patterns of non-enforcement" were distinguished by even the *Chaney* Court from isolated decisions not to act based on legitimate factors such as resource scarcity or case selection criteria.[48] Administrative efforts to ignore statutory intent by invoking the executive's otherwise broad prosecutorial discretion is clearly repugnant to the Constitution's vesting of legislative authority in Congress. Whatever one believes prudent policy dictates, the executive is never justified in pursuing policy against express commands of Congress.

The judiciary's conservative critics are correct to point out that Congress has recently resorted to writing complex, technically detailed, agency-forcing statutes. But, this is because there has developed a lack of confidence in the executive's good faith efforts to implement congressional policy. Debate about the prudence of agency-forcing statutes must therefore reach deeper than merely criticizing Congress for micromanaging, it must examine what compels Congress to use such provisions.

The judiciary in large part has been a bystander in the growing dispute between Congress and the executive over administrative discretion. Whatever might be said of particular lower federal courts, the Supreme Court has displayed great deference to executive discretion. The sweeping nature of the Court's decisions in *Vermont Yankee*, *Chevron*, and *Chaney* can hardly be construed as judicial usurpation of administrative authority. Instead, the Court has deferred to the executive except where Congress has given it reason to act otherwise.

Congressional Intent and Agency Obligation

It is not surprising that the courts' critics have ignored the source of the judiciary's increased involvement in administrative policymaking. After all, they are interested in arguing that the courts have thwarted democratic policymaking by placing illegitimate restraints on the executive. To make this argument, however, they must show that judges routinely misconstrue or ignore congressional intent to promote their own policy preferences. Here is where the conservative critique fails.

It is true that courts have on occasion altered statutory meaning to fit changing times and circumstances, especially in politically controversial areas of law. The most often cited examples of "judicial tailoring" of statute are the affirmative action cases. In *United Steel Workers v. Weber* (1979), for example, the Supreme Court upheld race conscious policies under Title VII of the 1964 Civil Rights Act, even though there was overwhelming evidence that congressional sponsors of the act had unequivocally denied it would allow positive discrimination.[49] Even Justice Harry A. Blackmun, who joined the *Weber* majority, conceded that legislative history did not support the Court's interpretation of Title VII, but instead that "additional considerations, practical and equitable, only partially perceived, if perceived at all by the 88th Congress, support the conclusion reached by the Court."[50] Justice John Paul Stevens, writing for the Court in 1987, reached the same conclusion about Congress's 1964 intent, but still upheld the use of race- and gender-based quotas in *Johnson v. Santa Clara Transportation Agency* (1987).[51] The Court's liberty with congressional intent also became controversial in *Patterson v. McLean Credit Union* (1989) when the Court reconsidered a 1976 ruling, *Runyon v. McCrary*, which rendered a highly questionable interpretation of an 1861 civil rights statute so as to allow suits against private parties for damages in race-bias cases.[52]

Even these examples of judicial infidelity to legislative intent, however, hardly reveal a judiciary acting unilaterally to subvert the policies of the elected branches. In previous cases, Justice Department attorneys urged the Court to adopt the statutory interpretations in question. For instance, the Court's interpretation of the 1861 Civil Rights Act in *Runyon* had been advanced in a brief filed by Solicitor General Bork during the Ford administration.[53] The Court's interpretation of the 1964 Civil Rights Act in *Weber* and *Johnson* was consistent with the stance supported by the department's brief a year before in *Bakke*.[54] In addition, in many of these cases claims to statutory rights were buttressed with claims under the equal protection clause which offered residual support for the Court's more flexible statutory constructions. Moreover, whatever the original meaning of these statutes, it is clear that Congress tacitly supported the judicial adaptations. When the Rehnquist Court handed down a series of decisions in 1988–89 paring back the use of disparate impact analysis and narrowing its earlier interpretations of civil rights statutes, Congress responded by passing the 1991 Civil Rights Act reversing the Court. (The 1991 act was a slightly amended version of legislation passed by Congress in 1990 but was vetoed by President Bush.[55])

Finally, whatever judicial infidelity to legislative intent has existed, such cases are the exception rather than the rule. To characterize the judiciary as ordinarily disregarding congressional intent is simply inaccurate. Indeed, for reasons which will be discussed below, the reverse is more often the case, especially during the deregulatory crusade launched by the Reagan administration in the 1980s. Judges increasingly have found themselves confronted with intentional agency evasion of statutory duty and have acted to protect congressional policy rather than subvert it. In the words of Judge Skelly Wright, the federal courts have tried "to see that the legislative purposes heralded in the halls of Congress, are not lost in the vast halls of the federal bureaucracy."[56]

Even conservative critics admit that recent developments in administrative law can be characterized by "judicial insistence on statutory duty." This is why they are concerned to make the otherwise curious argument that judicial appeal to statutory intent should not be binding on administrative agencies. Here we get to the heart of the issue, conservatives want to expand presidential policymaking vis-à-vis Congress by limiting judicial review of administrative action. Why should courts not intervene to require agency compliance with the law? Several arguments have been advanced to support judicial aggrandizement of presidential power at the expense of Congress. Three main strands of argument, however, are distinguishable and merit response.

Statutes as the Product of Subcommittee Government

The first line of argument assails Congress as an institution that is out of control. Reforms during the 1960s and 1970s decentralizing power in Congress led to a form of subcommittee government. Consequently, control over regulatory policy was stripped from Congress as an institution and captured by new "issue networks" consisting of liberal subcommittee chairs, overzealous congressional staffers, interest groups, and bureaucrats anxious to free themselves from White House control.[57] As important subcommittees were captured by liberals, congressional staffers drafted lengthy, complex legislation and legislative reports that purposely mischaracterized the overall goals and mood of Congress. Moreover, as the quantity and complexity of legislation emerging from subcommittees increases, individual members of Congress are less able to scrutinize legislation and the lengthy committee reports.[58] When sweeping regulatory measures were enacted, members of Congress never took the time to understand what they voted on or were duped into believing that the legislation was innocuous. Despite these developments, courts have eagerly utilized the language of lengthy committee reports or vague statutory provisions to invalidate bureaucratic efforts to effect presidential policy. Thus, political scientist Shep Melnick argues:

> When courts look to congressional intent to resolve ambiguity, they usually find the intent of the program advocates who dominate subcommittees. The real partners in the new administrative law, to put it bluntly, are the courts, subcommittees and those administrators who wish to be freed from the influence of OMB and the President.[59]

The argument that Congress lacks control over the policy it produces is even taken up by Justice Scalia who has argued that, "most members of Congress do not have time to read (committee reports). Such documents thus become devices of committee-staff prescription, used by the staff who write them to construct legislative history. They are not legitimate expressions of the congressional will."[60]

Politics inside Congress, however, can hardly justify administrative efforts to circumvent its authority as an institution. Merely because committees and subcommittees dominate the congressional process, it does not follow that Congress has lost control over the resulting policy. The argument that committee reports are invalid because they are authored by staff members and not voted upon is akin to suggesting that federal court opinions are invalid because they are authored by law clerks or administrative regulations can be ignored because they are not written by the President. Congressional staff members are part of the institutional process and function pursuant to Congress's authority. Representative Robert Kastenmeier recently remarked: "Why (committee reports) should not be given credibility, and validity . . . I don't know. It probably is the only definitive explanation of the bill outside the language of the bill itself."[61]

In addition, the description of an ignorant Congress blindly supporting subcommittee recommendations has been widely disputed.[62] Because legislation and subcommittee reports have increased in length and complexity does not mean that Congress is denied the ability to discern their consequences or meaning, or that individual members of Congress are easily duped. This description not only flies in the face of congressional norms of behavior, wherein members seek the trust of colleagues as a source of personal power, it also fails to account for the role of special-interest groups which critics otherwise believe are ubiquitous on Capitol Hill. Special-interest groups from both the left and right read the details of subcommittee legislation and the accompanying reports and are quick to alert Congress to their implications. Although legislators may not be able to read every detail of subcommittee recommendations, it does not mean that they have no understanding of the policies embodied or implied in them.

Statutory Uncertainty and Judicial Deference

A second argument raised against the use of statutory intent is that judges use a style of interpretation that ignores the pluralistic nature of legislation. Every statute undoubtedly embodies trade-offs and compromises between competing groups and congressional factions. This is especially true with respect to the sweeping regulatory legislation passed during the 1960s and early 1970s. These statutes, legal scholar Martin Shapiro has argued, have at least three different levels of legislative instruction: preambles and general provisions which announce broad "ambitious aspirations"; a more detailed level of standards which often contain "agency-forcing" and "technology-forcing" provisions; and a final level of "fudge clauses" or escape provisions representing legislative concessions to regulated industry groups.[63] The different layers in regulatory statutes are often inconsistent. A broad public purpose goal announced at the first level may not be matched by the standards set at the second and may even be qualified by the fudge provisions at the third.[64]

When judges use statutory duty they pick and choose the level of legislative commands they prefer.[65] According to Professor Shapiro, the problem is made acute by the acceptance of "postpluralist" or "postconsequentialist" jurisprudence, wherein judges "favor 'public regarding' or 'public interest' interpretations over those that register the concrete claims of particular groups." Such an approach to statutory interpretation fails to recognize the mosaic of legislative compromises. Consequently, when statutory language is ambiguous, judicial insistence on the most public regarding interpretation equates to nothing more than judicial insistence on the judge's personal preferences.[66] Courts should instead defer to the agency's interpretation. What judges should ask when reviewing agency action is not whether the agency has adopted the "best interpretation" but only whether it has adopted a reasonable interpretation.

This is precisely the standard of review adopted by the Court in *Chevron* and *Vermont Yankee*. So why do critics remain dissatisfied? The answer to this comes down to what is meant by "reasonable." The most obvious response is that "reasonable" is anything not "arbitrary or capricious," which is the standard established in 1946 by the Administrative Procedures Act (APA). Previous judicial interpretations of this standard found that to avoid being arbitrary and capricious agencies have to do more than merely avoid irrationality; they must make "reasoned decisions."

To ensure reasoned decision making courts have required agencies to take a "hard look" at relevant facts and information.[67] Courts have also insisted that agencies compile reviewable decision-making records demonstrating "dialogue" with interested parties and factual support for their determinations.[68] This type of review, which allows judges to pierce through the agency decision itself and examine the decision-making process, was implicitly accepted as part of the arbitrary and capricious standard by the Supreme Court in its *Chevron* and *Vermont Yankee* decisions.

Critics complain that under the guise of requiring reasoned decision making judges can force agencies to reach substantive policy outcomes. The APA, they argue, meant to limit judicial examination of agency reasoning. Shapiro claims that the arbitrary and capricious standard was intended to be only a "lunacy test"—allowing judges to overturn agency decisions only when so obviously defective that only a lunatic could have reached them.[69] In other words, agency decisions, not processes, should be the subject of review and agency findings should always be accepted unless they are so obviously irrational that they border on absurdity.

Such a standard, however, is not only imprudent, in effect allowing politically appointed administrators to ignore the technical advice of even their own agency experts, it also inaccurately portrays what Congress intended when it enacted the APA. Although it is true Congress saw the arbitrary and capricious standard as a restriction on judicial review, it must be understood in the context of what Congress hoped to accomplish through that restriction. Congress clearly did not want to abandon the administrative bureaucracy to unbridled partisan control. Rather, Congress, at the time of the APA's enactment, wanted a competent, neutral administrative bureaucracy that made decisions based on scientific fact and technical expertise.[70]

Against the backdrop of Supreme Court resistance to the New Deal during the 1930s, courts in 1946 still loomed as the greatest threat to a government of neutral competency. Congress assumed that executive branch agencies generally could be trusted to pursue, not obstruct legislative purposes. Hence congressional concern was not about judicial interventions per se, but about safeguarding government administration from the arbitrary and capricious influence of partisan whim and personal idiosyncrasy. Certainly nothing in the legislative history of the APA or the arbitrary and capricious standard suggests that Congress intended to allow administrators to disregard or violate clear congressional instructions.

Moreover, it is unclear how prescriptions for absolute deference under the APA could be squared with the judiciary's more general constitutional obligation to ensure executive compliance with the law. Using Professor Shapiro's own description of regulatory statutes, what choice do judges have when confronted with an agency that refuses to enforce regulations demanded by unambiguous language in the first two levels of statute? Shapiro presumably would have judges defer to administrative agency decisions which ignore these first two levels of law and focus only on the third "fudge factor" level because the executive chooses to do so. But there is no a priori reason why the more public-regarding levels of statutory meaning should be negated in order to be faithful to the private-interest level. Indeed, a dispassionate view would suggest the reverse—

that is, unless there is evidence to the contrary, Congress should be presumed to have acted in the most public-regarding manner consistent with the statute's language.

Finally, debate about precisely what is arbitrary and capricious under the APA misses the point. Even if we accepted a narrow definition, is it reasonable to assume that a decision violating clear legislative instructions or disregarding relevant facts is not arbitrary or capricious? Shapiro's lunacy test would give politically appointed executives carte blanche to ignore Congress and expert judgment in order to pursue partisan policies. What conservative critics really object to is not the degree of judicial review but the fact that review of agency action takes place at all.[71]

The realistic premise of their analysis is now bare. Why should executives not be held to the best interpretation of statute or the rule which best respects relevant facts? Shapiro argues that it is because there are no "best" or "right" answers. That is, there are no "neutral principles" of adjudication which yield a correct or best interpretation of statute. Nor are experts able to agree on scientifically neutral facts which in a similar vein would lead to the best policy conclusions.[72] Given the uncertainty of regulatory science and the political nature of law, the administrative process becomes merely a political game played by Congress and the President in which courts should not intervene. As Professor Shapiro tells us: "Instead of asking the agencies to put their uncertainties on the table so everyone can see that they are really making a policy choice, courts (inappropriately) demand that agencies pretend their decisions are correct science rather than prudential guesses."[73]

The argument that regulatory law and policy science are wrought with uncertainty and hence are inherently political has both a strong and a weak claim. The strong claim is that all policy-related decisions are "political" and therefore unreviewable from the standpoint of neutral principles. Because the indiscriminate nature of this claim destroys any method of evaluating government performance, a second, less ambitious claim is usually advanced. It argues that neutral principles of law and neutral facts are important, but only during the early stages of decision making when administrators are narrowing the range of possible alternatives. After the narrowing process is completed, however, administrators are still faced with multiple acceptable policy alternatives from which to choose. The choice at this final stage is essentially political, but narrowing the alternatives may be done by appealing to apolitical criteria.

Obviously, assumptions about the relativity of regulatory science and statutory interpretation may not be shared. Even if we accept these assumptions in the weak form, however, they do not lead to the prescription of wholesale deference to administrative action which Shapiro and others would have. The judge still has the duty of ensuring that administrators have properly limited policy options. When correctly understood, this is what is implied by judicial devices such as the hard look doctrine and the dialogue requirement. The insistence on reasoned decision making clearly does not force administrators to one inevitable policy conclusion. Rather, as the Supreme Court's decisions recognize, more than one alternative usually exists, but administrators must be able to demonstrate that their choices can be supported on grounds other than mere partisanship.

Statutory Intent and the Separation of Powers

A final objection to judicial insistence on statutory intent is lodged not in the APA, but in the separation of powers itself. For instance, Professor Jeremy Rabkin has argued that courts have ignored the separation of powers principles in administrative law disputes. In contrast to constitutional law, he says, in the administrative arena "the Supreme Court has been eager to make the federal courts into agents of Congress, holding executive operations to congressional intentions."[74] This not only violates the inherent logic of the Constitution, he points out, but "enforcing the will of Congress, of course, can often serve as an excuse for judges to enforce their own notions of good policy."[75] In cases such as *Chevron*, *Bowsher*, and *Chadha* the Supreme Court did rebuke lower courts for intruding on the executive, but, Rabkin complains, it nevertheless "took for granted that judges must hold executive operations to those standards which they can discern as being intended by the enacting Congress."[76]

For those familiar with the history of the separation of powers, this argument appears facetious. Professor Rabkin, however, defends his position in a curious way. He asserts that "any theory of popular sovereignty implicitly (and in its original Hobbesian version, quite explicitly) relies on a strictly positivist view of law."[77] Since the framers recognized natural law rights and opted for a system of institutional obstacles to constrain legislative majorities, they intended to restrict popular sovereignty.

At this point, Professor Rabkin makes a troubling jump. He argues that by equating the exercise of popular sovereignty with congressional action, the framers of the Constitution intended to limit congressional authority over the executive. The framers were not troubled by constraints on the legislature, "but instead argued quite explicitly that the will of the impulsive or selfish majorities ought to be obstructed in order to safeguard private rights and the public good." Thus, "what the demands for administrative adherence to enacted measures actually serve is inertia. Such inertia may be good for protecting private rights, but it does not obviously serve the public good, especially when circumstances change."[78] The argument is a complicated one; however, its thrust is that the separation of powers means to protect "energy" in the executive, which is understood as an executive free from legislative constraints that it deems to be contrary to the public good.[79]

This argument is unpersuasive for several reasons. The insistence that the doctrine of popular sovereignty rests on legal positivism is overly simplistic and ignores that doctrine's modern origin in the natural law assumptions of social contract theory.[80] Even Hobbes, who admittedly takes a thin view of natural law, nevertheless derived his entire theory from the individual's natural right to life.[81] Of course, by defining natural law so thinly Hobbes provided a justification for Royal absolutism, which may be the reason Rabkin cites Hobbes to support his own argument.

American government, however, is more indebted to Locke than to Hobbes for its constitutional philosophy. Locke's theory that sovereignty derives from the individual's natural rights is at the foundation of American constitutionalism. Rights are held as trumps against positive law. But within these natural law constraints, positive law, Locke argued, was strictly the province of the legislature.[82] When properly understood the relationship between popular sovereignty and legislative sovereignty is quite clear. Popular sovereignty was embedded at the constitutional level. Natural law restraints on legislative actions are implicit; hence the rights defined in the Constitution. The executive is not bound to follow statutes which violate those rights, not because the framers opted to limit popular sovereignty but because the Lockean theory of popular sovereignty implied natural law limitations.[83]

Of course, no one suggests that the executive should be left on its own to decide whether legislation violates constitutional rights; the separation of powers implies judicial responsibility for assuring government compliance with law. Regarding the "public good" where constitutional rights are not involved, however, Locke and the Constitution are both clear: The legislature, Congress, is sovereign in such matters.

Any serious attention to history would reveal that the theory of separation of powers, whether in its Lockean or later formulation derived from Montesquieu, was intended to bind executive ministers to the law, to ensure a government of law and not men. The American addition of checks and balances extended additional institutional safeguards on the formulation of law by sharing small portions of the legislative function with the executive. This mixture of power, however, is limited to explicit constitutional provisions. In the case of the President it is limited to the veto power. To argue that the checks and balances legitimize noncompliance with statutes, based solely on policy disagreement, turns the entire theory of separation of powers on its head.[84] More importantly, if judicial analysis of the separation of powers focused more heavily on the mixture of governmental power under the Constitution, the result would be a reduction of presidential power over administrative policy, not its expansion. Such a focus would undermine the formalistic analysis of the separation of powers which the Court has usually adopted, and when applied to Article I would permit a far greater role for Congress in oversight of the bureaucracy.[85]

Finally, presidential authority to control bureaucratic discretion ultimately hinges on the "faithful execution" clause.[86] Even if we admit to the broadest interpretation of discretion under this clause, it is "the law" in the end being enforced. Certainly no legitimate view of discretion permits the negation of clear legislative intent, whether the President thinks Congress is acting prudently or not.

The problem for those who would aggrandize presidential authority and allow the executive to ignore statutory commands is that their argument boils down to the assertion of an executive "dispensing power" of the kind the Constitution clearly rejects. In *Kendall* the Court made clear such discretion was not anticipated by the Constitution: "To contend that the obligation imposed on the President to see the laws faithfully executed, implied a power to forbid their execution, is a novel construction of the constitution, and entirely inadmissible."[87] The Court's opinion echoed an earlier ruling in *United States v. Smith and Ogden* (1806) wherein the federal court rejected the suggestion that the President could direct any action contrary to an act of Congress prior to a judicial ruling on its constitutionality.

> The President of the United States cannot control the statute, nor dispense with its execution, and still less can he authorize a person to do what the law forbids. If he could, it would render the execution of the laws dependent on his will and pleasure; which is a doctrine that has not been set up, and will not meet with any supporters in our government.[88]

These early judicial interpretations of the faithful execution clause find support in the history of the clause itself. The language of the clause undoubtedly came from the first article of the 1689 English Bill of Rights, which declared: "That the pretended power of suspending of Laws, or the Execution of Laws by Regal Authority, without Consent of Parliament is Illegal." This language was aimed at the seventeenth-century dispute between Parliament and the Stuart kings over the king's so-called dispensing power to void any law meeting his displeasure. The nature of this dispute was well known to the framers, and it is clear they intended to deny the American President any discretionary authority of the type the Stuarts claimed.[89] Senate legal counsel Michael Davidson points out that in *Smith and Ogden* and *Kendall,* the "courts drew a direct line from the powers denied to the Crown by the English Bill of Rights, through the Constitution, to a permanent restriction on the President that he could not impair the continuing operation of statute."[90]

The executive's authority unilaterally to dispense or ignore laws after the period for veto has passed has been uniformly rejected even by Attorneys General. In 1980 Attorney General Benjamin Civiletti stated categorically:

> The President has no "dispensing power." If he or his subordinates, acting at his direction, defy an Act of Congress, their action will be condemned if the Act is ultimately upheld. Their own views regarding the legality or desirability of the statute do not suspend its operation and do not immunize their conduct from judicial control.[91]

But, if the courts must always hold the executive to compliance with the law, what if the statute is unreasonable, unrealistic in its premises, or simply bad public policy? For instance, what should courts do when Congress mandates technology that is not yet available or regulatory goals that are simply unachievable? Would it not constitute "a perverse sort of legalism," critics have insisted, if judges require that statutes be fully enforced or statutory criteria fully observed in cases where standards are unobtainable or undesirable?[92]

The obvious objection to this is to ask whose definition of "public benefits" or "reasonableness" should count. Implicit in the argument is the assumption that is disputed: the executive acts reasonably and on behalf of the public good, Congress and judges do not.[93] If we leave this argument aside, however, Professor Rabkin does have a point, though it is much more limited than arguments about popular sovereignty. When Congress passes laws forcing technology or mandating aspirational standards, the executive enjoys greater freedom from judicial demands for compliance with law. If the technology or resources to reach statutory standards simply do not exist, judicial insistence to the contrary would be *lex ad absurdum*. Still, this is quite different from saying the executive is released of statutory obligation entirely. The fact that aspirational statutes cannot be complied with perfectly no more removes executive branch obligations than the fact that perfect justice is unobtainable diminishes government obligations to pursue it.

New Strategies of Presidential Policymaking

The point of the foregoing discussion is not to argue that the conservative critique of executive-judicial branch relations is entirely wrong. Federal courts have become more prominent actors in administrative policymaking. That is precisely why, as we will see, the Justice Department's role in administrative law has become more controversial. But the critique is in essential aspects incomplete. Its most important failure is not mischaracterization of judicial action but its failure to account for the impact of new presidential strategies of policymaking. Why have courts increasingly been thrust into administrative conflicts between the executive and Congress? Why has Congress turned to writing detailed, agency-forcing statutes? The answer revolves around the executive's use of administrative rather than legislative strategies of policymaking.[94]

The administrative presidency strategy evolved during the late 1960s within the context of electoral dealignment and divided government.[95] Two changes in normative theories of public administration coincided with these developments: First, the acceptance of the notion that Presidents should have greater control over structures and processes of government in order to meet the growing demands placed on that institution.[96] Second, the growing hostility to "subsystem" governments and the pluralistic assumptions of group-based politics.[97] As a result, prescriptions for neutral competence in government administration gradually gave way to calls for greater accountability.[98]

Presidency scholar Richard Nathan in 1975 described the Nixon administration's effort to centralize control of the bureaucracy through the use of appointments and central policy screening mechanisms such as the budget.[99] The objective of the new strategy was to bypass Congress and effect domestic policy directly through control of agency discretion. To this end, the administration appointed agency heads who were loyal personally to the President, it used policy-centralizing organizations such as the Office of Management and Budget (OMB) and the Domestic Policy Council to screen regulatory activities, and it used guerrilla-warfare tactics such as impoundments against legislative policies that it disapproved of. Although the strategy emerged during Nixon's first term, the Watergate scandal forced the administration's retreat, and it was aborted in the second term.

Nathan's original exposition of the administrative presidency strategy carried pejorative overtones. Coinciding with the downfall of the Nixon administration and the general apprehension of presidential largess, Nathan entitled his book *The Plot that Failed: Nixon and the Administrative Presidency*. Watergate led to a period when scholarly literature turned highly critical of the strong presidency model and of White House efforts to drive a wedge between the administrative apparatus and Congress. Both Presidents Gerald Ford and Jimmy Carter dedicated themselves to decentralizing administrative policymaking and to the return to a more cooperative relationship with Congress.[100] By the late 1970s, however, partly as a result of the perceived failure of the Carter administration, the strong presidency model was rehabilitated. With this came the rehabilitation of the administrative presidency strategy as well.[101] By 1983, in the new political environment of the Reagan administration, Nathan published a second version of his book—this time without pejorative overtones. Nathan now argued that "elected chief executives . . . and their appointees should play a larger role in the administrative process."[102]

Thus, Reagan became the first President to fully embrace the administrative presidency strategy. The circumstances of the Reagan administration were uniquely suited to it. Despite high levels of personal popularity, Ronald Reagan's legislative program received the lowest level of congressional support of that of any modern President.[103] Given these factors, it is no surprise that the administration turned to policymaking strategies aimed at circumventing Congress.

The Reagan administration's use of the strategy, especially in the areas of economic deregulation and civil rights, has been widely discussed in scholarly research. The Heritage Foundation's influential document *Mandate for Leadership* laid out the strategy in a detailed agency-by-agency analysis at the beginning of Reagan's first term.[104] With this blue print the administration hoped to hit the ground running.[105] Under Reagan, the administrative presidency strategy was transformed significantly from that employed by Nixon. For Reagan, the strategy was not so much an instrument of personal power as it was a method of institutionalizing ideological objectives. In political scientist Bert Rockman's analysis of Ronald Reagan's organizational style, he notes that the President "perfected the strategy." Nixon, he argues, had utilized the administrative presidency as a "mechanism designed to ensure responsiveness to him personally." For Ronald Reagan, it was "a mechanism to ensure responsiveness to a political agenda that Reagan, and certainly his followers, hoped would outlast his own tenure in office.[106]

The Reagan administration pushed the limits of discretionary appointments, cutting overall levels of career civil servants and increasing the number of political appointees.[107] In addition, departments and agencies not integral to the administration's policy agenda suffered staggering personnel cutbacks while those favored enjoyed sustained growth. Departmental losers included: Education (–34%), Housing and Urban Development (–23%), Labor (–23%), Energy (–22%), and Health and Human Services (–18%). Department winners were: Justice (+26%), Treasury, (+19%) and Defense (+14%).[108] Appointees even to low level positions in the bureaucracy were subjected to rigorous screening procedures to ensure ideological purity. This emphasis was not just to fill bureaucratic ranks with "true believers" who would pursue the administration's immediate policy objectives but also to credentialize conservatives.[109] There was also an attempt to shape policy from the top down by appointing highly loyal ideologues such as Edwin Meese, James Watt, and Ray Donovan as department heads. Efforts to achieve deregulation by appointing loyal conservatives to head regulatory agencies were even more pronounced. Thorne Auchter at the Occupational Safety and Health Administration, Raymond Peck at the National Highway Traffic and Safety Administration, Clarence Pendleton at the Civil Rights Commission, and Anne Burford at the Environmental Protection Agency, were all determined opponents of the regulatory laws their agencies were charged with enforcing.

The administration also emphasized the role of central policy screening mechanisms. Like the Nixon administration, Reagan flirted with new super-cabinet level bodies for controlling policy. Edwin Meese's elaborate system of six cabinet councils set up during the first term eventually collapsed under its own weight. During the second term the system was streamlined into two councils, one for domestic policy and one for foreign policy.[110] The reorganization and use of core management agencies such as the Office of Personnel Management (OPM) and the OMB for policy levers proved more successful. The perfection of the OMB budgeting process as a policy device under David Stockman in particular proved effective.[111] Under Reagan, OMB not only exerted control over administrative policy by screening agencies' prelegislative budget requests, it also was given influence over postlegislative policymaking. Executive Orders 12,291 (February 17, 1981) and 12,498 (January 4, 1985) required administrative agencies to obtain OMB cost–benefit analysis and clearance before issuing new rules and regulations.[112]

The consequences of the administrative presidency strategy on policymaking relationships within the executive branch are widely discussed in recent scholarship on the presidency. Richard Waterman recently examined the use of this strategy under the Nixon, Carter, and Reagan administrations.[113] Waterman, though an advocate of strong presidential leadership, is less enthusiastic than Nathan about the political value of the strategy. He points out that it can carry significant costs which will erode the President's base of political power for obtaining longer-term objectives.

Yet the impact of the administrative presidency strategy on the institutional relationship between the executive and other branches has not been fully recognized. Obviously, when administrative agencies are made the forums for interbranch confrontation they become vulnerable to increased judicial intervention. This explains why courts have become more prominent actors in administrative policymaking and why judicial insistence on statutory duty has become politically controversial.

The Department of Justice and the Administrative Presidency

Research on the administrative presidency has focused mainly on administration appointments and the use of the budget as a policy-centralizing mechanism. But the Justice Department has played a major, though largely overlooked, role in presidential strategies to control bureaucratic policymaking. In addition to its own statutory authority, the department's monopoly over government litigation has made it a particularly attractive target of presidential control. The Justice Department thus plays two roles in the administrative presidency—selectively enforcing its own statutory program and using its control of litigation to screen the access that other agencies have to the courts.

Selective Enforcement by the Department of Justice

Because the Justice Department's law enforcement role usually takes the form of litigation, it is especially vulnerable to a nonenforcement strategy by the administration. As previously discussed, the courts traditionally have been reluctant to review prosecutorial decisions. Besides the obvious interest judges have in avoiding unnecessary involvement in prosecution, the statutory basis for judicial review of prosecutorial discretion is more fragile than it is for agency rulemaking or other types of agency action.[114] Technical barriers such as lack of a public decision-making record and recognition that prosecutors weigh factors other than potential guilt or innocence have made courts more hesitant to override the general assumption of unreviewability. In cases such as *Cox*, *Nixon*, and *Chaney*, the courts have recognized that prosecutorial decisions require a balancing of factors that judges are ill-prepared to second guess.[115]

Separation of powers considerations that weigh in favor of judicial review of agency rulemaking also are not present in ordinary prosecutions which are less likely to have broad policy implications. In *Newman v. United States* (1967), for instance, the D.C. Circuit Court refused to review a U.S. Attorney's decision not to accept a plea bargain in a criminal case. Echoing the rationale of the *Cox* court, it said: "Few subjects are less adapted to judicial review than the exercise of the Executive of his discretion in deciding when and whether to institute criminal proceedings, or what precise charge shall be made, or whether to dismiss a proceeding once brought."[116]

Nevertheless a distinction can be made between the Justice Department's discretion in individual cases such as *Newman* and *Cox*, and prosecutorial discretion in the form of a blanket refusal to prosecute under a statute. During the 1970s the courts, faced with the Nixon administration's nonenforcement strategy, became much less hesitant about reviewing prosecutorial discretion of this blanket variety. In *Nader v. Saxbe* (1974), for example, the D.C. Circuit Court held that a Justice Department policy of refusing to bring prosecutions under the Federal Corrupt Practices Act was a reviewable decision. Since the executive's obligation is to "faithfully execute the law" the court reasoned that "the exercise of prosecutorial discretion, like the exercise of executive discretion generally, is subject to statutory and constitutional limits enforceable through judicial review."[117] By drawing a distinction between the exercise of prosecutorial discretion in specific cases and the setting of broad prosecutorial standards, the courts have recognized the latter can result in statutory abdication of the sort that the Constitution intends to prevent.

During the 1970s Congress also attempted to erect a counterweight against future use of the Justice Department in nonenforcement strategies by embedding private rights of action and fee shifting provisions in politically controversial statutes.[118] These provisions increase the scope of judicial oversight of bureaucratic policymaking by allowing public-interest groups to bring suits against recalcitrant administrators. The Civil Rights Attorneys Fees Award Act of 1976, in particular, aimed at countering the type of executive branch abdication of civil rights enforcement that occurred under the Nixon Justice Department.[119] By making it clear that "private attorneys general" would be adequately compensated for enforcing civil rights statutes, Congress created a potent independent source of enforcement authority outside presidential control. By thus expanding the number of prosecutors available to enforce federal statutes, Congress not only bypassed the courts' traditional resistance to reviewing prosecutorial discretion, it also gave the judiciary a vote of confidence as an overseer of administrative action.[120]

The most extreme example of executive nonenforcement occurs when the Justice Department refuses to defend, or decides to attack, a congressional statute that has been challenged in the courts. Although such refusals are relatively uncommon, they have occurred with increasing frequency during the past two decades. Whether the Justice Department has standing to attack the constitutionality of federal statutes is questionable. Nothing in its statutory or common law authority to represent the United States authorizes it.[121] Moreover, because the faithful execution clause cannot be construed to give the executive a general dispensing power, no constitutional standing exists for such a role.

The Justice Department's affirmative obligation to defend congressional statutes has been consistently recognized by Attorneys General themselves. Attorney General Palmer opined that it is "not within the province of the Attorney General to declare an act of Congress unconstitutional. . . ."[122] Likewise, Homer Cummings wrote: "ordinarily, I think, it does not lie within the province of a ministerial officer to question the validity of a statute which, insofar as he is concerned, merely imposes upon him a proper duty and has no bearing upon his constitutional rights."[123] More recently, Benjamin Civiletti said: "The traditional opinion has been that the Attorney General, in the due performance of his constitutional function as an Officer of the United States, must ordinarily defend the acts of Congress. . . . I subscribe fully to that position."[124]

Nevertheless in recent years the Justice Department has asserted two exceptions to its general obligation to defend congressional statutes. The department has refused to defend statutes which impinge upon the "constitutional prerogatives of the executive" and statutes which are "transparently unconstitutional."[125] The argument that the executive can refuse to defend statutes it deems unconstitutional is a more narrow claim than assertion of a general dispensing power, but it is vulnerable to the same types of objections. There is no evidence that the Constitution ever contemplated giving the executive such a power. Indeed the President was given the veto power for the specific purpose of enabling him to defend against such statutes. The framers, however, also provided that the veto could be overridden. This being the case, it seems unlikely that they intended the President to be left free to ignore or attack an act once signed or enacted over a presidential veto.[126]

A distinction should be drawn between the two exceptions asserted by the Justice Department. The argument that the executive can refuse to defend a statute on the grounds that it obstructs executive branch authority is more generally supportable in theory and tradition than the assertion it can reject statutes violating the Constitution in some other way. When the Attorney General attacks statutes on separation of powers grounds he functions in his statutory and constitutional role as advocate for the executive. Presidents since Jefferson and Jackson have asserted that their own definition of executive power should be given deference by the other branches. In the absence of the ability to present that view in litigation the President would be dependent upon congressional definition of his authority.[127]

The Justice Department first attacked federal statutes in the Supreme Court as violating the separation of powers in the *Myers* and *Humphrey's* cases. It did not exercise the discretion again until 1976 in *Buckley v. Valeo*. During the Reagan administration, however, the department filed briefs in three cases challenging congressional statutes on separation of powers grounds—*Chadha, Bowsher,* and *Morrison.*[128] To protect its own interest in such cases, in 1982 Congress made specific provisions for congressional counsel to routinely defend statutes when the Attorney General refuses to do so.[129]

The Attorney General's decision to attack a federal statute where no separation of powers claim is present raises quite different problems. In such cases there is no reason to believe that the President's interpretation of the Constitution should be given special consideration by the Justice Department.[130] The only basis for a Justice Department attack on statutes of this kind would be the Attorney General's duty to "support and defend the Constitution." Thus Benjamin Civiletti argued that the Attorney General:

> Must examine the acts of Congress and the Constitution and determine what they require of him; and if he finds in a given case that there is conflict between the requirements of one and the requirements of the other . . . the Attorney General could lawfully decline to enforce such a law; and he could lawfully decline to defend it in court. Indeed, he would be untrue to his office if he were to do otherwise.[131]

Given the higher law assumptions of American constitutional law this position is arguably correct. No officer is bound to enforce a statute that violates the Constitution. However, phrasing the dilemma in these terms begs the real question, which is whether the executive, without an authoritative judicial decision on constitutionality, can decline to enforce federal law. There is no evidence to suggest that the executive was intended to have such a power and its assertion would alter the balance between the executive and legislative branches.[132] Moreover, the line between constitutional and "transparently unconstitutional" statutes is difficult to draw. On what criteria should the Attorney General's judgment be based? The formal position adopted by the Justice Department is that the constitutionality of statutes is to be assumed unless "no professionally respectable argument can be made in defense of the statute." Such a standard is at best a question of judgment, and at worst an invitation for partisan misuse.[133]

As a practical matter Attorneys General have rarely used their discretion to attack a statute in a nonseparation of powers case. In *United States v. Lovett* (1946) the Justice Department refused to defend a statute which prohibited salaries from being paid to four executive branch officers who had earned Congress's displeasure.[134] The Justice Department joined in attacking the statute as a bill of attainder and as an unconstitutional removal of executive officials by Congress. The Supreme Court struck down the law on the latter grounds. Because the department intervened primarily on the separation of powers argument its position raised little controversy. Congress, after being notified by the Attorney General that he would not argue for the validity of the statute, employed private counsel to represent it.[135]

The only other time the Attorney General exercised this discretion in a case decided by the courts was in *Simkins v. Moses H. Cone Memorial Hospital* (1963).[136] In this case the department attacked the separate-but-equal provision of a federal hospital financing law.[137] The department's legal position in *Simkins* was undoubtedly correct. A year earlier the Supreme Court held that the validity of state-supported racial discrimination "is foreclosed as a litigable issue."[138]

Thus, the case could hardly be cited as a grievous abuse of discretion. Nevertheless, legal scholars have pointed out that the Court was "on shaky ground" when
it recognized the department's standing to intervene in such a case.[139]

The position of the Reagan Justice Department in a 1983 case, *League of
Women Voters v. Federal Communication Commission,* is even more problematic.[140] In this case the Justice Department notified Congress that it was unwilling to defend provisions of the Corporation for Public Broadcasting Act. The act
prohibited endorsement of political candidates by noncommercial licensees. The
department argued that the statute chilled First Amendment rights to free speech
and press and that "no argument could overcome this constitutional defect."[141] In
fact, there were powerful arguments made by members of Congress and by
attorneys within the Justice Department itself supporting the statute.[142] Unlike in
the *Simkins* case, the law was not "patently" or "transparently" unconstitutional.
The Justice Department's action was widely seen at the time as an invitation to
the courts to invalidate a law that the administration opposed on simple policy
grounds. Although the district court dismissed the suit for ripeness, the episode
led to calls for congressional action to clarify the department's obligations to
defend federal statutes.[143]

The Justice Department as a Screen of Agency Policymaking

As we noted in chapter 3, the Attorney General's opinion-writing authority and
statutory control over government litigation provides the White House with a
convenient handle on bureaucratic policymaking. In contrast to the prelegislative
role OMB plays, the Justice Department plays a postlegislative role, controlling
bureaucratic policy prior to and after it enters the judicial arena. By refusing to
bring enforcement suits or to authorize agency litigation, the Justice Department
can prevent policies that it disfavors from ever reaching the courts. Even when it
allows agencies to present their views, or when agencies have independent authority to represent themselves, Justice Department attorneys will often appear in
opposition. The department's formidable litigating experience and close relationship to the judiciary make this a real obstacle to agency use of the courts to free
themselves from White House control. Even independent regulatory commissions
can find this a difficult hurdle to a policy opposed by the administration. In the
Henderson case, for example, lawyers for the ICC found themselves left arguing for
separate-but-equal while Justice Department attorneys convinced the Supreme Court
to strike down the commission's policy on segregated railroads.[144]

Despite the political implications of Justice Department oversight of agency
litigation, surprisingly little research has been conducted on Justice–agency relations since Donald Horowitz's pioneering work more than a decade ago.[145]
Susan Olson updated some of Horowitz's analysis in a 1984 study.[146] But both
these scholars focused more on the question of the effectiveness of representation than on implications for political control of bureaucratic policy.

The strategic value of Justice Department litigating authority during periods of divided government has not been lost on the White House or Congress. As tensions between Congress and the President increase, congressional impatience with the Justice Department litigation monopoly and its willingness to authorize more active judicial oversight emerge. The increased intervention by the judiciary simultaneously increases the value of central control over agency litigation to the White House and pressures from inside agencies to be able to represent themselves before the courts. During the last two decades a struggle to control government litigation has ensued, mirroring the ebb and flow of the administrative presidency itself.

The Justice Department's post–New Deal monopoly over government litigation went without serious challenge until tensions emerged between the Nixon administration and Congress during the early 1970s. Then pressure to decentralize government litigation emerged both from Congress and from administrative agencies seeking greater freedom from the White House.[147] In 1970 the administration attempted to head off the rush for independent authority by having the Bureau of the Budget issue a memorandum to agencies and departments instructing them not to include requests for independent litigating authority in draft bills or reports on legislation going to Congress.[148]

Agencies and departments, however, continued to push for independent authority, especially in program areas vulnerable to White House incursions.[149] In the Occupational Safety and Health Act of 1970 (OSHA), Congress gave OSHA authority to represent itself, though it stipulated that "such litigation shall be subject to the direction of the Attorney General."[150] In 1972 amendments to the Longshoreman and Harbor Worker's Act, Labor Department lawyers were given authority to litigate in proceedings to review compensation orders. This time no mention was made of supervision by the Attorney General.[151] In the Clean Air Act of 1970,[152] the Clean Water Act of 1972,[153] and the Safe Drinking Water Act of 1973,[154] Congress gave the EPA authority to represent itself in litigation should the "Attorney General fail to provide legal representation as requested." Later, in the Toxic Substances Control Act of 1980, the EPA was also authorized to appear in court to obtain injunctive relief.[155]

The Justice Department's tarnished reputation following the Watergate episode posed a particular threat to its litigating monopoly. A 1974 study by the Administrative Conference of Justice–agency relations recommended that Congress delegate more independent litigating authority to agencies. In particular it suggested that control over litigation involving review of regulations and administrative orders, as opposed to prosecution and enforcement, should be returned to the agencies to prevent intrusive White House influence.[156] Horowitz in his study also suggested returning more authority to agencies, contending that it would result in better compliance with court directives.[157]

The Justice Department vigorously opposed these encroachments on its authority.[158] After Watergate, however, it could no longer count on the support of the White House to keep agency requests in check. Both Presidents Ford and

Carter hoped to avoid the appearance of White House domination of domestic policymaking. President Carter dismantled the Nixon administration's Domestic Policy Council which had been utilized to control cabinet agencies, and in its place set out to make "decentralized Cabinet consultation" the cornerstone of White House relations with the bureaucracy.[159] Though Carter's penchant for detail and his personal management style doomed this effort, the White House nevertheless remained supportive, at least in principle, to reforms aimed at policy insulation and decentralization.

Calls for decentralization of legal work became so alluring that in 1977 President Carter directed OMB to study the issue formally. The most direct result of the OMB review was establishment of the Federal Legal Council in 1979.[160] Chaired by the Attorney General, the council included representatives from all other major executive departments and agencies. Its primary task was to further consider and recommend ways to redistribute federal litigating authority.[161]

During the late 1970s adroit maneuvering by Attorney General Griffin Bell thwarted most major assaults on Justice Department authority.[162] When recommendations surfaced in Congress to allow agencies to represent themselves before the Supreme Court, Bell launched a counteroffensive. In one speech, entitled "The Attorney General: The Federal Government's Chief Lawyer and Chief Litigator, or One Among Many," Bell said:

> I do not favor the independence of regulatory agencies and government corporation in legal matters. I think that it is unseemly for two government agencies to sue each other. It requires the judicial branch to decide questions of government policy, a role never envisioned by our country's Founding Fathers. It is time-consuming and expensive. . . . It is clear that the Solicitor General must continue to perform his current function of representing all the executive departments and the independent regulatory agencies before the Supreme Court.[163]

Bell also moved behind the scenes to defuse agency requests for independent authority.[164] To head off statutory delegations of litigating authority Bell signed "bilateral memoranda of understanding" with several agencies. Such agreements, wherein the Attorney General administratively assigned specified areas of litigation to the agency, previously had been made only to the Department of Labor over complex and narrowly defined employment discrimination suits.[165] Now Griffin Bell used such devices as a way to stop Congress from making widespread exceptions to the Justice Department's statutory authority.[166] By signing memoranda the department could retain ultimate, if not day-to-day, control over government litigation and avoid statutory dismemberment.

Bell negotiated administrative agreements with the Department of Labor for litigation under the Employee Retirement Income Security Act of 1974 (ERISA), the Occupational Safety and Health Act of 1970 (OSHA), and the Farm Contractor Registration Act of 1974; with the EPA for litigation under 1977 amendments to the Clean Air Act; with the Department of Energy for litigation under the Emergency Petroleum Allocation Act in 1978; and with the Veterans Administration for litigation under the Veterans Rehabilitation and Education Amendment Act of 1980.[167] The cumulative impact of these agreements, combined with statutory delegations made by Congress, began to threaten seriously the Justice Department's ability to control agency legal policy. A 1982 study by the Office of Legal Counsel catalogued seventy-two separate exceptions to Justice Department authority, most of which had been made since the Nixon administration.[168]

By the late 1970s the White House was again seeking to find mechanisms for centralizing bureaucratic policymaking. In addition, Congress became less receptive to agency requests for decentralization. In the midst of an economic recession and rising budget deficits it began looking for ways to economize government operations, not create duplicative services within the bureaucracy. By 1980 these factors created a new environment in Washington, conducive to the Reagan administration's return to the administrative strategy and the Justice Department's role in such a strategy.

The Reagan Justice Department and the Administrative Strategy

Use of the Justice Department as a tool of administrative control did not originate with the Reagan administration. Richard Harris in 1970 described how the Nixon administration effectively used the Justice Department to pursue its policy agenda.[169] The Reagan administration, however, was the first to have worked out a formal strategy to involve the Justice Department in control of other administrative agencies. Before the administration took office the Heritage Foundation report identified the Justice Department as a key central agency. It recommended expanding its authority and making institutional changes to make it a more effective instrument of presidential control.[170] The administration followed much of this advice—during the Reagan years, ideologues were appointed to leadership positions at the Justice Department and its resources and budget were expanded. The institutional reorganizations that the department underwent during the first term also made it more responsive to central direction. The department's top leadership positions were consolidated, OIAJ was replaced with OLP, and a more partisan atmosphere was brought to the Solicitor General's office.

In addition, efforts to decentralize government litigation came to an abrupt end in 1980. The value of the department's centralized authority was well understood by the administration. The Heritage Foundation's report said bluntly:

> (The) President is ill-served by having too many agencies and departments making inroads on Justice's litigative authority. Litigation, after all, is one of the principal ways in which a President can attempt to control the broad outlines of federal policy—and one suspects that is precisely why Congress has been so generous in recent years in divesting Justice of its massive control.[171]

Figure 6.1. **Justice Department Authorization of Agency Litigation, 1955–1986**

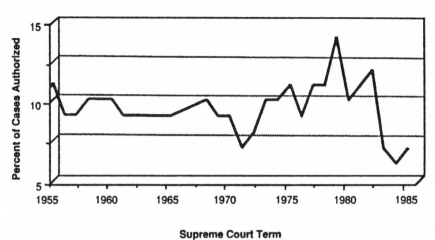

Supreme Court Term

Source: Annual Report of the Solicitor General (1956–1987).

The report concluded by proclaiming "the war against the Justice Department must be brought to a halt." Although the administration never issued an executive order reeling back authority won by agencies during the 1970s, as suggested by Heritage, it nevertheless made clear future decentralizations would not be tolerated. Edwin Meese explained that "restoring control over litigation was a White House priority. We sent word around that [agencies] should stop asking for litigating authority."[172] The Federal Legal Council was also given a centralizing, rather than a decentralizing role under the Reagan administration. Rather than looking at ways to divide litigating authority, it was used to establish legal policies in areas of shared bureaucratic interest such as Freedom of Information Act requests.[173] In 1982 the administration also issued a government-wide memorandum outlining the Justice Department's "plenary authority to conduct government litigation" and the administration's opposition to further erosion of its authority.[174]

The impact these changes had on Justice Department relations with Congress and the rest of the bureaucracy is difficult to measure. While it is clear that relationships became more strained, there is no systematic way to gauge the degree or nature of conflicts. Nevertheless, there is impressionistic evidence that the level and frequency of such conflicts increased dramatically during the Reagan years. Aggregate data on Justice Department authorization of agency suits, for instance, reveal that the Reagan Justice Department was more vigorous in limiting agency access to appellate review. Figure 6.1 illustrates the percentage of agency appeals to the Supreme Court authorized by the Justice Department between 1955 and 1986.

Between 1955 and 1968 the percentage of agency petitions authorized by Justice varied from 9 to 11 percent. The first significant decrease in authorizations occurred under the Nixon administration, when authorizations dropped to 7 percent in 1971. During the Ford and Carter administrations the Justice Department resumed a more lenient approach. In 1979 the percentage of authorizations reached a high of 14 percent, before dropping precipitously to a low of 6 percent in 1984 under the Reagan administration. Although no conclusion about the substance of legal positions being suppressed can be made from the data, it is clear that under Nixon and Reagan stricter controls were placed on agency resort to the courts.

There is also abundant anecdotal evidence suggesting increased Justice– agency conflict during the Reagan years. For instance, in the *Bob Jones* controversy the Justice Department not only alienated lawyers in the Solicitor General's office, it also angered the IRS. Ironically, in this case lawyers for the Justice Department argued that agency discretion should be limited by a stricter reading of statutory language and intent.[175]

The Justice Department's refusal to bring fair housing suits also brought it into conflict with attorneys at the Department of Housing and Urban Development (HUD). After filing an average of sixteen new housing discrimination cases each year under the Carter administration, the Justice Department failed to file a single case the first year of the Reagan administration. In 1982 HUD officials insisted, against the opposition of Assistant Attorney General William Bradford Reynolds, that the department file an *amicus* brief in *Havens v. Coleman*, a relatively minor suit in which the Court affirmed the standing of "testers" to sue under Title VIII of the 1968 Civil Rights Act.[176] Nevertheless, the department's reluctance to initiate fair housing actions continued to be a major source of friction between it and HUD throughout the administration's first term.[177]

Justice Department policy on affirmative action also brought it into conflict with other departments. When Attorney General Meese recommended in 1985 that Reagan scrap a twenty-year-old executive order requiring federal contractors to engage in affirmative action hiring practices, he was opposed by other members of the cabinet. Labor Secretary William Brock, in particular, attacked the Justice Department's position and took the lead in the successful campaign to convince Reagan to leave the order intact.[178]

The Justice Department's relationship with Congress deteriorated sharply during the Reagan administration. As noted above, the Reagan Justice Department asked the Supreme Court to overturn more congressional statutes than any previous administration, attacking federal laws in *Chadha*, *Bowsher*, and *Morrison*. And in at least two others cases in the lower courts, *League of Women Voters* and another entitled *Ameron, Inc. v. U.S. Army Corps of Engineers* (1986), it refused to defend statutes on grounds other than the separation of powers.

The *Ameron* case dealt with a statute signed by Ronald Reagan himself, the Competition in Contracting Act of 1984 (CICA).[179] The law permits companies to challenge federal contracting awards and allows the Comptroller General to freeze defense contracts for up to ninety days when an award is questioned. It became law as part of the larger Deficit Reduction Act of 1984. After signing the legislation, however, Reagan issued a statement that he was approving CICA under protest. Shortly thereafter an opinion by Attorney General William French Smith argued that the law was unconstitutional. On the strength of that opinion, OMB ordered federal agencies to disregard the law. When CICA was challenged in 1985, the Justice Department refused to defend it. Nevertheless, the law was upheld by the district court and later on appeal by the Third Circuit Court of Appeals. Despite this, the administration continued to refuse to recognize or enforce the provisions of CICA. Finally, during Justice Department authorization hearings in 1986, the chairman of the House Judiciary Committee, Peter Rodino, threatened to cut off Justice Department funding.[180] Threatened with a loss of funds, Attorney General Meese decided to capitulate and OMB rescinded its order.[181]

The Justice Department's civil rights policies also brought it into several direct confrontations with Congress.[182] As early as 1982 the department and Congress clashed over reextension of the Voting Rights Act.[183] The department attempted to remove a key provision in the act permitting minority litigants to use disparate impact evidence to challenge local voting practices. The administration's efforts were widely criticized and Congress voted to keep the disparate impact provisions in the act by a massive margin (389 to 24 in the House and 85 to 8 in the Republican-controlled Senate).[184] President Reagan eventually signed the reextension, but the Justice Department continued to refuse to use impact evidence to bring voting rights suits, or to reject local voting practices under the preclearance requirements under the act.[185]

The disparate impact issue was rekindled three years later when the Justice Department intervened in a voting rights case in North Carolina entitled *Thornburgh v. Gingles* (1985).[186] The Justice Department's *amicus* brief argued that in reextending the Voting Rights Act in 1982 Congress intended to limit the use of disparate impact evidence. The brief was a clear effort by the administration to "win in the courthouse battles it lost on Capitol Hill."[187] Infuriated by the department's brief, congressional sponsors of the 1982 law, including Republican Senators Robert Dole and Charles Grassly, filed their own *amicus* brief opposing the Justice Department's position.[188]

A more surreptitious challenge to congressional policymaking came in the form of Justice Department nonenforcement strategy. Although other Justice Department divisions have been criticized for relaxed or selective enforcement, the Civil Rights Division's record was the most egregious and controversial.[189] For example, suits filed by the special litigation section of the division, the section responsible for enforcing laws protecting the handicapped, dropped from twenty-nine in 1980 to zero in 1981, and only three were filed during the administration's entire first term. The general litigation division, responsible for enforcing school desegregation and fair housing laws, went from twenty-two suits filed in 1980 to only ten suits in 1981. The voting section, which is responsible for enforcing the Voting Rights Act, filed twelve suits during the last year of the Carter administration and only two during all four years of Reagan's first term.[190] The Office for Compliance and Review (OCR), responsible for ensuring federal agencies comply with nondiscrimination statutes, conducted ten separate audits between 1975 and 1980, but failed to conduct a single audit during all eight years of the Reagan administration.[191]

While nonenforcement strategies are more subtle than highly visible reversals of litigating positions in the Supreme Court, they are more effective in the long term because they are less immediately conspicuous.[192] The emasculation of the Office for Compliance and Review's auditing function, said its career head, "took away the most effective watchdog over discrimination which occurs within the federal government. With no records on compliance and no pressure from inside the administration it is impossible to say how much discrimination may have increased."[193]

While the administration's strategy allowed it to achieve many of its legal policy objectives during the first term, these successes came at significant cost to the Justice Department. By forgoing a legislative strategy and engaging in guerrilla warfare against Congress, the Justice Department created friction within the bureaucracy and isolated itself from congressional support. The department's relaxed enforcement of civil rights laws drew the ire of career attorneys and increased friction between them and political appointees. During the administration's first term two group letters by career attorneys protesting the "Department's disregard for law" were sent to the Attorney General and to Congress.[194] Moreover, the Civil Rights Division experienced a high number of resignations of its career attorneys and several highly publicized "protest resignations" as a result of its strategy.[195]

More importantly, Congress's response to the administration's strategy ultimately forced the administration to retreat from its more controversial policy stances and crippled the Justice Department. By the beginning of the second term the strain and distrust that had developed between the Justice Department and Congress was evident. Efforts by the department to remove private rights of actions and fee-shifting provisions in regulatory statutes were consistently rejected by Congress.[196] In 1985 three bills proposed by the Justice Department aimed at gutting the Civil Rights Attorneys Fees Awards Act of 1976 were rejected in the Republican-controlled Senate.[197] Congress also began working on legislation to reverse what policy gains the department was able to eke out of the courts in the area of affirmative action and employment discrimination.[198]

As congressional oversight intensified, clashes between the Justice Department and congressional oversight committees such as the Competition in Contracting Act (CICA) episode became more frequent.[199] In 1984, Meese's confirmation as Attorney General was delayed over a year. The administration's judicial nominations during the second term became subject to stricter scrutiny and more frequent rejections, with the Bork–Ginsburg defeat a particularly severe blow. In 1985, several Republican Senators joined Democrats in rejecting the nomination of William Bradford Reynolds to become Associate Attorney General.[200] This was the first time a nominee to that position ever failed to gain Senate approval.[201] And in 1987, after Congress began investigating Meese in connection with a defense contracting scandal, another independent counsel was appointed to investigate the Attorney General. Meese subsequently was forced to resign and the administration had to appoint a more moderate Attorney General. By 1988 morale at the department was at its lowest point since Watergate, public confidence in the department was shaken, and Congress had institutionalized a much tougher oversight process.[202]

The Reagan Justice Department may have left its most enduring mark, however, by precipitating the Supreme Court's decision in *Morrison v. Olson*, which may yet have a crippling effect on presidential authority over the bureaucracy. It is worth examining the events leading up to that decision in greater detail because they illuminate the Justice Department's role in the new style of administrative law conflicts.

The *Olson* case began as a conflict between Congress and the administration over enforcement of the 1980 Superfund law.[203] The law, which creates a Hazardous Substance Response Fund to be used by EPA for cleaning up toxic waste dumps, empowers the Attorney General to bring suit against waste generators to reimburse the fund for clean-up costs. Under the law, EPA identifies waste sites, uses federal funds to effect immediate cleanup, then refers the matter to the Justice Department for legal action to recover costs. This removal of litigating authority from general program implementation reflects the division of authority that usually exists between Justice and agencies.

The Reagan Justice Department was slow to bring reimbursement suits under Superfund. While there was dissatisfaction among the EPA's career staff with Justice's failure to prosecute Superfund cases, this was not the source of conflict; EPA administrators had also adopted a lax enforcement posture.[204] Instead, the conflict emerged when Congress began to investigate mismanagement of the Superfund, and the Justice Department refused to allow the EPA to turn documents over to Congress.[205]

To understand the Superfund conflict, some background on Reagan's EPA is necessary. The Reagan administration employed the administrative approach to the EPA from the beginning. Anne Burford, appointed to head the agency in 1981, shared the President's antiregulatory philosophy and was an outspoken critic of the environmental laws that EPA was charged with enforcing. Under Burford, the agency's budget was slashed, employment levels dropped, and regulatory action came to a standstill. The EPA divested massive amounts of enforcement authority to the states, and the number of prosecution referrals to the Justice Department decreased from 252 in 1980, to only 78 in 1981. Burford defended these drops by stressing the EPA's efforts to promote voluntary compliance with environmental laws.[206]

Although the administration's disabling of EPA allowed it to achieve many of its environmental deregulation goals early, the strategy ultimately backfired—its heavy-handed approach to the EPA drew an immediate and potent congressional response. By 1983, six separate congressional subcommittees were investigating the agency.[207] In the midst of investigations into mismanagement of Superfund, Burford and several other EPA officials, including Rita LaVelle, an assistant administrator in charge of the Superfund program, were cited for contempt of Congress and eventually resigned.[208] In their place the administration was forced to appoint a more moderate administrative team headed by William Ruckelshaus. Under Ruckelshaus the EPA's budget was restored, personnel was increased back to pre-1980 levels, enforcement referrals to the Justice Department increased, divestitures of enforcement authority were halted, and the agency's commitment to its regulatory mission was restored.[209] Like the consequences suffered by the Justice Department, the congressional counterassault on the EPA illustrates the political limits to the use of the administrative strategy as a policy instrument. The administration's environmental deregulatory goals were ultimately defeated by political opposition resulting from its administrative approach.[210]

The Department of Justice played a crucial role in the EPA controversy.[211] By early fall 1982 two separate House subcommittees were investigating EPA's Superfund management. As part of their investigations they requested EPA enforcement documents.[212] (Eventually the subcommittees discovered that Rita Lavelle had been "election-tracking" Superfund settlements in order to help Republican congressional candidates.[213]) Despite being aware of possible misuses of the Superfund, Burford was willing to cooperate with Congress. Burford's attitude, and the EPA's policy, was to provide Congress with all requested information. In the past the only restriction on the production of such documents was insistence that Congress keep them confidential if they contained "enforcement sensitive" or "case specific" information. Thus, after an initial review of the subcommittee requests, EPA officials expressed willingness to comply and began gathering the relevant material.[214]

Because the Justice Department's litigating role under Superfund was involved, however, the EPA was obliged to bring Justice into decisions about releasing the information. From the beginning the Justice Department took the lead role in deciding that some of the documents should be withheld. Throughout the controversy, Justice Department officials saw themselves as bringing the EPA's informational practices in line with a centralized policy on releasing enforcement sensitive documents to Congress. Department officials stressed that: "if individual agencies unilaterally were permitted to grant unrestricted access to agency information it would run counter to the perceived Executive Branch responsibility to protect certain constitutional privileges."[215]

After two months of negotiations between Justice, the EPA, and members of the congressional subcommittees, the Justice Department informed Congress that some 125 of the requested documents (approximately 5 percent of the subpoenaed material) would be withheld.[216] The Office of Legal Counsel also forwarded a memorandum to the President recommending that executive privilege be formally invoked.[217]

By mid-November both subcommittees issued subpoenas. President Reagan subsequently ordered Anne Burford to invoke executive privilege, and Attorney General Smith wrote letters to the subcommittees explaining the executive branch's position. On December 16, 1982, the full House charged Burford with contempt of Congress, the first-ever citation of an executive officer. Rather than instruct the U.S. Attorney in Washington, D.C. to turn the contempt citation over to a grand jury, as required by law, the Justice Department filed an extraordinary suit against Congress, *United States v. House of Representatives* (1983).[218] Briefs filed by the Justice Department argued that the separation of powers prevented Congress from subpoenaing information covered under a claim of executive privilege. Judge Smith of the D.C. District Court dismissed the suit, urging comity. Smith said: "Compromise and cooperation, rather than confrontation, should be the aim of the parties (and) . . . the two branches (should) settle their differences without further judicial involvement."[219] After extensive negotiations between Congress and the White House, a compromise was eventually reached in which the privilege claim was withdrawn and the documents were made available.[220]

The role of the Justice Department in escalating the conflict first into a claim of executive privilege and then into a lawsuit entangling the judiciary in a dispute between Congress and the President raises several questions. From the beginning it was clear that the EPA and Justice had different interests at stake. EPA officials, wishing to avoid unnecessary confrontation with oversight subcommittees, were seeking ways to compromise with Congress. Burford never supported the Justice Department's recommendation to invoke privilege and only relented to make the claim after being instructed to do so by the White House.[221]

The Department of Justice, on the other hand, saw an overriding interest in centralized control of agency release of enforcement related information to Congress. By mid-December 1982, department officials had developed a formal three-phase procedure for reviewing congressional requests for such information. With the Judiciary oversight subcommittees not immediately involved in the dispute, and EPA occupying the unenviable position of invoking privilege, Justice itself had little to lose and much to gain by escalating the confrontation. If the privilege claim succeeded it would shield the department's own lax enforcement of Superfund, provide a precedent for future withholding from Congress, and legitimize the department's screening of an important area of agency-congressional relations.

Throughout the controversy Justice Department officials were bad faith negotiators with Congress. Fearful that the EPA would capitulate to congressional pressure, Justice officials at one point instructed them to purge their files and send the Superfund enforcement documents to Justice. This would have prevented the agency from complying with congressional subpoenas while offering it a way out of confronting its oversight subcommittees. After being alerted to the plan, however, Congressman Dingel, chair of one of the subcommittees, sent a letter to the EPA stopping the purge.[222] During negotiations with Congress and in the memo sent to the President, the Justice Department also misrepresented the EPA's position on withholding the documents. The Justice Department implied throughout the affair that EPA was opposed to release of the information, even though agency officials had made known to the Justice Department on several occasions their desire to comply and avoid further confrontation.[223] Indeed, so far removed had the EPA become from the withholding process that even after it asserted privilege Burford did not know what documents were being denied.[224]

The lengths to which the Justice Department went to protect the administration from a scandal also raises serious questions. Justice Department officials knew that the subpoenaed documents revealed unethical and illegal conduct by EPA officials. They also knew that EPA officials had perjured themselves during congressional hearings. Yet the Justice Department still recommended the assertion of privilege. It filed documents and made statements which it knew to be inaccurate in the district court, and it gathered campaign contributor information on the congressional leaders involved in an attempt to insinuate that their effort to obtain the EPA documents was for the benefit of campaign contributions.[225]

In 1985 the House Judiciary Committee investigated the Justice Department's role in the EPA affair. Its report condemned the department's actions during the episode and criticized several Justice Department officials for obstructing the Judiciary Committee's own investigation.[226] Judiciary Committee Chairman Peter Rodino forwarded a copy of the report to the Attorney General with a formal request that he seek the appointment of an independent counsel to investigate whether three officials in particular—Theodore Olson, Assistant Attorney General for the Office of Legal Counsel, Charles Schmults, Deputy Attorney General, and Carol Dinkins, Assistant Attorney General for the Land and Natural Resources Division—had perjured themselves or otherwise obstructed the investigation. Rodino's request led to appointment of an independent counsel and eventually to a challenge of the 1978 Ethics in Government Act.

The Supreme Court's decision in *Morrison v. Olson*, which permits Congress to vest "core executive" functions in officials outside the President's removal authority, is the real point behind the EPA controversy. Waterman and others have argued that the Reagan administration's environmental policy objectives would have been better served by a less heavy-handed approach to the EPA. By focusing exclusively on the EPA and the administration's failure to achieve its policy objectives, however, the institutional consequences of the administrative strategy are obscured. The confrontation with Congress which was forced by

Justice had two long-term institutional consequences: First, Congress, doubting the executive's commitment to the enforcement of environmental laws, inserted new, strict agency-forcing provisions when it reauthorized the Superfund law in 1985.[227] These provisions will restrict both the EPA's and the Justice Department's future flexibility by constraining their discretion and providing the basis for future court challenges. Thus, judicial oversight of executive compliance with these statutes will increase.

Second, by escalating the conflict to the level of constitutional law, the Justice Department may have precipitated a mortal wound on the President's control of the bureaucracy. The incident prompted the introduction of legislation to reorganize the EPA as an independent agency with its head buffered from presidential removal.[228] Similar legislation has also been considered for the Justice Department.[229] Although Congress has thus far failed to enact such legislation, the Court's decision in *Morrison* has removed the most potent obstacle to such reforms in the future.

Conclusion

The development of the new system politics has significantly transformed the way policy is made in the United States. By institutionalizing divided government, the new politics has regularized interbranch conflict between Congress and the President over control of the administrative bureaucracy. This has increased the scope of judicial oversight of administrative policymaking and politicized administrative law.

Because of its strategic position between the courts, Congress, and other administrative agencies, the Justice Department is at the center of these new administrative law conflicts. The events leading to the Court's decision in *Morrison* illustrate the nature and consequences of that role. All aspects of the drama came together in a single episode: the employment of the administrative strategy against regulatory agencies; congressional retaliation through stricter oversight, investigation, and restriction of presidential authority; the Justice Department's screening of agency relations with Congress and the courts; and the executive's tendency to elevate policy conflicts into constitutional ones.

The complex interbranch and intrabranch relations of the new administrative law have been glossed over by conservative critics of the judiciary who seek to describe judges as usurping executive power. However, the constitutional obligations of the judiciary have forced it into the conflict over administrative control whether it wanted to be there or not. By ignoring the normative relationship between congressional statute and judicial duty, conservative critics mischaracterize the role of the courts and wind up with prescriptions that aggravate the problems they purport to be solving. If the goal is to limit the judicial role in administrative policymaking, the prescription should be for greater executive branch cooperation, not conflict with Congress. It is not necessary to emasculate the presidency in order to recognize that the Constitution requires Congress to be an active partner in administrative policymaking. Historically, strong Presidents are those who have led Congress, not circumvented it.[230]

Notes

1. For a discussion of this point see Richard Cortner, *The Supreme Court and the Second Bill of Rights* (Madison: University of Wisconsin Press, 1981).

2. See Norman Ornstein (ed.), *Congress in Change* (New York: Praeger, 1975).

3. For a discussion of the decline of southern Democratic power and the more liberal nature of Congress since the 1960s, see Norman Ornstein, Robert Peabody, and David Rohde, "The Changing Senate: From the 1950s to the 1970s"; Lawrence Dodd and Bruce Oppenheimer, "The House in Transition," in Dodd and Oppenheimer (eds.), *Congress Reconsidered*.

4. This composite picture of developments in administrative law can be followed in more detail in Richard Stewart, "The Reformation of American Administrative Law," *Harvard Law Review* 88 (1975), 1667; James DeLong, "Informal Rulemaking and the Integration of Public Law and Policy," *Harvard Law Review* 88 (1975), 262; Merrick Garland, "Deregulation and Judicial Review," *Stanford Law Review* 38 (1986), 1189; Rabin, "Federal Regulations in Historical Perspective," *Stanford Law Review* 38 (1986), 1278.

5. See Rabkin, *Judicial Compulsions*; Crovitz and Rabkin (eds.), *The Fettered Presidency*.

6. See R. Shep Melnick, *Regulation and the Courts: The Case of the Clean Air Act* (Washington D.C.: Brookings, 1983); "The Politics of Partnership," *Public Administration* 45 (November/December 1985), 654.

7. See Martin Shapiro, *Who Guards the Guardians: Judicial Control of Administration* (Athens, Georgia: University of Georgia, 1988), and "Prudence and Rationality Under the Constitution," in Gary Bryner and Dennis Thompson (eds.), *The Constitution and the Regulation of Society* (Provo, Utah: Brigham Young University Press, 1988).

8. Perhaps the best brief description of the "new critique's" separation of powers argument and the realistic assumptions behind it is found in Crovitz and Rabkin, *The Fettered Presidency*, 3–12.

9. Bickel, *The Least Dangerous Branch*, 16.

10. See Philip J. Cooper, "Conflict or Constructive Tension: The Changing Relationship of Judges and Administrators," *Public Administration Review* 45 (November/December 1985), 643.

11. Ibid.

12. Charles Jones, *An Introduction to the Study of Public Policy* (Monterey, Calif.: Brooks/Cole, 1984).

13. Lawrence O'Toole and Robert Mountjoy, "Interorganizational Policy Implementation: A Theoretical Perspective," *Public Administration Review* 44 (1984), 491; Daniel Mazmanian and Paul Sabatier, *Implementation and Public Policy* (New York: Scott Foresman, 1983); James Q. Wilson (ed.), *The Politics of Regulation* (New York: Basic, 1980); and Shapiro, *Who Guards the Guardians*.

14. See, for example, James Florio, "Congress as Reluctant Regulator: Hazardous Waste Policy in the 1980's," *Journal on Regulation* 3 (1986), 351.

15. Theodore Lowi, *The End of Liberalism* (New York: Norton, 1969).

16. See Weaver, *Decision to Prosecute*.

17. For a recent discussion of the growing conflict between the President and Con-

gress over control of administration, see William West and Joseph Cooper, "Legislative Influence v. Presidential Dominance: Competing Models of Bureaucratic Control," *Political Science Quarterly* 104 (1990), 581.

18. 5 U.S. (1 Cr.) (1803), 137.

19. 37 U.S. (12 Pet.) (1838), 524.

20. Ibid., 610.

21. See Martin Shapiro, "The APA: Past, Present, and Future," *Virginia Law Review* 72 (1986), 447.

22. See Judge David Bazelon's pronouncement of "a new era in the long and fruitful collaboration of administrative agencies and reviewing courts" in *Environmental Defense Fund v. Ruckelshaus*, 439 F.2d. (D.C. Cir. 1971), 589, 597. For a defense of the stricter judicial controls based on this theory see Stewart, "The Reformation of American Administrative Law," 1669 (1975); J. Skelly Wright, "Beyond Discretionary Justice," *Yale Law Journal* 81 (1970), 575, and Kenneth C. Davis, *Discretionary Justice* (Champaign-Urbana: University of Illinois Press, 1971).

23. *The Supreme Court, the Constitution, and Presidential Power* (Lanham, Md.: University Press of America, 1980), appendix 303–20.

24. Harold Bruff, "On the Constitutional Status of the Administrative Agencies," *American University Law Review* 36 (1987), 496.

25. For example, O'Connor, "The amicus curiae role," 257; Segal, "Amicus Curiae Briefs," 135; Chamberlain, "Mixing Politics and Justice," 379. See also the discussion in chapter 2.

26. For example, the Court took substantively the same position urged by Justice Department briefs in *Brown v. Board of Ed.*, 374 U.S. (1954), 483; *Baker v. Carr*, 369 U.S. (1962), 186; *Reynolds v. Sims*, 377 U.S. (1964), 533; and *Bakke v. California Brd. of Regents*, 483 U.S. (1978), 265.

27. For a discussion of the department's switch in civil rights cases under the Reagan administration, see Selig, "The Reagan Justice Department and Civil Rights," 785; and the reply by Reynolds, "The Reagan Administration and Civil Rights," 1001.

28. See Louis Fisher, "Micromanagement by Congress: Reality and Myth," in Crovitz and Rabkin, *The Fettered Presidency*, 139.

29. Bator, "Legalistic Constitutionalism," 265, 268.

30. See Shapiro, *Who Guards The Guardians*, 164–67. Shapiro's account of "the Supreme Court's jurisprudence in this area" is a brief discussion of only three cases, of which only one supports his claims (the three cases examined are *MVMA v. State Farm*, *Vermont Yankee*, and *Chevron v. NRDC*). In the latter two cases the Court held in favor of the administrative agency. Even Shapiro was forced to admit that Supreme Court opinions presented "a rather open field." That is why, he says, it "is more sensible to present the current tendencies in judicial review of agency rulemaking as general ideas than to try to parse the opinions of the Supreme Court in order to come up with a definite statement of precisely what the law is at the moment." What Shapiro means is that it is difficult to support his assumptions if we take a hard look at actual Supreme Court opinions.

31. 424 U.S. (1976), 319.

32. See *Bishop v. Wood*, 426 U.S. (1976), 341; *Ingraham v. Wright*, 430 U.S. (1977), 651; *Board of Curators v. Horowitz*, 435 U.S. (1978), 78; *Parham v. J.R.*, 422 U.S. (1979), 584; *Schweiker v. McClure*, 72 L. Ed 2d (1982), 1.

33. 435 U.S. (1978), 519.

34. See Morrison, "OMB Interference with Agency Rulemaking: The Wrong Way to Write a Statute," *Harvard Law Review* 99 (1986), 1075.

35. 104 S.Ct. (1984), 2778.

36. Ibid., 2782.
37. For a discussion of the *Chevron* standard, see Kenneth Starr, "Judicial Review in the Post-Chevron Era," *Yale Journal on Regulation* 3 (1986), 283.
38. Ibid., 294.
39. 463 U.S. (1983), 29.
40. For example, see Martin Shapiro's comments, in Bryner and Thompson (eds.), *The Constitution and the Regulation of Society*, 231.
41. 105 S.Ct. (1985), 1649.
42. 21 U.S.C. Sec. 352(f), (1982), 355.
43. 105 S.Ct., 1656.
44. For an argument that the Court has been too deferential to agency inaction see, Cass Sunstein, "Reviewing Agency Inaction after *Heckler v. Chaney*," *University of Chicago Law Review* 52 (1985), 653.
45. Florio, "Congress as Reluctant Regulator," 380.
46. Ibid., 352.
47. 480 F.2d (1973), 1159.
48. See 105 S.Ct., 1656; note especially concurrences by Justices Marshall and Brennan.
49. 443 U.S. (1979), 193; note especially Justice Rehnquist's dissent.
50. Ibid., 209.
51. 107 S.Ct. (1987), 1459.
52. 109 S.Ct. (1989), 2369.
53. See brief for the United States in 96 S.Ct. (No. 75–62), 2586.
54. See brief for the United States in 98 S.Ct. (No. 76–811), 2733.
55. See Biskupic, "Groups Look to Capitol Hill," 1479.
56. *Calvert Cliffs Coordinating Committee v. AEC*, 449 F.2d, 1111.
57. See Hugh Heclo, "Issue Networks and the Executive Establishment," in King (ed.), *The New American Political System*, 87; *A Government of Strangers: Executive Politics in Washington* (Washington D.C.: Brookings, 1977); Murray Weidenbaum, *Business, Government, and the Public* (Englewood Cliffs, N.J.: Prentice-Hall, 1981).
58. See R. Shep Melnick, "The Politics of Partnership," *Public Administration* 45 (November/December 1985), 655–56.
59. Ibid.
60. Scalia's remarks were reported by Katzmann, *Toward Institutional Comity*, 172.
61. Ibid., 173.
62. See the debate between Scalia, Kastenmeier, Michael Remington, and Stephen Breyer in Katzmann (ed.), *Toward Institutional Comity*, 170–75.
63. Shapiro, *Who Guards the Guardians*, 81–87.
64. Ibid., 88.
65. See Scalia's remarks in Katzmann, *Toward Institutional Comity*, 172.
66. Shapiro, *Who Guards the Guardians*, 121–27.
67. The "hard look" doctrine was first announced in *Greater Boston Television Corp. v. FCC*, 444 F.2d (1969), 841. See Cass Sunstein, "In Defense of the Hard Look: Judicial Activism and Administrative Law," *Harvard Journal of Legislation and Public Policy* 7 (1984), 51.
68. See *Florida Power and Light Co. v. Lorian*, 105 S.Ct. (1985), 1598.
69. Shapiro, *Who Guards the Guardians*, 56.
70. This is the traditional account of legislative intent behind the APA. See Walter Gellhorn, "The Administrative Procedure Act: The Beginnings," *Virginia Law Review* 72 (1986), 219. Shapiro recognizes that the APA and New Deal statutes attempted to make the bureaucracy "politically neutral" and "technologically expert" in Bryner and Thomp-

son (eds.), *Constitution and Regulation of Society*, 215–20. The work considered as the classic of the traditional administration orthodoxy is Luther Gulick and Lendall Urwick (eds.), *Papers in the Science of Administration* (New York: Institute of Public Administration, 1937).

71. The one exception critics allow is that courts are expected to protect "traditional" property rights, though here it is unclear why these rights are superior to others that might claim judicial protection. See Rabkin, *Judicial Compulsions* and Shapiro, *Who Guards the Guardians*.

72. See especially the discussion between Shapiro, Theodore Lowi, Aaron Wildavsky and Sheldon Wolin, in Bryner and Thompson, *The Constitution and Regulation of Society*, 238–49.

73. Ibid., 245.

74. Rabkin, *Judicial Compulsions*, 81.

75. Ibid.

76. Ibid.

77. Ibid., 82.

78. Ibid., 83.

79. Ibid., 102–3.

80. See C.E. Merriam, *History of the Theory of Sovereignty since Rousseau* (New York: Columbia University Press, 1900). That modern theories of popular sovereignty implied natural law restraints is clear. Preston King has written: "The 'classical' doctrine of (absolute) sovereignty proved far too absolutist to account accurately for the order obtaining in democratic states. . . . A sovereign democratic state is necessarily bound by some rules from which it cannot free itself." David Miller (ed.), *The Blackwell Encyclopedia of Political Thought* (Oxford: Basil Blackwell, 1987), 495.

81. Thomas Hobbes, *Leviathan*, chap. 14.

82. Locke of course goes to great pains throughout his *Second Treatise of Civil Government* to stress that the legislature must dominate the other branches of government: "there can be but one supreme power, which is the legislative, to which all the rest are and must be subordinate" (chap. 13, para 149). His much-quoted remarks about the separation of powers make clear why he believed in a strict separation of the legislative power from the executive: It may be, he said, "too great temptation to human frailty, apt to grasp at power, for the same persons who have the power of making laws to have also in their hands the power to execute them, whereby they may exempt themselves from obedience to the laws they make" (chap. 22, para. 143).

83. Ibid., chap. 13, para. 149.

84. The American theory of separation of powers is discussed in Malcolm Sharp, "The Classical American Doctrine of the Separation of Powers," 385; Vile, *Constitutionalism and the Separation of Powers*; W.B. Gwyn, *The Meaning of the Separation of Powers* (New Orleans: Tulane University Press, 1965); and G. Marshall, *Constitutional Theory*.

85. See Peter L. Strauss, "The Place of Agencies in Government: Separation of Powers and the Fourth Branch," *Columbia Law Review* 84 (1984), 579.

86. U.S. Const., art. II, sec. 3.

87. 37 U.S. (12 Pet.) (1838), 524, 612.

88. 27 Fed. Cas. (C.C.D.N.Y., 1806), 1192, 1230.

89. See Reinstein, "An Early View of Executive Powers and Privilege: Trial of Smith and Ogden," *Hastings Constitutional Law Quarterly* 2 (1975), 309.

90. See Michael Davidson, "Authority of the Justice Department to Deny the Validity of Acts of Congress", in U.S. Congress, House Committee on the Judiciary, *Hearings on Department of Justice Authorization and Oversight, 1981*, 96th Cong., 2d sess. (1981), 883, 892.

91. See letter from Benjamin Civiletti to Senator Max Baucus, July 30, 1980, printed in Ibid., 871, 876.

92. Rabkin, *Judicial Compulsions*, 94.

93. See Arthur Maass, *Congress and the Common Good* (New York: Basic, 1983); and William West and Joseph Cooper, "The Congressional Veto and Administrative Rulemaking," *Political Science Quarterly* 98 (1983), 201.

94. The "administrative presidency" strategy is an approach by which Presidents have attempted to alter the goals and objectives of federal agencies by seeking change directly at the administrative level. This is an alternative approach to policy development from the traditional legislative approach, whereby Presidents make recommendations to Congress and seek policy change by passage of legislation. The strategy has been widely discussed in political science literature; see especially Nathan, *The Administrative Presidency*; Terry Moe, "The Politicized Presidency," in Chubb and Peterson (eds.), *The New Direction in American Politics*; Waterman, *Presidential Influence*.

95. For a general discussion of the factors leading to the emergence of the administrative presidency and scholarly literature surrounding them see Waterman, *Presidential Influence*, 1–26.

96. See Terry Moe, "The Politicized Presidency," in Chubb and Peterson (eds.), *The New Direction in American Politics*.

97. See, for example, Marver Bernstein, *Regulating Business by Independent Commission* (Princeton, N.J.: University Press, 1955); and Theodore Lowi, *The End of Liberalism* (New York: Norton, 1969).

98. By the time massive new regulatory authority was being extended over areas like the environment and health and safety during the late 1960s and 1970s, the fear of "capture" or "bureaucratic unresponsiveness" kept agencies like the FDA, OSHA, and the EPA from being fashioned as independent commissions. Instead these new regulatory agencies were established squarely in the executive branch with their heads appointed by and serving at the pleasure of the President. Although presidential accountability was supposed to keep them from capture, the belief that regulatory agencies should be removed from partisan influences was not completely abandoned. These agencies were a new breed of government entity known as "independent agencies." How these entities were shielded from partisan pressure when their leadership was obviously vulnerable to White House control was never really clear. Somehow their administrators were supposed to operate in the uncomfortable halfway situation of resisting political direction while knowing their jobs relied on political grace.

99. Nathan, *The Plot That Failed: Nixon and the Administrative Presidency* (New York: Wiley, 1975).

100. For a history of White House–Cabinet relations since 1968, see Pfiffner, "White House Staff Versus the Cabinet," 666.

101. See Waterman, *Presidential Influence*, 9.

102. Nathan, *The Administrative Presidency* (1983), vii.

103. Levels of congressional support for recent administrations were reported in a study in *Congressional Quarterly*, January 7, 1989, 5.

104. Charles Heatherly (ed.), *Mandate for Leadership: Policy Management in a Conservative Administration* (Washington, D.C.: Heritage Foundation, 1981).

105. See James Pfiffner, *The Strategic Presidency: Hitting the Ground Running* (Chicago: Dorsey Press, 1988).

106. Bert Rockman, "The Style and Organization of the Reagan Presidency," in Charles Jones (ed.), *The Reagan Legacy: Promise and Performance* (Chatham, N.J.: Chatham House, 1988), 11.

107. Ibid., 10.

108. U.S. General Accounting Office, "Federal Employees: Trends in Career and Noncareer Employee Appointments in the Executive Branch," Fact Sheet for the Committee on Government Affairs, U.S. Senate, July 1987.

109. Rockman, "Style and Organization of Reagan Presidency," 9–10.

110. For a discussion of the cabinet council system see Peter Benda and Charles Levine, "Reagan and the Bureaucracy: The Bequest, the Promise and the Legacy," in Jones (ed.), *The Reagan Legacy.*

111. Ibid., 112–20.

112. For a discussion of these orders, see Alan Morrison, "OMB Interference With Agency Rulemaking: The Wrong Way to Write a Regulation," *Harvard Law Review* 99 (1986), 1040; and Christopher DeMuth and Douglas Ginsburg, "White House Review of Agency Rulemaking," *Harvard Law Review* 99 (1986), 1075.

113. Waterman, *Presidential Influence.*

114. Because there are no statutes specifically outlining the scope of review over government criminal prosecution, the jurisdictional basis for review must be sought in the generalized provisions of section 10 of the Administrative Procedure Act: "Agency action made reviewable by statute and final agency action for which there is no other adequate remedy in a court are subject to judicial review."

115. See *Heckler v. Chaney*, 105 S.Ct. (1985), 1649, 1655–56. For a general discussion of judicial capacity to review prosecutorial decisions, see Frank Easterbrook, "On Not Enforcing the Law," *Regulation*, January-February 1983, 14–16.

116. *Newman v. United States*, 382 F.2d (D.C. Cir. 1967), 479, 480.

117. 497 F.2d (D.C. Cir. 1974), 676, 679–80.

118. See Rabkin, *Judicial Compulsions.*

119. An excellent discussion of the intent and impact of this act is found in Susan Gluck Mezey, "Public Interest Litigation and the Civil Rights Attorney's Fees Awards Act: Attempts to Close the Barn Door," paper presented at the Annual Meeting of the American Political Science Association, Washington, D.C., August 31–September 4, 1988.

120. The debate regarding the general operation of these types of provisions can be seen in Karen O'Connor and Lee Epstein, "Bridging the Gap Between Congress and the Supreme Court," *Western Political Quarterly* 38 (1985), 238; and Bruce Fein, "Citizen Suit Attorney Fee Shifting Awards: A Critical Examination of Government-Subsidized Litigation," *Law and Contemporary Problems* 47 (1984), 211.

121. See Arthur Miller and Jeffrey Bowman, "Presidential Attacks on the Constitutionality of Federal Statutes: A New Separation of Powers Problem," *Ohio State Law Review* 40 (1979), 51; and "Executive Discretion and the Congressional Defense of Statutes," *Yale Law Journal* 92 (1983), 970. Particularly controversial is the department's standing to intervene as *amicus curiae* in private litigation to attack congressional statutes. Its statutory standing to intervene in cases where congressional statutes are challenged is found in 28 United States Code, section 2403 (1984). Commonly referred to as the "intervention statute," it requires courts to allow the Attorney General to intervene "in any action . . . wherein the constitutionality of any Act of Congress affecting public interest is drawn into question."

However, no support for the Justice Department's claim to standing can be found in the history of the intervention statute itself. It was enacted during the New Deal when federal statutes were being struck down by the Court in private litigation and Congress wished to empower the department to defend New Deal policies. Miller and Bowman, "Presidential Attacks," 57–58.

122. *Op. A.G.* 31 (1919), 475, 476.

123. 38 *Op. A.G.* (1935), 252, 253.

124. Letter from Benjamin Civiletti to Senator Max Baucus, July 30, 1980, reprinted in *Justice Department Authorization Hearings, 1981*, 871, 876.

125. Ibid. The first official statement of this policy was in Civiletti's letter to Senator Baucus. Three years later it was reiterated by Attorney General William French Smith, Press Release 5, May 6, 1982: "The Department of Justice has the responsibility to defend acts of Congress unless they intrude on executive powers or are clearly unconstitutional. . . ."

126. Michael Davidson notes in this respect: "The Framers thus conferred only one specific power on the President with respect to legislation he did not approve: he could veto it. . . . No evidence has been presented that the division of powers between Congress and the President thus established depended on whether the latter linked Acts of Congress to the law's constitutionality. The Framers were familiar with the idea that the constitutionality of laws could be disputed. In the Federalist No. 78, Alexander Hamilton discussed in detail the authority of the Judiciary to deny the validity of unconstitutional statutes. In contrast to the judicial authority in this context, no executive authority is suggested. Executive authority was provided through the veto, and only through the veto." Davidson, "Authority of the Department of Justice to Deny the Validity of Acts of Congress," in *Justice Department Authorization Hearings, 1981*, 889–90.

127. "Executive Discretion and the Congressional Defense of Statutes," 970, 974.

128. In addition the Justice Department has refused to defend or has filed briefs attacking federal statutes in several lower court cases, most of which deal with legislative veto provisions. See, e.g., *American Fed'n of Gov't Employees v. Pierce*, 697 F.2d (D.C. Cir. 1982), 303; *Consumers Union v. FTC*, 691 F.2d (D.C. Cir. 1982), 575; *Consumer Energy Council v. FERC*, 673 F.2d (D.C. Cir. 1982), 425; *Clark v. Valeo*, 550 F.2d (D.C. Cir.), 642; *McCorkle v. United States*, 559 F.2d (4th Cir. 1977), 1258; *Atkins v. United States*, 556 F.2d (Ct. Cl. 1977), 1028; *National Wildlife Fed'n v. Watt*, 571 F. Supp. (D.D.C. 1983), 1145; *Pacific Legal Foundation v. Watt*, 529 F. Supp. (D. Mont. 1981), 982.

129. 2 U.S.C. Sec. 288(e) (1982) authorizes the Senate Legal Counsel to intervene or appear, when authorized by the Senate, in any legal action "in which the powers and responsibilities of Congress under the Constitution of the United States are placed in issue." The House has made similar provisions to employ special counsel on an ad hoc basis to represent its interests before the courts. See, e.g., *INS v. Chadha*, 462 U.S. (1983), 9119 (special counsel employed); *National Wildlife Fed'n v. Watt*, 571 F. Supp. (D.D.C. 1983), 1145 (Counsel to Clerk of the House employed).

130. For a discussion of Justice Department refusals in these situations specifically see "Executive Discretion and the Congressional Defense of Statutes."

131. Letter from Civiletti to Baucus, *Justice Department Authorization Hearings, 1981*, 871.

132. Davidson, "Authority of the Department of Justice to Deny the Validity of Acts of Congress," in *Justice Department Authorization Hearings, 1981*, 885.

133. For a general discussion of the Justice Department criteria, see Schwartz, "Two Perspectives on the Solicitor General's Independence," 1119, 1154–57.

134. 328 U.S. (1946), 303. The Urgent Deficiency Appropriations Act of 1943, 57 Stat. 431 provided that the salaries of four "irresponsible, unrepresentative, crackpot, radical bureaucrats" be cut off.

135. 328 U.S., 315–16.

136. 211 F. Supp. (M.D.N.C. 1962), 628, rev'd 323 F.2d. 959 (4th Cir. 1963), cert. denied, 376 U.S. (1964), 938.

137. The Hill-Burton Act of 1946, 60 Stat. (1946), 1040, 1043.

138. *Bailey v. Patterson*, 369 U.S. (1962), 31, 33.

139. Miller and Bowman, "Presidential Attacks," 57.

140. 489 F. Supp. (C.D. Cal. 1980), 517.

141. See testimony of Alice Daniel, Assistant Attorney General for the Civil Division, in U.S. Congress, Senate Committee on the Judiciary, *Department of Justice Authorization and Oversight Hearings, 1981*, 96th Cong., 2d sess. 853–54.

142. Attorneys in the Justice Department's Office of Legal Counsel and in the Senate pointed out that there were strong arguments in favor of constitutionality. For a discussion of these arguments see "Congressional Defense of Statutes," 974–76.

143. See Ibid.

144. *Henderson v. United States*, 339 U.S. (1950), 826.

145. Horowitz, *The Jurocracy*.

146. Olson, "Challenges to the Gatekeeper."

147. See Horowitz, *The Jurocracy*, especially 107–16.

148. U.S. Bureau of the Budget, Circular No. A–99, "Direction and Control of Litigation" (June 30, 1970). The policy has been followed by the successor Office of Management and Budget.

149. Agencies requesting independent authority from Congress during the early 1970s included the Post Office, the Interior Department, Labor, HUD, HEW, the FDA, the EPA, and OSHA. See Horowitz, *The Jurocracy*, 107–16.

150. 29 U.S.C. Sec. 663 (1982).

151. 33 U.S.C. Sec. 921(a) (1982).

152. 42 U.S.C. Sec. 7605(a) (1982).

153. 33 U.S.C. Sec. 1366 (1982).

154. 42 U.S.C. Sec. 300j–9(f) (1982).

155. 15 U.S.C. Sec. 2603(e), 2604(e, 2606(e) (1982).

156. See John F. Davis, *Department of Justice Control of Agency Litigation*.

157. Horowitz, *The Jurocracy*, 121–27.

158. See "Memorandum from the Office of Legislative Affairs to the Deputy Attorney General: Encroachments on the Attorney General's Litigating Authority," May 23, 1975.

159. For an account of Carter's approach to the cabinet and bureaucracy, see Colin Campbell, *Managing the Presidency* (Pittsburgh, Penn.: University of Pittsburgh, 1986), 59–67.

160. Established by Executive Order 12146 (July 18, 1979).

161. For a discussion of Federal Legal Counsel's role, see Olson, "Challenges to the Gatekeeper," 77.

162. On the debate that was taking place inside the administration over Justice Department litigating authority, see Allison Stark, "When the Government Goes to Court, Who Should Speak for Uncle Sam?" *National Journal* (July 5, 1980), 1098.

163. The speech is printed in *Fordham Law Review* 46 (1978), 1049.

164. See "Bell to See GC's in Authority Debate," *Legal Times*, December 25, 1978, 3.

165. In 1939 Attorney General Frank Murphy delegated trial court responsibility for wage and hour suits under the Fair Labor Standards Act of 1938 to attorneys in the Department of Labor. Similar delegations were also made to the Labor Department for litigation under the Equal Pay Act of 1963 and the Age Discrimination in Employment Act of 1967.

166. Telephone interview with Griffin Bell, August 22, 1988.

167. A comprehensive listing of these memoranda is found in a report prepared for Attorney General Smith in October 1982 by Paul McGrath, Assistant Attorney General for the Civil Division, "Compendium of Department and Agencies with Authority Either by Statute or Agreement to Represent Themselves in Civil Litigation." See also *Justice Department Authorization Hearings, 1981*, 429.

168. Ibid.

169. Richard Harris, *Justice*.

170. See the section on the Justice Department by Michael Hammond in Heatherly (ed.), *Mandate for Leadership*, 403.

171. Ibid., 416.

172. Interview with Edwin Meese, August 20, 1988, Washington, D.C.

173. Olson, "Challenge to the Gatekeeper," 77–78.

174. The memorandum was the result of a massive study on the division of litigating authority prepared by Paul McGrath, Assistant Attorney General for the Civil Division, for Attorney General Smith in 1982. See McGrath, "Compendium of Departments and Agencies with Authority Either by Statute or Agreement to Represent Themselves in Civil Litigation," October, 1982.

175. See Brief for the United States in 461 U.S. 574 (No. 81–3), 12–41.

176. See Letter from Martine E. Sloan, Executive Director of the National Committee Against Discrimination in Housing, *Washington Post*, April 3, 1982, A–15.

177. The administration filed a total of eighteen cases during its first four years in office. U.S. Department of Justice, Case Docket for Complaints Filed January 20, 1981 through March 16, 1984 (the actual number of suits brought is twenty-four; however, six of these involved alleged racial steering of home buyers by real estate brokers in the Chicago area and therefore actually represented, in effect, a single case against a problem in one particular location).

178. For a discussion of the inter-administration debate see "Administration Ignites New Conflict Over Affirmative Action Enforcement," *Congressional Quarterly*, October 19, 1985, 2106; "Reagan Urging Curbs on Affirmative Action," *Congressional Quarterly*, February 15, 1986, 315.

179. See *Ameron, Inc. v. Army Corps of Engineers*, 787 F.2d (3rd Cir. 1986), 875.

180. See U.S. Congress, House Committee on the Judiciary, *Hearings on Department of Justice Authorization and Oversight, 1986*, 99th Cong., 1st sess. (1986), 67–72.

181. For an account of the conflict over CICA, see Murray Waas and Jeffrey Toobin, "Meese's Power Grab: The Constitutional Crisis No One Noticed," *New Republic*, May 19, 1986, 15.

182. For an account of the conflict between the administration and Congress over civil rights see Barbra Wolovovitz and Jules Lobel, "The Enforcement of Civil Rights Statutes: The Reagan Administration's Record," *Black Law Journal* (1986), 252.

183. See Elder Witt, "Reagan, Congress at Odds Over Voting Rights Changes," *Congressional Quarterly*, November 23, 1985, 2429.

184. For the reaction to the administration's proposal see Drew Days, "Turning Back the Clock: The Reagan Administration and Civil Rights," *Harvard Civil Rights and Civil Liberties Law Review* 19 (1984), 309, 337–339; A. Micherg, "A Thousand Days of Silence," *Human Rights* 11 (1984), 18.

185. William Bradford Reynolds formally announced the policy August 29, 1986, see "Justice Will No Longer Consider Discrimination in Approving Plans," *Los Angeles Times*, August 30, 1986, Pt.1–28.

186. 478 U.S. (1985), 30.

187. Interview with Nan Aaron, Director of the Alliance for Justice, August 20, 1988, Washington, D.C.

188. For a discussion of the *Thornburg* episode, see Caplan, *The Tenth Justice*, 240–244.

189. For an example of the criticisms typical of the Civil Rights Division's failure to enforce civil rights statutes, see Leadership Conference on Civil Rights, *Without Justice: A Report on the Justice Department and Civil Rights* (1982); and American Civil Liberties Union, *In Contempt of Congress and the Courts: The Reagan Civil Rights Record* (1984). For a defense of the administration's record, see U.S. Department of Justice, Civil Rights Division, *Enforcing the Law, 1981–1987* (1987).

190. Data on suits filed by the Civil Rights Division is taken from U.S. Department of Justice, Case Docket for Complaints Filed January 20, 1979 through March 24, 1984.

191. Information supplied to author by OCR, August 21, 1988. The interagency audits conducted prior to the Reagan administration included: the Manpower Administration's Employment Service Program in 1975; the Veterans Administration in 1975; the Food and Nutrition Service in 1975; the Department of Commerce in 1976; the Department of Transportation in 1976; the Department of Interior in 1977; the Employment and Training Administration in 1978; and the Farmers Home Administration of the Department of Agriculture in 1980.

192. See Dick Kirchten, "Government of Men," *National Journal* (February 20, 1982), 340.

193. Interview with Theodore Nickens, Deputy Chief for Program Compliance and Review Section, August 21, 1988.

194. See Michael Wines, "Administration Says It Merely Seeks a Better Way," *National Journal* (March 27, 1982), 536, 539.

195. A thorough account of employee turnover and protest resignations from the Civil Rights Division is in U.S. Congress, Senate Committee on the Judiciary, *Hearings on the Nomination of William Bradford Reynolds to be Associate Attorney General*, 99th Cong., 1st sess. (1985), 929–49.

196. For a general discussion of these efforts see Richard Larsen, "Current Proposals in Congress to Limit and to Ban Court-Awarded Attorneys Fees in Public Interest Litigation," *Review of Law and Social Change* 14 (1986), 523; Laura Macklin, "Promoting Settlement, Forgoing the Facts," *Review of Law and Social Change* 14 (1986), 575; Frances Zemans, "Fee Shifting and the Implementation of Public Policy," *Law and Contemporary Problems* 47 (1984), 187.

197. The measures were S.1580, S.1794, and S.1795, collectively known as "The Legal Fees Equity Act." For a discussion of the defeat of these measures and the defection of moderate GOP Senators, see Mezey, "Attempts to Close the Barn Door," 25–29.

198. See Biskupic, "Groups Look to Capitol Hill for Help on Civil Rights," 1479, and "Rights Bill Is Almost Ready After Long Debate," *Congressional Quarterly* (November 11, 1989), 3055.

199. See, for instance, Ruth Marcus, "Sparks Fly at Senate Hearing," *Washington Post* (June 1987).

200. All eight Democrats on the Judiciary Committee were joined by moderate Republicans Arlen Specter and Charles McC. Mathias in an eight to ten vote against confirmation.

201. Reynolds was later promoted to a newly created position called "Counselor to the Attorney General" which did not require Senate confirmation but in which he was given general supervisory responsibilities. See "Reynold's Promotion Angers Senate Democrats," *Congressional Quarterly* (May 23, 1987), 1077.

202. For a general picture of the discomfort afflicting the department, see Rowland Evans and Robert Novak, "Meese, Wallach and Malaise at Justice" *Washington Post* (April 11, 1988), A–22; Ruth Marcus, "Justice Officials Dispute Meese's Rosy Assessment," *Washington Post* (April 3, 1988), A–1; Ruth Marcus, "Top Justice Officials Quit," *Washington Post* (March 30, 1988), A–1; Al Kamen, "Attorney General's Problems Created Deep Malaise at Justice," *Washington Post* (July 27, 1988), A–1, A–10; Lois Ramono, "The Meese Manifesto," *Washington Post* (June 2, 1988), C–1, and "Resign, Ed Meese," *The New Republic* (November 9, 1987), 7.

203. Comprehensive Response, Compensation and Liability Act of 1980, Pub. L. No. 96–510.

204. The EPA and Justice Department's lax enforcement of Superfund and other environmental laws was investigated by the Senate Committee on Environment and Pub-

lic Works, *Fiscal Year 1983 Budget Review for the Environmental Protection Agency*, 97th Cong., 2d sess., 1982.

205. See U.S. Congress, *Subcommittee on Oversight, House Committee on Energy and Commerce, Investigation of the EPA: Report on the President's Claim of Executive Privilege over EPA Documents, Abuses in the Superfund Program and Other Abuses*, Committee Print No. 99-AA, 98th Cong., 2d sess. (1984), 160–64.

206. This account of the Reagan administration's treatment of the EPA is from Waterman, *Presidential Influence*, 115–33.

207. Ibid., 133–37.

208. See U.S. Congress, *House Committee on Public Works and Transportation, Contempt of Congress: Report on Congressional Proceedings Against Anne M. Gorsuch, Administrator, U.S. EPA for Withholding Documents*, House Report No. 97–968, 97th Cong., 2d sess. (1982), 6.

209. Waterman, *Presidential Influence*, 136–37.

210. Ibid., 137–43.

211. See U.S. Congress, House Committee on the Judiciary, *Report on Investigation of the Role of the Department of Justice in the Withholding of Environmental Protection Agency Documents from Congress 1981–1982*, 98th Cong., 1st sess., H.R. Rep. No. 99–435 (1985).

212. The Oversight Subcommittee on Public Works and Transportation (the Levitas Subcommittee) and the Oversight Subcommittee of the Committee on Energy and Commerce (the Dingle Subcommittee).

213. See *EPA Oversight Subcommittee Report* (1984).

214. See House Judiciary Committee, *Report*, 28–30.

215. Ibid., 23.

216. Ibid., 214–29.

217. See "Memorandum for the President from Theodore Olson," dated October 25, 1982.

218. 556 F. Supp. 150 (D.D.C., 1983). For a discussion of the Justice Department's role in this case, see Robert Palmer, "The Confrontation of the Legislative and Executive Branches," 331.

219. Ibid., 153.

220. See "Memorandum of Understanding," March 9, 1983, signed by Subcommittee Chairman Dingle and White House Legal Counsel Fred Fielding.

221. House Judiciary Committee, *Report*, 180–82.

222. See letter from Dingle to Robert Perry, October 8, 1982, in U.S. Congress, House Committee on Energy and Commerce, *Investigation of the ERA: Report on Abuses in the Superfund Program* (1984), 224.

223. House Judiciary Committee, *Report* (1985), 141.

224. Ibid., 229.

225. Ibid.

226. Ibid.

227. Congress's efforts to restrict EPA discretion in the wake of the Superfund controversy is discussed in Florio, "Congress as Reluctant Regulator," 351, and in "Superfund Reauthorization," *Congressional Quarterly Almanac* (1984), 309–13.

228. At least two measures were introduced to remove the EPA from presidential control, HR.1582 and S.547, 98th Cong., 2d sess. (1983).

229. Interview with Mark Gitenstein, Chief Majority Counsel, Senate Committee on the Judiciary, Washington, D.C., August 19, 1988.

230. See P.E. Arnold and L.J. Roos, "Toward a Theory of Congressional-Executive Branch Relations," *Review of Politics* 26 (1974), 140.

7

Conclusion:
The Politics of Justice

This book has examined the factors leading to the recent controversy surrounding the political role of the Attorney General. Throughout it has emphasized the impact that broader developments in the American political system have had on government legal institutions and the making of legal policy. The nationalization of governmental power, the judicialization of large areas of public policy, and the institutionalization of partisan conflict have raised the political value of federal legal policy. The Reagan administration's appreciation of the strategic value of legal policy led it to a thoroughly politicized view of the Justice Department. The rigorous screening of judicial nominees, aggressive use of government litigation, adroit exercise of rhetoric, and the use of the department to screen administrative policy were all part of a more comprehensive strategy.

Although Reagan's politicization of the Department of Justice was more systematic than that of any previous administration, it was not without precedent—other administrations have utilized the department to pursue their policy agendas. The extraordinary controversy surrounding government legal administration during the 1980s was primarily the product of other factors which made the political environment in which the Reagan Justice Department operated unique. First, the administration came to office on the heels of post-Watergate reforms aimed at depoliticizing legal administration and restoring the Attorney General's quasi-judicial status. The appointment of Edwin Meese in particular challenged the norms and conventions established under Attorneys General Edward Levi and Griffin Bell. Second, the extremely conservative nature of the administration's political agenda forced the Justice Department into a confrontation with a judiciary that, at the outset of the Reagan administration, was largely liberal, and was politically more independent than ever before. The New Right hue cast on Justice Department policy during the second term also caused friction within the conservative coalition itself. Finally, the Reagan administration's reliance on administrative, rather than legislative, strategies of policymaking alienated the Justice Department from congressional support even among moderate Republicans.

Was the administration's campaign to reshape American law and legal institutions successful? The administration was able to achieve many of its judicial goals. By the time Reagan left office in 1988, the lower federal courts were filled with young, conservative judges.[1] A solid conservative majority appeared to be in place on the Supreme Court,[2] and discussion of American jurisprudence had taken on board the conservative agenda.

The administration also realized many of its specific policy objectives. Relaxed enforcement of antitrust laws permitted a record number of mergers and corporate takeovers. The Supreme Court had begun placing new restrictions on affirmative action programs and imposing stricter evidentiary requirements in discrimination cases.[3] It chiseled away some of the protections in the area of criminal justice, establishing "good-faith exceptions" to the exclusionary rule and the *Miranda* right, and had become more permissive on capital punishment.[4] Finally, the Court allowed control over several areas of social policy, such as abortion, homosexual rights, and student speech to be returned to state and local government.[5]

Nevertheless, the administration's politicization of government legal administration had tremendous costs. The controversy that Meese's actions as Attorney General created led to congressional investigations of his conduct, the appointment of two separate independent counsels, and his eventual resignation. In the aftermath, the Reagan administration was forced to appoint a more traditional, moderate Attorney General, Richard Thornburgh, who devoted his first two years in office to restoring public confidence in the department and repairing its relationship with Congress.[6] Although changes in Justice Department policy were not dramatic, Thornburgh adopted a less confrontational style and attempted to defuse the highly charged political atmosphere surrounding legal policy that predominated during the 1980s. OLP's function was altered, the department's civil rights enforcement record improved, and in public speeches the Attorney General returned to discussing ordinary, even tedious topics.

The Reagan administration's heavy-handed approach to the Justice Department also produced a backlash from liberal interest groups. Groups monitoring the department's activities, such as the Alliance for Justice and the Leadership Conference on Civil Rights, enjoyed a surge in support during the 1980s and became key actors in blunting the administration's legal policy agenda in Congress and the courts. The involvement of these groups in recent confirmation battles surrounding judges and Justice Department personnel illustrates the influence that they have gained during the Reagan years.

Moreover, by forgoing a broad legislative effort, some victories the administration achieved in reshaping legal policy may prove temporary. Many of the Supreme Court's recent decisions upholding conservative policy reforms in civil rights, for instance, have been reversed by the 1991 Civil Rights Act.[7] Moreover, without statutory entrenchment, the reforms will have little staying power if the composition of the federal bench were to change under a future Democratic administration. In addition, as the federal courts have started to move in a more conservative direction a new judicial federalism has emerged in which state attorneys general and state courts have stepped in to protect rights and privileges formerly guarded in the federal courts.[8]

Far more important than policy setbacks, however, are the longer-term institutional consequences. Congressional oversight of the Justice Department became more intense in the wake of the Reagan administration. In particular, the Judiciary Committee has become more rigorous in screening Justice Department appointments. It rejected William Bradford Reynolds's nomination to be Associate Attorney General in 1985. In 1989, William Lucas, Bush's pick to be Assistant Attorney General for Civil Rights, became the first nominee to that position to be rejected by the Senate. Although Lucas would have been only the second black to fill the post, Senate Democrats opposed the appointment because Lucas lacked civil rights experience and supported many of the controversial policies pursued by Reynolds.[9] Attorney General Thornburgh also was forced to abandon his choice to become Deputy Attorney General. Thornburgh wanted to nominated Robert Fiske, Jr. to the post, but conservatives on the Judiciary Committee objected because Fiske had formerly served as chair of the ABA standing committee and had attracted conservative ire because the committee had been giving low ratings to Reagan's second-term judicial nominees. When the two ranking Republicans on the Judiciary Committee, Strom Thurmond and Orrin Hatch, both indicated they would oppose the nominee, the administration was forced to settle on Donald Ayer for the post instead.[10]

Senate screening of judicial appointments has changed even more markedly since the Reagan administration. The Senate, said Senator Patrick Leahy, has "rediscovered the advice and consent clause of the Constitution." It is widely agreed that the Bork confirmation battle marked a new era in the advice and consent function on judicial appointments.[11] The Senate has become much less hesitant to ask detailed questions of nominees and for the first time has asserted the right to reject a President's nominee based strictly on the candidate's political philosophy.[12] The Bush administration's nomination of David Souter to the Supreme Court to replace Justice Brennan indicates what effect this change will likely have on future nominations to the high court. Presidents will be tempted to appoint judges with little or no written record or political experience that could be exploited during the confirmation process and will advise them to be less frank during congressional hearings.[13]

Finally, the Reagan administration's aggressive use of the Justice Department to pursue its political agenda exacerbated the trends in interbranch relations which had led to the politicization of legal administration in the first place. The cumulative impact of the Reagan years is that more, not fewer, areas of public policy have been judicialized. In particular, the courts assumed a much greater role in the administrative process during the 1980s, and it is likely that disputes over control of the bureaucracy will become an even more important concern for courts during the 1990s.

Here is where recent conservative critics of the judiciary err. The best way to reduce the policymaking role of the federal courts is to encourage cooperation, not confrontation, between Congress and the executive. In a system that vests legislative authority in Congress, any model of strong presidential leadership cannot afford to set itself up as a competitor with Congress. If it does, the likely outcome will be stricter congressional control of administration and greater judicial oversight of the executive.

This may be the most important lesson to emerge from the controversy surrounding the Reagan Justice Department. After years of neglect, American scholars are returning to the study of institutions and institutional relationships as primary factors in shaping national politics. Certainly, this neglect added to confusion regarding the normative role of the Attorney General and the Department of Justice. New studies of institutions are particularly important in light of recent changes in the American political system which have institutionalized partisan and ideological conflict, thus transforming policy disputes into constitutional ones. Political actors now must weigh more carefully the long-term institutional consequences of their actions against any short-term policy objectives they hope to achieve. Even "realists" must admit that it would benefit conservatives little if short-term legal policy goals were accomplished at the expense of sacrificing presidential power over the bureaucracy in the long term. Recent separation of powers conflict should not, and cannot be understood simply as a series of unconnected policy disputes. The legal positions asserted by the Justice Department in *Bowsher* and *Chadha*, for instance, would be strange indeed if defended solely as disputes over policy.

Ultimately the political role of the Attorney General is determined by the constitutional-institutional framework in which he operates. The dysfunction created when a system that requires institutions to share power becomes overly confrontational is illustrated by the recent controversy surrounding the Justice Department and government legal policy. The American separation of powers works only when each branch is willing to act with comity toward the others. Although the American system does not permit the same degree of collaboration between branches that exists in the British system, greater comity and cooperation than recent experience suggests has in the past existed and can again exist.

Notes

1. See generally O'Brien, "The Reagan Judges," and Schwartz, *Packing the Courts.*

2. See Joan Biskupic, "Solid New Majority Evident as 1988–1989 Term Ends," *Congressional Quarterly*, July 8, 1989, 1694.

3. See *Richmond v. J.A. Croson*, 109 S.Ct. (1989), 706, and *Patterson v. McLean Credit Union*, 109 S.Ct. (1989), 2363.

4. See *United States v. Leon*, 468 U.S. (1984), 897; *Oregon v. Elstad*, 470 U.S.

(1985), 298; and *McCleskey v. Kemp*, 428 U.S. (1987), 278.

5. See *Webster v. Reproductive Services*, 109 S.Ct. (1989), 3040; *Bowers v. Hardwick*, 478 U.S. (1986), 186; and *Hazelwood School Distr. v. Kulhmeier*, 108 S.Ct. (1988), 562.

6. See John Moore, "The Justice Department: There's Nowhere to Go But Up," *National Journal*, June, 10, 1989, 1478.

7. See Joan Biskupic, "Rights Bill is Almost Ready After Long Delay, Debate," *Congressional Quarterly*, November 11, 1989, 3055, and "Groups Look to Capitol Hill for Help on Civil Rights," *Congressional Quarterly*, June 17, 1989, 1479.

8. For further discussion, see Ronald Collins and Peter Galie, "Upholding Rights Left Unprotected by the U.S. Supreme Court," *National Law Journal*, November 9, 1987, 32; Stanley H. Friedelbaum, *Human Rights in the States: New Directions in Constitutional Policymaking* (Westport, Conn.: Greenwood, 1988); and John Moore, "New Cops on the Beat," *National Journal*, May 23, 1987, 1338.

9. See Biskupic, "Lucas Comes Under Sharp Fire," 1871.

10. Biskupic, "Thornburgh's Bumpy Start Surprises Some on Hill," 2215; and Devroy, "Dispute on Justice Nominee Persists."

11. See Nadine Cohodas, "Reagan's Legacy Is Not Only on the Bench," *Congressional Quarterly*, November 26, 1988, 3392, and Ethan Bonner, *Battle For Justice: How the Bork Nomination Shook America* (New York: Norton, 1989).

12. On previous occasions when nominees have been rejected because of political differences the real reason for opposition was masked by other issues such as competence or racism. Bork was the first to have his nomination rejected solely on his political philosophy. For an argument against the Senate's newly established role, see Bruce Fein, "The President's Power to Appoint Federal Judges: A Popular Check on Court Usurpations," Washington Legal Foundations, Critical Legal Issues Working Paper Series—No. 1, August 1985.

13. See Eastland, "Anonymity: A Feather in Souter's Cap?"

8

Epilogue:
Reflections on Justice during
the Bush Administration

Just as this book was going to press, debate over federal legal policy was again thrust to the center stage of American politics. In 1991, the Senate and the White House became enmeshed in another devisive confirmation battle: the nomination of Clarence Thomas for a seat on the high court. This struggle coincided with the resignation of Richard Thornburgh and President Bush's appointment of William P. Barr to become the seventy-seventh Attorney General.

In addition, several books on the Justice Department and legal policies of the Reagan administration appeared. In the two most noteworthy works, William French Smith and Charles Fried wrote spirited apologies for the policies pursued by the Reagan Justice Department.[1] Like earlier studies, these works explicitly or implicitly view government legal offices as institutional shells, the roles of which are shaped by the individuals who occupy them. Thus, Fried and Smith make the same mistake as many of their critics: they assume that individual Attorneys General or Solicitors General are free to chose whether they will be partisan advocates for the administration's policies or neutral advisors on questions of law.[2]

Such freedom does of course exist at a certain level. By viewing legal policy as a by-product of the individuals who hold office, however, we obscure the role that larger institutional forces play in defining the scope and political context of legal policy. For instance, this book has argued that the Justice Department's sudden interest in civil rights litigation during the 1950s should be viewed against the increased importance that the northern black vote represented to presidential electoral coalitions, and the resistance of congressional southern Democrats to civil rights legislation. Likewise, the rhetorical attacks on the Supreme Court launched by John Mitchell or Edwin Meese become more interesting when one realizes how judicialization of large areas of social policy increased not just the political power but also the independence of the Court. The same is true of the Justice Department's

226

arguments in recent administrative law cases; these take on a new dimension when placed in the context of an electoral system that has given the Republican party a seemingly permanent lock on the White House and has entrenched Democrats in Congress.

Focusing on the macroinstitutional contexts of legal policymaking also yields insight into the activities and policies of the Bush Justice Department. Tarnished by the controversies of the Reagan years, the Justice Department in 1988 seemed poised to return to a more neutral, less partisan role. George Bush's moderate politics and Richard Thornburgh's reputation as a political pragmatist augured for a period of reform and depoliticization similar to that which accompanied the appointment Edward Levi in 1975.[3] The anticipated changes never took place, however, and the bipartisan goodwill accompanying Thornburgh's appointment quickly faded.[4] Instead, the policies of the Justice Department under Richard Thornburgh and William Barr have been continuations of those initiated during the Reagan years.

To be sure, less controversy has attached to Justice Department policies since Meese resigned in 1988. This is because Thornburgh inherited a department already purged of internal opposition to the conservative agenda and because he moved aggressively to restrict further scrutiny of Justice Department activities. Shortly after taking office, Thornburgh fired eleven of fifteen career officers in the Office of Public Information, the office that responds to queries from the press and public, and he reduced by a third the number of employees in the Office of Legislative Liaison.[5] Thornburgh also changed the format of the *Attorney General's Annual Report*, reducing its size and eliminating information on the department's case filings in the Supreme Court and on the screening of agency appeals, information previously made public in the *Report* since the 1920s. These moves, together with new procedures for approving interviews of departmental officials and steps to stop leaks to the press, halted the flow of information about Justice Department activities.[6]

By emphasizing policy areas of bipartisan consensus, Thornburgh was also able to improve the Justice Department's image. In the war on drugs, for instance, he was successful at increasing the Drug Enforcement Administration's budget by more than 40 percent and in winning ratification of a United Nation's convention aimed at improving international cooperation in curbing the drug trade.[7]

While these measures helped still public controversy, the devisive legal policies of the Reagan administration continued to haunt Justice Department relations with Congress. In addition to Senate rejection of William Lucas as head of the Civil Rights Division and the forced withdrawal of Robert Fiske Stone as Deputy Attorney General, Thornburgh also came under attack during his first year for failure to investigate allegations of fraud and abuse in the Department of Housing and Urban Development during the Reagan administration.[8]

Thornburgh's imperious style also strained relationships inside the Justice

Department. He was criticized for relying too heavily on a small clique of young aides he transplanted from Pennsylvania. These included David Runkel, who acted as both chief of staff and chief spokesman for the Attorney General, and Henry Barr, an advisor on criminal law who resigned under a cloud and was later convicted of illegal use of narcotics.[9] Deputy Attorney General Donald Ayer and another top assistant, Peter Nowinski, resigned in May 1990, alleging Thornburgh had undermined the Office of Professional Responsibility, which was investigating whether aides to Thornburgh leaked information about FBI probes of prominent Democrats. Thornburgh and Ayer also had clashed over sentencing guidelines that would have imposed stiffer fines on corporations convicted of crimes such as fraud or willful pollution. The guidelines, proposed by the United States Sentencing Commission, were supported in a letter written by Ayer in early 1990. Thornburgh later withdrew the letter after White House Legal Counsel C. Boyden Gray inquired about the guidelines on behalf of business leaders.[10]

Later, Thornburgh became the target of criticism for the Justice Department's failure to act earlier and more aggressively in the face of the B.C.C.I. (Bank of Commerce and Credit International) and the savings and loans scandals.[11] The escalating economic costs and protracted political fallout from these events proved particularly damaging. As a holdover from the Reagan administration, Thornburgh's relationship to President Bush and the White House power structure was tenuous from the start. As his support in Congress and the Justice Department evaporated he found himself increasingly isolated.

As Thornburgh's control over the administration's legal policy diminished, C. Boyden Gray's grew. In stark contrast to the second term of the Reagan administration, where Meese's close ties to the president undercut the White House legal counsel's influence and the Justice Department was able to drive legal policy, Gray's office became the central figure in the Bush administration's legal policymaking process. A close friend of the President's, Gray had served as Bush's legal counsel in the Vice President's office and began the administration as Bush's most trusted White House aide. A contributor to the Heritage Foundation's *Mandate for Leadership* series, Gray had close ties to the Federalist Society and other conservative legal groups. He surrounded himself with a highly talented staff of conservative young attorneys drawn from the ranks of the Federalist Society and from former clerks to conservative jurists such as Antonin Scalia and Robert Bork. These staff members included several attorneys with distinguished conservative pedigrees, such as his chief deputy, John P. Schmitz, the son of arch-conservative former California Congressman John G. Schmitz, and such as associate counsel Janet Rehnquist, daughter of the Chief Justice.[12]

Seen as the conservative epicenter in the administration, Gray and his staff took the initiative on issues ranging from civil rights, ethics, and judicial nominations to separation of powers. Gray's interest in transforming the federal judiciary, in particular, caused control over appointments to be tilted toward the

White House. With responsibility for judicial selection transferred out of the Office of Legal Policy and a less formal process in place at the Justice Department, Gray's office became the primary ideological screen in the administration. Gray assigned the task of researching judicial nominees to Associate Counsel Lee S. Liberman. A conservative activist, Liberman graduated from the University of Chicago School of Law, twice clerked for Scalia, and was a founding member of the Federalist Society. Liberman and Gray have played a role in appointments to all levels of the judiciary. But it was through nominations to the appellate courts, and especially the crucial selections of David Souter and Clarence Thomas to fill seats on the high court, that Thornburgh became increasingly marginalized and Gray's office became the primary actor.[13]

Gray also extended his influence inside the Justice Department by cultivating relations with other conservatives. He was in regular contact with Solicitor General Kenneth Starr. Starr, prior to accepting the Solicitor General's post in 1989, had been a counselor to William French Smith from 1981 to 1983 and was then appointed to the Circuit Court in Washington D.C. During his five years on the Circuit Court, Starr was allied with the conservative wing of the court and was a strong supporter of the Reagan administration's civil rights agenda.[14] Gray was also influential in getting a close friend, William Barr, appointed as Assistant Attorney General for the Office of Legal Counsel and later promoted to the Deputy Attorney General's post when Ayer resigned in 1990. With both Starr and Barr in regular communication with Boyden Gray, Thornburgh became a secondary player in formulating administration policy positions on major legal issues such as the 1990 Clean Air Act, the 1991 Civil Rights Act, and the administration's legal position on abortion counseling by federally funded clinics.[15]

Having failed to meet the expectations that accompanied his appointment, Thornburgh resigned in June of 1991 in order to run for a Senate seat in Pennsylvania that was left open by the death of John Heinz. Yet, even Thornburgh's resignation proved awkward. Having announced in May that he would be a candidate for the Senate, Thornburgh intended to stay until just prior to the special election held in November 1991. This would have made him the first Attorney General since Robert Kennedy ran for the Senate in 1964 to run for a federal office while still heading the Justice Department. When Senate Democrats objected to the ethics of a sitting Attorney General raising personal campaign funds, Thornburgh was forced to resign early.[16] The timing was ill-planned for the White House, which was left without an Attorney General during the controversial confirmation hearings of Clarence Thomas.[17]

In November 1991, William Barr was appointed to become the seventy-seventh Attorney General. Barr had worked as an Asian analyst for the Central Intelligence Agency until 1978, when he earned a law degree from George Washington University Law School at night, and went into private practice. In 1982 Barr took a position as a staff attorney in the Domestic Policy Council in the Reagan White House. It was there he met Boyden Gray, who later helped engineer his rise to the Deputy Attorney General's office. In that office he, Starr, and Gray became the administration's legal policy troika, an arrangement formalized with Barr's elevation to the Attorney General's post.[18]

In most areas Barr's legal views closely parallel Gray's. As head of the Office of Legal Counsel he was an ardent defender of presidential prerogative, and he is a strong supporter of efforts to restrict the rights of the accused.[19] During confirmation hearings, Barr drew opposition from abortion rights advocates for announcing that he disagreed with the Court's decision in *Roe v. Wade* and believed the right to privacy did not extend to abortion. However, the Senate Judiciary Committee, still in disarray from its handling of the Thomas hearings, was unwilling to embroil itself in another decisive battle with the White House. After pledging to consult more closely with Congress and to manage the Justice Department in a more open fashion, the committee approved him by a 14-to-0 vote and confirmation by the full Senate came on a voice vote on November 20, 1991.[20]

Despite the changes in style and personality in the Attorney General's office and despite the increased influence of the White House Legal Counsel, the substance of the Bush administration's legal policy agenda has changed little from that pursued under Reagan. In *amicus* participation in the Supreme Court, the administration has continued to urge the conservative positions developed during the Reagan administration.[21] Once again, the abortion issue is the clearest example of the administration's efforts to move the law to the right. In *Webster v. Reproductive Health Services* (1989), the Bush administration asked Charles Fried, who had resumed teaching at Harvard Law School, to return and argue the abortion issue before the Court.[22] For the second time in four years, the Solicitor General asked the Court to overturn *Roe v. Wade* and abandon the abortion right. Although the *Webster* Court refused to overturn *Roe*, it upheld for the first time a state law imposing substantive restrictions aimed at discouraging women from exercising the right to choice.[23]

The argument that "*Roe* was wrongly decided and should be overruled," was repeated by Solicitor General Kenneth Starr in a second abortion case that, as of this writing, is still pending before the court. In *Planned Parenthood of Southeastern Pennsylvania v. Casey* (1992), the Solicitor General argued that the Court should uphold a Pennsylvania statute that imposed restrictions on abortion similar to those struck down in the 1985 *Thornburgh* decision.[24] In a strange switch of bedfellows, however, the Solicitor General found himself siding with attorneys for the American Civil Liberties Union (ACLU). In former cases, the ACLU opposed any erosion of *Roe;* however, with Bush's appointment of Souter and Thomas to the Court, the ACLU had abandoned any hope that abortion rights would continue to be protected in the federal courts. Instead, it was seeking to turn abortion into a campaign issue in the 1992 presidential election by forcing the Court to overturn *Roe*.

In other areas of law, such as criminal justice and First Amendment cases, the administration also continued to press the Court for conservative reform. In *Arizona v. Fulminante* (1991), it argued that a coerced confession does not automatically taint a conviction.[25] In *McCleskey v. Zant* (1991), it argued that the Court should place new restrictions on the number of *habeas corpus* petitions that inmates on death row can file.[26] And in *Barnes v. Glen Theatre* (1991), it argued that states may ban nude dancing even in adults-only clubs.[27] In civil rights too, the Justice Department has continued its conservative attack. In *Wards Cove v. Antonio* (1989), *Patterson v. McLean Credit Union* (1989), and *City of Richmond v. Croson* (1989), the department argued and finally won a majority of the Court to accept its position that the use of disparate impact evidence under Title VI should be restricted.[28]

The Bush administration's judicial appointments, at all levels of the judiciary, have also remained at least as conservative as those of the Reagan administration. After three years in office, Bush had appointed 27 judges to the appeals court and 95 to federal district courts. The administration's appointments resembled those made during the Reagan years in every characteristic: 85 percent were men, about 90 percent were white, and about two-thirds had degrees from private law schools and a net worth in excess of $500,000. Most importantly, nearly 98 percent of Bush's nominees were Republican and more than one-third had worked for the Reagan administration. Moreover, the administration adopted a "farm team" approach to filling slots on the appeals court. Sixty-three percent were simply elevated from federal district court positions, nearly all of these had been original Reagan appointees.[29]

In its two Supreme Court appointments, the administration named David Souter to replace Justice Brennan in 1989 and Clarence Thomas to replace Justice Marshall in 1991. The appointments were crucial because they replaced two staunchly conservative jurists the heart of the liberal block of the Court that had resisted many of the legal positions of the Reagan Justice Department. With little or no record for opponents to attack, Souter sailed through the confirmation process. The nomination of Clarence Thomas, however, proved even more dramatic than the attempted elevation of Robert Bork four years earlier.

Thomas's record as the head of the Equal Employment Opportunity Commission (EEOC) during the Reagan administration and a year's service as a federal appeals court judge was more substantive and factious than Souter's. Still, his position on many major legal issues outside of the area of civil rights, such as abortion and criminal justice issue, were not well known. Learning from the Bork episode, Thomas provided antagonists few answers during Senate confirmation hearings, refusing to respond to questions about specific issues that might come before the Court. In addition, what opposition might have emerged based on Thomas' civil rights record was partially muted by the reluctance of some in the civil rights community to attack a black nominee, regardless of his ideology. After four days of hearings, which included testimony from more than 75 groups, Thomas' nomination survived a 7-to-7 vote by the Senate Judiciary

Committee, with every Republican member of the committee and Democrat Dennis DeConcini of Arizona voting for Thomas.[30]

Just two days prior to the scheduled full Senate vote on Thomas, however, opponents leaked news of a confidential FBI report regarding an alleged incident of sexual harassment by the nominee. The allegation, by Anita Hill, a black law professor and former aide to Thomas at EEOC, created a firestorm that culminated in two days of nationally televised hearings that attracted a larger television audience than the Super Bowl. Thomas, who flatly denied the allegations, salvaged his nomination by portraying himself as the victim of a conspiracy between special interest groups and liberals on the Judiciary committee. Indeed, the hearings damaged the committee itself more than the nominee. Having no female members, the committee was criticized by women as being insensitive for its treatment of Professor Hill and its failure to air the allegations earlier during the hearing process. Administration supporters, on the other hand, attacked the committee for conducting a public character assassination of Thomas without evidence.[31] With members of the committee split along partisan lines in their support of Hill and Thomas, the hearings lacked a sense of direction or fairness. Two days after their conclusion, the full Senate voted 52-to-48 to confirm Thomas, the closest Supreme Court confirmation vote in more than a century.[32] In the wake of the hearings, however, the committee was put on the defensive and, as the ease of Barr's confirmation demonstrates, became increasingly less effective in countering the administration's legal agenda.[33]

Once on the Court, both Souter and Thomas have voted consistently with the four Reagan appointees.[34] During the 1991 term, for instance, Souter voted with Rehnquist 79 percent of the time, O'Connor 80 percent of the time, Scalia 73 percent, and Kennedy 82 percent of the time. This can be contrasted with the liberal block of Marshall, Blackmun and Stevens, none of which Souter voted with more than 55 percent of the time. Moreover, in 5-to-4 bare-majority opinions, the four Reagan appointees and Souter constituted the majority in 5 of 21 cases, more than double the number of any other bare-majority block.[35]

Halfway through the 1992 term of the Court, Thomas has also allied himself with the Reagan block of justices. In his first four months, Thomas voted with Justice Scalia in every case in which they both participated.[36] In perhaps his most controversial opinion to date, *Hudson v. McMillian*, Thomas, joined only by Scalia, wrote a dissent arguing that the Eighth Amendment's ban on cruel and unusual punishment did not protect prisoners from beatings by guards unless the prisoners suffered serious injury.[37] In two other cases, Thomas joined the Reagan Court majority to adopt positions even more conservative than the ones urged by Bush's Solicitor General. In *Preseley v. Etowah County Commission* (1992), Thomas and the Court rejected the Bush administration's broad interpretation of Justice Department preclearance powers under the Voting Rights Act.[38] In *Lechmere v. NLRB* (1992), Thomas, writing for the majority, rejected the Bush administration's broad reading of the National Labor Relations Act as protecting union organizing efforts on private property such as supermarket parking lots.[39]

With the Supreme Court now upholding key elements of the conservative agenda, much of the controversy that formerly centered on Justice Department legal positions has now shifted to the Court itself.[40] While the Justice Department continues to file briefs urging major transformations in the law, such briefs become less interesting once a majority of the Supreme Court agrees with them, or, as in the Voting Rights Act case and the labor law case, when the majority takes positions even further to the right of the administration.

But if White House conflicts with the Court ended, legal policy conflicts with the Democratic Congress, particularly over control of the administrative bureaucracy, continued. The Heritage Foundation's *Mandate For Leadership III* recommended that the Bush administration undertake an even more aggressive effort than its predecessor in pursuing a White House strategy for deregulation. Among specific suggestions for "retaking control from Congress" was one that the administration revise E.O. 12291, which requires OMB review of agency rules, so as to "make presidential control over executive branch regulators explicit." It also suggested that the Justice Department seek appropriate cases to challenge the constitutional status of and "extend presidential control to the independent regulatory agencies." And finally, it recommended that the administration "develop a comprehensive litigation strategy for reasserting presidential control" over agency activity. Such a strategy should include:

> a) defending the President's assertion of control over regulatory decisions, b) challenging precedents that prevent rational decision-making and weaken presidential authority, and c) assuring that all significant filings by or on behalf of regulatory agencies are consistent in asserting the President's authority and defending his objectives.[41]

The Bush administration had little hesitation acting on these recommendations. Bush immediately activated a new Council on Competitiveness, headed by Gray and Vice President Dan Quayle. The Council serves as yet another White House screen of regulatory rulemaking and has the power to veto any agency regulation that has an "unnecessarily adverse effect on business competitiveness."[42] Despite this additional level of White House review, in January 1992 the President signed an order that imposed a three-month moratorium on all new regulations, allowing exceptions only for rules explicitly required by statute or are likely to be "beneficial to the economy." In April the White House order was extended an additional four months, and the Council has urged the President to make the rigid review process permanent, asserting that the Constitution grants the President unilateral control over the regulatory process.[43] Defended by both Gray and Barr, the new review process was criticized by congressional leaders, especially Representative John Conyers, Jr., Chair of the House Operations Committee, and Senator John Glenn, Chair of the Committee on Government Affairs, who argued that it unconstitutionally infringed on the ability of agencies to carry out their statutory duties.[44] If the process is made permanent, it is certain to be subjected to a court challenge that will only further ensnarl the judiciary in administrative processes.

More than its predecessors, the Bush administration has also used signing statements to gut congressional policies with which it disagreed. In the most egregious example of this practice, Boyden Gray circulated a statement interpreting the 1991 Civil Rights Act so as to gut several key provisions, even before the bill was signed.[45] The act, a congressional response to the Court's narrowing of *Griggs*, was the product of intense negotiations between the White House, which wanted to ensure that legislation would not force businesses to rely on racial quotas to avoid discrimination suits, and the Democratic Congress, which wanted to protect minority preference hiring programs and ensure that plaintiffs could use disparate impact evidence in discrimination suits. A measure specifically tailored not to force the use of employment quotas but nevertheless to allow disparate impact evidence, passed by Congress in 1990, but, under advice from Gray, Bush vetoed the measure. The following year, however, Senate Republican John Danforth, who had earlier led the administration's fight for Clarence Thomas, crafted a compromise bill that won White House approval. The White House shift was part of an apparent deal Danforth made for votes during the Thomas controversy. The 1991 bill included provisions nearly identical to the one vetoed a year earlier, except that it relied on vague language to settle a few key sticking points.[46]

Two days before the bill was to be signed, however, Gray circulated a draft of a directive that specifically attacked race preference policies and would have ended the use of preferences and quotas in federal hiring. The directive was clearly an attempt to achieve administratively what the administration was not able to achieve in its fight with Congress over the wording of the Civil Rights Act. Leaked reports of the draft statement unleashed a torrent of criticism from civil rights groups and congressional members from both parties, especially Danforth. Embarrassed by the controversy, Bush, in a rare repudiation of Gray, rejected the suggestion of ending federal affirmative action and denied any prior knowledge of Gray's draft statement.[47]

In a more important development, the Justice Department has continued its quest to get the Supreme Court to place more stringent limitations on lower court review of administrative action. The key to this effort has been Justice Scalia, who not only has championed broad application of the *Chevron* standards of deference to administrative agencies but also has continued to push a literalist or textualist approach to statutory interpretation. Scalia has argued that lower courts should ignore congressional intent altogether as a basis for reviewing administrative action. According to this view, all that is important is the language of statute, not Congress' efforts to explain what its statutes mean through committee reports or legislative histories. In at least two cases during the Court's 1991 term, *Wis-*

consin Public Intervenor v. Mortier,[48] dealing with a Wisconsin town's efforts to impose pesticide regulations, and *West Virginia Hospitals v. Casey*,[49] dealing with the award of expert witness fees in civil rights cases, Scalia chastised lower courts for relying on legislative history for construction of statutes. We are "a government of laws, not of committee reports" he said in *Wisconsin*.[50] This textualist approach to statutory interpretation, combined with the standards of maximum deference to agency interpretations of statute established in *Chevron*, gives full sway to conservative efforts to circumvent congressional policymaking and to replace it with presidential fiat.

The implications of judicial acceptance of these new standards of broad deference during periods of divided government became apparent in a 1991 case entitled *Rust v. Sullivan*. In *Rust* the Court used these standards to uphold the Bush administration's abortion gag-rule.[51] The rule, issued by the Department of Health and Human Services (HHS), restricted doctors working in federally funded clinics from engaging in abortion counseling or referral. The new rule radically altered the meaning of a twenty-year-old law, the Public Services Act of 1970, Title X of which prohibited the appropriation of federal funds to "programs where abortion is a method of family planning." For more than eighteen years, during four different presidential administrations, the statute had been interpreted by administrators and judges alike as restricting abortions only, not abortion counseling and referral.

In defending the administration's radical policy change, the Solicitor General argued that the Court should defer to HHS unless its rule could not be consistent with any plausible construction of the act. The Court agreed, and, consistent with the *Chevron* precedent, it concluded that when the plain language of a statute is ambiguous, as it was in this case, "we must defer to the (agency's) permissible construction of the statute."[52] Stunned by the Court's decision, both houses of Congress in November of 1991 passed legislation overturning the HHS rule. President Bush, however, vetoed the measure and the House of Representatives fell eleven votes short of the two-thirds margin required to override.[53]

In angry dissents, Justices Blackmun, Marshall, Stevens, and O'Connor pointed out that the Court's decision allowed HHS to reverse the most obvious interpretation of its statutory duty in order to adopt one that raised serious constitutional questions. For at least two of the dissenters, the administration's rule violated the First and Fifth Amendments by imposing content-based restrictions on the speech of Title X recipients, a condition, they argued, Congress clearly could not have intended.[54] More broadly, the dissenters argued, that in its haste to defer to the administration's anti-abortion policy preferences, the Court had abandoned its own long-standing canon of statutory construction requiring it to adopt the interpretation most consistent with the Constitution unless such a construction is plainly contrary to the intent of Congress.[55]

In this case, the Court, at the behest of the Justice Department, adopted standards of administrative review that not only condoned reversal of long-established interpretations of statutory meaning but allowed the administration to attach an otherwise unconstitutional condition to the receipt of public funds. Ironically, the gag-rule, upheld as a "plausible" interpretation of statutory intent, remains in force even after overwhelming majorities in Congress rejected it. The Court's willingness to abandon what it thinks Congress intended, defer to any interpretation of a statute adopted by the executive, even one that is constitutionally dubious, and then stand idly by while the President uses his veto to prevent corrective legislation must be viewed with alarm. As the *New York Times* editorialized, the practical effect of the Court's position is nothing short of permitting the administration to "make law backwards."[56]

Perhaps more than anything else, it is this broad-based assault on Congress' ability to control policy and the accompanying expansion of executive power that seems to be at the heart of the new alliance between the Justice Department and the conservatively aligned Supreme Court. In this respect, the politicization of the Justice Department during the Reagan and Bush administrations is different from previous periods. Its goal is institutional transformation through establishing a unified executive and a plebiscitary-style presidency, not simply realizing specific policy objectives. If this is so, its consequences will be less tractable and its implications potentially far more dangerous to the rule of law.

As the gag-rule case illustrates, the pressures emerging from the country's prolonged experience with divided government appear to be permanently warping those institutional structures that are intended to protect democracy and the rule of law. That the Justice Department has become the primary and most effective weapon in the quest to aggrandize presidential power may be reason enough for us to reexamine the option of an independent Attorney General. In the wake of *Morrison v. Olson*, the question should increasingly be formulated in terms of whether such independence would be politically *desirable* rather than constitutionally *possible*.

A more general evaluation of American political institutions also seems appropriate at this time. The modern controversy surrounding federal legal policy and the offices that make it is best understood as a symptom of larger ailments with our system. Even if party government were restored in the near future, if Democrats recaptured the White House or Republicans gained in the Congress, it is unlikely, absent extraordinary pressure such as existed in the wake of Watergate, that any President would voluntarily surrender authority or restore congressional power. Perhaps a more powerful executive is desirable, even necessary to a positive, regulatory state such as the federal government has become during the twentieth century. In short, what might be needed is a new constitution or at least a reassessment of the value of the separation of powers. Still, it would be better if we faced these questions honestly and avoid the collapse of faith in democratic government that has accompanied recent efforts by both branches to bypass the other.

Notes

1. William French Smith, *Law and Justice in the Reagan Administration* (Stanford, California: The Hoover Institution Press, 1991); Charles Fried, *Order and Law: Arguing the Reagan Revolution—A First Hand Account* (New York: Simon and Schuster, 1991).

2. This view is also taken by Nancy Baker in *Conflicting Loyalties: Law and Politics in the Attorney General's Office, 1789–1990* (Lawrence Kansas: University of Kansas Press, 1992). Baker's book offers a detailed history of the Attorney General's office focusing on the conflicting loyalty between law and politics. She argues that the role of the office is best understood by examining the type of incumbents who are appointed, whether they view themselves as partisan advocates, such as Hommer Cummings, Robert Kennedy or Edwin Meese, or as a "neutral" legal advisors, such as William Wirt, Harlan Fisk Stone or Griffin Bell.

3. "Controversy-Free Confirmation Expected for Thornburgh," *New York Times* (July 12, 1988); "Thornburgh Named Attorney General," *The Washington Post* (July 13, 1988); "Senate, 85 to O, Confirms Thornburgh to Succeed Meese," *The Washington Post* (August 12, 1988).

4. Joan Biskupic, "Thornburgh's Bumpy Start Surprises Some on Hill," *Congressional Quarterly* (August 26, 1989), 2215–18.

5. "Thornburgh Cutting Costs, Fires 20 Information Aides," *Salt Lake Tribune* (January 11, 1989); "Spokesmen Note Layoffs - Their Own," *The Washington Post* (January 11, 1989).

6. See Mary McGrory, "He Can Run, Be He Can't Hide: Dick Thornburgh's no-show in Congress," *The Washington Post Weekly* (July 29-August 4, 1991).

7. Sharon LaFraniere, "Thornburgh Brings Methodical Approach to Decision to Run," *The Washington Post* (June 5, 1991), A-16.

8. Biskupic, "Thornburgh's Bumpy Start Surprises Some on Hill," 2215–18.

9. Robert Bork discusses the politics behind the Fisk and Lucas controversies in "The Full Court Press: The Drive for Control of the Courts," *The American Enterprise* (January/February, 1990), 58–61.

10. "Justice Aide Quits Amid Tensions Over Thornburgh's Stewardship," *New York Times* (May 12, 1990), A-1.

11. David Johnston, "Conceding Delay at Justice, Nominee Defends Department on B.C.C.I. Case," *New York Times* (November 13, 1992), A-10.

12. W. John Moor, "The True Believers," *National Journal* (September 17, 1991), 2018–22.

13. *Ibid.*

14. Philip Shenon, "Selection of Starr Could Lead to High Court," *The New York Times* (February 2, 1989), A-15.

15. Moor, "The True Believers," 2018–22.

16. Dan Balz, "Debate Arises on Timing of Thornburgh Departure," *The Washington Post* (June 6, 1991), A-4.

17. LaFraniere, "Thornburgh Brings Methodical Approach to Decision to Run."

18. Sharon LaFerniere, "William Barr's Energetic Game Plan as Attorney General," *The Washington Post Weekly* (March 16–22, 1992), 31.

19. See Joan Biskupic, "Tough Enough of Too Soft," *Congressional Quarterly* (November 30, 1991), 3529.

20. David Johnston, "Barr Confirmed in Voice Vote As the 77th Attorney General," *New York Times* (November 21, 1991), A-10.

21. See Tim Smart, "Speak Softly and Carry a Big Right-Wing Agenda," *Business Week* (November 27, 1989), 115.

22. 109 S.Ct. 3040 (1989).

23. 492 U.S. 490 (1989).

24. As of this writing, the case is still before the Court, 112 S.Ct. (1992).

25. Brief for the United States as Amicus Curiae in Support of Petitioner, *Arizona v. Fulminante*, 111 S.Ct. 1246 (1991).

26. Brief for the United States as Amicus Curiae in Support of Respondent, *McCleskey v. Zant. 111 S.Ct. 1454 (1991)*.

27. Brief for the United States as Amicus Curiae in Support of Appellant, *Barnes v. Glen Theatre, Inc.*, 111 S.Ct. 2456 (1991).

28. 490 U.S. 642 (1989): 491 U.S. 164 (1989): 488 U.S. 469 (1989). Congress overturned these decisions by passing the Civil Rights Act of 1991.

29. Joan Biskupic, "Bush Boosts Bench Strength Of Conservative Judges," *Congressional Quarterly* (January 19, 1991), 104–107; Biskupic, "Bush Treads Well-Worn Path In Building Federal Bench," *Congressional Quarterly* (January 18, 1992), 111–13.

30. Joan Biskupic, "Thomas Hearings Illustrate Politics of the Process," *Congressional Quarterly* (September 21, 1991), 18–22.

31. For a discussion of the controversy surrounding the Judiciary Committee and the confirmation process following the Thomas hearings see Joan Biskupic, "Thomas Drama Engulfs Nation," *Congressional Quarterly* (October 12, 1991), 2948–57; Gloria Borger, "Judging Thomas," *U.S. News & World Report* (October 21, 1991), 33–36.

32. Joan Biskupic, "Thomas' Victory Puts Icing On Reagan-Bush Court," *Congressional Quarterly* (October 19, 1991), 3026–33.

33. Following the Thomas hearings the White House began limiting access to FBI background reports on court nominees and Senate Democrats created a task force to recommend changes to the confirmation process. One change that was recommended was that the president consult with the Senate on various candidates before a particular nominee is chosen. See Joan Biskupic, "Reviewing the Process," *Congressional Quarterly* (January 8, 1992), 113.

34. On the effect of Souter's appointment see Joan Biskupic, "1990–91 Term Marked by Surge In Conservative Activism," *Congressional Quarterly* (July 6, 1991), 101–103.

35. Justices voting statistics are taken from *Harvard Law Review* 105 (November 1991): 420.

36. Ruth Marcus, "Clarence Thomas: Fondest Dream, Worst Nightmare," *The Washington Post Weekly* (March 9–15, 1992), 32.

37. *Hudson v. McMillian,,* No. 90–6531, 112 S.Ct. (1992).

38. *Presley v. Etowah County Commission*, 112 S.Ct. 820 (1992).

39. *Lechmere v. NLRB*, 112 S.Ct. 841 (1992).

40. W. John Moore, "Tugging From the Right," *National Journal* (October 20, 1990), 2510–15: Marcus, "Clarence Thomas: Fondest Dream, Worst Nightmare."

41. Charles L. Heatherly and Burton Yale Pines, eds., *Mandate for Leadership III: Policy Strategies of the 1990s* (Washington, D.C.: The Heritage Foundation, 1990), 95–99.

42. Dana Priest, "The Secret (Maybe Illegal) Life of the Competitiveness Council," *Washington Post Weekly* (November 25, 1991), 33.

43. "Quayle Says Rule Review Is Saving U.S. $10 Billion," *New York Times* (April 3, 1992), A-7.

44. See Phillip A. Davis, "Outcry Greets Bush's Plan to Delay New Rules," *Congressional Quarterly* (January 25, 1992), 164–66; "Aides Urge Bush to Impose Moratorium on Regulations," *New York Times* (January 21, 1992), A-1.

45. Civil Rights Act of 1991 (PL 102–166).

46. For a discussion of the intent and major provisions of the 1991 Civil Rights Act

see "Civil Rights Act of 1991," *Congressional Quarterly* (December 7, 1991), 3620–22.

47. See Andrew Rosenthal, "President Tries to Quell Furor on Interpreting Scope of New Law," *The New York Times* (November 22, 1991), A-1.

48. 111 S.Ct. 2476 (1991).

49. 111 S.Ct. 1138 (1991).

50. *Ibid.*, 2490.

51. 111 S.Ct. 1759 (1991).

52. *Ibid.*, 1769.

53. Anthony Lewis, "How Freedom Died," *New York Times* (November 27, 1991), A-15.

54. Ibid., Blackmun and Marshall dissent, 1781–86.

55. Ibid., O'Connor dissent, 1788.

56. Editorial, "Making Law Backwards," *New York Times* (November 27, 1991), A-14.

Appendix:
Published Speeches and Articles by Attorneys General, 1925–1988[*]

Edwin Meese

"Bicentennial of the Constitution," *Federal Bar News & Journal* 34 (October 1987), 343

"Our Constitutional Design: The Implications for its Interpretation," *Marquette Law Review* 70 (Spring 1987), 381

"Speech before Third Circuit Conference," *Temple Law Review* 60 (Winter 1987), 835

"Toward a Jurisprudence of Original Intent," *Harvard Journal of Law & Political Policy* 11 (Winter 1988), 5

"Tribute to Hugo Black," *St. Louis University Public Law Review* 6 (1987), 187

"Tort Reform: Before National Legal Center for Public Interest," *Idaho Law Review* 23 (1986), 343

"The Law of the Constitution," *Tulane Law Review* 61 (April 1987), 979

"Promoting Truth in Courtroom," *Vanderbilt Law Review* 40 (March 1987), 271

"Remarks at Detroit College Commencement," *Detroit College Law Review* 4 (Winter 1986), 1161

"The Supreme Court of United States: Bulwark of a Limited Constitution," *South Texas Law Review* 27 (Fall 1986), 455

William French Smith

"Achieving Prison Reform," *Pennsylvania Bar Quarterly* 54 (October 1983), 180

"Framers Federalism," *New York State Bar Journal* 56 (April 1984), 8

"Immigration Law Reform: Proposals in 98th Congress," *San Diego Law Review* 21 (December 1983), 7

"Observations on the Establishment Cause," *Pepperdine Law Review* 11 (March 1985), 457

"Limiting the Insanity Defense: A Rational Approach to Irrational Crimes," *Missouri Law Review* 47 (Fall 1982), 605

---

[*]As indexed by *An Index to Legal Periodicals* (New York: Wilson Co.)

"Remarks on Law Enforcement on Law Day," *South Carolina Law Review* 34 (December 1982), 247

"Commencement Address," *Cal. W. Law Review* 19 (Spring 1983), 411

"New Directions in Department of Justice Enforcement of Antitrust Policy," *Antitrust Law Journal* 51 (Spring 1982), 93

"Federal Courts Have Gone Beyond Their Ability," *Judges Journal* 21 (Winter 1982), 3

"Urging Judicial Restraint," *ABA Journal* 68 (January 1982), 59

Benjamin Civiletti

"Q & A with Civiletti," *ABA Journal* 56 (October 1979), 1497

"Intelligence Gathering and the Law: Conflict or Compatibility," *Fordham Law Review* 48 (May 1980), 883

"Can the Same Person Prosecute and Defend," *Human Rights* 8 (Summer 1979), 28

"Prosecutor as Advocate," *New York State Law Review* 25 (1979), 1

Griffin Bell

"Crisis in the Courts—A Proposal for Change," *Vanderbilt Law Review* 31 (January 1978), 3

"The Judicial Tenure Act," *Trial* 13 (November 1977), 21

"Improvements in the Administration of Justice," *Texas Technical Law Review* 10 (1979), 53

"Improving the Administration of Justice," *Pennsylvania Bar Quarterly* 48 (October 1977), 502

"New Directions in Administration of Justice: Department of Justice Response to the Pound Conference," *ABA Journal* 64 (January 1978), 48

"The Pound Conference and Department of Justice Followup," *FRD* 76 (January 1978), 320

"The Attorney General—The Government's Chief Lawyer or One Among Many," *Fordham Law Review* 46 (May 1978), 1049

"Electronic Surveillance and Fee Society," *St. Louis University Law Journal* 1 (1979), 23

"Immigration," *San Diego Law Review* 15 (December 1977), 200

"Federalism," *Tol Law Review* 9 (Summer 1978), 615

Edward Levi

"Improvements in the Judicial System" (Pound Conference address), *FRD* 70 (June 1976), 79

"Address at the University of Chicago," *University of Chicago L.S. Record* 22 (Fall 1976), 14

"Address at the Chicago Bar Association," *Chicago Bar Record* 58 (August 1976), 6

"New Approaches to Justice" (Civil Rights), *Pennsylvania Bar Quarterly* 46 (October 1975), 404

"Some Aspects of Separation of Powers," *Columbia Law Review* 76 (April 1976), 371

"Confidentiality and the Democratic Process," *Record* 30 (June 1975), 323

"Law Day Address" (Privileges), *Nebraska Law Review* 55 (1975), 35

"The Department of Justice: Some Thought on Its Past, Present and Future," *Illinois Bar Journal* 64 (December 1975)

William Saxbe

"Building a New Confidence at the Department of Justice," *New York State Bar Journal* 45 (November 1973), 455

"New Approaches to Justice," *Pennsylvania Bar Quarterly* (October 1973)

Elliot Richardson

"On Behalf of Obligations," *Lincoln Law Review* 8 (1973), 109

"The Guarantee Clause: Proposal for an Electoral Commission," *American University Law Review* 25 (1973), 1

Richard Kleindienst

"Government Lawyers" (Symposium), *Federal Bar Journal* 32 (Winter 1973), 1

"Is Crime Being Encouraged," *Review of C Abo. PR.* 34 (May 1973), 225

John Mitchell

"In Quest of Speedy Justice," *Judicature* 55 (November 1971), 139

"In Quest of Speedy Justice," *University of Florida Law Review* 24 (Winter 1972), 230

"Not Will But Judgement," *ABA Journal* 57 (December 1971), 1185

"The Duty to Decide," *Catholic Law* 18 (Winter 1972), 2

"Idea for Consensus," *Trial* 6 (June 1970), 14

"New District of Columbia Court System," *American University Law Review* 20 (December 1970), 12

"Free Press & a Fair Trial," *Illinois Bar Journal* 59 (December 1970), 282

"Remarks on Eavesdropping," *Kentucky State Bar Journal* 35 (July 1971), 26

"First Amendment and Dissent," *New York State Bar Journal* 42 (December 1970), 687

"Restoring the Finality of Justice," *Alabama Lawyer* 32 (October 1971), 367

"Law Day Address," *South West Law Journal* 25 (May 1971), 235

"Defending the Supreme Court," *District of Columbia Bar Journal* 37 (July 1970), 33

"Address before the ABA Antitrust Section," *ABA Antitrust Law Journal* 38 (1969), 219

"Address on Antitrust," *Georgia State Bar Journal* 6 (August 1969), 92

"Bail Reform and the Constitutionality of Pre-trial Detention," *Virginia Law Review* 55 (November 1969), 1223

"Violence in America and the Right to Dissent," *Tennessee Law Review* 37 (February 1969), 129

Ramsey Clark

"Address on the Administration of Law," *FRD* 44 (May 1968), 152

Nicholas deB. Katzenbach

"Address on Antitrust," *Antitrust Bulletin* 10 (December 1965), 933

"Address on Civil Rights at Emory University," *Journal of Public Law* 14 (1965), 243

"Equal Treatment in the Enforcement of the Law," *Journal of Criminal Law* 56 (December 1965), 498

"The President's Law Enforcement Commission Urges the Legal Profession's Cooperation," *ABA Journal* 52 (November 1966), 1013

"Extending Legal Services to the Poor," *Brief Case* 23 (February 1965), 148

Robert Kennedy

"Criminal Justice," *William & Mary Law Review* 5 (1964), 167

"Antitrust Aims of the Department of Justice," *New York Law F.* 9 (March 1963)

"Civil Rights and the South," *North Carolina Law Review* 42 (December 1963), 1

"Criminal Investigation and the Fifth Amendment," *Notre Dame Law Review* 38 (1963), 627

"What is a Crime?" *University of Florida Law Review* 16 (Fall 1963), 143

"Three Weapons Against Organized Crime," *Crime & Delinquency* 8 (October 1962), 321

"Address on Jurisprudence," *Fordham Law Review* 30 (February 1962), 437

"Halfway Houses Pay Off," *Crime & Delinquency* 10 (January 1964), 1

"Respect for Law," *ABA Journal* 48 (January 1962), 31

"Address on Parole and Penology," *FRD* 30 (August 1962), 442

"Justice Is Found in Hearts & Minds of Men," *Fed Prob.* 25 (December 1961), 3

"The Department of Justice and the Indigent Accused," *Journal American Jud. Society* 47 (January 1964), 159

William Rogers

"The United States Automatic Reservation to the Optional Clause: Jurisdiction of the International Courts of Justice," *Int. & Comp. Law Quarterly* 7 (October 1958), 758

"Our Great Goal of Peace Under Law," *ABA Journal* 45 (November 1959), 1181

"Constitutional Law: The Papers of the Executive Branch," *ABA Journal* 44 (October 1958), 941

"The Problem of School Segregation: A Serious Challenge to American Citizens," *ABA Journal* 45 (January 1959), 23

"Desegregation: The Citizens' Responsibility," *Cornell Law Quarterly* 45 (Spring 1960), 488

"The Most Important Task of All," *New York Cnty. Bar Bull.* 15 (April 1958), 181

"Judicial Appointments in the Eisenhower Administration," *Journal American Jud. Society* 41 (August 1957), 38

"Address on the Department of Justice," *West Virginia Bar Journal* 73 (1957), 69

Herbert Brownell

"Brownell Expresses Views on the Hoover Commission," *ICC Journal* 23 (December 1955), 195

"Delays in Litigation," *Chicago Bar Rec.* 38 (April 1957), 295

"Rationale of Federal Antitrust Enforcement," *Catholic University Law Review* 6 (May 1957), 129

"Statement before the Senate Banking Committee on Statutes Governing Financial Institutions," *Antitrust Bulletin* 2 (April 1957), 519

"Protecting Civil Rights," *Chicago Bar Record* 39 (November 1957), 55

"Bill of Rights: Liberty and Law are Inseparable," *ABA Journal* 41 (June 1955), 517

"John Marshall—The Chief Justice," *Cornell Law Quarterly* 41 (Fall 1955), 93

"The Problem of Backlogs: A National Shortcoming in the Courts," *ABA Journal* 42 (March 1958), 213

"United States Supreme Court: Symbol of Just Government," *ABA Journal* 42 (November 1956), 1032

"Freedom and Responsibility of the Press in a Free Country," *Fordham Law Review* 24 (Summer 1955), 178

"Press Photographers and the Courtroom," *Nebraska Law Review* 35 (November 1955), 1

"Law in the Settlement of Disputes Between Nations," *Connecticut Bar Journal* 31 (December 1957), 346

"Federal Suppression of Labor Racketeering: A Report," *South West Law Journal* 9 (Summer 1956)

"National Conference on Parole: Scope & Purpose," *Federal Probl.* 20 (June 1956), 5

"On the Separation of Powers," *Dick. Law Review* 60 (October 1955), 1

"The Attorney General Reports," *New York S. Bar Bull.* 28 (February 1956), 94

"Lawyers and a Government of Law," *Record* 13 (April 1958), 188

"Improving Our System of Justice," *Fed Prob.* 17 (December 1953), 8

"The Separation of Powers and Immunity from Self Incrimination," *Federal Bar Journal* 14 (June 1954), 5

"Immunity from Prosecution vs. Self Incrimination," *Tulane Law Review* 28 (December 1953), 1

"Training Programs of the Department of Justice," *Journal Legal Education* 6 (1954), 563

"As a Newcomer Sees the Department of Justice," *Record* 8 (May 1953), 219

"Public Security and Wire Tapping," *Cornell Law Quarterly* 39 (Winter 1954), 195

James McGranery

J. Howard McGrath

"Improvement in the Administration of Justice," *Maryland State Bar Journal* 56 (1951), 289

"Address before the Canadian Bar Association," *Canadian Bar Journal* 33 (1950), 19

"The Communist Threat," *Women's Law Journal* 36 (Fall 1950), 14

"Pressing Problems to Concern the Lawyer," *Georgia Bar Journal* 13 (May 1951), 399

"Relation of Department of Justice to the Interstate Commerce Commission," *ICC Journal* 18 (November 1950), 83

Tom Clark

"The Attorney General's Manual on Administrative Procedure," *ICC Journal* (Fall 1984)

"Your Attorney General," *Virginia State Bar Journal* 57 (1946), 351

"Civil Rights Address," *National Bar Journal* 6 (March 1948), 1

"A Federal Prosecutor Looks at Civil Rights," *Columbia Law Review* 47 (March 1947), 175

"Subversive Tendencies in the United States," *New York State Bar Journal* 71 (1948), 173

"Recent Improvements in the Federal Judicial System," *Dicta* 23 (December 1946), 269

"The National Crime Situation," *California State Bar Journal* 49 (1946)

"Government Liability for Use of Patented Inventions," *Temple Law Quarterly* 20 (July 1946), 1

"National Sovereignty and Dominion over Lands Underlying the Ocean," *Temple Law Quarterly* 20 (July 1946), 1

"Justice and the Administration of Justice," *Maryland State Bar Journal* 50 (1945), 236

"Administrative Law," *Nebraska Law Review* 25 (March 1946), 79

"Administrative Law," *Nebraska State Bar Journal* 36 (1945), 79

"Should There Be a Uniform Federal Procedure for All Government Agencies?" *Journal of the Bar Association of the District of Columbia* 12 (October 1945), 239

"The Office of Attorney General," *Tennessee Law Review* 19 (Fall 1946), 150
"Fitting the Punishment to the Criminal," *Iowa Law Review* 31 (January 1946), 191

Francis Biddle

"Aspects of the Work of the Attorney General," *New Jersey S. Bar Y.B.* 33 (1945)
"The Department of Justice: The War Effort," *West Virginia Bar Journal* 59 (1943), 130
"Administrative Law," *ABA Journal* 27 (November 1941), 660
"Civil Rights in Times of Stress," *Bill of Rights Review* 2 (1941), 13
"Civil Liberties," *American Law S. Rev.* 9 (April 1941), 881
"The Powers of Democracy," *California State Bar Journal* 29 (1941)
"Government and the Public," *Federal Bar Journal* 4 (May 1941), 149
"Law in the War Effort," *Tennessee Law Review* 17 (December 1942), 532
"Thinking in War-Time," *Boston University Law Review* 22 (April 1942), 199
"Remarks about the Department of Justice," *Vermont Bar Journal* 36 (1942), 42
"A War Message to the Bar," *Pennsylvania Bar Quarterly* 13 (April 1942), 138

Robert Jackson

"Democracy Under Fire," *Law Society Journal* 9 (November 1940), 301
"The Federal Prosecutor," *Journal Am. Jud. Society* 24 (1940)
"The Federal Prosecutor," *Journal of Criminal Law* 31 (1940), 3
"Address on International Law," *New York State Bar Journal* 65 (1942), 434
"The Challenge of International Lawlessness," *ABA Journal* 27 (November 1941), 690
"International Order," *ABA Journal* 27 (May 1941), 275
"The Law Above Nations" *American Journal of International Law* 37 (April 1943), 297
"Government Counsel and Their Opportunity," *ABA Journal* 26 (May 1940), 411
"Mobilizing the Profession for Defense," *ABA Journal* 27 (June 1941), 350
"A Program for Internal Defense of United States," *New York State Bar Journal* 63 (1940), 679

Frank Murphy

"Civil Liberties," *United States Law Review* 73 (April 1939), 198
"Progress in Democracy," *American Labor Legal Review* 29 (June 1939), 61
"The Test of Patriotism," *Natural Law Guild Quarterly* 2 (October 1939), 165

Homer Cummings

"Address on the Administration of Justice," *North Carolina Bar Journal* (1938), 149
"Nature of the Amending Process," *George Washington Law Review* 6 (March 1938), 247
"The Value of Judicial Conferences in the Circuits," *ABA Journal* 24 (December 1938), 979
"Reforming Federal Criminal Procedure," *Connecticut Bar Journal* 12 (July 1938), 197
"Unsolved Problems of Monopoly," *United States Law Review* 72 (January 1938), 23
"A Rounded System of Judicial Rule Making," *ABA Journal* 24 (May 1938), 513
"A Rounded System of Judicial Rule Making," *Law Society Journal* 8 (November 1938), 293
"A Rounded System of Judicial Rule Making," *United States Law Review* 72 (July 1938), 337

"Modernizing Federal Procedures," *ABA Journal* 24 (August 1938), 625
"They All Come Out," *Law Society Journal* 8 (1938), 212
"The Right Arm of Statesmanship," *ABA Journal* 23 (January 1937), 7
"Progress Toward a Modern Administration of Justice," *ABA Journal* 22 (April 1936), 345
"Progress Toward a Modern Administration of Justice," *United States Law Review* 70 (March 1936), 239
"The American Constitution Method," *ABA Journal* 22 (1936), 24
"The American Constitution Method," *United States Law Review* 70 (January 1936), 10
"A Nation was Brought Into Being," *United States Law Review* 70 (September 1936), 491
"Address on Courts, Criminal Law and the Legal Profession," *New York County Law Y.B.* (1934), 406
"Address on Practice & Procedure," *ABA Journal* 21 (January 1937), 7
"The New Home of Department of Justice," *Federal Bar Journal* 2 (February 1934), 73
"Immediate Problems for the Bar," *Oklahoma State Bar Journal* 5 (February 1934), 8
"Immediate Problems for the Bar," *ABA Journal* 20 (April 1934), 212
"The Lawyer Criminal," *ABA Journal* 20 (February 1934), 82
"Modern Tendencies and the Law," *ABA Journal* 19 (October 1933), 576

William Mitchell

"Methods of Amending the Constitution," *Law & Banking* 25 (Summer 1932), 265
"The Supreme Court in Washington's Time," *ABA Journal* 18 (April 1932), 341
"Reform in Federal Criminal Procedure," *ABA Journal* 18 (December 1932), 732
"Appointment of Federal Judges," *Minnesota Law Review* 2 (Winter 1931), 105
"Abdication by the States of Powers Under the Constitution," *ABA Journal* 17 (November 1931), 811
"Appointment of Federal Judges," *Com Law Journal* 37 (1932), 319
"Appointment of Federal Judges," *ABA Journal* 17 (August 1931), 569
"Address on the Department of Justice," *ABA Journal* 16 (January 1930), 9
"Address on the Department of Justice," *New York County L. Y.B.* (1929), 301

John Sargent

"Commercial Arbitration," *Com. L. League Journal* 34 (1929), 628
"The Common Law," *Boston University Law Review* 11 (Winter 1931), 348
"Importance of Law Observance," *Pennsylvania B. Journal* 308 (1927)
"Law Enforcement and Prohibition," *American Law Review* 60 (Spring 1926), 782
"Law Enforcement and Prohibition," *ABA Journal* 12 (August 1926), 736
"The Lawyer and His Practice," *ABA Journal* 11 (July 1925), 593

Selected Bibliography

Books

Abraham, Henry J. *Justices and Presidents: A Political History of Appointments to the Supreme Court.* Oxford: Oxford University Press, 1974.

Anderson, John. *Eisenhower, Brownell and the Congress: The Tangled Origins of the Civil Rights Bill.* Birmingham: University of Alabama Press, 1964.

Atiyah, Patrick and Summers, Robert. *Form and Substance in Anglo-American Law: A Comparative Study in Legal Reasoning, Legal Theory and Legal Institutions.* Oxford: Oxford University Press, 1987.

Baker, Leonard. *Back to the Back: The Duel Between FDR and the Supreme Court.* New York: Macmillan, 1967.

Ball, Howard. *Courts and Politics: The Federal Judicial System.* Englewood Cliffs, N.J.: Prentice-Hall, 1987.

Ball, Howard; Krane, Dale; and Lauth, Thomas. *Compromised Compliance: Justice Department Implementation of Section 5 of the 1965 Voting Rights Act.* Westport, Conn.: Greenwood, 1982.

Beale, Howard K., ed. *Diary of Edward Bates.* New York: Faber, 1933.

Bell, Griffin and Ostrow, Ronald. *Taking Care of the Law.* New York: Morrow, 1982.

Berger, Raoul. *Executive Privilege.* Boston: Harvard University Press, 1974.

_____. *Government by Judiciary.* Boston: Harvard University Press, 1977.

Berkson, Larry and Carbon, Susan. *The United States Circuit Judge Nominating Commission: Its Members, Procedures and Candidates.* Chicago: American Judicature Society, 1980.

Bickel, Alexander. *The Least Dangerous Branch: The Supreme Court at the Bar of Politics.* New York: Bobbs-Merrill, 1962.

_____. *The Supreme Court and the Idea of Progress.* New Haven, Conn.: Yale University Press, 1978.

Biddle, Francis. *In Brief Authority.* Garden City: Doubleday, 1962.

Bonner, Ethan. *Battle for Justice: How the Bork Nomination Shook America.* New York: Norton, 1989.

Bork, Robert H. *The Tempting of America.* New York: Free Press, 1990.

Brown, R.G. and Chafee, Z. *Report Upon the Illegal Practices of the United States Department of Justice.* Washington D.C.: National Popular Government League, 1920.

Bryner, Gary and Thompson, Dennis, eds. *The Constitution and the Regulation of Society.* Provo, Utah: Brigham Young University Press, 1988.

Burnham, Walter Dean. *The Current Crisis in American Politics.* New York: Oxford University Press, 1982.

Campbell, Colin. *Managing the Presidency*. Pittsburg, Pa.: University of Pittsburg, 1986.

Caplan, Lincoln. *The Tenth Justice: The Solicitor General and the Rule of Law*. New York: Vintage, 1988.

Cater, Douglas. *Power in Washington*. New York: Random House, 1964.

Chubb, John and Peterson, Paul, eds. *The New Direction in American Politics*. Washington, D.C.: Brookings, 1985.

_____. *Can the Government Govern*. Washington, D.C.: Brookings, 1989.

Cohen, Stanley. *A. Mitchell Palmer: Politician*. New York: DaCapo, 1972.

Cook, Fred. *The FBI Nobody Knows*. London: Mcmillan, 1964.

Corwin, Edward. *The President: Office and Powers*. New York: New York University Press, 1957.

Crovitz, L. Gordon and Rabkin, Jeremy, eds. *The Fettered Presidency*. Washington, D.C.: AEI, 1989.

Cummings, Homer and McFarland, Carl. *Federal Justice*. New York: Macmillan, 1937.

Daugherty, Harry M. *The Inside Story of the Harding Tragedy*. New York: Churchill, 1932.

Davis, John. *Department of Justice Control of Agency Litigation*. Washington, D.C.: Administrative Conference of the the United States, 1975.

Davis, Kenneth C. *Discretionary Justice*. Champaign-Urbana: University of Illinois Press, 1971.

Department of Justice Manual. Englewood Cliffs, N.J.: Prentice-Hall, 1989.

Dodd, Lawrence and Oppenheimer, Bruce. *Congress Reconsidered*. New York: Praeger, 1977.

Duram, James. *A Moderate among Extremists: Dwight D. Eisenhower and the School Desegregation Crisis*. Chicago: Nelson-Hall, 1981.

Easby-Smith, James. *The Department of Justice: Its History and Functions*. Washington, D.C.: Lowdermilk & Company, 1904.

Eastland, Terry. *Ethics, Politics and the Independent Counsel: Executive Power, Executive Vice*. Washington, D.C.: National Legal Center, 1989.

Edwards, J. Ll. J. *Law Officers of the Crown*. London: 1964.

Eisenstein, James. *Counsel for the United States*. Baltimore: John Hopkins Press, 1978.

Epstein, Jason. *The Great Conspiracy Trial*. London: Faber, 1970.

Ewald, W. Bragg, Jr. *Eisenhower the President: Crucial Days, 1951–1960*. Englewood Cliffs, N.J.: Prentice-Hall, 1981.

Fenno, Richard. *The President's Cabinet*. Cambridge: Harvard University Press, 1959.

Fish, Peter. *The Politics of Federal Judicial Administration*. Princeton, N.J.: Princeton University Press, 1973.

Fisher, Louis. *Constitutional Conflicts between Congress and the President*. Princeton, N.J.: Princeton University Press, 1985.

Foley, Michael. *The New Senate*. New Haven, Conn.: Yale University Press, 1980.

Freeman, J. Lieper. *The Political Process*. New York: Random House, 1965.

Gawthorp, Lewis. *Bureaucratic Behavior in the Executive Branch*. New York: Free Press, 1969.

Ginsberg, Benjamin and Shefter, Martin. *Politics by Other Means*. New York: Basic, 1990.

Ginsberg, Benjamin and Stone, Alan, eds. *Do Elections Matter?* Armonk, N.Y.: M.E. Sharpe, 1986.

Goodwin, John. *What Happens When Organized Genius is Applied to Government*. Washington, D.C.: Hammond, 1924.

Grossman, Joel. *Lawyers and Judges: The ABA and the Politics of Judicial Selection*. New York: Wiley, 1965.

Gwyn, W.B. *The Meaning of the Separation of Powers.* New Orleans: Tulane University Press, 1965.

Harris, Richard. *Justice: The Crisis of Law, Order and Freedom in America.* London: Bodley Head, 1970.

_____. *The Fear of Crime.* New York: Praeger, 1969.

Heatherly, Charles, ed. *Mandate for Leadership: Policy Management in a Conservative Administration.* Washington, D.C.: Heritage Foundation, 1981.

Heclo, Hugh and Salamon, Lester. *The Illusion of Presidential Government.* Boulder, Colo.: Westview, 1982.

Higgs, Robert. *Crisis and Leviathan: Critical Episodes in the Growth of American Government.* Oxford: Oxford University Press, 1987.

Hodgson, Godfrey. *All Things to All Men: The False Promise of the American Presidency.* New York: Doubleday, 1980.

Horowitz, Donald. *The Jurocracy.* Lexington, Mass.: D.C. Heath, 1977.

_____. *The Courts and Social Policy.* Washington, D.C.: Brookings, 1977.

Huston, Luther. *The Department of Justice.* New York: Praeger, 1967.

Huston, Luther; Miller, Arthur; Krislov, Samuel; and Dixon, Robert. *Roles of the Attorney General of the United States.* Washington, D.C.: AEI, 1968.

Jackson, R. *The Machinery of Justice in England.* 7th ed. London, 1977.

Jaworski, Leon. *The Right and the Power: The Prosecution of Watergate.* Houston, Tex.: Gulf Publishing, 1976.

Katzmann, Robert A., ed. *Judges and Legislators: Toward Institutional Comity.* Washington, D.C.: Brookings, 1988.

Kernell, Samuel. *Going Public: New Strategies of Presidential Leadership.* Washington, D.C.: Congressional Quarterly Press, 1986.

King, Anthony, ed. *The New American Political System.* Washington, D.C.: AEI, 1978.

_____. *New American Political System.* 2d ed. Washington, D.C.: AEI, 1990.

King, Donald and Quick, Charles, eds. *Legal Aspects of the Civil Rights Movement.* Detroit: Wayne State University, 1965.

Kleindienst, Richard. *Justice.* New York: Praeger, 1985.

Kluger, Richard. *Simple Justice.* New York: Random House, 1977.

Kovaleff, Theodore. *Business and Government During the Eisenhower Administration: A Study of the Antitrust Policy of the Justice Department.* Athens, Oh.: Ohio University Press, 1980.

Kurland, Philip. *Politics, the Constitution and the Warren Court.* Chicago: University of Chicago, 1970.

Langeluttig, Albert. *The Department of Justice in the United States.* Baltimore: John Hopkins Press, 1927.

Loomis, Burdett. *The New American Politician.* New York: Basic Books, 1988.

Lowi, Theodore. *The Personal President: Power Invested, Promise Unfulfilled.* Ithaca, N.Y.: Cornell University Press, 1985.

Lownthal, Max. *The Federal Bureau of Investigation.* New York: William Sloan, 1950.

Lunch, William. *The Nationalization of American Politics.* Los Angeles: University of California Press, 1987.

MacDermott, J. *Protection from Power under English Law.* London: Stevens, 1957.

Macedo, Stephen. *The New Right v. The Constitution.* New York: Basic Books, 1986.

Mackenzie, G. Calvin. *The Politics of Presidential Appointments.* New York: Free Press, 1980.

Madison, James. *The Federalist.* Edited by Max Beloff. Oxford: Blackwell, 1948.

Malbin, Michael, ed. *Money and Politics in the United States: Financing Elections in the 1980s.* Washington, D.C.: AEI, 1984.

_____. *Parties, Interest Groups, and Campaign Finance Laws*. Washington, D.C.: AEI, 1980.

Mann, Thomas and Ornstein, Norman, eds. *The New Congress*. Washington, D.C.: AEI, 1981.

March, James and Olsen, Johan. *Rediscovering Institutions*. New York: Macmillan, 1989.

Marshall, Burke. *Federalism and Civil Rights*. New York: Columbia University Press, 1964.

Marshall, Geoffrey. *Constitutional Conventions*. Oxford: Oxford University Press, 1984.

_____. *Constitutional Theory*. Oxford: Clarendon Press, 1971.

Maass, Arthur. *Congress and the Common Good*. New York: Basic, 1983.

McFeeley, N. *Appointment of Judges: The Johnson Presidency*. Austin: University of Texas Press, 1987.

Melnick, R. Shep. *Regulation and the Courts: The Case of the Clean Air Act*. Washington, D.C.: Brookings, 1983.

Mikva, Abner J. *Report of the Lawyer's Review Committee to Study the Department of Justice*. 1971.

Nathan, Richard. *The Administrative Presidency*. New York: Wiley, 1983.

_____. *The Plot That Failed: Nixon and the Administrative Presidency*. New York: Wiley, 1975.

Navasky, Victor. *Kennedy Justice*. New York: Atheneum, 1977.

Neff, Alan. *The United States District Judge Nominating Commissions: Their Members, Procedures and Candidates*. Chicago: American Judicature Society, 1981.

Neustadt, Richard. *Presidential Power: The Politics of Leaders*, 3d ed. New York: Wiley, 1980.

Noggle, Burl. *Teapot Dome: Oil and Politics in the 1920's*. Baton Rouge: Louisiana State University Press, 1962.

North, Witney Seymour, Jr. *United States Attorney*. New York: Morrow, 1975.

O'Brien, David. *Judicial Roulette: Report of the Twentieth Century Task Force on Judicial Selection*. New York: Priority Press, 1988.

_____. *Storm Center: The Supreme Court in American Politics*. 2d ed. New York: Norton, 1990.

Overstreet, Harry and Banoro. *The FBI in Our Open Society*. New York: Norton, 1969.

Panetta, Leon and Gall, Peter. *Bring Us Together, The Nixon Team and the Civil Rights Retreat*. Philadelphia: J.B. Lippincott, 1971.

Peele, Gillian. *Revival and Reaction: The Right in Contemporary America*. Oxford: Clarendon Press, 1984.

Pfiffner, James. *The Strategic Presidency: Hitting the Ground Running*. Chicago: Dorsey Press, 1988.

Quirk, Paul. *Industrial Influence in Federal Regulatory Agencies*. Princeton, N.J.: Princeton University Press, 1981.

Rabkin, Jeremy. *Judicial Compulsions*. New York: Basic Books, 1989.

Reichley, James A., ed. *Elections American Style*. Washington, D.C.: Brookings, 1987.

Richardson, Elliot. *The Creative Balance*. London: Hamish Hamilton, 1976.

Richardson, James, ed. *Messages and Papers of the President*, 4 vols. New York: Bureau of National Literature, 1897–1925.

Rohde, David and Spaeth, Harold. *Supreme Court Decision Making*. San Francisco: Freeman, 1976.

Schlesinger, Arthur. *Robert Kennedy and His Times*. London: Andre Deutsch Ltd., 1978.

Schmidhauser, John. *Judges and Justices: The Federal Appellate Judiciary*. Boston: Little, Brown, 1979.

Schwartz, Herman. *Packing the Courts: The Conservative Campaign to Rewrite the Constitution*. New York: Scribners, 1988.

Scigliano, Robert. *The Supreme Court and the Presidency.* New York: Free Press, 1971.

Seidman, Harold. *Politics, Position and Power: From the Positive to the Regulatory State.* 4th ed. New York: Oxford University Press, 1986.

Shapiro, Martin. *Who Guards the Guardians: Judicial Control of Administration.* Athens, Ga.: University of Georgia, 1988.

Simon, James. *In His Own Image: The Supreme Court in Richard Nixon's America.* New York: David McKay, 1973.

Sundquist, James. *The Decline and Resurgence of Congress.* Washington, D.C.: Brookings, 1981.

_____. *Politics and Policy: The Eisenhower, Kennedy, and Johnson Years.* Washington, D.C.: Brookings, 1968.

Vile, M.J.C. *Constitutionalism and the Separation of Powers.* Oxford: Oxford University Press, 1967.

Waterman, Richard. *Presidential Influence and the Administrative State.* Knoxville: Tennessee University Press, 1985.

Weaver, Suzanne. *Decision to Prosecute: The Antitrust Division in the United States Department of Justice.* Boston: MIT Press, 1978.

Weidenbaum, Murray. *Business, Government, and the Public.* Englewood Cliffs, N.J.: Prentice-Hall, 1981.

White, G. Edward. *Patterns of American Legal Thought.* Oxford: Oxford University Press, 1978.

White, Leonard. *The Federalists.* New York: New York University Press, 1948.

Whitehead, Don. *The FBI Story.* New York: Random House, 1956.

Wilson, James Q. *The Politics of Regulation.* New York: Basic, 1980.

Articles and Chapters

Aranson, Henry. "Judicial Control of the Political Branches: Public Purpose and Public Law." *Cato Journal* 4 (1985).

Arnold, P.E. and Roos, L.J. "Toward a Theory of Congressional-Executive Branch Relations." *Review of Politics* 26(1974).

Ball, Howard. "Confronting Institutional Schizophrenia: The Effort to De-Politicize the U.S. Department of Justice, 1974–1976." Paper presented at the President Ford Conference, Hofstra University, April 7, 1989.

Barker, Lucius. "Third Parties in Litigation: A Systematic View of the Judicial Function." *Journal of Politics* 29 (1967).

Barnett, Randy. "Judicial Conservativism vs. a Principled Judicial Activism." *Harvard Journal of Law & Public Policy* 10 (1987).

Bator, Paul. "Legalistic Constitutionalism and Our Ineffective Government." In Jeremy Rabkin and Gordon L. Crovitz (eds.), *The Fettered Presidency.* eds. (Washington, D.C.: AEI, 1989).

Bell, Griffin. "The Attorney General: The Federal Government's Chief Lawyer and Litigator, or One Among Many." *Fordham Law Review* 46 (1978).

_____. "Office of the Attorney General's Client Relationship." *Business Law* 36 (March 1981).

Bellot, Hugh H.L. "The Origin of the Attorney-General." *The Law Quarterly Review* 25 (1909).

Berttozzi, Mark. "Separating Politics from the Administration of Justice." *Judicature* 67 (1984).

_____. "The Special Counsel Law." *Congressional Quarterly* (December 19, 1987).

Bickel, Alexander. "The Decade of School Desegregation: Progress and Prospects." *Columbia Law Review* 64.

Biskupic, Joan. "Thornburgh's Bumpy Start Surprises Some on Hill." *Congressional Quarterly* (August 26, 1989).

_____. "Groups Look to Capital Hill for Help on Civil Rights." *Congressional Quarterly* (June 17, 1989).

_____. "Lucas Comes Under Sharp Fire at Confirmation Hearings." *Congressional Quarterly* (July 22, 1989).

Bonafede, J. "Smith Moves to Shed His Image as an Invisible Attorney General." *National Journal* (March 6, 1982).

Bork, Robert. "The Problems and Pleasures of Being Solicitor General." *Antitrust Law Journal* 42 (1973).

Brennan, William H. "The Constitution of the United States: Contemporary Ratification." *South Texas Law Review* 27 (1986).

Brigman, W.E. *The Office of the Solicitor General of the United States.* Ph.D. diss.: University of North Carolina, 1966.

Bruff, Harold. "Special Prosecutor Case a Balancing Act." *Legal Times* (July 4, 1988).

_____. "On the Constitutional Status of the Administrative Agencies." *American University Law Review* 36 (1987).

Buckley, Frank. "The Department of Justice—Its Origin, Development and Present Day Organization." *Boston University Law Review* 5 (1925).

Burns, Heywood. "The Federal Executive and Civil Rights." In Friedman, Leon (ed.), *Southern Justice*. New York: Pantheon, 1965.

Caldeira, Gregory and Wright, James. "Organized Interests and Agenda Setting in the Supreme Court." *American Political Science Review* 82 (1988).

Cannon, Bradley. "Defining the Dimensions of Judicial Activism." *Judicature* 66 (1983).

Cannon, Lou and McAllister, Bill. "Meese Announces Resignation Says Probe 'Vindicated Him.' " *Washington Post* (July 6, 1988).

Carr, Ronald. "Mr. Levi at Justice." *University of Chicago Law Review* 52 (1985).

Casper, J. Gerhard. "The Supreme Court and National Policy Making." *American Political Science Review* 70 (1976).

Chamberlain, Ronald. "Mixing Politics and Justice: The Office of Solicitor General." *Journal of Law and Politics* 4 (1987).

Church, George. "A Solid Yes to Affirmative Action." *Time* (July 14, 1986).

Civiletti, Benjamin. "Post Watergate Legislation in Retrospective." *South West Law Journal* 34 (1981).

Clark, Ramsey. "Enduring Constitutional Issues." *Tulane Law Review* 61 (1987).

Clark, David. "Adjudication to Administration: A Statistical Analysis of Federal District Courts in the Twentieth Century." *Southern California Law Review* 55 (1981).

Clark, Tom C. "The Office of the Attorney General." *Tennessee Law Review.* 19 (1946).

Cohodas, Nadine. "Reagan Seeks Relaxation of Antitrust Laws." *Congressional Quarterly* (February 1, 1986).

"Congress Moves to Amend Special Counsel Law." *Legal Times* (January 12, 1987).

Cooper, Philip J. "Conflict or Constructive Tension: The Changing Relationship of Judges and Administrators." *Public Adminstration Review* 45 (November/December 1985).

Corwin, Edward. "Progress of Constitutional Theory." *American History Review* 30 (1925).

_____. "Tenure of Office and the Removal Power under the Constitution." *Columbia Law Review* 27 (1927).

Cortner, Richard. "Strategies and Tactics of Litigants in Constitutional Cases." *Journal of Public Law* 17 (1968).

Cox, Archibald. "Executive Privilege." *University of Pennsylvania Law Review* 122 (1974).

Currie, David. "Misunderstanding Standing." *Supreme Court Review* (1981).

Dahl, Robert. "Decision-Making in a Democracy: The Supreme Court as a National Policy-Maker." *Journal of Public Law* 6 (1957).

Davidson, Roger H. "Breaking Up Those 'Cozy Triangles': An Impossible Dream?" In Susan Welch and John Peters (eds.), *Legislative Reform and Public Policy*. New York: Praeger, 1977.

Days, Drew. "Turning Back the Clock: The Reagan Administration and Civil Rights." *Harvard Civil Rights and Civil Law Law Review* 19 (1984).

DeLong, James. "Informal Rulemaking and the Integration of Public Law and Policy." *Harvard Law Review* 88 (1975).

Devroy, Ann. "Dispute on Justice Nominee Persists." *Washington Post* (June 22, 1989).

Dworkin, Ronald. "Political Judges and the Rule of Law." *Proceedings of the British Academy* 64 (1978).

Easby-Smith, James. "Edmund Randolph—Trail Blazer." *Journal of the Bar Association D.C.* 12 (1945).

Easterbrook, Frank. "On Not Enforcing the Law." *Regulation* (January-February 1983).

Eastland, Terry. "Anonymity: A Feather in Souter's Cap?" *Los Angeles Times* (July 28, 1990).

———. "Reagan Justice: Curbing Excess, Strengthening the Rule of Law." *Policy Review* (Fall 1988).

Edwards, J.Ll.J. "The Integrity of Criminal Prosecutions—Watergate Echoes Beyond the Shores of the United States." In P. Glazebook (ed.), *Reshaping the Criminal Law*. London: Stevens & Sons, 1978.

Egan, Michael J. "Carter's Merit Selection." *Trial* 13 (1977).

Eisenberg, M. and Teitel, Ruti G. "Rex Lee Selectively Abandons Judicial Restraint." *Legal Times* (April 30, 1984).

Elliff, John T. "The United States Department of Justice and Individual Rights, 1937–1962." Ph.D. diss., Harvard University, 1967.

Ellis, Richard. "Limits of the Lightning Rod: Eisenhower, Brownell, Southern Whites, and Civil Rights." Presented at the 1989 Meeting of the Western Political Science Association, Salt Lake City.

Elman, Philip. "The Solicitor General's Office, Justice Frankfurter, and Civil Rights Litigation, 1946–1960: An Oral History." *Harvard Law Review* 100 (1987).

Evans, Rowland and Novak, Robert. "Meese, Wallach and Malaise at Justice." *Washington Post* (April 11, 1988).

"Executive Discretion and the Congressional Defense of Statutes." *Yale Law Journal* 92 (1983).

Fahy, Charles. "The Office of the Solicitor General." *American Bar Association Journal* 28 (1942).

Farlie, John A. "The United States Department of Justice." *Michigan Law Review* 3 (1905).

Fein, Bruce. "Citizen Suit Attorney Fee Shifting Awards: A Critical Examination of Government-Subsidized Litigation." *Law and Contemporary Problems* 47 (1984).

Fine, Ralph. "The Politics of Justice." *American Bar Association Journal* 59 (1973).

Fisher, Louis. "Is the Tenth Justice an Executive or a Judicial Agent? Caplan's Tenth Justice." *Law and Social Inquiry* (1990): 601.

Florio, James. "Congress as Reluctant Regulator: Hazardous Waste Policy in the 1980's." *Journal on Regulation* 3 (1986).

Fowler, Gary. "Judicial Selection under Reagan and Carter: A Comparison of Their Initial Recommendation Procedures." *Judicature* 67 (1984).

Fritchey, Charles. "Watch on the Attorney General." *Harper's Magazine* (November 1967).

Gailey, Phil. "Politics and the Attorney General." *New York Times* (April 21, 1985).

Glazer, Nathan. "The Imperial Judiciary." *The Public Interest* (Fall 1975).

Goldman, Sheldon. "Reaganizing the Judiciary." *Judicature* 68 (1985).

_____. "Reagan's Judicial Appointments at Mid-Term: Shaping the Bench in His Own Image." *Judicature* 66 (1983).

_____. "Reagan's Judicial Legacy: Completing the Puzzle and Summing Up." *Judicature* 72 (1989).

_____. "Characteristics of Eisenhower and Kennedy Appointees to the Lower Federal Courts." *Western Politics Quarterly* 19 (1965).

Gottschall, John. "Eisenhower's Judicial Legacy." *Legal Studies Forum* 9 (1985): 251.

"Government Litigation in the Supreme Court: The Roles of the Solicitor General." *Yale Law Journal* 78 (1969).

Griffith, J. "Putting Politics in its Place at the Justice Department." *Fortune.* (October 1973): 228.

Griswold, Erwin. "The Office of the Solicitor General: Representing the Interests of the United States Before the Supreme Court." *Missouri Law Review* 34 (1969).

Heinberg, John. "Centralization in Federal Prosecution." *Missouri Law Review* 15 (1950): 244.

Hightower, James. "From Attornatus to the Department of Justice—An Historical Perspective." Reprinted in *U.S. Congresss.* Senate. Committee on the Judiciary. Subcommittee on the Separation of Powers, *Hearings on Removing Politics from the Administration of Justice.* 93d Cong., 2d sess., 1974.

Hodder-Williams, Richard. "Advancing the Administration's Agenda Through Litigation." Paper presented at the Annual Meeting of the American Politics Group, Lady Margaret Hall, Oxford, England, January 3–5, 1986.

Hutchinson, Dennis J. "Unanimity and Desegregation: Decision-Making in the Supreme Court." *Georgia Law Journal* 68 (1979).

"Immunity of the United States Attorney General." *Journal of Criminal Law* 71 (1980).

"Interview With Charles Fried." *Washington Lawyer* (May 1987): 48.

Jenkins, John A. "The Solicitor General's Winning Ways." *American Bar Association Journal* 69 (1983).

Jones, Sir Elwyn. "The Office of Attorney-General." *Cambridge Law Journal* 27 (1969).

"Judicial Lobby Legislation." *Congressional Quarterly* (October 24, 1987).

"Justice Department Gets a Just Man." *The Economist* (January 25, 1975).

"Justice Will No Longer Consider Discrimination in Approving Plans." *Los Angeles Times* (August 30, 1986)

Kamen, Al. "Attorney General's Problems Created Deep Maiaise at Justice." *Washington Post* (July 27, 1988).

Kennedy, R. "A Reply to Philip Elman." *Harvard Law Review* 100 (1987).

Key, Sewall. "The Legal Work of the Federal Government." *Virginia Law Review* 25 (1938).

Key, Sewall and LeSourd, Francis. "The Struggle of the Attorney General to Retain His Powers." Department of Justice Main Library Manuscript 43–0846, 1937.

Kurland, Philip. "Judicial Review Revisited: Original Intent and the Common Will." *Cincinnati Law Review* 55 (1987).

Lacovara, Philip. "The Wrong Way to Pick Judges." *New York Times* (October 3, 1986).

Landes, William and Posner, Richard. "The Independent Judiciary in an Interest-Group Perspective." *Journal of Law and Economics* 18 (1975).

Larsen, Richard. "Current Proposals in Congress to Limit and to Ban Court-Awarded Attorneys Fees in Public Interest Litigation." *Review of Law and Social Change* 14 (1986).

Larson, Arthur. "Has the President an Inherent Power of Removal of his Non-Executive Appointees?" *Tennessee Law Review* 16 (1940).

Lauter, David. "Lee Reflects on His Tenure as Solicitor General: 'We Won a Lot More Than We Lost.' " *National Law Journal* (May 13, 1985).

Learned, Henry. "The Attorney General and the Cabinet." *Political Science Quarterly* 24 (1909).

Lee, Rex. "Lawyering in the Supreme Court: The Role of the Solicitor General." *Supreme Court History Society Year Book* (1985).

_____. The Provinces of Constitutional Interpretation." *Tulane Law Review* 61 (1987).

Macklin, Laura. "Promoting Settlement, Foregoing the Facts." *Review of Law and Social Change* 14 (1986).

Malone, R.L. "The Department of Justice: The World's Largest Law Office." *Americal Bar Association Journal* 39 (1953).

Marcus, Ruth. "Sparks Fly at Senate Hearing." *Washington Post* (June 1987).

_____. "Justice Officials Dispute Meese's Rosy Assessment." *Washington Post* (April 3, 1988).

_____. "Top Justice Officials Quit." *Washington Post* (March 30, 1988).

Mayer, Michael S. "Eisenhower's Conditional Crusade: The Eisenhower Administration and Civil Rights." Ph.D. diss., Princeton University, 1984.

McClellan, James. "A Lawyer Looks at Rex Lee." *Benchmark* 1 (1984).

McConnell, Michael. "The Rule of Law and the Role of the Solicitor General." *Loyola Los Angeles Law Review* 21 (1988).

McCree, Wade R., Jr. "The Solicitor General and His Client." *Washington University Law Quarterly* 59 (1981).

Meador, Daniel. "Role of the Justice Department in Maintaining an Effective Judiciary." *Annuals AAPSS* 462 (1982).

_____. "The President, the Attorney General and the Department of Justice." Paper presented at the White Burkett Miller Center, University of Virginia (January 4, 1980).

Melnick, R. Shep. "Prudence and Rationality Under the Constitution." *The Constitution and Regulation of Society*. Provo, Utah: Brigham Young University Press, 1988.

Meyer, Lawrence. "Levi: Liberal with a Taste for Restraint." *Washington Post* (February 5, 1975).

Mezey, Susan Gluck. "Public Interest Litigation and the Civil Rights Attorney's Fees Awards Act: Attempts to Close the Barn Door." Paper presented at the Annual Meeting of the American Political Science Association, Washington, D.C., August 31–September 4, 1988.

Micherg, A. "A Thousand Days of Silence." *Human Rights* 11 (1984).

Miller, Arthur and Bowman, Jeffrey. "Presidential Attacks on the Constitutionality of Federal Statutes: A New Separation of Powers Problem." *Ohio State Law Review* 40 (1979).

Morrison, Alan. "OMB Interference with Agency Rulemaking: The Wrong Way to Write a Regulation." *Harvard Law Review* 99 (1986).

Moss, Debra Cassens. "The Policy and Rhetoric of Ed Meese." *American Bar Association Journal* (February 1987).

Navasky, Victor. "The Politics of Justice." *New York Times Magazine* (May 5, 1974).

_____. "The Attorney General as Scholar, Not Enforcer." *New York Times Magazine* (September 7, 1975): 13.

Nealon, Rita W. "The Opinion Function of the Attorney General." *New York University Law Review* 25 (1950).

Neff, Alan. "Breaking with a Tradition: A Study of the U.S. District Court Nominating Commissions." *Judicature* 64 (1981).

Neuborne, Burt. "In Lukewarm Defense of Charles Fried." *Manhattan Law* (October 20–26, 1987).

"No-buy Pledges: Effects of Inadequate Disclosure and the Role of the Attorney General." *Brooklyn Law Review* 50 (1984).

O'Brien, David. "The Reagan Judges: His Most Enduring Legacy." In Charles Jones (ed.), *The Reagan Legacy: Promise and Performance.* Chatham, N.J.: Chatham House, 1988.

O'Connor, Karen. "The Amicus Curiae Role of the United States Solicitor General in Supreme Court Litigation." *Judicature* 66 (1982).

O'Connor, Karen and Epstein, Lee. "The Rise of Conservative Interest Group Litigation." *Journal of Politics* 45 (1983).

_____. "Bridging the Gap Between Congress and the Supreme Court." *Western Political Quarterly* 38 (1985).

Olson, Susan. "Comparing Justice and Labor Department Lawyers: Ten Years of Occupational Safety and Health Litigation." *Law and Policy* 7 (1985).

_____. "Challenges to the Gatekeeper: The Debate over Federal Litigating Authority." *Judicature* 68 (1984).

_____. "The Political Evolution of Interest Group Litigation." In Gambitta, J. (ed.), *Governing Through the Courts.* Beverly Hills: Sage & Palmer, 1981.

Orren, Karen. "Standing to Sue: Interest Group Conflicts in the Federal Courts." *American Political Science Review* 70 (1976).

Palmer, Robert. "The Confrontation of the Legislative and Executive Branches: An Examination of the Constitutional Balance of Powers and the Role of the Attorney General." *Pepperdine Law Review* 11 (1984).

Parris, Judith. "Merit Selection of Federal Judges." Library of Congress, Congressional Research Service (December 20, 1979).

Pfiffner, James. "White House Staff versus the Cabinet: Centripetal and Centrifugal Roles." *Presidential Studies Quarterly* 16 (1986).

Price, J. "What Price Advocacy." *New York Times* (October 25, 1987).

"Problems at Justice." *National Journal* 33 (1970).

"Prying Informants Files Loose from the Hands of the Attorney General." *Howard Law Journal* 22 (1979).

Putzel, Henry. "Federal Civil Rights Enforcement: A Current Appraisal." *University of Pennsylvania Law Review* 99 (1951).

Rabin, Robert. "Federal Regulations in Historical Perspective." *Stanford Law Review* 38 (1986).

Ramono, Lois. "The Meese Manifesto." *Washington Post* (June 2, 1988).

_____. "Resign Ed Meese." *The New Republic* (November 9, 1987).

Reese, Grover III. "Questions for Supreme Court Nominees: Excluding the Constitution." *Georgia Law Review* 17 (1983).

"Removing Politics from the Department of Justice: Constitutional Problems with Institutional Reform." *New York University Law Review* 50 (1975).

"Reynold's Promotion Angers Senate Democrats." *Congressional Quarterly* (May 23, 1987).

Reynolds, William Bradford. "The Civil Rights Establishment Is All Wrong." *Human Rights* (Spring 1984).

_____. "The Reagan Administration and Civil Rights: Winning the War Against Discrimination." *University of Illinois Law Review* (1986).

Rhodes, I.S. "Opinions of the Attorney-General." Revised. *American Bar Association Journal* 64 (September 1978).

Rockman, Bert. "The Style and Organization of the Reagan Presidency." In Charles Jones (ed.), *The Reagan Legacy: Promise and Performance.* Chatham, N.J.: Chatham House, 1988.

Rogers, William. "Judicial Appointments in the Eisenhower Administration." *Judicature* 41 (1957).

Rogovin, Michael. "Reorganizing Politics Out of the Department of Justice." *American Bar Association Journal* 64 (June 1978).

Rosenbaum, J. "Implementing Federal Merit Selection." *Judicature* 61 (1977).

Rosenbloom, David. "Public Administrators and the Judiciary: The New Partnership." *Public Administration Review* 47 (January-February 1987).

Sanders, Elizabeth. "The Presidency and the Bureaucratic State." In Michael Nelson (ed.), *The Presidency and the Political System*, 2d ed. (Washington, D.C.: CQ Press, 1988).

Scalia, Antonin. "Vermont Yankee: The APA, The D.C. Circuit, and the Supreme Court." *Supreme Court Review* (1978).

Schlundt, Richard. "Civil Rights Policies in the Eisenhower Years." Ph.D. diss., Rice University, 1973.

Schnapper, Eric. "Becket at the Bar—The Conflicting Obligations of the Solicitor General." *Loyola Los Angeles Law Review* 21 (1988).

Schwartz, Joshua. "Two Perspectives on the Solicitor General's Independence." *Loyola of Los Angeles Law Review* 21 (1988).

Segal, Jeffrey. "Amicus Curiae Briefs by the Solicitor General During the Warren and Burger Courts." *Western Political Science Quarterly* 41 (1988).

Selig, Joel. "The Reagan Justice Department and Civil Rights: What Went Wrong." *University of Illinois Law Review* (1985).

Shafer, Byron. "The New Cultural Politics." *Political Science* 18 (1985).

Shapiro, Martin. "The APA: Past, Present and Future." *Virginia Law Review* 72 (1986).

_____. "On Predicting the Future of Administrative Law." *Regulation* (May 1982).

Sharp, Malcolm. "The Classical American Doctrine of the Separation of Powers." *University of Chicago Law Review* 2 (1935).

Silverstein, Mark and Ginsberg, Benjamin. "The Supreme Court and the New Politics of Judicial Power." *Political Science Quarterly* 102 (1987).

Slotnick, Elliott. "The U.S. Judge Nominating Commission." *Law and Society Quarterly* 1 (1979).

Smith, Roger M. "Political Jurisprudence, the New Institutionalism, and the Future of Public Law." *American Political Science Review* 82 (1988).

Sobeloff, Simon. "The Law Business of the United States." *Oregon Law Review* 34 (1955).

"The Solicitor General and Intragovernmental Conflict." *Michigan Law Review* 76 (1977).

Solomon, Burt. "Meese Sets Ambitious Agenda that Challenges Fundamental Legal Beliefs." *National Journal* (November 23, 1985).

Stark, Allison. "When the Government Goes to Court, Who Should Speak for Uncle Sam?" *National Journal* (July 5, 1980).

Starr, Kenneth. "Judicial Review in the Post-Chevron Era." *Yale Journal on Regulation* 3 (1986).

Stern, Robert. "The Solicitor General's Office and Administrative Agency Litigation." *ABA Journal* 46 (1960).

Stevens, John P. "The Supreme Court of the United States: Reflections after a Summer Recess." *South Texas Law Review* 27 (1986).

Stewart, Richard. "The Reformation of American Administrative Law." *Harvard Law Review* 88 (1975).

Strauss, Peter L. "The Place of Agencies in Government: Separation of Powers and the Fourth Branch." *Columbia Law Review* 84 (1984).

Sullivan, Donald Francis. "The Civil Rights Programs of the Kennedy Administration: A Political Analysis." Ph.D. diss., University of Oklahoma, 1965.

Sunstein, Cass. "In Defense of the Hard Look: Judicial Activism and Administrative Law." *Harvard Journal of Legislation and Public Policy* 7 (1984).
_____. "Reviewing Agency Inaction after Heckler v. Chaney." *University of Chicago Law Review* 52 (1985).
Taylor, Stewart. "Ties of Attorney General to Chief." *New York Times* (January 30, 1984).
Thatcher, Thomas. "Genesis and Present Duties of the Office of Solicitor General." *American Bar Association Journal* 17 (1931).
"Thornburgh and Sessions Clash over Congressional Meetings." *Washington Post* (March 11, 1989).
Toobin, Jeffrey. "Meese's Power Grab: The Constitutional Crisis No One Noticed." *New Republic* (May 19, 1986).
Warren, Charles. "New Light on the Federal Judiciary Act of 1789." *Harvard Law Review* 37 (1923).
Wasby, Stephen. "Arrogation of Power or Accountability: Judicial Imperialism Revisited." *Judicature* 65 (1981).
Werdegar, Katheryn. "The Solicitor General and Administrative Due Process: A Quarter Century of Advocacy." *George Washington Law Review* 36 (1968).
West, William and Cooper, Joseph. "Legislative Influence v. Presidential Dominance: Competing Models of Bureaucratic Control." *Political Science Quarterly* 104 (1990).
_____. "The Congressional Veto and Administrative Rulemaking." *Political Science Quarterly* 98 (1983).
Wildavsky, Aaron. "The Past and Future Presidency." *The Public Interest* (Fall 1975).
Wilkins, Richard. "An Officer and an Advocate: The Role of the Solicitor General." *Loyola Los Angeles Law Review* 21 (1988).
Wines, Michael. "Administration Says It Merely Seeks a Better Way." *National Journal* (March 27, 1982).
Witt, Elder. "Reagan vs. Court: A Continuing Crusade." *Congressional Quarterly* (July 20, 1985).
_____. "Reagan's Arguments Rebuffed by High Court." *Congressional Quarterly* (July 12, 1986):.
Wolvovitz, Barbra and Lobel, Jules. "The Enforcement of Civil Rights Statutes: The Reagan Administration's Record." *Black Law Journal* 9 (1986).
Wright, Skelly J. "Beyond Discretionary Justice." *Yale Law Journal* 81 (1970).
Zemans, Frances. "Fee Shifting and the Implementation of Public Policy." *Law and Contemporary Problems* (1984).

Documents and Reports

American Bar Association. Report of the Special Committee to Study Law Enforcement Agencies. *Preventing Improper Influence on Federal Law Enforcement Agencies* (1976).
American Civil Liberties Union. *In Contempt of Congress and the Courts: The Reagan Civil Rights Record* (1984).
National Association of Attorneys General. Committee on the Office of Attorney General. *Selection of the Attorney General of the United States* (May 1974).
United States Congress, House of Representatives. House Committee on the Judiciary. *Hearings on the Solicitor General's Office.* 100th Cong., 1st sess., 1987.
_____. House Committee on the Judiciary. *Independent Counsel Amendment Act of 1987.* H. Rept. 316, 100th Cong., 1st sess., 1987.
_____. House Committee on the Judiciary. *Hearings on Department of Justice Authorization and Oversight.* 99th Cong., 1st sess., 1986.

_____. House Committee on the Judiciary. *Report on Investigation of the Role of the Department of Justice in the Withholding of EPA Documents.* H. Rept. 99–435, 98th Cong., 1st sess., 1985.

_____. House Committee on the Judiciary. *Special Prosecutor Legislation: Hearings on H.R. 2835.* 95th Cong., 1st sess., 1977.

_____. House Committee on Energy and Commerce. *Investigation of the EPA: Report on Abuses in the Superfund Program.* Comm. Print No. 99-AA, 98th Cong., 2d sess. 1984.

_____. House Committee on the Judiciary. *Hearings on Investigation of the Department of Justice.* 82d Cong., 2d sess., 1952–1953.

_____. House Committee on Rules. *Attorney General A. Mitchell Palmer on Charges Against the Justice Department by Louis Post and Others.* 66th Cong., 2d sess., 1920.

_____. House Committee on Public Works and Transportation. *Contempt of Congress: Report on Congressional Proceedings Against Anne M. Gorsuch, Administrator, U.S. EPA for Withholding Documents.* House Report No. 97–968. 97th Cong., 2d sess., 1982.

United States Congress, Senate. Senate Committee on Government Affairs. *Study on Federal Regulation: Regulatory Organization.* Vol. 5, 95th Cong., 2d sess., 1977.

_____. Senate Committee on Government Operations. *Hearings on S. 495: Watergate Reorganization and Reform Act.* 94th Cong., 1st sess., 1977.

_____. Senate Committee on Government Affairs. *Public Officials Integrity Act: Hearings on S. 555.* 95th Cong., 1st sess., 1977.

_____. Senate Committee on Government Affairs, Subcommittee on Oversight of Government Management. *Special Prosecutor Provisions of Ethics in Government Act.* 97th Cong., 1st sess., 1981.

_____. Senate Committee on the Judiciary. *Hearings on Judicial Selection and the Reagan Administration.* 100th Cong., 2d sess., 1988.

_____. Senate Judiciary Committe. *Hearings on the Nomination of Robert H. Bork to be an Associate Justice of the United States Supreme Court.* 100th Cong., 1st sess., 1987.

_____. Senate Committee on the Judiciary. *Hearings on Edwin Meese to be Attorney General.* 98th Cong., 2d sess., 1984 and 99th Cong., 1st sess., 1985.

_____. Senate Committee on the Judiciary. *Hearings on the Nomination of Justice William H. Rehnquist to be Chief Justice of the Supreme Court.* 99th Cong., 2d sess., 1986.

_____. Senate Committee on the Judiciary. *Hearings on the Nomination of Justice Antonin Scalia to be Associate Justice of the Supreme Court.* 99th Cong., 2d sess., 1986.

_____. Senate Committee on the Judiciary. *Hearings on the Nomination of William Bradford Reynolds to be Associate Attorney General.* 99th Cong., 1st sess., 1985.

_____. Senate Committee on the Judiciary. *Hearings on the Nomination of Edwin Meese III to be Attorney General.* 98th Cong., 2d sess., 1984.

_____. Senate Committee on the Judiciary. *Hearings on Ethics in Government Act Amendments.* 97th Cong., 2d sess., 1982.

_____. Senate Committee on the Judiciary. *Hearings on the Nomination of Judge Sandra Day O'Connor to Serve as an Associate Justice of the Supreme Court.* 97th Cong., 1st sess., 1981.

_____. Senate Committee on the Judiciary. *Department of Justice Authorization and Oversight Hearings.* 96th Cong., 2d sess., 1981.

_____. Senate Committee on the Judiciary. *Hearings on the Selection and Confirmation of Federal Judges.* Part 1, 96th Cong., 1st sess., 1981.

_____. Senate Committee on the Judiciary. *Hearings on the Nomination of Griffin H. Bell to be Attorney General.* 95th Cong., 1st sess., 1977.

_____. Senate Committee on the Judiciary. *Hearings on the Nomination of Edward H. Levi to be Attorney General.* 94th Cong., 1st sess., 1975.

_____. Senate Select Committee on Intelligence. *Intelligence Activities and the Rights of Americans.* 94th Cong., 2d sess., 1976.

_____. Senate Committee on the Judiciary. *Hearings on the Nomination of Elliot L. Richardson to be Attorney General of the United States.* 93rd Cong., 1st sess., 1924.

_____. Senate Committee on the Judiciary, Subcommittee on the Separation of Powers. *Removing Politics from the Administration of Justice.* 93rd Cong., 2d sess., 1974.

_____. Senate Judiciary Committe. *Hearings on the Nomination of Richard Kleindienst to be Attorney General.* 92d Cong., 2d sess., 1972.

_____. Senate Judiciary Committe. *Hearings on the Nomination of Robert F. Kennedy to be Attorney General.* 87th Cong., 1st sess., 1961.

_____. Senate Committee on the Judiciary. *Hearings on Reorganization of the Federal Judiciary.* 75th Cong., 1st sess., 1937.

_____. Senate Select Committee on Investigation of the Attorney General. *Hearings on Attorney General Harry M. Daughtery.* 68th Cong., 1st sess., 1924.

United States Department of Justice. *Annual Report of the Attorney General* 1872–1988.

_____. Civil Rights Division. *Enforcing the Law* (1981–1987)

_____. Office of Legal Counsel. "Memorandum Opinion for the Attorney General Re: Role of the Solicitor General." Opinions of the Office of Legal Counsel 1 (1977).

_____. Office of Legal Policy. *Report to the Attorney General: The Law of Pretrial Interrogation* (February 1986).

_____. Office of Legal Policy. *The Search and Seizure Exclusionary Rule.* (February 1986).

_____. Office of Legal Policy. *Original Meaning of Jurisprudence.* (March 1987).

_____. Office of Legal Policy. *Wrong Turns on the Road to Judicial Activism* (September 1987).

_____ Office of Legal Policy. *Redefining Discrimination: "Disparate Impact" and the Institutionalization of Affirmative Action* (November 1987).

_____. Office of Legal Policy. *Economic Liberties Protected by the Constitution* (March 1988).

_____. Office of Legal Policy. "Myths and Realities—Reagan Administration Judicial Selection." Memorandum from the Office of Legal Policy (May 17, 1988).

Index

Aaron, Nan, 155
ABA. American Bar Association
Abortion issues, 57, 146, 148, 149, 230, 235. *See also* specific court cases
ACLU. *See* American Civil Liberties Union
Adams, John Quincy, 49
Adams v. Richardson (1973), 139, 180
Administrative Division, 34
Administrative law, 172–210
  conflicts in, 174–81
  congressional intent, 181–90
  presidential policies, 190–209
Administrative policymaking, 72–79, 190–200
Administrative Procedures Act (1946), 176, 178, 184, 185, 186, 212*n.70*, 215*n.114*
Admiralty and Insular Affairs Division, 30–31, 33–34. *See also* Civil Division
Affirmative action, 34, 103, 148, 181, 202, 204, 234
Age Discrimination Employment Act (1967), 217
Agency policymaking, 178, 181–90, 197–200, 214*n.98*. *See also* specific agency names
Agricultural Adjustment Act (1933), 124
Agriculture Department, 73
Akerman, Amos, 22
Akron v. Akron Center for Reproductive Health (1983), 148, 149, 169*n.210*
Alexander v. Holmes (1969), 139
Alliance for Justice, 155
American Bar Association (ABA)
  civil rights, 131

American Bar Association (ABA) *(continued)*
  executive-judicial alliance, 124, 140
  judicial selection, 61, 63, 64, 65
  Reagan administration, 151, 152, 154
  See also National Bar Association
American Civil Liberties Union (ACLU), 126, 155, 230
American Enterprise Institute, 7, 138
Ameron, Inc. v. U.S. Army Corps of Engineers (1986), 202
Amicus curiae briefs ("friend of the court"), 60, 68–69, 86*nn.138, 141*. *See also* specific cases
Anderson, John, 132
Antitrust Division, 30, 31, 102–3, 151
Antitrust laws, 148, 175
APA. Administrative Procedures Act (1946)
Appointments Clause, 97, 108, 109
Arizona v. Fulminante (1991), 231
Articles of Confederation, U.S., 15, 91
Assistant Attorney General, 25, 26, 29, 30, 34, 87*n.155*
Assistant to the Attorney General, 30, 32, 33. *See also* Deputy Attorney General
Associate Attorney General, 36
Atiyah, Patrick, 14, 89
Attorney General, British, 11–14
Attorney General, U.S.
  administrative policymaking, 72–79
  British office compared with, 11–14
  centralization issues, 22–25, 73–79
  confirmation process, 4, 6, 143–44, 150, 166*n.162*, 168*n.216*
  current role, 36–40

Cornell W. Clayton is Assistant Professor of Political Science at Washington State University. A former Truman Scholar, he has also taught at the University of Utah. He received his M.Phil. from Oxford University in 1990.